THE HERITAGE OF PERSIA

Bibliotheca Iranica
Reprint Series

[Unnumbered]
Qajar Iran
Edited by
C. E. Boswroth and Carole Hillenbrand

(No. 1)
The Heritage of Persia
Richard N. Frye

Forthcoming
(No. 2)
**The Diary of H. M. [Naser al-Din Shah of Qajar]
the Shah of Persia During His Tour Through Europe
in A.D. 1873**
Translated by: J.W. Redhouse
Preface by: Carole Hillenbrand
Reprinted from the original 1874 edition.

Bibliotheca Iranica
Reprint Series No. 1

THE HERITAGE
OF PERSIA

Richard N. Frye

Mazda Publishers
Costa Mesa, California
1993

Library of Congress Cataloging-in-Publication Data

Frye, Richard Nelson, 1920-
  The Heritage of Persia / Richard N. Frye.
    p. cm. -- (Bibliotheca Iranica: Reprint Series No. 1)
  Includes index
  Originally published: Cleveland : World Pub. Co., 1963.
  1. Iran--history--to 640.   I. Title. II. Series.
  DS275.F7 1993   93-34039
  935--dc20   CIP

ISBN:1-56859-008-3

10 9 8 7 6 5 4 3 2

انتشارات مزدا

CONTENTS

Introduction

Part One: Land Of Contrasts

Introduction to things general and specific 1
The geographical background of history 7
People change and people remain 10

Part Two: Iranian Traditions

The Aryan background..................................... 17
Zoroaster and his message 28
Sagas of the East 35
Iran and Turan 42
Social structure 53

Part Three: Iran and the west

The heritage of the ages 62
Upstart dynasts 75
The rise of Persis... 85
The crisis of empire.. 94
The one world of the Achamenids. The court and bureaucracy...... 102
Economic life... 119
Religion under the later Achamenids 124
The fall of the Achamenids 129

Part Four: L'Iran Extérieur

Alexander the Great and his legacy........................... 143
Seleuçid centralism 149
The Hellenistic heritage 161
The extended cultural area 173
The Graeco-Bactrians...................................... 182
Gandhara and Western influences........................... 189

Part Five: The Adaptable Arsacids

    A forgotten dynasty 199
    Origins 201
    The road westwards 205
    Parthia and Rome 208
    The Government and bureaucracy of the empire 212
    Literature and culture 218
    Foundations of Zoroastrianism 220
    The Kushans and the East 223
    The traditions of Persis 226

Part Six: Heirs of the Achaemenids

    Ardashir and the cycle of history 236
    The imperialism of Shapur 241
    Heresies and the church 248
    The glory that was Iran 254

Part Seven: The Persian Conquest of Islam

    Disintegration of the old order 268
    Islam versus Iran 274
    Central Asian particularism 279
    Orthodoxy in Fars 283
    The new Persian renaissance 286

MAPS 293

NOTES TO MAPS 296

APPENDICES 298

BIBLIOGRAPHY 301

INDEX 311

To my Iranian Friends
(Afghans, Baluchis, Kurds, Ossetes, Persians, Tajiks)

LIST OF ILLUSTRATIONS

1 The entrance to the Palace grounds at Persepolis

2 Shah's tented camp at Persepolis

3 Lion and bull carving from Persepolis

4 Investiture of Shapur at Naqsh-i Rustam

5 Shapur's victory over Valerian

6 Royal Assyrian lion hunt

7 Fragments from a Sasanian Palace (showing a boar hunt)

8 King Peroz hunting boars

9 The large Buddha at Bamiyan

ACKNOWLEDGMENTS

The author and publishers would like to thank the following for supplying, or for giving permission to reproduce, the photographs in this volume: J. Allan Cash, plates 1, 2; British Museum, plate 6; R. N. Frye, plate 9; Paul Popper Ltd, plates 3, 5; Philadelphia Museum of Art, plate 8; Smithsonian Institution, Freer Gallery of Art, Washington D.C., plate 4; Weidenfeld & Nicholson Archives, plates 6, 7.

INTRODUCTION

THE present book falls into the category of 'scientific-popular', to use current Russian terminology. This means that a general subject is presented for students and the public, but that the treatment is based on the latest scholarly work in the various fields covered in the book. The inclusion of maps, bibliography and illustrations makes the volume suitable for classrooms as well as for readers who wish to acquaint themselves with the pre-Islamic history of Persia and some of the many problems in that history. It is hoped that *The Heritage of Persia* will show the remarkable continuity of culture, from the time the Iranians came upon the plateau until the Islamicisation of the land in the tenth century A.D. The later story, down to the present, is much better known than the early history of Persia, and the same vitality of ancient traditions holds true even in our own day.

I have tried to present various points of view on problems discussed in the book and I have sought to maintain a dispassionate approach to partisan theories. I have not hesitated to repeat old well-established theories, even though they seemed prosaic compared to more recent clever or brilliant surmises, which though possibly plausible, had no concrete evidence behind them. My main criterion in supporting one theory as opposed to others has been simplicity. More evidence is reconciled in a similar fashion by one hypothesis than another, as in the natural sciences; so here I choose the less complex. Although human actions are frequently not simple or uncomplicated, yet the guide of simplicity, in my opinion, is the best one to follow in most scholarly activity.

Several new approaches to the pre-Islamic history of Iran are proposed in this book. One is the general thesis that the history of Zoroastrianism can best be understood as the grafting on to the religious beliefs of the majority of Iranians the teachings of the minority of the followers of the prophet Zoroaster, rather than as the accommodation of aberrant, archaic beliefs to the message of the Gathas. Scholars have been seeking to understand how the followers of Zoroaster could have accepted the Younger Avesta with the glorification of *haoma* and of practices against which the prophet railed. The question should be rather of how the majority of the people, following priests who recited the ancient theogonies of the Younger Avesta, adopted the teachings of Zoroaster into their beliefs. A new vista for the explanation of many religious problems opens as a consequence.

Another general position, which is different from the usual view, is the extension of the ancient history of the country down to the tenth century A.D. In my opinion those 'Persian nationalists' who extolled in their writings the glories of ancient Iran under the Abbasid caliphate, on the whole were not seeking to destroy Islam but to establish it on a wider, international basis, rather than to leave it limited to an Arab religion with a culture and civilisation based on the bedouin background. For me, those who first wrote Persian in Arabic script were really *'avant-garde'* Muslims, who performed a service for Islam by enriching it with non-Arabic literature and culture. This perspective, I believe, helps to solve many minor problems which were especially difficult of solution according to the traditional view that the Persians developed a 'renaissance' against the Arabs, by extolling ancient Persian traditions against Islam.

Inevitably certain minor points are treated in this volume which might better have been omitted, but the author begs the reader for indulgence in the former's scholarly pursuit of matters, as well as etymologies of words, which needed more than the mere statement, 'this is so', or 'I believe this'. I regret the impossibility of giving a full scholarly apparatus, with sources for all statements, but I wish especially to note my position on the ever-vexing problem of transcriptions of Oriental words. Specialists do not need precise transliterations of the words quoted in this book, for they know as well as I what is under discussion. Diacritical marks and deformations of names known to the general reader may give more trouble than help, and simplicity need not detract from scholarly worth. Therefore, I beg the specialist to excuse the absence of long marks on the vowels of certain words, even though on others I felt obliged to give a more precise transliteration.

Finally, I wish to thank those who have helped me with the

manuscript, above all to Mark Jan Dresden of the University of Pennsylvania who read all of the manuscript giving me valuable hints and corrections. Needless to say, neither he, nor anyone save myself is responsible for errors. Dietz Otto Edzard of Munich University read the German version of the first part and saved me from some errors in Mesopotamian matters. Others are mentioned in footnotes, and to all a sincere thanks. I hope that the volume will prove interesting and useful to many readers.

RICHARD N. FRYE

Cambridge, Massachusetts

INTRODUCTION TO SECOND EDITION

The first edition has been long out of print and the need for a second edition has been felt by many students who wanted a compact volume on ancient Persia but showing the transition to an Islamic culture. It was not, however, possible to rewrite the book or to make extensive additions. Rather mistakes have been corrected and the work has been brought up to date especially the bibliography. Reviews of the first edition especially the one in the *Vestnik Drevnei Istorii* for 1965 by M. Dandamaev and G. Koshelenko, have been very useful. Obviously some points of view briefly expressed in the present work would need much elaboration to justify them, for which unfortunately there is no space. The excellent Russian translation of the first edition by V. Livshits and E. Zeimal under the title *Naslediye Irana* (Moscow, 1972) contains much additional bibliography which could not be included in the second edition. This second edition was prepared at the Asia Institute of Pahlavi University in Shiraz, where I was the director for five years, and many bibliographical items were not present. For omissions the author begs the indulgence of the reader. It is hoped, however, that the second edition with corrections will prove to be as useful as the first was in its time.

RICHARD N. FRYE

Shiraz

Preface to New Printing of *The Heritage of Persia*

One could always add to any writing after a few years but I am both surprised and happy that in this case little needs to be revised. Only a few corrections are made below according to the page numbers:

p.12 and 48. One should distinguish between northern and southern Bactria divided by the Oxus (Amu Darya).

p.31. The article by Shahbazi is "The 'Traditional Date of Zoroaster' Explained," BSOAS, 40 (1977), 29-30.

p.114. More likely than a list of satrapies is simply a tax list.

p.115. The Persians, as ruling people, at *first* were exempt from taxes.

p.137, note 23. The meaning and derivation of the term Parsua is uncertain.

p.139, note 57. Another possible translation is 'farms.'

p.141, note 83. The *karanos* in Anatolia seems to have been a 'super' general over the satraps.

p.210. The term **frataraka* should be translated as 'governor.'

p.232. For *'xopxyix'* read *'xoragia'*.

p.244. Kesh (present Shahrisabz) should be read for Kashgar.

p.250, (last line). For 'which is likely' read 'more likely in the early years.'

p.263. For 'last' read 'first translation.' Cf. Frye, *The History of Ancient Iran* (Munich, 1984), p. 368.

p.296. Many cities can now be added to this list; cf. R. Gyselen, *La géographie adminstrative de l'empire Sassanide, les témoinages sigillographiques* (Paris, 1989).

In the bibliography for many new references cf. R. Frye, *The History of Ancient Iran* (Beck Verlag, Munich, 1984) and M. Boyce, *A History of Zoroastrianism,* 3 vols. (E. J. Brill, Leiden, 1975-1991).

Richard N. Frye
Brimfield, MA.
1993

1 LAND OF CONTRASTS

Introduction to Things General and Specific

To anyone who has travelled in Persia, two features of the landscape seem ever present, mountains and aridity. It is true that centres of population are found in usually small, sometimes fertile river valleys, while broad plains are not absent. But the plateau which is the major part of the country is predominantly rocky and dry and it was so in historic times as it is at the present day. Just as the desert has always had a great impact on the Arab, so the features of his land have exerted a strong influence on the Persian. In our modern civilisation, usually shielded from the vagaries of the weather and even from mere contact with nature, we tend to forget the often decisive role that nature has played in the destinies of people more dependent on weather and on the soil of their immediate surroundings than we are.

At the same time that one should not underestimate the importance of environment on the lives of men the other extreme of over-emphasising the geographical basis of history might also lead to wrong conclusions. An individual's heredity, his upbringing in a family, his loyalties to clan, tribe and nation, the interplay of various traditions, all tend to make the study of history amazingly complex. If we were able to rationalise peoples' 'solidarity complexes', as the sociologist might say, perhaps we could at least understand in some measure why people and nations acted as they did. Unfortunately, many if not most of the 'solidarity complexes' are irrational and difficult to classify and analyse. Yet the expansion of knowledge is attended by constant attempts to classify or reclassify and to understand what is often irrational. So it is, I believe, with our understanding of history, and Persia's history is no exception. Generalisation, then, cannot be avoided in writing any history. Although we try to understand

1

the past by finding parallels, by tracing the continuity of institutions and beliefs in a given area down through the centuries, some generalisations we make will be subject to question and dispute. But generalisations must be made, and inferences and probabilities will be amply forthcoming, for the history of ancient Persia abounds in problems and uncertainties. Furthermore, although the author does not fully subscribe to the view that only with the coming of the Arabs and Islam did the Persians learn to understand and to write history, still the paucity of records makes the task of studying the ancient history of Persia extremely difficult, especially when it is compared to ancient Greece or Rome.

There may be a certain advantage, albeit dubious, in the very scarcity of sources for Persian history, since every shred of evidence from Persia's past becomes more significant than, for example, a similar object, inscription, or word would be in the fuller, more literary histories of classical antiquity. The works of the archaeologist, the art historian, epigraphist and numismatist cannot be overlooked in constructing an early history of the Persians, and indeed the specialised studies of individual art objects, single words in an inscription or a rare coin, may provide inestimable help with more general questions of history. For this same reason it should be remembered that new sources of information, or a new site excavated by the archaeologist, may profoundly change our ideas on the ancient history of Persia. This may prove at times frustrating but it is also exhilarating to know that the past, like the natural sciences now and in the future, has no frontiers.

Persia, of course, is a designation we obtained from the Greeks, who knew perfectly well that Persia meant the province of the Achaemenian empire where the Persians lived in the land of the Aryans. Aryan, with an approximate derived meaning 'noble, lord', seems to have been the general designation of those people, speaking eastern Indo-European tongues or dialects, who migrated into the lands between the Ganges and Euphrates rivers at the end of the second and the beginning of the first millennium BC. Both in India and the West they were conscious of their difference from the settled peoples over whom they came to rule. For those who went to India, the (home) land of the Aryans lay to the north-west of the subcontinent. For those who went all the way to Mesopotamia the land of the Aryans was in the East, but

2

also at home, just where they settled. Ancient authors knew that the Persians and Medes were Aryans, and the sources do use the term 'Aryan' for both.[1] In the far-flung Achaemenid empire the term (Old Iranian) *aryānām khshathram* 'land (or kingdom) of the Aryans', was probably not in general use since the term is nowhere attested. Later, after the fall of the Achaemenid empire, in Greek sources, there appears to be a confusion, and also an identity of 'Aryan' with the important province in the eastern part of the Achaemenid empire called *Haraiva* in Old Persian and *Aria by Herodotus and others.[2] With the expansion of the Parthians it would seem that the term *Aria, or Ariane in Greek sources, expanded as well so that it finally becomes 'greater Aria', equivalent to 'realm of the Aryans', which is the term the Sasanians used for the extended homeland of their empire, *Eranshahr*.[3] The use of the word Iran for the modern country is thus a continuation of the ancient term.

To avoid confusion I would propose the following nomenclature for the pre-Islamic period of time. 'Greater Iran' would include the entire area where Iranian languages were spoken in historical times and where the culture could be characterised as predominantly 'Iranian'. Parts of Trans-caucasia, Central Asia, north-west India, and Meso-potamia, as well as the plateau, including the modern states of Afghanistan and Persia, belong to 'Greater Iran'. To distinguish between the core or heartland, Iran proper (modern Afghanistan and Persia) and the peripheral area, I believe the French term for the latter, *l'Iran extérieur*, should be adopted. Of course, the frontiers must be imprecise for we follow cultural criteria rather than political boundaries; for example, the capital of the Sasanian empire, Ctesiphon near modern Baghdad, was surely considered by the Sasanians as situated in *Eranshahr*. At the same time, it would seem that certain areas on the Indian Ocean today included in the political boundaries of Persia, were not considered part of Iran before the Sasanians. In this book although we shall be concerned primarily with Iran proper, the areas where the culture of Iran was dominant, on the other hand Central Asia and north-west India cannot be overlooked. In-deed, they are integral parts of the story. The term 'Persia' will be used for the modern country, or for the same area in antiquity, the province, of course, being Persis or Fars.

The temporal limits of our investigation cannot be strictly fixed any more than the geographical boundaries. The main part

3

of our study will be concerned with the Achaemenids, Parthians and Sasanians, from the sixth century BC to the sixth century AD. But in order properly to understand the Achaemenids, their predecessors the Medes, and even earlier peoples and eras should be investigated. A search for origins, or what came earlier, will not go beyond the limits of this study, but the extension of our concern to the tenth century AD will require an explanation.

There is no doubt about the incomparable importance of the coming of Islam not only to Iran but also to the entire Near East. The history of that part of the world can be divided into two periods, pre-Islamic and afterwards. Not even the consequences of Alexander the Great's conquests and the resulting Hellenism of the third and second centuries before our era, or the comparable impact of the West today, can equal the influence of Islam in the lands between the Mediterranean and the Indus river. Yet one should not date the end of ancient Iran with the Arab conquest of the country in the seventh century. As long as Islam was an Arabian religion with Arab *mores* and the like, Iran was not conquered by Islam. It is only in the tenth century AD when we find a New Persian literature, written in the Arabic alphabet, which perhaps more than any other factor brings the ancient traditions of Iran into the culture of Islam, that we can speak of a new era. For New Persian literature is not only Persian but, more striking, it is also Islamic. After this time Iran is irrevocably Muslim, and the revolts or separatist movements during the caliphate, incorrectly but conveniently called manifestations of 'Iranian nationalism', were for the most part Islamic. Indeed, in a real sense the petty Iranian dynasts were in many ways more champions of Islam than anti-Muslim Persian patriots, as they have sometimes been characterised. In freeing Islam from the exclusive attachment to the Arabic language and the Arab bedouin background, the Persians did much to universalise Islam and thus to expand and preserve it. For this reason it is not unreasonable to extend the ancient history of Iran to the tenth century AD when the Islamic history of *Iran* begins. This does not conflict with the history of the *Arabs in Iran* from the seventh to the tenth century of our era, which is another matter, and is discussed in my book *The Golden Age of Persia*.

The above exposition does not tally with the observation of a prominent modern Persian that although history begins with Islam for the Arabs it ends with Islam for the Persians. While there is a grain of truth in most general statements, this one, it

4

seems, owes its origin to twentieth-century nationalism rather than to a considered study of history, and if one is speaking of historiography, again the tenth century is the time of most change.

One could make a strong argument that before Islam chronological history as we know it from the Greeks or the Muslims did not exist in Iran. But this raises wider problems and it is not the place here to discuss the differences and changes in the *Weltanschauung* of various peoples. Some scholars have proposed a fundamental opposition between the 'cyclical' theory of history of the Indo-European peoples and the 'linear' theory of the Semitic peoples. Others have emphasised the great changes in a given society, especially in its conception of history with which we are here concerned, as, for example, when the belief in a messiah or saviour challenged hoary authority based on revelation (the Near East) or based on reason (the Greeks). Then, as we learn from Christianity, the messiah can be either the beginning or the end of history for that society. It is not that these questions are unimportant or uninteresting; they are relevant to our discussion of history or historiography in pre-Islamic Iran and should not be ignored. But they must be relegated to a necessary background of assumptions on which we build our structure of the history of ancient Iran. Suffice it to say that one should not forget that the approach to history in the ancient Orient was quite different from our own. What we may regard as tales or myths were believed by others as part of a religion, hence effectively 'real' in meanings other than ours. Other societies and other ages may seem very close to ours yet have different values and different approaches to problems from our own.

Furthermore, many Oriental peoples, the Iranians and Indians among them, were more concerned with religion than with history, and this is revealed in extant writings from ancient Iran and India. Religion, I believe, is not concerned with 'truth', neither universal 'logical' truth, such as two and two are four, nor specific 'natural' truth, such as the physical, observable characteristics of this book. Religion rather is an act of belief or faith of a group of human beings throughout history, and consequently it is more difficult to analyse or even to study than the man-determined 'truths'. The texts or sources of Iranian and Indian history must be studied with this in mind.

Can we trust our sources, then, and what are they? The nature and value of our sources vary in time, as do our methods in

5

using them. I mean, for example, that as soon as written records are present they not only greatly add to our knowledge, but they change the significance of objects of material culture, art and architecture, excavated by the archaeologist. The writings set the framework into which the rest must be fitted. With written records the all-important potsherds from pre-literate times decidedly lose their former importance in telling of waves of invasions of new peoples. Also, reconstructions of comparative philology may lose some of their assumed cultural and social significance with the discovery of texts revealing unexpected developments of meaning and significance in individual words. So the comparative value of our sources changes. Obviously the increase in numbers of written records not only further reduces the importance of archaeology but differentiates new disciplines such as art history, architecture and numismatics. The methods of the historian must change with his tools. A coin commemorating a victory of Charlemagne over the Saxons is surely much more important than a coin struck by Prussia in honour of a victory in the war of 1870. The historian of Charlemagne cannot fail to consider numismatics in his researches while the historian of 1870 need never have heard the word. The historian of pre-Islamic Iran, then, must not neglect any scraps of information of any kind relating to his subject. There is a danger, however, of assessing the importance of a word in an ancient inscription far beyond its historical significance, while the *argumentum e silentio* is a particularly obnoxious hobgoblin in this field.

The basic sources for our study are, in the first instance, the writings in various Iranian languages; in the oldest period the inscriptions of the Achaemenid kings, primarily Darius and Xerxes, in three languages, Old Persian, Elamite and Akkadian, and the religious book the Avesta. For the Parthian era we have only scattered inscriptions, and later texts written in the Parthian language long after the fall of the Parthians, and mainly dealing with Manichaeism. The early Sasanian kings give us imperial inscriptions, sometimes in three languages, Middle Persian, Parthian and Greek. Then we have a predominantly religious literature of the Zoroastrians written in Middle Persian and commonly called Pahlavi, or Book Pahlavi. Most of this literature, however, was written after the Arab conquest of Persia, while the earliest extant manuscripts of such works are much later in time. The documents in Sogdian, Khotanese Saka and Khwarezmian from Central Asia, not to mention the Parthian and Middle Persian fragments from there, have opened new vistas in our knowledge of Iranian culture and civilisation. Finally, we have books written in New Persian, or in Arabic by Persians, which give much information about pre-Islamic Iran.

The most important foreign sources are classical, mostly in Greek, a few in Latin. Herodotus, Xenophon and the historians of Alexander the Great, primarily Arrian, are valuable for the Achaemenids, while the geographers Ptolemy and Strabo and the historian Pompeius Trogus in the epitome of Justin are especially significant for the history of the Parthians. Under the Sasanians the history of Agathius in Greek and the Latin work of Ammianus Marcellinus should be mentioned. Finally, Armenian and Syriac sources are of special relevance to the Sasanians. Other sources, from China, India, Egypt and Palestine play a decidedly minor role in elucidating the history of pre-Islamic Iran, and any new information they have, not found in other sources, is relatively scanty. These, in brief, are our chief sources, assisted by archaeology and sister disciplines. With them a history of two millennia must be reconstituted, and the gaps far exceed the few brief glimpses of history given by the sources. We have not even a fragmentary net with great holes in it but merely bits of information which must try to fit together into some framework.

The Geographical Background of History

In the centre of the Iranian plateau are two desolate salt deserts, the Dasht-i Kavir and the Dasht-i Lut. They act as a barrier between east and west, diverting large groups of migrating peoples either eastward towards India or westward towards Mesopotamia. Skirting the northern edge of the Dasht-i Kavir was a trade route which came from the lowlands of Mesopotamia where the Tigris and Euphrates rivers approached one another by ancient Ctesiphon or modern Baghdad. The road headed for the Iranian plateau through modern Kirmanshah, Hamadan, Tehran, and then followed the northern edge of the Kavir, at Herat branching north-east to Merv, Bukhara, Samarkand and on to China, or turning south to Seistan, east to Qandahar and over the mountains to the plains of the Indus river. These routes have been not only the time-honoured roads of trade but also of invasion. Other routes ran from Tehran or Hamadan north to Azerbaijan, Armenia and on to the Black or Caspian Seas, or southward to Isfahan and Fars province. But the main road of history was the east-west one mentioned above, called in its various parts the great Khurasan road, or the silk route to China, as well as other names.

Away from the roads in the mountains people frequently found refuge from invading, pillaging hordes or the passage of local armies. In the east, the rugged ranges of the Hindu Kush provided an ideal *refugium* for tribes and peoples unwilling to accept domination by low-landers, or fleeing from religious or political persecution. Certainly the great variety of dialects and languages in the large mountain area of what is today eastern Afghanistan and north-west Pakistan indicates an even greater extension of the ancestors of the Kafirs and other Indo-Iranian mountaineers to the west of their present homes. Mere communication in this rugged terrain was always difficult, so it is not surprising that the diversity of these people was always a more striking characteristic than their homogeneity. It seems the mountains used to be more wooded than they are today, but wood still remains the basis of building and it is also the most commonly used medium of art or sculpture in that mountain area. Never a rich land, in the earliest history it was perhaps most noted for the ruby and lapis-lazuli mines of Badakhshan.

While speaking of refuge areas, to the south in several regions, including the relatively isolated valley of present-day Kalat, one finds the Brahuis, a people speaking a Dravidian tongue, and representing most probably the descendants of the pre-Aryan inhabitants of eastern Iran. Certainly the Iranian Baluch tribes who gave their name to the vast area between the Indus river and the Persian Gulf in one direction, and the Indian Ocean and the Persian cities of Kirman and Bam with the Afghan towns of Farah and Qandahar to the north on the other, did not occupy this area before the tenth century AD. Why they should have occupied this area at all is a question a visitor might well ask, for the aridity, heat and desolation of the present can hardly have been much better in ancient times. Dwelling-rooms deep underground were needed to escape the summer heat in antiquity as today. The rocky, barren soil required deep wells and underground channels to bring water to the fields then as now, while the date palm was and is the staff of life. Nomads, or those dedicated to a semi-nomadic way of life, could flourish here but hardly others more settled.

Another minor 'refuge area' was the area of eastern Persia

8

called in early Islamic times Kohistan and at present the Afghan-Persian frontier area. But here the mountains were not so high as farther east, nor was the land so unproductive as farther south. The climate too was more temperate.

The impressive Elburz mountains, with their highest peak, Mt. Demavend (5,760 metres), separate the Iranian plateau from the narrow coastal strip on the Caspian Sea below sea level. The contrast between the plateau and the coastal plain is extreme, for the coast is a jungle where tigers used to roam in considerable numbers. Malaria, rice, and exotic tropical plants made the coast a different world with the arid plateau seemingly far away. The mountains and tropical lowlands formed a kind of museum where old traditions and practices could be preserved away from changes on the plateau. For the plateau people the mountains and jungles were a strange, forbidding land where the demons and strange beasts reputedly lived.

The Caucasus mountain range is probably the most variegated ethnological and linguistic area in the world. It is not a melting pot, as has been said, but a refuge area *par excellence* where small groups have maintained their identity throughout history. The descendants of the Mediaeval Alans, a Scythic Iranian people, live in the North Caucasus today and are called Ossetes. Iranian cultural influences were strong among the Armenians, Georgians and other peoples of the Caucasus and many times in history large parts of this area were under Persian rule. So it well deserves to be mentioned in a survey of Iran.

Finally, we have the mountainous refuge areas of western Iran, where today the Kurds, Lurs and others live, in the Zagros mountains. From the dawn of history this rugged land bordering the fertile plain of the Tigris and Euphrates rivers was a source of worry for the people of Mesopotamia. Nomads or mountaineers from the east frequently raided and plundered the rich cities of the lowlands.

One may thus conclude that the plains were the melting pots of various peoples while the mountains provided isolated areas where different religious beliefs (or heresies), old traditions and customs could be maintained in comparative isolation from the great arenas of history. All of this serves to make the study of Iran fascinating as well as to explain its history.

Today on the plateau only in north-west Persia, in the province of Azerbaijan, is dry farming practicable, and it must have been substantially the same in the past. Elsewhere irrigation

9

is required, and in order to preserve the precious water from evaporation under a hot sun, or to lead it safely through porous soil, a remarkable system of underground canals was evolved. In western Iran called *qanat* and in eastern Iran *kariz*, the irrigation canal is ancient in Iran for Polybius mentions its existence in great numbers in Media.[4] Such underground canals, of course, exist elsewhere, in Arabia, North Africa and perhaps even in pre-Columbian South America, but they have been developed most in Persia, some today extending underground for miles from their sources. The construction and maintenance of such conduits is quite an engineering feat requiring experienced specialists.

One may make a general observation that the land has not changed appreciably in historic times and much the same conditions which help to determine the mode and manner of life on the plateau now also prevailed in antiquity. Iran is a land of contrasts. In a small mountain valley one may find growing apple or peach trees while a short distance away in an oasis of the central deserts date palms or citrus fruit trees are prominent. Desolate and barren sand or stones may be separated from a colourful, fragrant garden by only a mud wall. The mud wall, too, can separate a tough, weather-beaten caravan leader from a delicate, soft denizen of such a private paradise.

People Change and People Remain

Who are the people of Iran today and who were they in the past? Human beings are differentiated primarily by their languages. By language a man is taught and by language he expresses himself. When we remember that in the excavations of Mohenjo-Daro, a very old pre-Aryan site in the lower Indus river valley, brachy-meso- and dolicho-cephalic skulls were found, perhaps 4,000 years old, then any attempt to differentiate races in Iran, at least in historic times, is hardly possible. This is not to reject the work of physical anthropologists, but for our purposes in Iran we do not need to go beyond the general racial designations of Mongoloid, Negroid and Caucasoid, with some subdivisions of the last. Mongoloid and Negroid peoples came to Iran for the most part in Islamic times, the former as Turks and Mongols, the latter primarily as slaves from Africa via Arabia. The existence of Negritos in coastal areas of south Persia, however, may testify to an aboriginal population perhaps to be connected with Negritos in the East Indies or Polynesia. The population of Iran may be

10

classified on the whole as Caucasoid, with all three sub-groups, Nordics, Alpines and Mediterraneans present. The Alpines, or 'round heads' predominate, and they may be further divided into Armenoids and Iranoids (called the Iranian or Scythian sub-race by some anthropologists). Attempts to link a racial group with a certain migration of peoples have been made by anthropologists and archaeologists, but certainly by the first millennium BC, if not long before, they are all greatly mixed. So we should turn our attention instead to linguistic and pastoral-agricultural groups.

In order to study the land and people of Iran in antiquity one might well heed parallels in the early Islamic period before the Turkish invasions, when there are more sources than before to help in the reconstruction of a picture of pre-Islamic Iran. From these sources one may generally conclude that the areas of Iran occupied by nomads in the recent past were also occupied by nomads in antiquity. It is true that in some districts town and settled life seems to have been more developed in the past than at present, but the reverse also was true, which does not invalidate the general proposition above. There were, and still are, certain areas which could support a settled life to such an extent that they might be termed 'centres of political power', where more or less self-contained states could arise. The fact that they did exist in the past testifies to the viability of tradition, geography and other circumstances making for a unity.

Beginning in the south-west is the plain of Khuzistan where the Elamites held sway in ancient times. Although properly speaking just an extension of the Mesopotamian plain to the east, historically, because it was an *extension* to the east, and because of frequent access to the plateau, Khuzistan has been intimately associated with the plateau. This association may date from 'pre-historic' times when the Elamites extended into Fars province. The Karun river and its tributaries made cultivation possible and consequently Khuzistan was a centre of civilisation and political organisation.

The people of Fars, ancient Persis, a series of valleys and plains mainly running north-west to south-east, were capable of expansion, as evidenced several times when unified under aggressive rulers. Such rulers had to exert themselves mightily, however, to obtain unity in the province, but once achieved there was a reservoir of manpower with both agricultural and pastoral wealth on which to draw. From the time of the Achaemenids Fars has remained the 'heart of Persia' in the minds of the people.

The real heart of Persia according to geography, however, is the area of modern Hamadan-Tehran-Isfahan, roughly included in ancient Media. Being located inside 'the bowl of the plateau', communications between the three cities were perhaps easier than elsewhere. Strategically also this is the area most open to invasion, and east-west trade flowed through Media. Life on the inner slopes of the Zagros or Elburz mountains was not too difficult for the farmers while wide plains sloping down to the salt deserts in the centre of the bowl provided excellent pasture for horses and cattle. Yet this area has not had the unity of tradition of Fars, and the basis for unified political rule, followed by expansion, seems to have been less evident here than in Fars.

The land around the Lake of Urmia, the centre of Azerbaijan, perhaps provided the richest conditions for a livelihood on the plateau. Here the population, denser than in the other provinces of Persia, has been important and active since antiquity. But Azerbaijan too was on trade routes over the Caucasus as well as on an east-west route to the Black Sea. Armies marched over these routes as did migrating tribes, and unity was hard to organise. In the past as today, Azerbaijan was never a completely 'Iranian' land, as we shall see.

The extensive eastern province called Khurasan under Islam can best be divided into three parts, the centre with Herat on the Harī-Rūd (river), the eastern part or Bactria with its capital at Balkh (near present-day Mazar-i Sharif), and the western part from the Caspian Gates located to the east of present Tehran, eastward to Mashhad, the capital today of the Persian province. This elongated area was the 'land of the rising sun' as its name implies, always exposed to invasions from Central Asia. Bactria, or the plain of Turkestan, as the Afghans call it today, drew its wealth from the land watered by the Oxus river, and was the cultural centre for a large area dominated by mountains to the north, east and south. Trade over the mountains to India in the south, China to the east and Central Asia to the north funnelled through Bactria to Persia proper. A strategic area, Bactria was also a centre of wealth which at times provided the basis of empire for its own sons.

Herat, in the fertile valley of the Hari-Rūd, was even more at the centre of routes going to all points of the compass. In a certain sense Herat represented the easternmost extension of the Iranians, for in antiquity, to the east, over the rugged Hindu

12

Kush mountains in the present-day Kabul-Ghazni-Qandahar area, were peoples best characterised as Indo-Iranians albeit with the latter element dominant.

Western Khurasan with various capitals from Hecatompylos in the west to Nishapur in the east has been too much like a highway to have any traditions of unity like Fars. It is in effect the bridge between eastern and western Iran. It is over this bridge that peoples have passed, moving westward for the most part. There have been no compelling reasons, geographical or historical, to bring the people of this part of Khurasan together, and while nomads have moved through to establish kingdoms to the west, the rulers of Khurasan have more frequently come from western Iran.

Other centres of population should be mentioned, although they have not loomed as large in history as the areas mentioned above. In Central Asia the oases of Merv, Bukhara, Samarkand and the Ferghana Valley have been important trading centres of considerable strategic importance on the 'silk road' to China. To the south, Seistan, the country around the Hamun lake and the Helmand river, provided an opportunity for a settled population to flourish and multiply in a plain away from mountains. Further upstream to the east on the foothills of the tributaries of the Helmand, in present-day Qandahar, ancient Harahuvati or Arachosia as the Greeks called it, the land was rich enough to support a large settled population.

Finally, the coastal plain on the southern shores of the Caspian Sea by its isolation from the plateau induced a kind of unity among its inhabitants. In spite of contacts and invasions both ways, the jungle and the plateau remained apart, as though in different worlds.

From the above it will be seen that the dominant characteristic of organised, settled life in Iran is its 'oasis character', its isolation from close contacts with the outside. Throughout history Persian families have lived in houses surrounded by high walls endeavouring to retain their privacy. The same tendency is repeated on a larger scale with the tribe, or even the province (or geographical area). The sometimes fierce individuality of the Persian and the lack of unity in his country have been most characteristic of him through the ages. One is tempted to ascribe the failure of the late Reza Shah to settle the nomads of his country to his inability first to deal with the clan or tribal spirit still alive in the rest of the population. Otherwise the

13

tribes might have been absorbed. To outsiders it seems as though the settled folk with their extended family loyalties are little removed in this respect from the tribesmen whose first, allegiance is to their tribe. Is this not an important reason for the fall of ephemeral states which were established in the Orient by great leaders able to command widespread loyalty to their persons, but whose successors were unable to continue the bond which held subjects together? Tribes in Iran are not all nomadic; some are settled but the same psychology of allegiance remains even after their way of life has been changed.

Between the oases in Iran lies much territory. Some of it can be irrigated and tilled by villagers but most of it is too dry for farming and little water is available for irrigation. Here the nomads can live, but they must move with the seasons and follow their herds. From the beginning of written records the conflicts between steppe and sown have echoed through the history of Iran. So it is today with the Persians as it was 3,000 years ago, and the great pastoral areas must have been much the same then as now. The southern Zagros mountains are crossed time and again by Bakhtiyari tribes and Lurs. To the north the tribally organised Kurds are for the most part settled while the Turkish tribes to the south, the Qashqais, Afshars and others have probably only replaced former Iranian-speaking tribes. Farther south and east to the Indus river are the Baluchi tribesmen, predominantly nomadic, who came from the north-west after the tenth century AD replacing Brahui or other non-Aryan nomads. The Afghan-Pakistan frontier today can hardly have supported a different kind of population in the past from the nomadic Pathans or Pashto/Pakhto speakers of today. However, 2,000 years ago the Indo-Iranian population, now restricted to the high mountains of present Nuristan, Chitral, Swat and such, must have extended to the south of the Kabul river and west of Bamiyan.

The steppes of Central Asia were ever the abode of nomads, first Iranian Scythians then later Turks, and these fierce horsemen kept the settled people of Khurasan on the alert with raids and migrations from the north. If one wonders how the Turks could have migrated through Iran from Central Asia to Anatolia without imposing a Turkish character on Khurasan, one may suppose that the oasis-dwelling Persians locked their gates and from behind thick walls told the nomads to continue westward. Village and town life cannot be recent in Iran; it must be very ancient. But, of course, the Iranians themselves were nomads

14

who came on to the plateau where other people had long been settled.

Anthropologists tell us that pastoralism is a developed form of life appearing later than settled, agricultural society, which itself followed the hunting stage. If this is accepted, then one may surmise that the ancestors of the Indians and Iranians adopted pastoralism after having been acquainted with agriculture in their earliest homeland. Moving south they conquered settled folk from whom they again learned of agriculture but on a much more developed scale. In the subcontinent of India and on the plateau of Iran the invaders were absorbed, but they gave their languages and traditions to the conquered natives. The traditions of a migrating, pastoral people lingered long in the new homelands, in a milieu probably similar to that which we find with the settled Arab with his often nostalgic feeling for the bedouin of the desert, the 'true Arab'. One should remember this in reading the ancient religious books of the Iranians and the Indians, for the tenor of all these books is derived from an early pastoral society and not a settled culture. Yet we learn about the pastoralists from the settled people, for the latter had the stability, the time and the desire to record the stories and the hymns recited by the nomads. In writing the hymns and lays of the warrior bands the sedentary scribes usually transformed what they heard to conform to some literary canon. So we have preserved in a sense 'interpretations' of the originals. Throughout history the steppe and the sown have existed side by side in Iran, frequently with little understanding or appreciation of one by the other.

Our view of the most ancient history of Iran, then, must be conditioned by these general observations as well as by a series of danger signals in drawing inferences from sparse and scattered information. Surmises and deductions must be made, however, following the general criteria of fitting as much of the given data as possible into a pattern, and of trying always to be as simple as possible. As does the natural scientist, so shall we endeavour to hold these criteria as guides for our reconstruction of the heritage of Persia.

NOTES

1 Herodotus VII. 62. Moses of Khoren I. 29, uses the term *arik* 'Aryan', as well as *mar-* and *med-* for the Medes.

15

2 The ethnica alone is attested in Herodotus III.93; VII.66 and in Arrian VII.6.3, but we may reconstruct ★ Aria for modern Herat. The Babylonian form of the name was *a-ri-e-mu*, possibly the origin of the Greek ★ Aria or Areia (Aramaic *'ryk* may refer to 'Arya or Aryan').

3 The district of Herat, called Harev *hlyw* in Middle Persian, has maintained its name from antiquity, and the name should not be linguistically confused with Arya though there might be historical reasons, under the Parthians, for the Greeks to coalesce Arya and the district which they called Aria.

4 Polybius, *Historia*, X.28.

2 IRANIAN TRADITIONS

The Aryan Background

Imagine that all evidence of the existence of Rome, its history, the Latin language, archaeological remains and references in later languages, had not existed, while the sole source for reconstructing the Latin language was the family called Romance languages in their modern forms. Would anyone be able to deduce that the original home of the Romance languages was a small area in west central Italy? How much would an *Ursprache,* reconstructed from Roumanian, French, Italian, Spanish and Portuguese resemble Latin? The difficulties in restoring a supposed Indo-European mother tongue would be even greater than the hypothetical case above. Yet this is what linguists have done. Rules of phonetic changes have been formulated, modified and multiplied until just as in the natural sciences where the proof of the pudding is in the eating, so in Indo-European comparative philology we have a system which in its general premises and methods does work. Frequently challenged by the discovery of new languages, such as Indo-European Hittite, the discipline has succeeded in accommodating seeming aberrations and thus vindicating the reliability of the method used. Because of this success other areas of study such as art history and comparative religions look to linguistics for possible guidance in methods of investigation. This is only consistent with the quiet, unassuming, present (as compared with certain nineteenth-century tendencies) progress of natural science to the understanding of the world about us in our own day.

Therefore, the basis of investigation of the pre-literary history of the Iranians must be comparative philology, with other relevant disciplines at least taking their cues from the study of language. In order to learn about the unknown mother language (Aryan or Indo-Iranian) we question the children (Old Persian and Avestan) whom we know; but also one should investigate the nephews (proto-Slavic, proto-Germanic, etc.) to learn of the common grandmother (Indo-European *Ursprache*) which will in turn help in understanding all the children and grandchildren. Of course this relationship must be assumed, it being understood that the affiliations are not simple but often subject to dispute. One might even argue that a proto-Aryan language is not needed, but only Indo-European and Avestan-Old Persian and Old Indian. Such matters, however, are beyond the scope of this book.

The original Indo-European language, while artificial in that it has been created by linguists, is none the less more than a convention of common features found in various daughter and grand-daughter languages. It might be characterised as a tool which gives the most adequate explanation of the divergencies found in all the languages of the family. Membership in the family is claimed by modern spoken and ancient written languages which have common features of vocabulary and grammar. To put it in another way, the placement of languages in the family is determined by conformity to general 'laws' of morphology and phonetics. Phonetic changes are paramount in classifying the languages. Some languages, of course, changed more in certain aspects of phonology or morphology than others, making it difficult to draw neat divisions and categories between languages. One must remember that 'the phonetic laws or the laws of general, historical morphology are not sufficient to explain any fact; they present the constant conditions which regulate the development of linguistic facts'.[1] In spite of many *caveats* in using the methods of comparative philology, and in spite of the hypothetical nature of the original Indo-European language, spoken by an unknown people with an assumed social and religious, as well as linguistic, unity, we must none the less build on the Indo-European theory *faute de mieux*. Before turning to the civilisation of the Indo-Europeans, especially their religion, a few words should be devoted to the dialectology of the presumed Indo-European original language.

It is obvious in studying various dialects of any present-day language that the area where a certain phonetic change, a special word or syntactic development occurs is usually not identical to the area of another change. If one would make maps of various areas of isoglosses between dialects of a given language and then superimpose them on one another, the result would be

18

exceedingly complicated. If one applied the same method to the Indo-European languages relative to the *Ursprache* the result would be much more confusing. In certain matters, for instance the augment on certain past tenses, Greek, Armenian and Indo-Iranian would agree while other Indo-European languages would be different. Slavic, Baltic and Albanian preserve an original *e* which is changed to *a* in Indo-Iranian, and there are many other such concordances in various groups of Indo-European tongues. So one could trace many lines of isoglosses among the Indo-European languages and they would cross in countless cases. Still one must not despair but continue to make classifications of the Indo-European languages in order to further their study. And one may assume a dialectical division within common Indo-European before the dispersal of the people speaking the *Ursprache*. Perhaps one should avoid the word dialect and only say that certain tendencies to innovation or change existed in one group and otherwise in the other. We can hardly say that the original tongue was divided into 'centum' and 'satem' dialects on the basis of phonetic 'laws' about changes in the Indo-European palatals and velars. This is not our concern, but coming to the subfamilies such as Balto-Slavic and Indo-Iranian one is on firmer ground. Before turning to Indo-Iranians, however, we may consider a few questions in regard to the society and religion of the undispersed Indo-Europeans.

Based on the reconstructed language some scholars have naturally proceeded to reconstruct the material culture, the state of the family and society, and above all the religious beliefs of the Indo-Europeans. If one presupposes a unity of language, a unity of social and religious beliefs would easily follow. Much has been written about the material culture of the Indo-Europeans but there is neither space, nor is it appropriate here to go into involved questions in this sphere. One may guess that the Indo-Europeans before dispersal were on the threshold of the age of metals because of the existence, and yet uncertain meanings, of derivatives from Indo-Europeans *aios* 'metal', Latin *aes* 'bronze, copper', Sanskrit *áyas* 'iron' (a later development), and others.[2]

Presumably the Indo-Europeans had domesticated the horse (Indo-European *ekuos)* and were acquainted with agriculture (Indo-European root *ar*—'to plough'). [3] Beyond these general observations we hardly can go further.

The social organisation of the Indo-Europeans is more difficult to reconstruct. Presumably they knew the forest as well as the steppe. One might draw parallels with primitive peoples, nomads or with speakers of other families of languages, but one must be very careful in interpreting parallels, for they are but parallels and nothing more. For example, it might prove fruitful to compare the Altaic peoples (Turko-Mongols) with the Indo-Europeans since the former came to the steppe from the forests of Siberia, became nomadic, and, as the Indo-Europeans did, invaded the Near East. Even though the Altaic peoples expand and migrate in relatively late historic times, our knowledge of their early society is grossly inadequate, making the drawing of parallels difficult. From what we know of the Indo-Iranians, the Dorians in Greece, and Indo-European invaders elsewhere, we may assume that they were all fierce and warlike. Probably they had a tight, organised society similar to the Turks and to most migratory peoples, but this helps us little. The family was most likely patriarchal, and the chief unit in society was probably the extended family or 'great house' (Indo-European *ueik, *uoikos). A comparison of Lithuanian *veszpats* 'lord', Sanskrit *viśpáti* 'head of the clan', and Latin *vicus* 'village', does not tell us much, however, about Indo-European society. One may assume that the society must have been closely bound up with religion, and it is to this domain that we turn next.

The religion of the ancient Indo-Europeans has received much attention of late and controversy about it is rife among scholars. The theory of Max Müller and his school, which proposed that celestial phcnomena lay behind the myths and religion of the Indo-Europeans, is no longer accepted although some of his many ideas have been, with very little change. The brief remarks by Meillet, warning of vague indications leading to inflated illusions, indicate the limited conclusions one may draw from methods of comparative philology to elucidate religion, and they remain a classic presentation of the problem.[4] The Indo-European word for god or divinity is *deiwos*, perhaps conceived individually as a luminous, shining sky deity. It is not the place here to discuss the problems of the 'heaven father,' Jupiter in Latin, *dyáus pitá* in Sanskrit, and the words for day, *dies* in Latin, etc. Suffice it to say that the Indo-Europeans considered the sky, sun and many celestial and natural phenomena, to be divine and the divinities were probably represented by their ordinary names, thus giving a common and a particular noun for each. For example, in Old Slavic the god Perun is the god of thunder, while the word for the phenomenon of thunder itself was

20

the same root, preserved even today in Polish *piorun*, or even closer in Lithuanian *Perkunas* 'thunder god' and *perkunas* 'thunder'. But the Indo-Europeans probably also conceived of their gods as social phenomena become divine, as Indo-Iranian *mitra* 'contract', and *Mitra*, the god of contracts according to Meillet and others. The god, then, we may say, is a phenomenon, natural or social, as well as a magical force connected with his name. Further, we find no common Indo-European words for cult, priest or sacrifice, and this may indicate that each tribe or group of Indo-Europeans had its own cult. It is possible that there was a parallel development of religion in the position of the Druids among the Celts and the Brahmins of India, as well as linguistic parallels of terms of religion among Indo-Iranians and Italo-Celts, but these are general or uncertain theories which cannot lead us to the details of an original Indo-European religion.[5] Meillet expressed it well when he said that more than any other history, the history of religions had need of texts written in the language of the people under study, which in effect precluded a study of the religion of the original undivided Indo-Europeans.[6]

The school of Georges Dumézil, however, has opened new vistas of investigation and discussion on the problems of Indo-European folklore and religion. Briefly, the general position of Dumézil may be described as a new approach to ancient religions; the ideology and spirit of ancient religions must be emphasised rather than their ritual and external manifestations. For Dumézil the ideology of a religion is found in its theology, mythology, sacred literature and sacerdotal organisation. For him, if the Indo-European people had a community of language before they separated, then they must also have had a common ideology.

In ancient India, Iran and elsewhere, Dumézil found that the 'ideology' of a tripartite division of society parallel to a tripartite classification of the gods was prominent. After further study he concluded that this ideology was fundamental in the religious beliefs of all the Indo-European daughter peoples and not to be found elsewhere. Within the tripartite division there was, moreover, a duality, which was also a fundamental concept in the ideology of the Indo-Europeans. The three divisions of the ideology could be described both as cosmic and as social 'functions', the highest that of sovereignty, with two aspects, juridical and magical, as the duality within the tripartite division. Among the Aryans, then later the Indians, Mitra and Varuṇa

21

represented respectively the juridical and magical aspects of the first function, the province of priests. The second function, the martial spirit or force, was the domain of the warriors with the god Indra, while the third function, that of fecundity or growth, was the concern of farmers and husbandmen. This, in a few words, represents generally the theory of Dumézil, albeit with many developments and minor conclusions from the above-mentioned premises.

At the outset, one may welcome the new interest in the study of the religion of the Indo-Europeans which has grown partly as a result of controversy over Dumézil's theories. Further, one may warmly greet his attempts to find an order or system in beliefs hitherto characterised as 'primitive beliefs' or 'nature worship', which told us very little. His general influence has also stimulated work in comparative folklore and mythology, some of which is of great interest and value.[8] In the Iranian field Dumézil's theories have been followed by several scholars in the attempt to elucidate various aspects of the Zoroastrian religion.[9] Although his opponents decry his general theory and methods, they attack even more the widespread consequences of his insistence that 'the duality in a tripartite division' penetrates all corners of the society, religion and culture of the Indo-European daughter peoples. It is, they say, as if the ideology of the Trinity so dominated Christians that their political thought, art, and of course all religious beliefs, were to be understood on the basis of a trinity. It must be emphasised that there is no *direct evidence* written or otherwise, for the validity of Dumézil's theories, only his inferences. But just as with conversion to a new faith, passions run high, and he has succeeded in convincing some scholars that 'the Indo-European tripartite division is today a fact, which it would be just as foolish to deny as, for example, the correspondence of Latin *rex*, Sanskrit *rājan* and Irish *ri*.[10] Other scholars remain as unpersuaded as they were of the pronouncements of J. Hertel who tried to find fire at the basis of all Aryan beliefs.[11] Perhaps Meillet's admonition above is still the best guide to a difficult and even misleading subject, and with this remark we may leave the Indo-Europeans.

One is on safer territory with the Indo-Iranians or Aryans, and a real relationship between the Indians and Iranians may be assumed, probably closer than between any other two Indo-European families of languages. It is not only from related vocabulary and grammar that we can postulate an Indo-Iranian

22

unity, but many religious and social concepts stem from a common origin, and, of course, both peoples used the term 'Aryan' for themselves. So we may reconstruct a common Aryan language and then derive from it common Indian and common Iranian, although this is still hypothetical. From Indian further derive the language of the Vedas and other tongues of India, while from Iranian derive Avestan in its two dialects, the language of the Gathas and the language of the Younger Avesta, as well as Old Persian of the inscriptions of the Achaemenid kings. Our oldest, indeed our only factual evidence of the Aryans, apart from possible archaeological attributions to them, is found in cuneiform records. We learn of the Aryans first in the Near East.

It would seem that the Aryans entered the Mesopotamian cultural area from the highlands to the east. Whether they came to the Iranian plateau from the north via the Caucasus or from Central Asia is uncertain, possibly by both routes but probably mainly from the latter. From cuneiform sources one could surmise that Aryan bands first came into Mesopotamia with the general movement of peoples after the death of Hammurabi in the seventeenth century BC. This is also the time of the expansion of the Hurrians, a people whose linguistic and ethnic affiliations are puzzling; in any case, they were not Indo-Europeans. They formed an important empire called Mitanni, and it is principally among the Mitanni that Aryan names and words occur.[12] Many personal names of Mitanni rulers which appear in the El-Amarna letters and in Hittite documents can be recognised as Aryan, but their etymologies are for the most part uncertain because of possible different readings or interpretations. In a famous treaty between the Hittite ruler Suppiluliuma and the Mitanni king, Mattiwaza, about 1370 BC, the Aryan gods Mitra, Varuna, Indra and the twin Nāsatyas are mentioned. Thus in the Mitanni kingdom Aryan gods were worshipped as well as Mesopotamian deities, which would indicate an Aryan element, but probably only among the rulers. While there is no doubt about the identification of the names of the deities in the treaty, much has been written about the significance of and in-terpretation of the names. In addition to personal names and the names of gods several Aryan words relating to horse training and numerals have been deciphered in records of the Mitanni Kikkuli from the Hittite site of Boghaz Köy in Anatolia. Although most of the words seem more Indian in form than Iranian, or even Aryan,

23

the two words which at first appear explainable *only* as Indian in form are *aika* 'one', and Varuṇa.[13] The former, I suggest, was really the Aryan form for 'one'[14] close in meaning to another Aryan word **aiva* 'the same, identity, exactly' (Indian *eva*), which was taken by some Iranians in Old Persian and Avestan for 'unity, one', and maintained to this day in some of the Pamir dialects and in Pashto. So *aika*- and Varuna could be considered real Aryan forms, or dialect forms from that general period, and we may conclude that there were bands of Aryan warriors rather than Indians who preceded the later main wave of Aryans, and who established states in the Near East in the middle of the second millennium BC. Presumably others invaded India in the same period. Again this surmise is based on the 'Aryan' hypothesis which is subject to criticism.

It would seem that these early Aryans were absorbed by the indigenous populations of western Iran and Mesopotamia and only the arrival of the Iranians later led to the 'Iranisation' of the land which bears their name. The pottery and objects uncovered by archaeologists have not been of great help in reconstructing the period of invasion of the Iranians, for it is extremely difficult, if at all possible, to assign certain strata in various sites on the plateau to the Iranian invaders with the material objects as representative of their culture. Our chief sources for this period are the Avesta, and the neighbouring literature of the Vedas. From them by inference and analogy one can reconstruct, though often tenuously, certain features of the life of the early Iranians.[15] The study of the phenomenology of religion and cultural anthropology can assist us, especially in setting the stage or background for our understanding.

Before turning to the Iranians, our proper concern, a few general remarks about the Aryans, the hypothetical undivided Indo-Iranians, may be helpful. One may at the beginning assume that the Aryans were in a nomadic stage of life, or perhaps better characterised as herdsmen who knew about agriculture. It is not necessary to discuss the care of cattle, for cattle seem to have been the staff of life for the Aryans as the camel was for the Arabs. Both in the Gathas and the Vedas cattle appear as a prime source of nourishment and wealth, and as significant in religion. Metals were known but certainly were quite rare. The horse and war chariot, as we learn from the Vedas, were very important in warfare. Agriculture was at least known to the Indo-Iranians before their separation from other Indo-Europeans and many

24

grains and other domesticated plants were eaten.[16] In social organisation, as might be expected of pastoralists, the clan (Avestan *zantu*, Sanskrit *jánah* 'race' and *jantú* 'offspring', Latin *genus*) was the most important unit. Whether a larger unit, such as the people or nation or race, had any significance, is dubious, even though the embryonic concepts may well have existed. Since pastoralists or nomads at the present and throughout history have been conspicuous for their lack of well-defined classes or castes, their form of life militating against strict specialisation, a tripartite composition of people (in the clan?) into those concerned with religion, the larger group of warriors, and the majority of herdsmen or just common folk is unproven. Again, the concepts may well have existed, but their influence on the ordering of society is unknown. [17]

The religion of the Aryans is also a matter of some controversy. If one may assume that the Indo-Europeans believed primarily in gods of nature, then the Aryans were probably on the brink of a change where the old nature gods like **dyāuš*[18] were losing their status to more personalised gods such as the Vedic Indra. It is generally accepted that the religion of the Aryans, if it can be reconstructed at all from any later texts, is best reflected in the Vedas. Later in India we find certain 'Aryans' who do not follow the Vedic religion, and we may assume that even before they went their various ways the un-divided Aryans were not uniform in their beliefs.[19] It is interesting to note in passing that the old pagan religion existed in Sweden side by side with Christianity in the eleventh century AD, and a reasonable explanation for the lack of conflict between them is that Christianity was intolerant in matters of belief but indulgent in regard to other traditions and practices, while the heathen would not exclude a member from their ranks if he believed as a Christian as long as he practised their rites.[20] It would seem that cult, marriage taboos, purification ceremonies and the like were the outstanding characteristics of the religion of the Aryans. Forces of nature were revered but probably in different ways; possibly some held to a henotheism while others were polytheists. But a change seems to have taken place among the Aryans which may well have been ethical as well as cosmological. It may have been a reflection into heaven of the conditions and aspirations of the Aryan people personalising their gods, and thus developing further an Indo-European tendency. Certain suggestions can be made.

25

Some of the gods, particularly those known as the Ādityas in the Vedas, may be understood as personifications of the ideas which their names mean. Thus, as we have seen, Mitra the god is the personification of *mitra* 'contract', Aryaman of *aryaman*, 'hospitality', Varuṇa of *varuṇa* 'true speech, oath', all of them abstract conceptions made into concrete deities, the guardians of those concepts which were so essential to the functioning of the universe.[21] Here we are far beyond primitive beliefs concerned with nature, and rather in a milieu of concern with the psychology of man, really with an overwhelming attention to man, his relation to other man and to himself. We may assume that some common Indo-European eschatological concepts, and myths to explain them, were reworked or developed by the Aryans when they settled among peoples of a higher civilisation in India and western Iran. The problem of the origin of myths, such as the flood motif, and the beginning of Indo-European epics is very involved, and it would lead us far afield. However, we should look briefly to the texts from India to help us with observations on the Aryan religion.

The hymns of the Rig Veda are sacrificial hymns directed to the gods when a rite is performed. The recitation and the sacrifice were parallel, or rather at certain points in the recitation certain acts were performed. One reason the hymns are difficult to understand is that they presupposed a knowledge of the ancient mythology in all who partook of the rites. There is no evidence that there were any idols or images; rather the power of words was central in the rites. There does not seem to have been any hierarchic order in the Vedic pantheon even though certain gods are more in the foreground or in the texts more important. Possibly some Aryans did think of one god as supreme, or even as the sole, ultimate reality. We must not forget that the hymns were written down later by the Brahmins to glorify the Brahman caste or their warrior patrons, and an idealised picture may be what we have rather than a source for the actual situation in Rig Vedic times.

A central figure in the Rig Veda is the god Indra, who might be characterised as the apotheosis of the Aryan man. Some of the hymns exuberate in ecstatic feeling about the god, even more powerful in the original language with metre; take for example Rig Veda 10.153, 2-5:.[22]

'Thou, Indra, art born from power, strength and vitality. Thou, bull, art really a bull.

26

Thou, Indra, art the Vṛtra killer. Thou has expanded the sky. Thou hast held up the heaven with strength.

Thou, Indra, carriest in thine arms thy glorious, shining (?) weapon sharpening it with thy strength.

Thou, Indra, art stronger than all creatures. Thou has extended thyself into all realms.'

Indra is the patron of the warrior bands of the Aryans, leading them to victory. If Indra is the hero of the Rig Veda, the drinking of *soma,* deified as a god *Soma,* is the central rite of the hymns. How the drink was prepared, and what its qualities were, occupies many stanzas of the hymns. We are not sure precisely what the *soma* plant was which produced an intoxication in those who consumed it, possibly to be compared with the ambrosia of the Greek gods, but we may be fairly sure that Indian *soma,* Avestan *haoma,* played an important role in the ritual life of the early Iranians as well as the Indians.

The Aryans did split, however, the Indians moving to the great plains of the subcontinent where they found numerous settled folk living in towns, relatives of the builders of such cities as Mohenjo-Daro and Harappa. Although these enemies of the Aryans are ill-regarded in the hymns, surely the conquerors learned much from the conquered *dasyu*—whom they despised. Although the caste system became fixed at a later date, we may assume that there was a considerable mixture of populations in India in earlier times. In Iran, however, the situation was different, for the real centres of settled life were in Mesopotamia to the west and the population on the plateau must have been relatively sparse. Since the Aryan bands in India fought among themselves as well as against the non-Aryan native population, we can assume the same for the Aryans in Iran, and there must have resulted considerable mixtures of various peoples. Generally speaking then, we can assume that there were deviations from Aryan society by both Iranians and Indians, perhaps more with the former than the latter.

Some peoples of the Hindu Kush mountains and the western Himalayas, represented by present-day speakers of Dardic and Kafir dialects, might be classified as a third group of Aryans parallel with Iranians and Indians, or possibly they could be subsumed under the Indian category. Our knowledge of this remote area is still rudimentary and much work remains before an adequate classification of all the languages and dialects can be made. Needless to say, work in this area will be of great

27

significance for any reconstruction of the pre-history of the Indo-Iranians. Incidentally, this mountainous refuge area also has a non-Indo-European language, Burushaski, spoken in Hunza, which may be the last remnant of languages once spoken over a large territory before the Aryans came upon the scene. Attempts to prove a connection of Burushaski with Caucasian languages or Basque in the Pyrenees are interesting if inconclusive.[23]

One can tentatively propose the following general distribution of the Aryans about the seventh century BC when the Medes and Persians had attained their final resting grounds. In Azerbaijan and western Iran, the Medes and other Iranian newcomers were in contact with a settled majority of non-Indo-European speakers represented by Urartians, Mannaeans, Hurrians, etc., possibly related somehow to the Palaeo-Caucasian or 'Japhetic' languages of the present-day Caucasus. Also present were other Indo-Europeans, principally the first bands of the Armenians coming from the west, and possibly fragmentary remains of previous Aryan invaders. To the south the Persians and other Iranian invaders found the land occupied by Elamites and related non-Indo-European speakers. Farther east were probably Dravidian peoples in Makran, Seistan and Sind, represented today by their descendants, the Brahuis.[24] The relation of these peoples with the Elamites is uncertain but some connection is not improbable. Finally, in the Hindu Kush mountains were remnants of the people driven there by earlier Aryan migrations into India. In the course of centuries these non-Indo-Europeans were pushed more and more into isolated valleys by Iranians from the west and Indians from the south and east until the last group is now represented by the Burushaki speakers in the high and isolated valleys of Hunza. Such was the general picture when Zoroaster appeared.

Zoroaster and His Message

Zarathushtra, or Zoroaster, as the Greeks called him, presents many problems, and it is discouraging that after so many years of research we do not know when or where he lived or even precisely his teachings. One may marshal the evidence and conclude that he was not one thing or did not live at a certain period, but positive information about the prophet and his time is conspicuous by its absence. Let us attempt to gather material relating to him, trying to group the less uncertain data first, and

28

finally coming to some tentative conclusions.

It is highly probable that Zarathushtra is not a figment of the imagination and that he did exist. Arguments that he was created to match prophets in other religions, or that the Avesta was a late forgery, are really unacceptable and we only need to follow history to refute them. The form of his name is also plausible among the names one would expect in an ancient society somewhere in Iran. The name Zarathushtra might be explained as 'he who can handle camels', although other etymologies have been proposed. In the Avesta we learn about his clan of Spitama and the closely related family of Haechataspa, indeed about his daughter and friends, and from the later Middle Persian commentaries we even learn the names of his father and mother. None of this, however, helps us with the *history* of Zoroaster, especially his time and place. We must turn primarily to the Gathas, presumably the words of the prophet, and to later sources and general considerations, to aid us in placing Zoroaster in history and geography.

To determine the date of Zoroaster we have no historical data to help us, and we can only say that most probably he lived before the Achaemenid empire. To further determine the time we should look at the evidence of the Gathas, Greek sources, and later Zoroastrian tradition subdivided into the tradition of the Pahlavi books and the tradition as found in Islamic sources. These we should try to bring into harmony, or at least we should come to a probable estimate of his dates from all of them.

The Gathas, 'verses or poems', were undoubtedly preserved by memory for centuries before being written down. The seventeen verses or five groups of verses, known collectively as Gatha, belong together by virtue of similarity in metre and archaic language. Certain features of the language of the Gathas, and of the Younger Avesta as well, are more archaic than corresponding features in Vedic Sanskrit.[25] but this, of course, does not mean that the Gathas are therefore older in time than the Rig Veda, since as a parallel in Altaic languages modern Mongolian in many features is 'more archaic' than the oldest Turkish, and Arabic is in the same relation to Hebrew.

Greek sources are not encouraging either. Xanthos of Lydia, the oldest source (fifth century BC) places Zoroaster 600 (or 6,000) years before Xerxes, and other Greek authors are more extravagant.[26] From the classical sources we gain no precision at all, only that Zoroaster lived in great antiquity. Obviously they had no accurate knowledge of his history, but we should explain even this lack. Some of the sources which give numbers in the thousands can be explained as reflecting an Iranian mythical world age number — an eschatological doctrine. [27] Did the Greeks reproduce this, or other extreme dates on Zoroaster, because the Persians fooled them, either intentionally or because they themselves believed it, or was Zoroaster so removed from the West in time or space that a myth about him was all that was known? If the Persians tried to fool the Greeks, then how is it that no indication of the real state of affairs leaked out to the Greeks, and why did the Persians try to fool the Greeks? In answer to the first question, it is unlikely that the Persians could keep true information from the Greeks, and if they did try, it can hardly be explained as pure perversity or a desire to sanctify Zoroaster by a hoary age. What then is the conclusion to draw from the Greek sources? One probably could say that the Greeks got their information from Persians who themselves did not know the date of Zoroaster. From the Greek sources, a date of, say, 1,000 BC might seem a shade more reasonable for Zoroaster than 600 BC, but this is speculative. The burden of bringing more evidence seems to rest on Iranian sources, or the Zoroastrian tradition.

Since the chronology of the ancient Near East before the Achaemenids is mostly based on the Egyptian king lists and anything outside the hieroglyphic-cuneiform cultural areas is hardly datable, it follows that the non-literary Iranians could not be expected to have a chronology of Zoroaster unless they kept genealogical lists like the Hebrews, which apparently was not the case. It would not be unreasonable to assume that the ancient Iranians, even shortly after Zoroaster's death, could not place him chronologically, at least in relation to any of the great events occurring in Mesopotamia or possibly even in western Iran. But later Zoroastrian tradition, followed by Islamic authors such as al-Bīrūnī, gives a precise date for Zoroaster, 258 years before Alexander the Great.[28] Many scholars have rejected this date, while others have accepted it as genuine. [29] Not long ago an impressive attempt was made to substantiate the date based on the reasonable assumption that the followers of Zoroaster counted the years from a significant moment in the life of the prophet, and when 258 years had passed in the era of Zoroaster, a great calamity occurred, the death of Darius, the last Achaemenid king, and the accession to power of Alexander the Great. This would mean 258 years subtracted from 330 BC or 588

BC for the year one of reckoning on the part of Zoroaster's followers.[30] It is interesting to observe that the dating of Buddha is apparently secured in a similar manner by reference to later traditions assigning events in Buddha's life to so many years before the reign of Aśoka. But actually it is only a later tradition and based on an assumed date of the Buddha rather than on Aśoka. One need not be reminded that the date 588 BC, which could be assumed to have been the date Zoroaster converted King Vishtaspa, when tradition says the prophet was forty-two years old, is based on a number of assumptions which might be criticised. Further tradition says the prophet was seventy-seven when he died, so if one prefers fixed historical dates for Zoroaster based upon reasonable *assumptions* and late Zoroastrian *traditions*, then 628-551 BC is the best theory we have. Otherwise, one may prefer to believe that the date is about the eighth or seventh century BC but not determined. If we could find evidence from outside the Zoroastrian tradition, which tradition assumes that the Zoroastrians had a clear 'era' reckoning from the time of the prophet, until Alexander so shocked them that they changed their outlook to date their prophet so many years before Alexander, then it would be easier to accept a more precise date for Zoroaster.[31]

It is true that the number 258 is curious, hardly apocalyptic or fitting into an eschatological system. Yet the negative reckoning, so many years before Alexander, presupposes the existence of an era of reckoning from some event in Zoroaster's life by his followers. As far as we know the Seleucid era was the first dating by a fixed year which was widely accepted. On the other hand, the followers of Zoroaster may have been well ahead of their time in adopting an 'era of Zoroaster', counting from the date of his conversion of Vishtaspa, possible echoes of which may survive in the Pahlavi book *Bundahishn* (ed. Anklesaria 240.1) where an era of the 'acceptance of the religion' *(padtriftan-i din)* is implied. The *Bundahishn*, of course, was written over 1,200 years after Alexander, but the mere fact that the apocryphal reign of Vishtaspa is said to have lasted for ninety years after the 'acceptance of religion' is hardly a support for a presumed 'Zoroastrian era'. Needless to say, we are still much in the dark. Shapur Shahbazi, in an unpublished article, however, has shown that the date 258 is based on calculations from Babylonian sources and is unreliable.

The homeland of Zoroaster has also raised great

31

controversies which are by no means all resolved. Most scholars now agree that he lived and taught in eastern Iran. Late Zoroastrian tradition placed the prophet in Azerbaijan, but the geographical horizon of the Avesta is limited to eastern Iran, and the transfer of his activities to western Iran at a later date can be explained by political circumstances. It is true that one may fit the *mythical* geography of the Avesta with the Aryan homeland of *Airyāna Vaējah*, into Azerbaijan, or for that matter elsewhere in Iran, but the geographical picture of the Avesta is not very helpful. One may say, however, that the legends and stories about Zoroaster's activities, not his birth, seem to be more specific when localised in the east than the stories localised in the west. For example, the story of the planting of a cypress tree in Kishmar in Khurasan to commemorate the conversion of Vishtaspa is old and widespread. Another tradition has him born in Raga, mediaeval Rayy, near Tehran, with a *hegira* to the east where he converts Vishtaspa. Furthermore, there is no apparent reason why Zoroaster should be moved to the east if in fact he lived in the west, while the reverse is more plausible since eastern Iran was subjected to invasion from Central Asia many times and was lost to Iranian rule for long periods. There is a Zoroastrian tradition that the prophet was killed in Bactria, but other traditions place his activity elsewhere in the east. One may guess that he was active in the Herat area with connections south to Seistan, east to Bactria (Balkh) and north to Merv.

Linguistic evidence too would tend to place the prophet in eastern Iran. Historically, one would expect that the Avesta, with its mythology and heroic epic features blending into the general eastern Iranian sagas which we shall shortly discuss, would be composed in a language close to that spoken in the Aryan homeland. That homeland may have been in Transoxiana, or even more to the south in the Herat area. Just as the Indians wherever they went in the sub-continent preserved the Vedic hymns in the old traditional language no matter what changes happened in their various dialects, so the Iranians wherever they went on the Iranian plateau preserved theogonies to Mithra and other Aryan gods. I suggest that the Iranian tribes of Persians, Medes and others, at the time of their wandering to their later homes, recited hymns to the gods similar in content and *language*, which would be the language of the old homeland *Airyāna Vaējah*. The tribes which went to western Iran gave their tongues to the indigenous population of Elamites, Hurrians or the

32

like, and consequently their dialects began to lose distinctions of grammatical gender and a general breakdown of the languages started. Before this happened, however, a prophet appeared in the east preaching in an archaising, conservative idiom of the dialect possibly of the Herat area, the language of the Gathas. This sounded more lofty and authoritative than the Avestan idiom used everywhere by 'priests' praying to Mithra, Ardvisura or other deities. Later when Zoroaster's teachings spread all over Iran other priests simply attached his hymns in the Gathic dialect to the common hymns in 'younger' Avestan. This probably happened under the Achaemenids, and we shall discuss this later.

To return to the two languages, or better characterised as dialects, Gathic and Avestan, the former the language of the Gathas, the latter the tongue of the 'Younger Avesta', they would best fit into the area between the central deserts and the mountains of Afghanistan. Since the contents of the Younger Avesta have connections with the eastern Iranian epic traditions, we may say that in content as well as language, both parts of the Avesta point to eastern Iran. This does, not mean, however, that the hymns of the Younger Avesta were only recited or sung in eastern Iran. Indeed parts of the Younger Avesta, particularly the Vendidad or Videvdat 'the anti-demonic law', may well have been composed in western Iran by the Magi, who seem to have been the priests of the Medes and later of all western Iranians. If this be true then the Magi may have known the Avestan language before Zoroaster. The Magi were probably influenced in ritual and practices by the indigenous population and by the ancient cultures of Mesopotamia while their counterparts in the east, the *zaotars*, remained truer to Aryan practices. But this is turning away from Zoroaster himself. Before turning to the historical, or better, epical milieu of eastern Iran at the time of Zoroaster, something should be said about his life and teachings.

We have said that Zoroaster does not appear in a vacuum, for we learn about his family, friends and enemies from the Avesta and from later Zoroastrian tradition.[32] Furthermore, as we shall shortly see, the prophet is placed among the epical, pre-historical kings of eastern Iran in an orderly picture of this pre-literary period in the sagas of the people. Because of this order, much, or even most of it may be historical, but we do not know. The age of Zoroaster seems to correspond with the phenomenological characterisation of an age when the gods have descended upon earth bringing an end to mythology, and the beginning of epic, the heroic age of Iran. The family and relations of Zoroaster need not detain us beyond the remark that the names are in general what one would expect in ancient, eastern Iran, though any royal connections among the ancestors of the prophet are suspicious, and I for one suspect them.

Zoroaster was probably a priest of the old Aryan religion, for he calls himself a *zaotar* (Indian *hotar*) in the Gathas (Yasna 33.6). Since he retained this ancient word and did not give it a bad sense, one may suppose he retained the old institution of the Aryan 'priest' in his new religion. He also retained the old poetic form, for the metre of his Gathas is similar to that of the Vedas. He further exalted the concept of *asha*, 'truth', the *rta* of India, and further used words in the same sense as in the Vedas. But Zoroaster is more; he is a prophet who preaches a new gospel not accepted by his own people. We obtain glimpses of opposition to him and then the prophet's *hegira* and chilly reception elsewhere (Yasna 51.12), and finally his acceptance by Kavi Vishtaspa and the success of his preaching. So Zoroaster was a prophet who found favour not at home but among others. In what way did his message differ from ancient beliefs and customs?

One difference between the Gathas and the Rig Veda is the different relation between the worshipper (this is Zoroaster himself in the Gathas) and the deity. The familiar tone of the Gathas strikes one at once, especially in Yasna 44 where the verses begin, 'I ask you, tell me truly oh Ahura (Mazda)'. The deity is like a partner in discourse with the prophet, and this is new with Zoroaster. His followers too are not neglected, so one senses a possible social base for Zoroaster's preaching. Whether one can distinguish between the followers of Zoroaster as peaceful shepherds with flocks of cattle and his enemies as fierce nomads who steal and slaughter the cattle of their foes, is perhaps reading too much into the words of Zoroaster. What stands out in the teaching of the prophet is the dualism of Good and Evil and the great importance of man as an arbiter between them. Whether he raised his dualism as a protest against existing monotheism is uncertain, but most people would agree that he was first and foremost a prophet with high ethical ideals and persuasive ideas. With which ideas did Zoroaster move the hearts of his contemporaries? Study of the Gathas led a recent translator to the following remarks.[33]

'He took over belief in the Ahuras from his predecessors. It is likely he transformed that belief; perhaps even created the name

34

Ahura Mazda and interpreted the Ahuras as personifications of the qualities of Ahura Mazda. But it was hardly possible with such theological discussion to set an entire people in religious motion. The favoured position of *asha*, which was also honoured by Zoroaster's opponents, is not new, nor is veneration of the cow, which Zoroaster already had ascribed to Fryana, the mythical ancestor of Kavi Vishtaspa. Perhaps even the dualism in substantial points had already been worked out by Zoroaster's predecessors. What is then the distinctive concept which Zoroaster brought out above all the cow-centred Magi and Brahmins, and which made him one of the great world founders of a religion? It is really the knowledge of the directly imminent beginning of the last epoch of the world, in which Good and Evil would be separated from one another, which he gave to mankind. It is the knowledge that it lies in every individual's hand to participate in the extirpation of Falsehood and in the establishing of the kingdom of God, before whom all men devoted to the pastoral life are equal, and so to re-establish the milk-flowing paradise on earth.'

Zoroaster's teachings must have made a great impression on his followers so that they memorised his sayings and passed them on to their children. There may have been prose explanations of the concise verses of Zoroaster like the commentaries on the sayings of Buddha, but unfortunately these Gathic commentaries have not survived, which makes our present understanding of the Gathas very difficult. Yet the power and intensity of feeling in the verses may be sensed even in translation, as for example Yasna 44.3-4:

> This do I ask Thee, Oh Lord, tell me truly;
> Who is the creator, the first father of Righteousness?
> Who laid down the path of the sun and stars?
> Who is it through whom the moon now waxes now wanes?
> All this and more do I wish to know, Oh Wise One.

> This do I ask thee, Oh Lord, tell me truly;
> Who holds the earth below and the sky as well
> from falling? Who (created) the waters and the plants?
> Who harnesses the (two) coursers to wind and clouds?
> Who, oh Wise One, is the creator of Good Mind?

Sagas of the East

The Persians are a people with an epic tradition which is surely very old. There are many problems in tracing the legends in the New Persian *Shahname*, or book of kings, back to Parthian, Achaemenian or Aryan times, and the changes or layers in

35

various stories throughout the ages are almost impossibly difficult to determine. One may, however, come to some general conclusions which would serve to clarify the role of the epic in pre-Islamic Iran.

Mythology is intimately bound up with the beginning of epic literature, for the former is concerned with the acts of the gods, and the latter with the heroic deeds of men. Just as later bards wove various stories of different dates with little regard to chronology into a unified epic, so the earlier priests recited hymns to the gods, and they, or associates, composed stories about the gods. As in the mythology of Japan where the descendants of the Sun goddess came to earth and ruled it, so in ancient Egypt and elsewhere the rulers are of divine origin. Among the Aryans, however, we do not find evidence for divine kingship. One may suppose that the undivided Aryans had a mythology but not yet an epic. After the separation of Indians and Iranians the new contacts of both, the former in the subcontinent and the latter in western Iran and Mesopotamia, may well have changed the outlooks of these people, now in more settled, more secure surroundings, to a more prosaic or pragmatic *Weltanschauung* which the heroic life which engenders epics lacked. In one place, however, the Aryan homeland, conditions propitious to the development of the epic continued. I suggest that circumstances and milieu were more favourable to the flowering of the epic in eastern Iran and Central Asia than elsewhere in the area covered by Iranians. It is inherently probable that the Iranians wherever they went had a common mythology, for even with the Indians there are parallel myths and names, such as the Iranian Yima and Indian Yama, an earthly first king or king of the dead, Iranian Thraetaona, Indian Traitaná, and others. Now it may well be, as some scholars have argued, that a common Indo-European eschatology engendered common stories and motifs in the later oral literature of some of the daughter languages, but few of these languages have an epic tradition. Persian is one and the *Shahname* is recited by countless people even today. The beginning of an epic tradition in Iran may have coincided with the appearance of the prophet Zoroaster, which event surely influenced the later development of the epic. If there had been no Zoroaster the epic might have developed as in India or among the Germanic peoples, or it might have died out under the rule in Iran of the Greeks or later the Arabs. If Zoroaster had appeared about the time of Christ and had been so willed he might have destroyed the old mythology and the epic with it. These are all 'ifs' and one may suppose that Zoroaster appeared at a time and place which almost ensured his inclusion in a developing epic. For the Iranian epic, as found in the *Shahname* and other variations of it, can be said at least to be in harmony with the Zoroastrian religion as it developed, if it were not actually 'Zoroastrianised', as is most likely.

Much has been written about the place of origin of local epic traditions or of various motifs in an all-Iranian epic tradition. This has led to a general conclusion about the Iranian epic, that it is really composed of two epic traditions, but there is some difference about the classification or nomenclature of these two traditions. One scholar called them the mythical tradition and the tradition of the eastern Iranian rulers, or the 'religious' and the 'national' traditions.[34]   Another postulates a 'Zoroastrian' and a 'nomadic' epic tradition.[35] The main problem here, I believe, is the different history of the epic in eastern and western Iran and its accretion by the addition of various local cycles. I have already proposed that all Iranians had a common mythology but not a common epic, at least not until the rule of the eastern Parthians spread over all of Iran. There is no evidence that stories of the eastern rulers or *kavis* were sung or recited in western Iran under the Achaemenids. Presumably there were local 'epics' about the ancestors of local rulers, but the inclusion of Zoroaster in the particular cycle of the *kavis* of eastern Iran probably helped to make that cycle the basis for the earlier part of the all-Iranian epic of later times. Furthermore, the stories of the eastern *kavis* may well have been more exciting and more heroic than others elsewhere, for any epic is primarily concerned with heroic deeds, religion being secondary.

One may suppose then that the Iranian epic was basically an eastern cycle of stories, the 'legendary' ancient history of eastern Iran with the prophet Zoroaster included in it as part of that history. There may have been stories in western Iran similar to some in the east in the time of the Achaemenids, such as the love story of Zariadres and Odatis, told by the Greek, Chares of Mytilene, but this proves nothing about the borrowing of motifs from east by west. Generally speaking, unless proper names can be traced as borrowed forms, the possibility of a common heritage or parallel development of story themes must always be present. One scholar has convincingly shown that the Kayanian cycle stories were not generally known everywhere in Iran until the

37

Parthians spread them and the Sasanians collected them and recorded them. [36] Of course, it is very difficult to follow the changes in stories and adaptations from other sources; for example, the attempts of Christensen to attach the Rustam stories in Seistan to the feudal lords of the Suren family and the Godarz tales to the Karen family, both in Parthian times, are plausible but cannot be proved. [37] In any case, we may say that the eastern Iranian Kayanian heroic cycle is the main source for the later all-Iranian epic. Since Zoroaster belonged to the Kayanian milieu the Zoroastrian religious leaders adopted the cycle as part of their lore or ancient history. While one may postulate a religious epic cycle and a national, or secular epic cycle, they are so intermingled later that the *Shahname* could be regarded as both the secular and religious history of the Zoroastrian religion by a Zoroastrian priest in recent times. Obviously the priests were not the only persons who kept the epic alive. Bards and minstrels entertained rulers and aristocracy by reciting epics down the ages. If one is concerned with literature, religion plays an insignificant role in the epic, but if one studies religion then contrariwise the tales are unimportant. That epics existed outside the purview of Zoroastrianism is indicated by an independent cycle, that of the Scythians, represented in a modern form by the legends of the Iranian Ossetes in the north Caucasus. Apparently these Iranians were untouched by Zoroastrianism, for there is no parallel word for 'demon, evil spirit', *dev*, which exists in other Iranian languages. [37a] One may consider their Nart tales as an epic and undoubtedly there were other cycles no longer existent. We will return to the epic when discussing the Parthians and Sasanians, but the next matter for consideration here is the historical material in the stories of the Kayanids and other ancient heroes of Iran.

The sources for the Iranian epic are the Avesta, the Pahlavi books and New Persian or Arabic works; the last are the most detailed but they are based on Pahlavi writings, while the Avesta does not have the detail or developed chronology of later times. The systematisation of the legendary history of Iran was carried out under the Sasanians when the real history had been forgotten. This legendary history was the real ancient history of Iran for the Sasanians. Here we are not concerned with the 'historical' versus the 'religious' tradition and disengaging elements of both, because only what was considered as ancient history by the Persians is germane to our task of reconstructing the history. In the developed Epic, or the 'secular' tradition as represented in Firdosi and other later authors, the first dynasty to rule the world was called Pishdadian, founded by a certain mythical king, Hoshang, Haoshyanha of the Avesta, and ended by an equally legendary king called Uzav.[38] The personages in this dynasty, whose names appear in the Avesta but in no real chronogical or dynastic order, are half mythical and half epical, partaking of gods and heroes. The old myths are presented as history in the epic but there is nothing historical in this dynasty and one can only speculate on the origin of the names of the rulers and their significance. There is no real chronology but there is a mythical or cosmological order based on a millennium reckoning or the eschatology of the Zoroastrians.

According to this scheme the world is divided into three ages of 3,000 years each. The first period is a golden age of the rule of Ahura Mazda. Then come 3,000 years of warfare with Evil, a time of troubles. At the end of this period comes Zoroaster who brings a new force into the fray, which tips the scales to Ahura Mazda, and at the end of this age, 9,000 years from creation, comes the renovation of the world.[39] Whether this millennium conception is derived from an ancient Aryan belief that 12,000 years is the time of existence of the world between creation and destruction, remains an open question. It is not improbable that there were other theories of the time span between creation and the end of the world but there is no space here to investigate these involved questions.

The next dynasty in the Epic would be similar to the preceding one were it not for the last ruler to bear the title of *kavi*, by which all of the monarchs of the dynasty are known, Kavi Vishtaspa, the patron of Zoroaster. His place in the list of kings attaches the entire dynasty in a sense to history. The word *kavi* is found in India as the priest who is a seer, conversant with magic, or one who is initiated into mysteries, also a sage or poet. In Iran the name is applied in the Avesta to eight rulers in the dynasty in order, Kavata, Apivahu, Usadan, Arshan, Pishinah, Byarshan, Syavarshan and Hausravah, all with the title Kavi prefixed to their names.[40] Then comes Kavi Vishtaspa, not mentioned with the others but rather as one *kavi* among many. Furthermore, he is the last ruler to bear the title in all of our sources. Contemporary with Vishtaspa are other *kavis*, opponents of Zoroaster, and since they are always linked with the *karapans* or 'mumblers', other priests who opposed the prophet, one could assume that the *kavis*

39

also had priestly functions. One may suppose then that the *kavis* were some kind of 'priest-kings' of eastern Iran, who upheld the ancient Aryan rites and practices. One may go further and assume that one family of *kavis* became strong enough to exert a hegemony over surrounding *kavis*. There is no evidence for this except the theme of a large unified empire or state in the epic tradition. We must ask if there is any other evidence for the existence of a *kavi* empire in eastern Iran in pre-Achaemenid times.

From the geographical circumstances in Central Asia and eastern Iran, one would not expect to find there a unified empire but rather a confederation of oasis states and tribes, if any unity existed at all. On the other hand, increasing knowledge about the past of this part of the world has made the existence of a large state here not all improbable. Before the extensive Soviet excavations in Central Asia, our conception of eastern Iran and Central Asia was of a land mainly without cities and inhabited mostly by nomads. Excavations in the large oases of Merv, Bukhara, Khwarezm, and elsewhere have changed this view, for we learn of the existence of great irrigation canals and large settlements in the first half of the first millennium BC. The material culture was probably not as developed as in western Iran but it was well into the Iron Age with artistic painted pottery.[41] The state or level of building techniques in these settlements is not altogether clear, but the discovery of walls and fortifications implies the development of settled life to an advanced degree, possibly to kingdoms or states of appreciable size. At the same time the number of horse trappings found might indicate the importance of nomads, who may have been the military mainstay of an east Iranian state, or states. Archaeology, then, would seem to confirm the picture of society in the Avesta of nomads and settled folk frequently at odds with each other.

From classical sources one might assume one of three possible states ruling in eastern Iran before the Achaemenids, an extension of the empire of the Medes eastward, a Bactrian kingdom, or a Khwarezmian kingdom. The kingdom of the Medes will be discussed in the next chapter; suffice it here to say that there is no real evidence that it extended into Khurasan beyond vague references in Ctesias to Assyrian rule as far as Bactria, and Median influence in the east.[42] Ctesias' notion that Zoroaster was a Bactrian king is of interest, but the reading of the name 'Zoroaster' is uncertain. Eastern Iranians may have served

40

in Median armies as allies, but proof of Median overlordship is lacking. The existence of an independent Bactrian kingdom in eastern Iran while the Medes were consolidating their rule in western areas has been supported by many scholars. Archaeology again would support the contention that extensive irrigation canals and towns with citadels in the Bactrian plain were developed under a central organisation, a Bactrian state, as suggested by Ctesias.[43]

The case for a Khwarezmian state was first presented by Markwart, who studied a passage in Herodotus (III.117) which dealt with a river Akes.[44] The results of this study have been concisely stated by Henning as follows:[45]

'According to this story, which Herodotus gives, presumably from Hecataios, the Khwarezmians, in the old days, possessed the valley of the Akes, i.e. the Harī-Rūd and its continuation, the modern Tejen. They exercised some measure of suzerainty over the Hyrcanians, the Parthians, the Sarangians of Seistan, and the Thamanaeans of Arachosia. Both Merv and Herat were then occupied by the Khwarezmians, whom Hecataios, in one of the few fragments of his work that have come down to us, places to the east of the Parthians.

'We can thus be fairly certain that there was a state in eastern Iran which centred around Merv and Herat and co-existed with the Median Empire; which was led by the Khwarezmians and abolished by Cyrus, who deprived them of their southern provinces, whereupon they gradually retired to their northern possessions along the River Oxus.

Henning further proposes that the relatively swift and easy conquest of eastern Iran by Cyrus the Great presupposes the existence of a large state or group of states. Otherwise the conquest would have taken a much longer time. If we follow this line of argument, however, one might add that the absence of later revolts against the Achaemenids, except in Darius' first year when rebels were everywhere, would suggest a background of Median hegemony or some western rule in eastern Iran. In the same view, it is not easy to believe that Cyrus put an end to the Khwarezmian state ruled by Vishtaspa, the patron of Zoroaster, because there are too many imponderables and no real evidence. At the present we can only say that there probably were at least two states or rather confederations in eastern Iran before the Achaemenids, with centres in Bactria and Herat. Further, the

41

Median empire probably had relations with one or both and possibly exercised some sort of influence over one or both, although there is no proof. [46] Kavi Vishtaspa and Zoroaster fitted into the Herat confederation then *before* it became unified, if it ever really did, and they did not necessarily have anything to do with Cyrus. The possibility that Bactria reached prominence only under the Achaemenids, and after the fall of a Khwarezmian state as suggested by Markwart, is an attractive theory but again without evidence.

So our history of eastern Iran before the Achaemenids is scanty and conjectural. The sagas of the epic for this period are unreliable as history, but they provide a framework for the heroic age which did not require history. A recurring motif of the epic, however, should be examined — the struggle between Iran and Turan.

Iran and Turan

The wars between Iran and Turan occupy many pages in the Iranian epic, and certainly this antagonism has served to exemplify Zoroastrian ideals of good and evil. The conflicts of steppe and sown, light and darkness, of the *ashavan*, followers of Zoroaster, and the *dragvant*, followers of Ahriman, are all summed up in the struggle between Iran and Turan. This pattern of opposition is a continuous tradition in the epic from the time of the conflict of the Aryans and non-Aryans, during the invasions of the former, down to the days of Firdosi when the Turks were invading the Near East. It is possible that in Islamic times the Turks were really equated with a Tur people of an earlier age, since the designation 'Turk' is probably a plural Tur-k, with the word 'Tur' designating some totem among the Ur-Turks of Central Asia. Hence Turkic Tur-k would equal Iranian Tur-an, also a plural. The history of the word 'Turan', scanty though it is, however, must be investigated.

The name Tur appears several times in the Avesta as Tura, and the earliest mention of the Tura people, never a district, is in Yasna 46.12 of the Gathas where the descendants of Fryana the Tura are mentioned. In Yasht 13 (the Fravardin Yasht) 143, the Zoroastrian followers of the Airya, and the Tura, Sairima, Saini and Daha peoples are mentioned. The first three names were explained in Sasanian times, if not before, as descendants of three brothers Erech, Salm and Tuch, the Iranian counterparts of the Biblical Shem, Ham and Japheth. We may tentatively identify the three peoples as Aryans or Iranians proper, Sarmatians of South Russia and Turans. The Saini are unknown and the Daha, presumably the Dāsá of the Rig Veda, may be identified with the Dahae of classical authors, or nomads living in present day Turkmenistan east of the Caspian Sea. The Tur people may have been a group or tribe of Iranian nomads in Central Asia whose name came to be applied to all nomads in that general region. It is possible further that the small district of Khwarezm in Sasanian times called Tur, represents a survival of the old tribal or generic name. Markwart suggested that the Tura people were identical with the Massagetai, an important nomadic folk known to Greek authors living east of the Caspian Sea, but this again is only conjecture.[47] The district of Turan in present Baluchistan, the *twgrn* in the Parthian version of Shapur's (Shahpuhr) great inscription from after AD 260, may reflect a movement of the Tura to the south. Most scholars reject any connection between the two, but it is not impossible that there was a real connection. The significant fact is the continuous tradition from ancient times of an opposition between Iranians and non-Iranians in the eastern part of the country or in Central Asia. This coincided with the religious belief of Good and Evil. Although the Tura in the Avestan age were most probably Iranian, perhaps the memory of struggles with aborigines played a part in the development of the epic. Later, of course, the Turks conveniently took the role of the great enemies of Iran.

The extent of influence of the Iranian epic is shown by the Turks who accepted it as their own ancient history as well as that of Iran. In the earliest 'Turkic dictionary' extant, the eponymous ancestor, or the hero, of the Turks of Central Asia, Alp Er Tonga, is identified with Afrasiyab, the principal 'Turanian' enemy of Iran in the Iranian epic.[48] Tonga is probably to be identified with the wolf totem, or the symbol *par excellence* of the Turks. Afrasiyab appears in several places in the Avesta with the form of his name Frangrasyan. There he is a semi-mythical figure, a kind of historicised evil spirit or dragon, one who holds back water (from Iran), indicating the great importance of water for the life of the country. In Yasht 5.41 of the Avesta Frangrasyan prays to the goddess Ardvisura Anahita to grant him the *hvarnah-* or the 'imperial glory' (of Iran), which she does not do. He further is represented as a great opponent of the Zoroastrians who are Iranians. The Turks were so much influenced by this cycle of stories that in the eleventh century AD we find the Qarakhanid dynasty in Central Asia calling itself the 'family of Afrasiyab', and so it is known in Islamic sources.

We have mentioned *hvarnah- above, which has been an important tradition or symbol for the Persians throughout their long history. A semantic development of the word was probably from a meaning of 'shining, radiant' to 'good fortune' and to khvarrah. written as a Semitic ideogram *GDH* in Middle Persian, with a particular meaning 'kingly glory or majesty'[49] The word khvarənah apparently has no cognate in Indian languages but perhaps the Indian word kṣatra in its meaning 'charisma of rule' included the concept of khvarənah. The Iranian cognate word khshathra may be paralleled by the Indian rāj. although khshathra has a specifically Zoroastrian sense as one of the Amesha Spentas or attributes or 'persons' of Ahura Mazda. So the hvarnah- or khvarrah/farn 'the imperial glory of Iran' has remained a symbol or what might be called 'mystique' for the Persian people probably from the time of Zoroaster down to the present. This 'mystique' has throughout history also contributed to the stability of the institution of the Shahan Shah in Persia.

To return to the peoples of eastern Iran, the Avestan evidence cannot be used as a basic source, rather only in confirmation of other material. The distribution of various Iranian tribes in Achaemenid times must have obtained in the period just previous to the accession of Darius. In his inscriptions the great king enumerates the peoples of his empire, and it is from this list as well as from Herodotus that we can try to reconstruct a map of eastern Iran at the time the Achaemenid kings made their far-flung conquests.

The eastern Iranians were divided into many tribes or peoples', which settling on the land gave their names to various districts. Thus Sogdiana was named after the Sogdians as Pars or Persis was probably named after the Parsa people. In Central Asia, outside of the oases, lived nomads called generically 'Saka' by the Persians. [50] It was probably their mode of life rather than any ethnic or linguistic features which differentiated them from their settled neighbours, the Sogdians, and Khwarezmians and others. As the Persians, and then the Greeks, learned more about Central Asia, especially after the Achaemenid empire was firmly established, the various Sakas were distinguished from each other. The etymology of the name 'Saka' is uncertain but Bailey proposes the meaning 'men', from a root sak. 'to be powerful, skilful', attested in the Rig Veda as an epithet of 'men'.[51] Many scholars had accepted a meaning of 'dog' for Saka as a tribal totem on analogy with the Turkified Mongol tribe of Nogay, meaning 'dog' in Mongolian. [52] The Greeks knew these people as Scythians, which latter term might be a 'West Scythian' designation of the nomadic people who invaded South Russia from the east in the eighth century BC, and who were known in the Bible as Ashkuz (which was mis-written as Ashkenaz). It is, of course, difficult to ascertain the ethnic geography of the vast area from the plains of South Russia to the borders of China in the early pre-Achaemenid period, but one may suppose that the Sakas-Scythians were undifferentiated by the settled people of the Near East as later the various Turkic peoples were all considered to be 'Turks'.

The conquests of Cyrus, and especially Darius, added to knowledge about the peoples of the northern steppes. Nomads had invaded Iran, probably over the Caucasus, in the time of Median hegemony, as we shall see, and one may assume that some of them remained in their new homes without necessarily being absorbed by the settled population. In Herodotus (III.92) for example, the Orthokorybanti, presumably a nomadic folk in the tenth satrapy of Media, may be identified with 'pointed hat Saka'(below), if one explains the Greek word as *orthos* plus *korys* 'upright helmet' with *bant* or *pant-* uncertain. (Compare Greek *kyrbasia*). In the Achaemenid inscriptions three groups of Saka are distinguished, the Saka *paradraya* 'beyond the sea' probably in South Russia rather than near the Aral Sea where some Soviet savants have located them, the Saka *tigrakhauda* 'pointed hats (or helmets)', and the Saka *haumavarga* 'the *haoma* revering Saka'? The last-named Sakas, called Amyrgioi by the Greeks, inhabited the eastern part of Central Asia, probably from Ferghana into Chinese Turkestan. Although the meaning of the name is uncertain, derivatives of it may survive in some Pamir languages of today. The identification of these Sakas with the name is uncertain, derivatives of it may survive in some Pamir languages of today. [53] The identification of these Sakas with the later Sakaraukai who invaded Bactria in the second century BC is possible since both came from the same area, but there is no linguistic proof of the identity of the two names as Markwart tried to show. [54]

The Saka *tigrakhauda* are pictured on reliefs and seals; one of their leaders, called Skunkha, is unmistakably portrayed on the rock relief of Darius at Behistun. These Saka may be located in West Turkestan, possibly to the east of the Aral Sea, although their range may have extended to the Caspian Sea. Whether these Saka are identical with the 'Sakas of the plain', while the *haumavarga* Sakas are the 'Sakas of the swamp' (or 'farthermost limits') as an Egyptian inscription puts it, is difficult to determine.[55]

Even more confusing is the story in Herodotus (I.201) how Cyrus lost his life in combat with the Massagetai, who (IV.11) also previously had driven 'the Scythians' into Europe. Since they occupied part of the same territory one may tentatively include the Massagetai under the 'pointed hat Saka', although the latter name is surely a Persian descriptive designation. The appelation 'Massagetai', however, presents problems, especially as we find the name only in classical sources and not in any Iranian writings. Attempts to explain the name as 'fish eaters', or the like (comparing Avestan *masya* 'fish'), or as 'great Sakas' or 'great Getai' have not been convincing.[56] Since some of these nomads may have ranged within the ken of the Chinese, one might expect some reference to them in Chinese sources, but it is only from the first century BC that the Chinese took an interest in West Turkestan, and even then identifications of Chinese words or renderings of foreign names are very difficult.

The settled people most closely in contact with the Sakas were the Khwarezmians and the Sogdians. Although Khwarezm in Islamic times was identical with Khiva and the delta of the Oxus river south of the Aral Sea, there is some question whether the Khwarezmians were located in this area in pre-Achaemenid times, or even when Darius carved his inscriptions. From the passage in Herodotus probably from Hecataios, quoted above, corroborated by a sentence in Arrian, the historian of Alexander the Great, we may assume that the Khwarezmians were living south of the Qara Kum desert as neighbours of the Parthians and others, possibly near the present towns of Quchan in Persia and Ashkabad in Turkmenistan. The area of Khiva was not uninhabited at this time as the archaeological researches of S. P. Tolstov have amply shown, but we have no written sources about the inhabitants. The Khwarezmians moved northward sometime during the existence of the Achaemenid empire, for Alexander the Great knew them in the country of the lower Oxus. Then they seemed to have belonged to a confederacy with the Massagetai and other tribes.[57] No explanation of the name, either as connected with the 'sun' or as 'good land' or the like has satisfied scholars.[58] The rediscovery of the mediaeval Khwarezmian language has been one of the great achievements of Iranian scholarship in recent years. Continuing intensive Soviet archaeological investigations in Khwarezm will surely reveal more about the people and their culture in the future.

The Sogdians are much better known than their neighbours thanks to literary remains in the Sogdian language. They inhabited the oases of Bukhara, Samarkand and probably part of the rich Ferghana valley and other neighbouring areas. They seem to have been merchants and traders in early times as they were in the first centuries of the Christian era and later. It may have been the conquest of Alexander the Great which started a diaspora of the Sogdians eastward, all the way to China. The Sogdians were closely related to the Bactrians in customs and culture including language. Indeed Strabo (724) declares the linguistic difference was small among most of the eastern Iranians, which is corroborated by the *Shih-chi*, or historic records compiled during the Han dynasty in the first century BC.[59] The oldest form of the name of the country, in the Old Persian inscriptions, is Sugd with variants, but we find -*l*- for -*gd*- in Chinese and Tibetan forms of the name, possibly indicating dialect variations within Sogdian. It should be noted, however, that the $d > l$ change is prominent in many east Iranian languages. The linguistic concordances between Sogdian, an east Iranian tongue, and Old Persian, a west Iranian language, may indicate an ancient geographical contiguity of the two peoples before the Persians migrated south-west.[60] In the Avesta Sugd or Sogdiana, used adjectivally, is found preceding the word *gava* or 'settlement', hence the possible origin of the later mythical title *gopat shah* in Pahlavi books.[61] Regarding the material culture of the Sogdians, and for that matter other settled 'eastern Iranians', Soviet archaeological excavations indicate that the seventh century BC was a period of the development of extensive irrigation systems, then as now the source of wealth and security for the peoples of Central Asia [62] Irrigation and agriculture in general are highly commended in the Avesta and the archaeological evidence indicates a fairly well organised society which built and maintained the irrigation dams and canals. The chief city of Sogdiana was Samarkand which we shall meet with later.

In addition to Sogdians *per se* there were other tribes in Central Asia. The name Ferghana has been derived from the

Parikani,[63] mentioned in Herodotus (III.92; VII, 68 and 86) as people in Persia as well as in Media and Baluchistan, but the Chinese designation *Ta wan* and other names for the area raises the question whether tribal names are invariably behind territorial or provincial names.[64] By studying place names, however, one may trace the movements of tribes; for example, the town of Amul on the Oxus has the same name as a city in Tabaristan south of the Caspian Sea, and both are probably connected with the Mardoi or Amardoi tribe found elsewhere in Iran. Suffice it to say that the movement of the tribes was generally from east to west and one should not be surprised to find names appearing in Persia with parallel forms in Central Asia.

The oasis of Merv was a great cross-roads of trade and of migrating tribes from earliest times. The explanation of the name as 'meadow' presents difficulties, but it would not be an inappropriate designation for the oasis on the flat lands where the present Harī-Rūd debouches. Merv was the military centre of the Persians for their north-east frontier during the Sasanian empire and the Arabs maintained it likewise during their conquests in Central Asia throughout the Umayyad Caliphate. At the time of the Arab conquest in 682 Sogdians, Khwarezmians and others had colonies in the city of Merv, and so it must have been in earlier times. Under Cyrus Merv (Old Persian *Margu-*) was naturally part of the satrapy of Herat, while Darius put it under Bactria.

Bactria (Old Persian *Bākhtri-*, an Iranian but non-Persian form of the name) was a fertile country, the present pláin of Afghan Turkestan south of the Oxus river or Amu Darya. The chief city had the same name, which may have been derived from the name of the river Bactrus (Pliny VI.48, 52), according to Markwart.[65] The chief city of Bactria like Merv was strategically located, commanding routes south over the Hindu Kush mountains to India east to China and north to Sogdiana. The land of Bactria was the most important satrapy in eastern Iran under the Achaemenids, and later was the centre of the post-Alexander Greeks who established a kingdom here and then proceeded to the conquest of north-west India. The Bactrians must have spoken an east Iranian tongue similar to Sogdian, but successive invasions of the rich plain between the Oxus river and the mountains changed the composition of the population, so we know nothing about the ancient inhabitants. The mountains of

Badakhshan were probably the only source of the lapis-lazuli of the ancient world, and if this is true the Bactrians must have been in contact with the Near East from very early times for articles of lapis-lazuli are found in Egyptian and Mesopotamian tombs of the second and third millennia BC. Possible pre-Achaemenid relations between the Medes and Bactrians have been mentioned. When Darius became king the satrapy of Bactria was loyal to him when most of the other satrapies were in rebellion.

The mountain folk of the Hindu Kush in this early period were probably undergoing Indianisation from the south and east and Iranisation roughly from the north and west. This mountainous area, including the Panjshir-Ghorband and Kabul valleys, it would seem, was the satrapy of Sattagydia (Old Persian *Thatagu-*) under Darius, and the province of Paropanisadai of Alexander the Great. The latter name is the old Iranian name of the Hindu Kush *uparisaina-* 'above the eagle', while Sattagydia is likely to be an appellation given to it by the Achaemenid Persians.[66] One might further identify the area of Sattagydia, or at least part of it with a place-name in the Avesta, Ishkata, in the Mithra Yasht.[67] That area was inhabited by a people called Parutas, also recorded by Herodotus (III.91). Somewhere to the east of them lived the Dadikai and the Paktyes (Herodotus III.91; VII.67). The former have been identified with the present Dardic-speaking people, the latter with the Pathans, while the Parutas (meaning 'mountaineers'?) or Aparytai have been related to the present Afridi tribesmen of north-west Pakistan. All of these identifications are mere guesses and not proved, although one or more may be correct. A number of scholars have objected to the Pathan or Pashto/Pakhto=Paktyes equation, G. Morgensterne proposing instead a derivation of Pashto < Parswana or Parsa.[68] The widely spread name Parsa brings a new element into the problem to which we may briefly diverge.

The earliest occurrence of 'Parsa' is found in Assyrian cuneiform records of the ninth century BC in the form Parsua, a district of imprecise location probably north of modern Kirmanshah in western Persia. The peoples of Parsua are mentioned a number of times in Assyrian annals as enemies subdued by Assyrian armies. About 640 BC we find Cyrus I called *shar parsuwash* or 'ruler of Parsa', now located to the south on the borders of Elam probably in present Fars. The two names are probably identical, but is 'Parsa' an Iranian name or is it a pre-Iranian place-name from which the Persians took their own name and transplanted it to the south as an ethnic name? In favour of the latter we have Herzfeld's suggestion that Assyrian *parsua* descends from a form *parakhshe* of the third millennium BC. Yet it is a rather weak and unproven assertion.[69] Dyakonov made an attractive proposal that in Parsa, Parsua and Parthava we have three forms of an Old Iranian *parsava* 'rib, side, frontier', related to Indo-European *perk* 'rib, breast', Avestan *parasu*, Ossetic *fars* 'side, frontier'. All three areas are on the sides or frontiers of Media, to the south (Parsa), east (Parthava) and west (Parsua), hence the common name with no need to presuppose Persians migrating from north to south.[70] It is quite possible that the names of the Persians and Parthians represent dialectical differences (*th* and *s*) and we have basically the same people, while the *parsua* of Assyrian texts could represent *parsava*. Further analysis would make Old Persian Parsa really a Median word for real Old Persian *Partha*, while Old Persian Parthava would stand for Median *Parsava*. This is ingenious but it places too much importance on the Median designation of a land or people as a rib > side > frontier area. It is more probable that we have an ethnic name in Parsa, an Iranian people who moved to Fars province giving it their name, but also a segment of them moving to the frontier of Mesopotamia while others remained in eastern Iran. Thus might one explain a remark of al-Bīrūnī that the Khwarezmians and Persians were closely related, as well as the above-mentioned Old Persian-Sogdian linguistic similarities, and third, a possible origin of names such as the Paktyes and the Pasiani who invaded Bactria from the north in the second century BC. These nomads have been identified as Parsa or Persians who belonged to the Massagetai confederacy with the Khwarezmians, and were simply Persians who had not gone south centuries previously with their brothers.[71] Although the assumed presence of 'Persian' speakers in eastern Iran would help to clarify a number of historical problems, at the present state of knowledge we can hardly reconstruct a history of such peoples.

The etymology of *parsa*, in addition to the theory above, has been variously proposed as 'war-axe people', comparing Indian *parasú-* 'axe', an explanation open to question since the word for axe may be Sumerian in origin.[72] The explanation of Parthava~Parsa~Pashto as 'land, earth' (Sanskrit *prithivi-*) is not likely. To return to Sattagydia, it undoubtedly caused the Achaemenids difficulties as well as modern scholars, albeit in a different manner.

The Gandhara area of modern Peshawar and Jalalabad may have overlapped Sattagydia, especially in the lowlands, but since Gandhara was surely Indian it need not detain us in our survey of the ancient eastern Iranians.

Arachosia (Old Persian *harahuvati,* corresponding to Sanskrit *sarasvati* 'rich in rivers') was the well-named land of present southern Afghanistan, the valley of the Upper Helmand (Avestan *Haētumant* 'rich in dams') and the tributaries where the Thamanai (Herodotus III.93, 117) lived. This ethnic name is only found in Herodotus unless the region of Anauon, the modern Farah area in Afghanistan, in Isidore of Charax, *Parthian Stations* 16, can be emended to read Thamanai. Although the name vanishes, unless it be preserved in the town name Chaman, east of modern Qandahar, the people of Arachosia must have been settled agriculturists from an early time in this fertile land comparable to Bactria in the north. Similar to Bactria in the north, Arachosia was the centre of Achaemenid rule over neighbouring tribes to the south and east and Darius was fortunate to have a loyal satrap who, after a number of battles with rebels sent against him from· the west, was able to consolidate the rule of the new king.

The lower course of the Helmand river and the Hamun lake was occupied by the Zrangai (Old Persian *Za)ra(n) ka,* with local Z- for Old Persian *d-*), which name has been explained as 'sea land' by many scholars, unsuccessfully, I believe. The name survived into Islamic times as Zarang, the capital of the country. The Hamun lake area played an important role in Zoroastrian tradition and as the homeland of the hero Rustam. By geography and history it has been connected with Arachosia and the upper Helmand rather than with Fars province or the west. The invasion of Saka tribes in the second and first centuries before our era undoubtedly changed the population for their name was applied to the land which it has held to this day, Seistan. In pre-Achaemenid times as today it is a land where the steppe and sown are intermingled and nomads are on all sides of the lake which used to be large in winter while almost vanishing in the late summer.

South of Arachosia and Seistan was primarily non-Aryan land, and the peoples in this satrapy of Darius called Maka were, according to Herodotus (III.93; VII.68), the Mykoi (Old Persian *Maka*), Outioi (Old Persian *Yautiyā*) and the Parikanioi. The first gave their name to present Makran 'Maka coast', and the last named were the mediaeval Parikhan or Bariz of the Arabic geographers.[73] The Yautiyā or Yuti were probably the ancestors of the Jut nomads of Kirman in Islamic times, not to be confused with the Zutt or gypsies.[74] The large area between the Indus river in the east to the Persian Gulf in the west, the Indian Ocean to the south and the central deserts and the wastes south of the Helmand river and Seistan to the north was only slowly penetrated by Iranians, and it was non-Iranian land under the Achaemenids though in part ruled by them. To conclude this survey of eastern Iran we should turn to the Parthians and to Herat.

Parthia (OP *Parthava*) was the territory of the present province of Khurasan in Persia, including Hyrcania at the south-east corner of the Caspian Sea, when Darius ascended the throne. We have already mentioned the possibility of a dialectal variation of Parsa in the name Parthava, but the invasion of the Parni nomads shortly after Alexander the Great changed the ethnic and probably the linguistic nature of the people of the province, although the later Parthian language of inscriptions and documents is basically the language of the land Parthava with Parni elements added to it. According to Strabo (XI.508, 515) the Parni belonged to the Dahi (Daas in Strabo) group of tribes, mentioned in the Old Persian inscription of Xerxes as Daha, presumably later Dahistan, directly east and south east of the Caspian Sea. The Parthians were said to be related to the Scythians by a number of classical authors, and this must apply to the Parni and other nomads who ruled over Parthia adopting the language and name of the settled folk.[75] As nomads adopting settled culture the Parni were probably more conservative in language and customs than other Iranians. This may be reflected in archaic forms of some words in Parthian writing recalling Old Persian orthography. That Parni or Aparni is related to the word *apar* 'above, high', hence 'highlanders', is not impossible though not over-convincing.[76] It was probably under Parthian rule, an age of Oriental chivalry, that the early legends of the rulers and heroes of eastern Iran were revived and given a Parthian flavour in many instances. The Parthian language came to be called the *pahlavānik* 'heroic' language and the Parthians themselves 'heroes'.

Herat (OP *Haraiva*) has been mentioned previously as the heartland of eastern Iran. Since the river bears the same name as the country or province, one may assume that the river name is the original. This area, I believe, was the main separation point of the Aryans, those going to India and those moving westwards. Greek authors as early as Herodotus confused the name of the river-province with the general name 'Aryan', although there may have been some realisation of a difference in the two names by the use of 'Areioi' and 'Arioi', although the variant readings follow no pattern. Strabo (XI.515) calls the river Arios and Ptolemy (VI.17, 2) Areias, and the country is Aria and Areia respectively. The explanation of the river name as 'flowing', comparing Sanskrit *sárati* 'flows' is possible. It may be that the 'Persians of the East' were concentrated in Herat province, or that the inhabitants considered themselves more particularly as 'Aryans' because of the place of their land in Iranian (and Zoroastrian) tradition. In any case, after Alexander's conquests we find an interesting development of the term Aria to Ariane, probably first by Eratosthenes (Strabo XV.723), and then the extension of the restricted area Ariane to include all of eastern Iran from the central deserts to the Indus River but excluding Bactria and northern lands. This Ariane was the *Aryanshahr* ruled, not by the Seleucids but principally by the Parthians when Eratosthenes lived and wrote *circa* 220 BC.

There were undoubtedly other tribes, and other districts not included in the above survey of eastern Iran, but even so the complexity of the map and the importance of eastern Iran, the 'homeland of the Iranians' should be recognised, something not always done in the past.

Social Structure

It may not be inappropriate here to discuss briefly the social structure of the Iranians as revealed in the Avesta, Old Persian inscriptions and scanty notices from classical sources. Many scholars have divided the social organisation 'vertically' and 'horizontally'. By the former is meant the place of an individual in ever larger units, as family, clan, tribe, while 'horizontal' structure means his place in a class society, determined by occupation or birth, such as artisan class, lower aristocracy or the like. Obviously the latter division exists only in a settled, civilised society, for nomads on the march have little of this kind of 'class structure'. With the rise of the Achaemenids we are on the threshold of the development of a 'horizontal' organisation of society, at least outside of Media, which may have entered this stage earlier.

The question of the widespread existence of a matriarchal society among Indo-Europeans or Aryans does not concern us here. Traces of it cannot be found among the Iranians of the seventh-sixth century BC although tales of Amazons and the influence of women in the Orient are not lacking in classical sources. The patriarchal clan, with the important relationships on the male side, was the principal unit of Iranian society, for the smaller family and the larger tribe were secondary. One might express the 'vertical' structure of Iranian society in the following manner (the correlations, of course, are not perfect, *khshathra*, for example, is by no means clearly 'nation'):

	Avesta	Old Persian terms	Darius (as an example)
1. family	*nmāna*	*taumā-*	= son of Vishtaspa
2. clan	*vis-*	*vith-*	= Achaemenid
3. tribe	*zantu*	**dantu-*	= Pasargadai
4. province or country	*dahyu-*	*dahyu-*	= Parsa
5. nation or people	*khshathra-*	*khshassa-*	= Arya

(In eastern Iran numbers four and five probably fell together into a confederation of tribes under a *kavi*.)

A further identification of the first three terms in Avestan with three Gathic words, proposed by Benveniste, has been modified by Thieme who, instead of equating the two series, would say that in the *nmāna* 'house' lives the *khvaētu* 'the family'; in the *vis-* 'settlement' lives the *varəzāna* 'the clan', and in the *zantu-* 'the territory of the tribe' lives *airyaman* 'hospitality', or 'those with whom one is connected by hospitality' [77] This is an important analysis by Thieme which has interesting ramifications in the religious sphere, but showing here a clear continuity from Aryan times. Numbers four and five above have to do with rule and rulers, a somewhat different relationship between members of a society and their 'national rulers'. New conceptions of rule over settled people, new traditions and a new charisma will have influenced the Iranians settling down in new homes, especially in western Iran. Here too the clan lost its importance in favour of the family on the one hand and the tribe or nation on the other, which is not unexpected.

The later 'caste system' of India or 'class system' of Sasanian Iran is not found here, but slaves, servants and 'nobility' do exist.

54

The 'horizontal' organisation of society before the settlement of the invaders can be surmised by inference. It would seem that the young adult Persian male, the head of his small family and able to bear arms, was called in Old Persian *maryaka or martka—. This word in an inscription on the tomb of Darius at Naqsh-i Rustam has been interpreted as 'menial' since the Akkadian term used in translation of the Old Persian means that, but because of cognates in various Indo-European languages, and the later development within Iranian, we are justified in considering the Akkadian 'servant' as a secondary meaning. The original sense would be the warrior, the old backbone of the clan, and a servant of the leader in the same sense that the officers of the Achaemenid king were called his slaves. It is true that this secondary sense of 'slave' or 'menial' also survived in some present Pamir languages, but I still consider the translation of Old Persian *maryaka by 'menial' as misleading; the servants and slaves were another group.

The menials may have been divided into two groups, domestic servants and foreign slaves. For the latter we may have a designation in the Old Persian *grda, attested in Elamite tablets from Persepolis kur-tash, and in Aramaic grd. This word, from the Indo-European root *gherdh-'to surround, to girdle', possibly represents prisoners of war or slaves who were bound to labour. From the Elamite tablets of Persepolis, however, it would seem that kur-tash was a generic name for 'worker', qualified by a designation of the special kind of artisan or worker. Or one might consider the *grda as domestic slaves, comparing Sanskrit grhah 'house'. In the Aramaic papyri from Egypt and from the Persepolis Treasury tablets, it would further appear that workers on the Egyptian estates of the Achaemenid princes and on the buildings at Persepolis were neither solely Persians nor, it would seem, completely free men. [78] They seem to have been mostly foreign, although 'freemen' in corvée labour or free specialists or overseers cannot be excluded. So the *grda- could well be for the most part foreign slaves while domestic servants, menials, or possibly (Iranian) slaves in another context (as Tokharian manne according to Bailey) would be the Old Persian māniya, interpreted as domestic servants or slaves (compare Greek dmos). Even though the Elamite word kur-tash is used in the inscription of Behistun to translate Old Persian māniya, which would mean that the old Persian term *grda- and Old Persian māniya were synonyms, one would expect some difference in meaning of the

55

two terms. The above conjecture would apply to Iran in general, but under the early Achaemenids I suspect that the *grda- were originally the slaves on the royal or princely estates, which term later spread all over the empire for all workers of various categories, while *māniya* remained in use only in Iran. Of course, a slave in antiquity, or for that matter in the Orient later, was rarely a chained hauler of stone and water under a lash. Some slaves were skilled artisans or highly educated or held positions of responsibility. The question of slavery within the Iranian tribes is obscure, but it probably existed in some form. One might hazard a conjecture that in this early slave or menial group one has the incipient fourth estate of later Sasanian society, the artisans and the merchants. Rather, one might suppose that contact with the Assyro-Babylonian world caused a revision in the 'ideal' of society of the Iranians, which brings us back to Dumézil.

That the 'ideal' society under the Sasanians was a system of four classes, priests, warriors, scribes and bureaucrats, and finally artisans and peasants, is fairly well attested. Also from the Avesta, a previous quadripartite division of society might also be inferred, but in Avestan times there was hardly any bureaucracy or scribal class as under the Achaemenids or later. In the Avesta the peasants, or *vāstryōshān*, as they are called in Book Pahlavi, were separate from the artisans or *hutukhshān*, thus making four classes. According to Dumézil this Avestan quadripartite division of society was developed from an Indo-European and an Aryan tripartite division of society. Dumézil might be right, but there is no proof, and one may wonder how actual any division of society really was throughout the early history of Iran. Did the division of society as found in the Avesta really exist, or was it only a theory or even merely a tendency towards such a division? Another question at once arises: did slaves or servants fit into the division? Obviously one can always find some sort of distinction between various groups in a society, but only in India do we find clear caste divisions. In Iran one may conjecture that the division of society in general was a part of Zoroastrian religious teachings held up as an ideal and that slaves did not enter this ideal society. Iranian ideas of social organisation must have changed when the Iranians came into close contact with the Mesopotamian culture area where settled people had developed certain norms of society over the centuries. Under such circumstances, the persistence of any Indo-European ideology about social classes into Achaemenid times is rather unlikely. We shall return to questions of society under the Achaemenids. In eastern Iran the pastoral, tribal society of the Aryans must have lasted into Achaemenid times, whereas in western Iran the pastoral mores of the conquerors shortly underwent changes. In neither case, however, should we assume a well organised division of society on ancient Indo-European principles according to Dumézil. The Iranian nomads, for such we may call the pastoralists who migrated to the Iranian plateau, would not easily have followed the principles of a settled society conveniently divided into recognised classes or castes. It may be that later Zoroastrians harked back to an Indo-European tradition of society of hoary antiquity, which had been neglected for centuries by the Iranians, but this raises further questions which cannot be answered.

After this brief survey of eastern Iran we may turn our attention to western Iran, where we are in a different milieu, with cuneiform sources which can be checked by each other. In short, we are in history.

NOTES

1 A. Meillet, *Linguistique historique et linguistique générale* (Paris, 1921), 15.

2 Cf. J. Pokorny, *Indogermanisches Etymologisches Wörterbuch* (Bern, 1959), 15.

3 *Ibid.*, 62.

4 A. Meillet, 'La religion indo-européenne', in *op. cit.*, 323-334. The following remarks follow Meillet to whose general conclusions I, for the most part, subscribe.

5 J. Vendryes, 'Correspondances entre l'Indo-iranian et l'italo-celtique', *Mémoires de la société de linguistique*, 20 (Paris, 1918), 272.

6 Meillet, *op. cit.*, 323.

7 A good summary of Dumézil's position can be found in his *L'idéologie tripartite des Indo-Européens* (Brussels, 1958). See also C. S. Littleton, *The New Comparative Mythology* (U. of California Press, 1966).

8. E.g. S. Wikander, 'Germanische und Indo-Iranische Eschatologie', *Kairos, Zeitschrift für Religionswissenschaft*, 2 (1960), 83; 'Från Bråvålla till Kurukshetra', *Arkiv för Nordisk Filologi*, 75 (1960), 183; A. V. Ström, *Das indogermanische Erbe in den Urzeit- und Endzeitschilderungen des Edda Liedes Voluspa', Atken des X. Internationalen Kongresses für die Geschichte der Religionen* (Marburg, 1961).

9 E.g. M. Molé, 'La structure du premier chaptre du Videvdat', *Journal Asiatique* (1951), 283, and J. Duchesne-Guillemin, *The Western Response to Zoroaster* (Oxford, 1958).

10 G. Redard in *Kratylos*, I (1956), 144.

11 J. Hertel, *Die Methode der arischen Forschung* (Leipzig, 1926).

12 The Hittite and Assyrian records are sometimes confusing in their nomenclature, for 'Hurrian' and 'Mitanni', as well as other designations, seem to be used interchangeably. Cf. P. Thieme, 'The Aryan Gods of the Mitanni Treaties', *Journal of the American Oriental Society*, 80 (1960), 301-317.

13 Cf. M. Mayrhofer, 'Zu den arischen Sprachresten in Vorderasien', Die Sprache, 5 (1959), 77-95. Corresponding forms for 'one' would be: Aryan ★ aika, Ur-Iranian ★ aika, Indian eka. I propose another line of descent for Avestan and Old Persian from Indo-European ★ oiuo, Aryan ★ aiva, with a ka ending in Old Persian. But ★ aiva-ka > Middle Persian ēvak > New Persian yak is another problem; perhaps a more direct descent ★ uika ⇒ yak, as Avestan aēxa ⇒ yax 'ice' is to be preferred. Varuṇa presents difficulties, but both 'Ur-Iranian' and Aryan forms would be from ★ var-, as an Avestan reconstruction ★ vouruna would parallel Avestan vouru- < Ur-Iranian ★ varu- 'wide'. Cf. E. P. Hamp, 'Varuṇa and the suffix -una', Indo-Iranian Journal, 4 (1960), 64. Cf. also Thieme (above) 301.

14 Of course we may have a dialect division in Indo-European both ★ oiqo and ★ oiuo influencing the later developments. We follow here Brugmann and the ★ Indo-European- ★ Aryan hypothesis although it may require revision.

15 We are concerned here with the cultural-historical data to be gained from the sources rather than with the philological exegesis of the texts or linguistic questions of vocabulary, grammar or syntax.

16 Indicated by Sanskrit kṛṣi- 'agriculture', Avestan Karšu-, as well as other relevant words. We have suggested above that the Aryans were Indo-Europeans who became nomadic and then reverted to pastoralists-agriculturists when they arrived at their new homes. The other alternative would place the separation of the Aryans from the other Indo-Europeans just at the beginning of their acquaintance with agriculture, which would explain the different agricultural words in Indo-Iranian from other Indo-European languages.

17 Cf. R. N. Frye, 'Georges Dumézil and the translators of the Avesta', Numen, 7 (1960), 161 foll.

18 Pokorny, op. cit., 184.

19 Cf. W. Rau, Staat und Gesellschaft im alten Indien (Wiesbaden, 1957), 17.

20 H. Ljungberg, Hur Kristendom kom till Sverige (Stockholm, 1946), 27.

21 P. Thieme, Mitra and Aryaman (New Haven, Connecticut, 1957), 59, 61.

22 Translation after K. Geldner, Der Rig-Veda, 3 (Cambridge, Massachusetts, 1951), 384; text ed. T. Aufrecht 2 (Bonn, 1877) 445. Geldner's translation of the third line above by 'den gleichgewillten (Gegenstand des) Preises, die Keule', is somewhat over-poetic.

23 H. Berger, 'Die Burushaski-Lehnwörter in der Zigeunersprache', Indo-Iranian Journal, 3 (1959), 17. Also Münchener Studien zur Sprachwissenschaft, 9 (1956) 4 foll.

24 I do not accept the theory that the Brahuis are a group of Dravidians who migrated from the Deccan to Makran in historic times.

25 For example, the Aryan diphthong ai is preserved in Avestan, while in Vedic Indian it became e. Cf. A. Meillet, 'Sur le texte de l'Avesta', Journal Asiatique (1920), 187 foll., and Mémoires de la société de linguistique, 18 (Paris, 1913), 377.

26 The classical sources are conveniently assembled in A. V. W. Jackson, Zoroaster (New York, 1898), 152-157. Cf. C. Clemen, Die griechischen und lateinischen Nachrichten über die persische Religion (Giessen, 1920).

27 As explained in many modern writings, for example, in H. S. Nyberg, Die Religionen des alten Iran (Leipzig, 1938), 28.

28 Sources in Jackson, op. cit., 157.

29 The date 258 is considered apocalyptic by Nyberg, op. cit., 33-34, and

historical by E. Herzfeld, *Zoroaster*, I (Princeton, 1947), chapter one.
30 W. B. Henning *Zoroaster* (Oxford, 1951), 41.
31 Cf. O. Klima, *'The Date of Zoroaster'*, *Archiv Orientální* 27 (Prague, 1959), 558. On p. 564 he proposes the date of Zoroaster as 784-707 BC.
32 Cf. Jackson, *op. cit.*, 19-22.
33 H. Humbach, *Die Gathas des Zarathustra*, I (Heidelberg, 1959), 74.
34 A. Christensen in *Handbuch der Altertums-Wissenschaft, Kulturgeschichte des alten Orients*, Dritter Abschnitt, Erste Lieferung (Munich, 1933), 217, and his *Les Kayanides* (Copenhagen, 1932), 69.
35 I. Gershevitch in E. B. Ceadel, *Literatures of the East* (London, 1953), 56.
36 M. Boyce, *'Zariadres and Zarēr'*, *Bulletin of the School of Oriental and African Studies*, 17 (London, 1955), 474.
37 A. Christensen, *Les Kayanides* (Copenhagen, 1932), 138.
37a. Cf. V. I. Abev, *'The Pre-Christian Religion of the Alans'*, *Papers presented by the USSR Delegation, XXV International Congress of Orientalists* (Moscow, 1960), and E. Benveniste, *Études sur la langue ossète* (Paris, 1959), 138.
38 Hoshang was the grandson of Gayomart, the first man (and king) according to Firdosi. Uzav or Zav, Uzava in the Avesta, was the father of Kavata according to the *Bundahishn*. The genealogies are mixed and uncertain.
39 Cf. J. Duchesne-Guillemin, *'Le commencement et la fin du monde selon les mazdéens'*, *Akten des X Internationalen Kongresses für die Geschichte der Religionen* (Marburg, 1961).
40 The origin of the title *kavi* is unclear. Perhaps it meant among the Aryans the leader of a tribe who performed religious rites, reciting the proper hymns to the gods, as K. Barr, *Avesta* (Copenhagen, 1954), 206, suggests. In Middle Persian of the books, or Pahlavi, we find the form *kay* < *khuvya*, Avestan *kavaya*, hence the name Kayanids.
The names of the eight *kavis* in Pahlavi are: Kai Kavad, Kai Apiveh, Kai Kaus, Kai Arish, Kay Pishin, Kay Vyarsh, Siyavush, and Kai Khusrav. Kaus, Arish, Pishin and Vyarsh are said to have been brothers, which statement does not inspire confidence in the historicity of the dynasty.
41 See the interesting discussion on irrigation and on pre-Achaemenid political organisation in V. M. Masson, *Drevnezemledelcheskaya kultura Margiany* (Moscow, 1959), 122-135.
42 *Ctesiae Fragmenta*, ed. C. Müller (Paris, 1828), 14. Diodor II.2.5.
43 See M. M. Dyakonov, *'Slozhenie klassovogo obshchestva v Severnoi Baktrii'*, 19 *Sovestskaya Arkheologiya* (1954), 129.
44 J. Markwart, *Wehrot und Arang* (Leiden, 1938), 8.
45 *Zoroaster, op. cit.*, 42.
46 Median contact with or influence in eastern Iran is suggested by the story of Zariadres and Odatis, found in Athenaeus (F. Jacoby, *Fragmente Gr. Hist.* no. 125, fr. 5, vol. IIB, and pp. 660-661), where two brothers rule Iran, Hystapes in Media and Zariadres eastern Iran up to the River Jaxartes or Syr Darya. Also the names Bactria (Bākhtrish) and Drangiana (Zranka) in the Old Persian inscriptions are Median (*z* for *d* and *tr* for *sh*) rather than Persian in form, indicating a Median contact before the Achaemenids. Finally, the institutions of the Medes borrowed by the Persians suggests that the Median empire was not a loose confederation but a far-flung empire.
47 J. Marquart, *Ērānshahr* (Berlin, 1901), 157.
48 Mahhmūd al-Kāshghaŕi, *Kitāb Dīvān Lughāt al-Turk*, 3 (Istanbul, 1335/1917), 110.

49 Cf. H. W. Bailey, *Zoroastrian Problems in the Ninth Century Books* (Oxford, 1943), 1-78. The form*hvarnah- is an Old Iranian reconstruction, Avestan *khvaranah*. The Old Turkish or even Altaic equivalent of the charisma of kingship was a prototype of the later Turkish word *qut-*. See also J. Duchesne-Guillemin, *'Le xvardnah', Annali Institut Orientale di Napoli* 5 (1965), 19-31.

50 Herodotus VII. 64, and Pliny *nat. hist., 50.*

51 H. W. Bailey, *'Languages of the Saka',* in B. Spuler, ed. *Handbuch der Orientalistik,* I, 4 *Iranistik* (Leiden, 1958), 133, where he compares Daha and Alemanni as examples of 'men' as a tribal name.

52 A. J. van Windekens, *'Les noms des Saces et des Scythes', Beiträge zur Namenforschung,* I (1949), 98-102, tries to connect *saka* < Iranian ★*svaka* with 'Scythian' through an Indo-European root ★(*s*)*keu-* 'to watch'. This was attacked by O. Szemérenyi, *'Iranica', ZDMG,* 101 (1951), 212, who unconvincingly derived *saka* from an Iranian root ★*sak-* 'go, flow, run', but more convincingly held that an Iranian ★*Skutha*=Scythian 'archer', derived from an Indo-European root ★*skeud-* 'to shoot'.

53 Bailey, *op. cit.,* 132. See also V. A. Litvinskij, *'Sakā haumavargā, Beiträge zur alten Geschichte und deren Nachleben, Festschrift für Franz Altheim,* 1 (Berlin, 1969), 115-26.

54 J. Markwart, *Das erste Kapital der Gatha ushtavati* (Rome, 1930), 43.

55 G. Posener, *La première domination perse en Égypte* (Cairo, 1936), 185. The 'pointed helmet' warriors of Yasht IX.30, of the Avesta cannot be identified safely with the Sakas, for the Sogdians too had 'pointed hats', as we learn from the Old Turkish inscriptions (Tonyuquq Inscription, line 46).

56 J. Marquart, *Untersuchungen zur Geschichte von Eran,* 2 (Leipzig, 1905), 78.

57 Strabo XI.513, discussed in W. W. Tarn, *The Greeks in Bactria and India* (Cambridge, 1951) 479, 540.

58 See R. Kent, *Old Persian* (New Haven, 1950), 177. S. P. Tolstov, *Auf den Spuren der Altchoresmischen Kultur* (Berlin, 1953), 89, connected the word with the Hurrians of ancient Mesopotamia, hardly to be taken seriously.

59 Ch. 123 is translated in J. De Groot, *Chinesische Urkunden zur Geschichte Asiens,* 2 (Berlin, 1926), 35, and F. Hirth, in *JAOS,* 37 (1917), 89 foll.

60 W. B. Henning, *'Mitteliranisch'* in B. Spuler, *Handbuch* (note 51), 108.

61 I. Gershevitch, *The Avestan Hymn to Mithra* (Cambridge, 1959), 176, and H. W. Bailey in *Bulletin of the School of Oriental Studies,* 6 (1932), 951.

62 M. M. Dyakonov, *'Drevnyaya Baktriya',* in *Po Sledam Drevnikh Kultur* (Moscow, 1954), 328, and the *Istoriya Uzbekskoi SSR,* 1 (Tashkent, 1955), 37.

63 *Istoriya, op. cit.,* 39, and E. Herzfeld, *Zoroaster,* 2 (Princeton, 1947), 449. Cf. I. M. Dyakonov, *Istoriya, Midii* (Moscow, 1956), 338, note 4, 349, 360.

64 J. Markwart, *'Die Sogdiana des Ptolemaios', Orientalia,* 15 (1946), 295.

65 J. Markwart, *A Catalogue of the Provincial Capitals of Eranshahr* (Rome, 1931), 34.

66 J. Marquart, *Untersuchungen* (note 56), 73, 177. He notes that in paragraph 6 of the Behistun inscription the Babylonian and Elamite versions have words derived from Old Persian ★*para-uparisaina* 'land in front of (south of the Hindu Kush) mountains'. Herzfeld's not original suggestion in *Archaeologische Mitteilungen aus Iran,* 1 (Berlin, 1929), 99, that Sattagydia is the Punjab, and further that Sattagydia is derived from Sapta Sindhava

raises problems, since for him the Hindu- of the Old Persian inscriptions would then be modern Sind on the lower Indus river. Darius may have ruled parts of both the Punjab and Sind, but probably for the Persians 'India' was the land along most of the Indus river.

67 Cf. Gershevitch, *op. cit.*, 174-175.

68 Article '*Afghanistan*', in *Encyclopaedia of Islam*, 2 ed.

69 Herzfeld, *Zoroaster*, 728.

70 I. M. Dyakonov, *Istoriya Midii* (Moscow, 1956), 69. See also E. A. Grantovskii, '*Drevneiranskoe etnicheskoe nazvanie* ★ *Parsava-Pārsa*', *Kratkie Soobsheheniya Instituta Narodov Azii*, 30 (Moscow, 1961), 3-19.

71 W. W. Tarn, *The Greeks in Bactria* (note 57), 294.

72 W. Eilers, '*Der Name Demawend*', *Archiv Orientálni*, 22 (1954), 357; and 24 (1956), 188. It is uncertain whether Akkadian *eilakku* means 'axe'.

73 W. Eilers *apud* W. F. Leemans, 'Trade Relations of Babylonia', *Journal of the Economic and Social History of the Orient*, 3 (1960), 29, proposes the etymology *Mak-kirān* 'Maka coast' for Makran, while Maka itself would be the Iranised form of the ancient place name ★ Makan, Sumerian *Má-gan*. This is the best explanation I have found for the name, yet a problem remains for this presupposes an Old Iranian ★ *Maka-karana* meaning 'end or frontier of the Maka', rather than 'coast'. Furthermore, the difference between Akkadian *Ma-ak* for Old Persian *Maka* and the Akkadian name *Ma-ka-na* for *Magan* is troublesome. On the Bariz cf. Herzfeld, *Zoroaster*, 734.

74 Markwart, *A Catalogue, op. cit.*, 77.

75 Cf. Benveniste, '*L'Eran-vež, etc.*' BSOS 7 (1934), 274.

76 Eilers, *op. cit.*, 373.

77 P. Thieme, *Mitra and Aryaman* (New Haven, 1957), 80.

78 Gershevitch in *Asia Major*, 2 (1951), 141-142, with remarks by Henning and Bailey, and G. R. Driver, *Aramaic Documents of the Fifth Century B.C.* (Oxford, 1957), 63. See also M. A. Dandamayev, '*Foreign Slaves of the Achaemenid Kings and their Nobles*', *Trudy 25 Mezhdv-narodnogo Kongressa Vostokovedv*, 2, (Moscow, 1963), 147-54. On OP ★ *maryaka* see H. W. Bailey in *Rocznik Orientalistyczny*, 21 (1957), 66.

3 IRAN AND THE WEST

The Heritage of the Ages

The Egyptians and Babylonians had centuries of history behind them when Persians first appear on the Near Eastern stage. Time-honoured institutions and beliefs had acquired religious sanction with widespread recognition and acceptance; the peoples of Mesopotamia, for example, had law books even before the time of Hammurabi. The great age of the god-pharaohs in Egypt was long past but Egyptian culture and civilisation continued as before. Centralised empires and feudal states had risen and fallen, and one might find a precedent for almost any political or social development of later times in an earlier period in the Near East.

The influence of Egypt and Mesopotamia, especially the latter, was felt by surrounding peoples and certainly most strongly on the Iranian plateau. In Anatolia the protocols, the form of legal oaths, trial by ordeal and others, had all been well fixed by the Hittites, having been borrowed from Mesopotamia. Babylonian cuneiform served as a *lingua franca*, a language for diplomatic intercourse, for treaties and for trade, and it was adapted to other languages and even other linguistic families, such as Urartian and Hittite.

In addition, as we have seen, since the middle of the second millennium BC Indo-Europeans with their horses and chariots were no strangers to the Near East. The Indo-Europeans, however, were not present in sufficient numbers at the beginning to impose their languages or mores on the settled folk. They were, however, participants in the expansion of the Hurrians in the seventeenth century BC over the northern part of the 'Fertile Crescent' from Mesopotamia to the Mediterranean Sea, and they certainly were active in the founding of scores of small 'Hurrian' principalities. It should be noted in passing that the Hurrian expansion brought a new pantheon into the Near East, such as the god Teshup and others, which was joined to the ancient deities of the area. The Aryan gods of some of the ruling class have already been mentioned, but they do not seem to have had an extensive influence, and we do not hear of them later until a few reappear when the Iranians arrive.

From about 1500 to 1150 BC a people called the Kassites from the Iranian plateau ruled in Babylonia. They too must have had contacts with Indo-Europeans to judge from some names of their deities and rulers. But the Kassites lost themselves in Babylonia much as the Mitanni in northern Mesopotamia and Syria at this same time were vanishing into the local populations. With the military occupation of large areas of southern Mesopotamia by the Elamites about 1150 BC the Kassites disappear, to be followed by a native Babylonian dynasty and a kind of Babylonian renaissance.

Perhaps the most important developments in the Near East at the turn of the millennium and for several centuries thereafter were the Aramaean ethnic expansion and the Assyrian political expansion. The Assyrians had previously shown evidence of their power and ability, and even under Tiglathpileser I of the Middle Assyrian kingdom, *circa* 1100 BC, who left many inscriptions, one can see the groundwork for the later cruel practices of the Assyrian kings which made their names so hated then and throughout history. Adad Nirari II, ruling about 900 BC, began Assyrian expansion by conquering small Aramaean states which had been established in northern Syria, and by using mass murder, terror and deportation of people to spread fear of Assyria. We cannot follow the fortunes of the Assyrian kings, many of whom are mentioned in the Bible, for the record is a bloody and monotonous one. Assurnasirpal II (883-859) records how he flayed rebels and hung their skins from the walls. Salmanasar III (858-824) fought against the empire of Urartu to the north and in Syria, spreading death and destruction wherever he went. Booty and slaves poured into Assyria which became a bureaucratic, centralised military state. One of the greatest Assyrian kings was Tiglathpileser III (745-727) who conquered the Aramaean state of Damascus, northern Israel, and sent armies deep into Iran to the Bikni mountain, which has been identified as Mt. Demavend near Tehran, but more likely is an identification with Mt. Alvand near Hamadan. It is remarkable that this military state produced a succession of able rulers who

63

were also soldiers and conquerors. A general of King Salmanasar V who revolted and became king under the name Sargon II (721-705) brought Assyria to its peak. The capital of Urartu, Tushpa probably on Lake Van, was captured and Urartu was ravaged, after which it did not recover. All of Syria and Palestine was brought under submission to Assyria and Babylonia was made an Assyrian province. Under Sanherib Babylon revolted and was destroyed, while under Asarhaddon (680-669) Egypt was conquered. Assurbanipal, the last great ruler of Assyria, captured Susa and smashed the power of Elam, but Assyria's own power declined rapidly after Assurbanipal's death and in 612, a memorable date in history, Nineveh, the Assyrian capital, fell to the Medes and the Babylonians, the latter now known as Chaldeans.

The Aramaic-speaking nomadic people who settled in southern Babylonia and founded small principalities during the period of Assyrian expansion in the north can be called Chaldeans (Kaldu). All around the 'Fertile Crescent' from the twelfth century BC Aramaic-speaking nomads infiltrated and took power, forming small principalities, perhaps the foremost one of which in Syria was the territory of Damascus. In the Old Testament we read of the struggles of David and Solomon against the Aramaeans. In Mesopotamia the Assyrian annals mention the Arumu as well as the Kaldu, so one may conclude that the Aramaeans were well ensconced here as they were on the other side of the Syrian desert. Their movement into the 'Fertile Crescent' resembles that later of the Arab tribes before Islam into the same territory. In Mesopotamia as in Syria, the Aramaeans were subjected to Assyrian aggression and suffered much from Assyrian rule. In one respect, however, they conquered their masters, for the cuneiform writing of the Assyrians, based on the ancient forms of the writing of Sumer and Akkad gave way to Aramaic writing, an alphabetic script far more practical for writing on parchment and papyri than the cuneiforms on mud. The Aramaic language, too, became the new *lingua franca* from Egypt to Persia.

Let us return briefly to the Assyrians who, in the first four centuries of the millennium, were changing the face of the Near East by violence, as the Aramaeans had done and were doing by infiltration into the settled lands. By Assyrian conquests and mass deportations the peoples of the Near East were mixed as they had never been before. Ancient local cultures were destroyed or transplanted and inevitable syncretism in most phases of culture followed. Religions which had been rooted in a particular locality for generations now found adherents all over the Assyrian empire. When Babylon was razed to the ground by Sanherib (Sennacherib) in 689 the great statue of the city god Marduk and his cult was simply transplanted to Assur; Babylonians who had been settled in Samaria in Palestine, however, continued to worship Nergal. The Assyrian army too was more like a professional rather than a citizens' army; for example, Ionian mercenaries served in the army of Sanherib. As a result of the deportation and extermination policies of the Assyrians the 'national resistance' of the peoples of the Near East was seriously weakened, an important factor in later Persian successes. One cannot deny certain advantages of the *Pax Assyriaca,* for trade flourished and great works of building and irrigation were undertaken by the Assyrian kings. Perhaps one might go further and say that a new kind of state was born in the common bondage to Assyria, a new state which none the less in all its traditions looked to the Sumerian-Akkadian past. For such ancient protocols as the titles 'king of all', 'king of Sumer and Akkad', 'king of the four world directions', were taken seriously by the Assyrian kings. Yet in spite of this respect for tradition which saved Babylon on several occasions because of Assyrian respect for history, the acts of the Assyrians were forming a new era in history. If this change is not apparent in Assyrian antiquarian interests, such as the library of Assurbanipal where the classics of the past were copied and preserved, none the less the stage was prepared for the 'one world' of the Achaemenids. An 'international' bureaucracy and an 'international' army were perhaps the two most important legacies of the Assyrians.

The imperial art of the Assyrians also provided a source of inspiration for the future. Not that Assyrian art is particularly original, for Babylonian and Hittite art traditions are apparent behind it. Still, the life and energy in the imperial stone reliefs and on seals is striking, and we are fortunate in having preserved for us so many of the former showing scenes of war and hunting with the great Assyrian king the central figure (fig. 6). Imperial and religious architecture was grandiose with apparently some new features such as coloured tiles for the walls, later a prominent feature in Achaemenid Susa. The literature of Assyria for the most part is not of high merit. Commentaries on ancient writings, astrology, magic and oracles, to which Asarhaddon was especially addicted, fill the cuneiform tablets. Astronomy was perhaps more developed than previously, but the majority of the texts are rather dull lists of cities conquered, tribes subdued, captives taken and horrible punishments meted out to them which are anything but edifying.

References have been made to the Iranian plateau and to Elam, so to complete the survey of the pre-Iranian age, Elam, the Mannaeans and Urartu must be discussed. Since they in whole or part occupied the Iranian plateau, they are obviously of more interest to the history of Iran than even Assyria.

The Elamites were known by the Persians as Uja or Huja after a mountain people to the east of Susa probably closely related to, or even a part of, the Elamites. Classical authors knew them as Uxii (a mistake by Alexander's historians for Uzii?) found in the modern name Khuzistan. Elam appears early in history but little is known about it. One of the rulers of the first dynasty of Kish in Mesopotamia is reported to have conquered the land of the Elamites, but even this earliest report of them is uncertain. Possibly the Elamites were related to other peoples to the north of them in Luristan, the Lullubi, Kassites (the Kossai of Greek sources) and the Guti, and it is a reasonable conjecture to suppose that a close ethnic and cultural relationship existed among all of the peoples living in western Iran in the second millennium BC as formerly among the 'painted pottery' population of the preceding millennia. It is difficult, however, to draw any sure conclusions from 'pre-historic' archaeological excavations on the plateau such as Tepe Giyan near Nihavend, the Tepe Sialk near modern Kashan, but the same pottery in various sites might indicate a uniform culture if not the same people. The name 'Japhetic' has been given to the languages in the area of western Iran which were neither Semitic nor Indo-European, among which Elamite is one, but this classification tell us little. One may suppose that the Elamites were related to other ancient, pre-Iranian peoples on the plateau and that the Elamites themselves came on to the plains from the eastern mountains. The ancient Elamite capital of Anshan has been found north of the Marv Dasht plain and is now under excavation by archaeologists. In any case, the Elamites had a long history and acted as the intermediaries between mountains and plains. They were greatly influenced first by the Sumerians in southern Mesopotamia, probably the inventors of writing, and then by the Semitic Akkadians.

It is impossible to detail the history of Elam here, and much

66

is unknown since it is reconstructed primarily from Akkadian cuneiform tablets, but Elam had some features of interest different from the small states of Mesopotamia, with whom the Elamite princelings warred. The role of the woman in ancient Elamite society seems to have been conspicuous, for the right to the throne was transmitted through the mother. Brother-sister marriage was practised, possibly the origin of Achaemenid and later general Zoroastrian consanguineous unions. The divinisation of the king is uncertain, but the descent of kingship from brother to brother, instead of father to son, seems to be peculiar to Elamites, though not unknown elsewhere in different times and places.[1] The recovery of many statuettes from Elamite sites indicates the importance of the mother goddess in Elamite religious beliefs. Undoubtedly Elamite culture, if not the Elamites themselves, penetrated far to the east on the Iranian plateau before the coming of the Iranians. As evidence there is an ancient Elamite rock relief at Naqsh-i Rustam near Persepolis almost obliterated by a later Sasanian rock carving. Furthermore Elamite was the language of the records at Persepolis under Darius, an indication of the presence of many Elamites as inhabitants of the region. We may suppose that there was an important Elamite influence on the Persians, perhaps to be compared to the local Iranian influence on the Turkish invaders of Azerbaijan so many centuries later. Fars province may have been the homeland of the Elamites.

Most of the political history of Elam must have been concerned with the occupation or conquest of large areas of Persia on the plateau, and constant raids westward against the inhabitants of Mesopotamia. About 1175 BC a king of Elam, Shutruk-Nakhunte, captured the great and ancient city of Babylon carrying back to Susa his capital great booty, among which was a diorite stone engraved with Hammurabi's law code, excavated by the French in 1901. Following an Elamite tradition, statues of the deities of various cities conquered by the Elamites, such as Marduk of Babylon and Nana, goddess of Uruk, were brought to Susa where the patron deity of the city, Inshushinak, held sway. It is not the place here to discuss the changing fortunes of the gods of Elam, of the many problems of designation such as 'king of Anshan and Susa', indicating either a summer and a winter capital, or perhaps even a dual monarchy, of the use of Akkadian and Akkadian influence in Elam, and many other questions. After 1100 BC Elam is in decline and is not mentioned in sources, the spotlight of history having turned to the north.

When the Elamites reappear in history in the seventh century BC it is as a conglomeration of principalities friendly or more often hostile to Assyria. The final result of years of intrigues and partial success at times against Assyrian power was the decision of Assurbanipal to ravage and crush the country. About 636 Susa was sacked; its famous ziggurat was razed to the ground and statues of the deities of the Elamites were carried to Assyria. Elam was finished as a power in the world.

Undoubtedly traces of Guti, Lullubi and Kassites continued to exist in the mountains of Luristan during the neo-Assyrian empire. The Kassites (Kossai) were chastised in their mountains by Alexander the Great, but the other two are not found in later sources. The name 'Guti' or 'Quti', as Assyrian sources would have it, is difficult to define, for in the third and second millennium BC it refers to a people centred in Kurdistan, while later it is more difficult to determine. Perhaps we have remnants of the Guti conquerors of Babylonia (*circa* 2100 BC) living in a more restricted area to the east of Assyria in the time of Salmanasar and the middle Assyrian kingdom a thousand years later.[2] The later archaising Assyrian sources sometimes use the term widely, perhaps in an ancient sense, covering the inhabitants of the Zagros mountains including Urartians and Mannaeans. One must always be careful with ancient, cuneiform names, for the temptation to relate tribal or ethnic names to later geographical names is great and it can lead to error. Furthermore, designations sometimes change greatly; for example, the name Magan in cuneiform texts of the third millennium BC may designate a country on the Persian side of the Persian Gulf (the name Maka/Makran has been compared with it), but in the first millennium BC it is used for Egypt!

About 1928 the first 'Luristan bronzes' reached European museums and now almost every museum in the world has a collection or has refused to acquire the plentiful objects.[3] The very quantity of the small bronze objects has led some sceptics to question the authenticity of many of the bronzes, but the possibility of verifying the report that they were all found by peasants in tombs is small, since every even suspected grave in Luristan must have now suffered exhumation. In spite of many problems surrounding the bronzes one may summarise our knowledge about them. First, most of them are obviously intended for a nomadic folk, or at least for people who highly regarded the horse, since the vast majority of bronzes are bridle or harness pieces, bits, rings for reins, and the like. Daggers, swords of various kinds, cult objects, pins, axes, belt buckles and arrowheads are represented in great numbers, all pieces which might be carried by nomads. Second, they mostly come from Luristan, presumably from shallow graves, but few have been scientifically excavated. The bronzes have not been found in quantity elsewhere in Mesopotamia or Iran. Third, they come from an area and presumably from a time when the Kassites and related folk were living in Luristan. Beyond this, scholars differ in their interpretation of the bronzes. Two remarks come to the non-specialist in this domain, the resemblance of many of the objects to Mesopotamian prototypes, and the resemblance of others to the 'Scythian style' of the art of the Eurasian steppes. An example of the former would be a mythical combat between a hero and an animal — the 'Gilgamesh story', of the latter certain bracelets ending in animal heads touching one another, and axe blades held in the jaws of an animal as the socket.[4] One may conjecture that the art of the bronzes of Luristan is a local production of metal workers, with art motifs derived basically from local patterns, perhaps descended from the painted pottery motifs, with many Mesopotamian influences. The question immediately arises whether the metal workers were nomads, but this is a rather unlikely supposition. For whom were the bronzes made and when? Godard, one of the principal authorities on the bronzes, dates the great bulk of them from after the end of Kassite rule in Mesopotamia about 1200-1000 BC when Hittite metallurgists could have come to the Zagros mountains following the fall of Hittite power. But he goes further by postulating a development of the Kassite art of Luristan by the Mannai (Mannaeans) who in turn passed this art to the Scythians when they occupied Media about 680 BC. Then the Scythians brought it to South Russia where the Sarmatians imposed a new taste on it, thus explaining the Scythian-Luristan connections.[5] Ghirshman, on the other hand, dates the majority of the Luristan objects to the eighth and seventh centuries, or even later, with the Scythians and Cimmerians being those for whom the objects were made.[6]

Although the majority of the 'Luristan bronzes' could well have been made in our own century, the wide variety of objects and motifs would suggest a problem in distinguishing 'Luristan bronzes' from 'bronzes found in Luristan' or even general 'ancient Iranian bronzes'. For this reason the 'extended chronology' of Godard for *all* bronzes from Luristan might have an edge over the 'small chronology' of Ghirshman, unless by the latter we refer only to those bronzes made for Scythians. Other possibilities do exist but until archaeologists go to Luristan and properly investigate this matter *in situ* one must withhold judgment. The excavations of Louis Vanden Berghe in Luristan should illuminate many of the problems. An earlier 'settled' style and a different, later 'nomadic' style, both in the same area cannot be excluded, but the methods of manufacture remain local.

A word should be said here of the attractive theory of Herzfeld that the Lullubi, Guti, Urartians and Elamites were all members of one ethnic and linguistic group called Kassi, or Caspians. He considers the names *Kossai* in Greek sources, *Kissi* in Herodotus (III,91, etc.), and Kassite to refer to a generic term for all the people, from the base **kas-*, with *-p* as a plural ending. [7] The relationship may be real, but it is unattested by any evidence that the plural *-p*, found in Elamite, was universal, for it is not found, as far as I know, in Hurrian or Urartian, which would be almost required for such an etymology of the 'Caspian' Sea. There is no evidence that the Caspians mentioned by Strabo and other classical authors were simply Kassites, though no doubt the Kassites did extend far and wide. The country of the people called Ellipi on the upper Karkha river valley in the mountains north of Elam appears *circa* 900 BC and the Assyrians directed many expeditions there. It has been suggested that these are simply Elamites, reading **Ellu-me for Elli-pe, and to be equated with the Elymais of Seleucid times and later, but Elymais was actually more to the south. [8]

The Mannai, who lived in present Iranian Kurdistan, have received much attention of late because of the discovery of magnificent art objects attributed to them. The objects apparently came from one treasure hoard found by peasants near the village of Ziwiye close to the town of Sakkiz after the end of World War II. Many objects of gold, silver, bronze and ivory were recovered, some of them broken or divided by the discoverers, and they present a medley of art styles. The ivory plaques and carvings are Assyrian, similar to ivories found at Nimrud in Mesopotamia. The gold bracelets, plaques and a pectoral show 'Scythian', Assyrian and local styles, while pottery, silver objects and bronze show the same influences. In this we have a most interesting art collection from the heart of the Mannai country dating sometime between the ninth and the middle of the seventh century BC.⁹ What do we know of the Mannai who lived south of Lake Urmia?

From Assyrian sources it would seem that Mannai meant a nation or confederation of peoples and tribes, while the Urartian inscriptions speak of Mannai as a state or kingdom. That the political organisation of the Mannai was unusual, perhaps an oligarchy, is possible, but not sure. ¹⁰ Whether the language(s) spoken in the Mannai territory were like Elamite or Urartian-Hurrian is difficult to determine, but from the forms of place names one may suggest the probability that Elamite was a close relative. In the Bible the kingdoms of Ararat, Minni and Ashkenaz are mentioned in Jeremiah 51.27 as coming up against the Assyrians (Babylon), and the second has been identified with the Mannai for the form of the word is perhaps to be read Menni. The Mannai were absorbed by the Medes, or rather they are later overshadowed by their rulers in the Median empire. For centuries, however, the Mannai had resisted Assyrian armies seeking horses and booty or seeking to impose Assyrian rule on the Iranian plateau. The history of the Mannai flows into that of the Medes and we shall hear more of them below.

Finally, before turning to the Medes, we must not neglect the important state of Urartu, a rival of Assyria and centre of a distinctive culture. Excavations in Soviet Armenia have revealed much more about this ancient folk than was hitherto known. In Assyrian documents from the twelfth century BC to the time of Sargon (died 705) the term Nairi for the territory north of Assyria between the Van and Urmia lakes occurs many times. Nairi would appear to be a general term designating land ruled by many kings, although a more restricted area may be intended in later Assyrian usage. Since it is now established that Urartian and Hurrian are sister languages, the derivation of the term 'Nairi' in Assyrian sources from an earlier Hurrian region, Nahria north-west of Assyria, as suggested by Melikishvili, appears probable. ¹¹ Together with the term 'Nairi', more often Assyrian sources speak of the state of Urartu which was their powerful opponent. This is probably a local name, maybe of a tribe near Assyria. The term Urartu is widespread but various forms of the name cause problems. It is found in several places in the Bible as Ararat, and in the Qumran 'Dead Sea' texts as *(h)urart-*, further in the Babylonian version of the Behistun inscription as Urashtu (where Old Persian and Elamite have Armenia), in Armenian as Airarat, and in Herodotus (III.94 and VII.79) as Alarodi. The Urartians, in their almost four hundred preserved inscriptions, called their entire country Biainili, probably an ancient indigenous term.

The history of Urartu goes back to the time of the Hurrian expansion and the Mitanni empire when Hurrian ethnic elements probably expanded into the Armenian mountain area. At the close of the second millennium BC the various tribes in the Lake Van area were organised into a political unity, and from Assyrian sources we hear of Urartian expansion. Salmanasar III in the first year of his rule (circa 858 BC) led an expedition against Urartu and its ruler Aram. By his time the political centre of gravity of Urartu had shifted from the upper reaches of the Upper Zab river south-east of Lake Van to Lake Van itself where the capital Tushpa was probably situated on the eastern shore. The main centre for the principal deity of Urartu, the god Khaldi, however, was the city of Ardini, or Musasir, as the Assyrians called it, located in the oldest centre of Urartu near present Rovanduz. The names of many kings of Urartu are known, Menua who successfully fought the Assyrians about 780 BC, Argishti his son, Rusa, which was also the name of the last king of Urartu, and others. In the middle of the eighth century BC the kingdom of Urartu was at its height. The son of Argishti, Sarduri II, who ruled about 760-730 BC called himself 'king of kings' and ruled a kingdom from the land of the Mannai south-east of Lake Urmia, which he subdued, almost to the Black Sea and the Kura river to the north. His troops advanced into northern Syria but came into conflict with the energetic Assyrian king Tiglathpileser III who defeated them. The Assyrians took the offensive and maintained it under Sargon II.

There is no space to discuss Sargon's eastern and northern campaigns, but a few details are interesting. About 716 he subdued the Mannai and the following year he put down a revolt instigated by Urartu. Later the land of Urartu was invaded and ravaged in all directions, and the religious centre of Musasir was taken and sacked, which event, according to the Assyrian sources, caused King Rusa of Urartu to commit suicide. From this blow Urartu really never recovered even though peace was made with Assyria. Cimmerians and Scythians from north of the Caucasus invaded Urartu and it is possible that the northern part of Urartu finally fell to the onslaughts of northern invaders, although the date *circa* 590 BC is given as the fall of the city of Tushpa to the Medes.[12] Because of the discovery of Scythian objects (arrow-heads and the like) in Karmir Blur (ancient Teishebaini), the excavator Piotrovskii proposed that this city was destroyed by invaders from the north of the Caucasus.[13] Apparently the Urartians recovered from this blow, since we find them conquering areas in present-day Iranian Azerbaijan under King Argishti around 700 BC. In any case, Urartu disappears about 600 years before our era and in its place we find in the north the Georgians and elsewhere the Armenians ruled by the Medes. Whence came the Armenians?

It is now generally accepted that the Armenians came into the land which bears their name from Anatolia. Their Indo-European language is probably closely related to the language of the Thracians, and among extant languages less so to Albanian. The name 'Armenia' was probably taken from a district into which the invaders came, thus *Arm* plus suffix -*ini* [14] The term 'Hayy' by which Armenians call themselves is generally thought to be the same as the land and people in eastern Anatolia called *Haia-sa* in Hittite records. [15] It is possible that in Achaemenid times the Armenians were divided into two groups, an 'Armenian' confederation in the east with Urartian elements in it and the 'Hayy' tribes in the west, as Piotrovskii (p. 129) suggests, but this is subject to dispute. In any case, the Urartians were replaced by the Armenians who remain to the present day.

Of course there must have been other peoples in what is today Persian Azerbaijan before the Achaemenids, but we can only speak of the principal groups known from our sources. The extension of Ibero-Caucasian languages, the modern representatives of which are Georgian, Abkhazian, Circassian, etc. to the south in early times is unknown but not unlikely. The discovery of a clay bulla in Karmir Blur indicates the presence of Aramaic writing on parchment or papyrus[16]; furthermore, the expansion of the Aramaeans brought them into the mountains south of Lake Van and they must have mixed with the local population. To the east of Urartu lived various tribes up to the Caspian Sea but it would be most hazardous to try to identify or place the names geographically. More important is the culture and civilisation of Urartu itself, for it must have been dominant all over this area, and it has been suggested that one must look for the origins of much of Achaemenid art, architecture and even state protocol and writing in Urartu.

73

The architecture of Urartu is unusual, so also for that matter is later Armenian architecture. Since the use of large stones without mortar for walls enclosing a terrace as at Masjid-i Sulaiman and Persepolis to the south has been attributed to Urartian influence, a word concerning this is in order.[17] The ruins of Urartian strongholds with large stones, and fortunately building inscriptions on some to identify them, exist in some numbers in the Armenian highlands. The older constructions do have walls, or usually surviving only the bases of huge 'cyclopean' stones while later sites have smaller stones and baked brick walls. The nearest relatives of Urartian architecture, in its use of columns in a colonnade and generally in stone work, are to be found in Anatolia, while the brick work is Mesopotamian in origin. In general, however, the specialists on Urartian architecture derive its monumental proportions in royal palaces or citadels from the contemporary Assyrian prototypes.[18] The Urartian caves at Lake Van and the irrigation canal system, traces of which still survive, attest to the energy and power of the Urartian state. That Urartian architecture had an influence on later Armenian style and techniques has been proposed by Armenian scholars and probably with good reason. Smaller arts of ivories, sculpture, generally speaking, may be classified as provincial Assyrian in conception and style.

The Urartians were famous for their metal work, especially bronzes, and it has been suggested that Urartian metal-workers even found their way to Etruria in Italy.[19] In metal work, however, the Urartians were continuing an old tradition of other peoples of western Iran. It seems that Urartian weapons and armour were famous, confirmed by excavated helmets and swords of exceptional quality, showing good use of rich ore deposits of various metals in the Armenian mountains. Urartu then was not a great centre from which influences radiated as was Assyria, but some influence on the Medes (and Persians) is not only possible but probable.

The principal god of the Urartians was Khaldi, but an inscription from near Van gives the names of sixty-three gods and fifteen goddesses with the number of sheep, bulls or cows sacrificed to each one. The gods were represented in art in human form, and may have had special symbols, for the sun disk of the Assyrian gods Ashur and Shamash also appears in Urartu, probably representing Shivini, the Urartian sun god. In the religion we find no apparent prototypes of later Iranian religions, but with the writing and inscriptions it may be possible to find parallels.

The oldest inscription in the language of Urartu is from the end of the ninth century BC. Before that we find inscriptions in Assyrian, so the writing system for Urartian was probably borrowed from Assyrian in the ninth century BC. The existence of an earlier hieroglyphic script has been attested, but it cannot have been widely used. [20] The style of Urartian inscriptions is conventional and laconic like the Assyrian inscriptions, especially the pre-Sargonid texts, but possible influences of a Hittite or Hurrian chancellery are not impossible. As far as Urartian influence on Old Persian is concerned, one can see a similarity between the oft-repeated Urartian phrase 'for the god Khaldi I accomplished these deeds in one year', and Darius' inscription at Behistun (IV.59-60), 'this which I did, I did in one and the same year by the help of Ahura Mazda'. Also Wolfgang Kleiss has indicated that Urartian temples provided the prototype for the Achaemenian structures called the Zindan at Psargadai and the Kavbah of Zoroaster at Naqsh-i Rustam. The question of borrowings, however, is difficult and involved, though the possibility exists.

Upstart Dynasts

The Iranians were comparative newcomers to the Near East and we must try to trace their early movements. Since an Iranian can be defined only as one who spoke an Iranian language we must seek written records to determine the presence of Iranians at an early epoch. The assignment of objects of material culture in archaeological sites to a certain ethnic or linguistic group is extremely difficult for many reasons, among them the persistence of old traditions and the imagination and inventiveness of the human mind. An art historian may trace the inter-connections of the motifs on prehistoric vases from Persepolis, Tepe Giyan, Sialk and elsewhere, but the 'pre-dominance of decoration over representation' as a criterion for the individual style of Iran can be traced throughout Persian history, and is not a very useful guide. [21] Although we are obviously on shaky ground in the early period at least a suggestion about the expansion of the Iranians must be made.

It is probable that Iranian expansion into the Zagros mountain area began in the tenth century BC but Iranian personal names have not been found earlier than 879 BC, and mention of the Medes occurs for the first time in a record of a campaign of Salmanasar III in 836-835 to the east.[22]   Shortly before this time the Parsua are mentioned and both notices, of Parsua and of the Medes, indicate geographical areas with more or less settled people rather than migrating tribes. Much has been written about the designation 'Parsua' and the wanderings of the Persians. Another term, Umman-Manda used in Assyrian and Babylonian sources, can be dismissed as a generic term for nomads or even 'barbarians', although Umman-Manda is used especially for the Medes later, or possibly for Scythians, or combinations of both peoples. The term has caused controversy but need not detain us. The older, generally accepted hypothesis on the wanderings of the Parsua or Parsa was that they came from over the Caucasus or from eastern Iran to the area south of Lake Urmia, then they moved to the area of Luristan above Elam and finally moved on to Persis or Fars, where they eventually settled. This reconstruction is based upon occurrences of the word Parsua or Parsuash/Parsumash, referring to these areas according to Assyrian texts. We have discussed the matter above, and one may add the suggestion that the word simply means 'knight or hero', hence any petty Iranian chief.[23]   An exasperating problem in reconstructing a map of western Iran in the eighth and seventh centuries BC is the great numbers of small kinglets or lords, mentioned in Assyrian annals, most of whom commanded only a few thousand warriors. The lack of any political unity may also reflect various ethnic groups with a consequent difficulty in determining the Iranian predominance in any state or people. The Parsua in the north were of no particular historical importance, so we can leave these Persians, if such they were, until the rise of the Achaemenids in the south. The main actors on the stage of history in the north are the Medes.

The Medes were organised in tribes as frequently at war among themselves as they were opposing settled kingdoms such as Urartu, the Mannai and Assyria. The existence of fortified towns or 'castles' in the land of the 'mighty Medes' is attested by Assyrian records, for Assyrian troops captured many of them in their frequent raids on to the plateau. The Assyrians sought horses from the plateau for their cavalry, and the Medes were famous for their horses. The Assyrians also may have had strategic aims in mind in some of their raids; for example, an expedition in 744 BC subdued many princelings to the south of Urartu, which land in turn was the goal of Assyrian arms the following year. As a result of the 744 expedition two new provinces of the Assyrian empire were organised on the plateau, Parsua and Bit Khamban, the former probably north of the age-old caravan route from the plains to modern Kirmanshah, the latter to the south of it. Cyrus II and the Achaemenids, I believe, had nothing to do with this Parsua. It may be true that in the years 744-737 Assyrian troops reached as far as the central salt deserts of Iran, for they did penetrate far into the interior in search of horses. The identification of place-names in the eastern campaigns of the Assyrians has taxed the ingenuity of Assyriologists, but conjecture rather than any proof is the rule. For example, a district called Zikertu, possibly to be located in modern Persian Azerbaijan between Tabriz and Miyaneh, has been identified with a Median tribe, the Sagartians, or Asagarta in Old Persian, but linguistic difficulties exist. We have a picture of many disorganised tribes or local rulers in Media in this period.

Sargon II continued Assyrian pressure on the Medes, Urartu and those Mannai hostile to Assyria. We hear of a certain ruler associated with the Mannai called Dayaukku or Deioces who, as a result of a campaign against the Mannai by Rusa of Urartu (*circa* 716), joined the Urartians, but was defeated and captured and sent by the Assyrians into exile in Syria.[24] Also under Sargon Israelite and Syrian prisoners were settled in Babylonia and probably in parts of the Zagros mountains as well. Before the consolidation of Median power the two greatest enemies of Assyria on the plateau were Elam in the south and Urartu in the north and the policies of the Assyrians were directed against one or the other with the small principalities acting as pawns between the great powers. The Elamites had been busy with internal quarrels and were generally weak, but a series of rulers in the eighth and seventh centuries BC took the lead in opposing Assyria from the south. In 690 BC the Elamites organised a coalition of Elam, Babylon, Aramaean tribes, Parsuash, Anzan, Ellipi and others against Assyria but the coalition did not last. Parsuash cannot be the Assyrian province of Parsua, but most likely is later Persis or part of it. Anzan or Anshan at this time may have been independent of Elam in the mountains to the eastward, but specific boundaries cannot be determined, nor can one be certain of changes in the area covered by the name.

With the death of Sargon the attention of the Assyrians was turned elsewhere away from the Iranian plateau. This respite, together with an ever-present Assyrian threat, led to the formation of a confederation of Median princes which was the background of the empire of the Medes. The leaders in the movement for unity were followers of the chief Dayaukku. His territory was probably situated near modern Hamadan in the heart of Media. But just at this time, the turn of the century *circa* 700 BC, the ethnic and political situation was disturbed by the invasion of the Cimmerians followed by the Scythians.

The Cimmerians (Assyrian: Gimirrai, Bible: Gomer in Cappadocia) lived in South Russia before the eighth century BC, but neither their extent nor their origin is clear. They were known to their neighbours the Greeks who settled in the Crimea and South Russia, but they were also known as invaders in Anatolia in the seventh century, who ravaged the Phrygian kingdom of King Midas about 675 BC (Herodotus I.6,15). That they made themselves at home in Cappadocia is attested by the Bible and by the Armenian name for Cappadocia Gamirkᶜ (Moses of Khorene, *History*, ed. Tiflis, 219). It is probable that the Cimmerians were not Iranian but possibly were related to the Thraco-Phrygian peoples.[25] In the Near East their activities are centred mostly in Cappadocia and in Azerbaijan, especially in the kingdom of the Mannai, where, however, they may have been confused with Scythians. The earliest mention of them in the Near East is in Assyrian annals, speaking of Rusa I of Urartu and his campaign about 715 BC into the land of the Gimirrai, at that time northwest of Urartu. Asarhaddon defeated them, together with some Scythians in 679 BC and shortly afterwards Cimmerian troops are found in the hire of Assyria.[26] Other Cimmerians proved troublesome and Assyria had to fight several times against them mostly in Anatolia, for in Azerbaijan the Cimmerians were soon replaced by a more formidable foe, the Scythians or Ishkuza (from a form *shkudha?*) for the Assyrians.[27]

Herodotus (IV.12) tells how the Scythians, invading South Russia from the east of the Caspian drove the Cimmerians across the Caucasus mountains and followed them into Media. They must have there joined forces, for the two appear together, and in the Akkadian version of the Behistun inscription the Cimmerians are found in place of the Sakas of the Old Persian and Elamite versions. The Mannai took advantage of the presence of the warlike invaders to make them allies, but by 673 probably all Mannaean territory was lost to Assyria which in turn sought allies among the Medes. This move seems to have been successful only as long as Asarhaddon lived, and even at the end of his rule he was worried by the attempt of a Median chieftain, Kashtaritu (Old Persian Khshathrita, a throne name for Fravartish or Greek Phraortes) to unite the Medes against Assyria, which was in 673.[28] It is likely that the Scythians too established a kingdom at this time for we hear of a King Ishpakai who was killed in battle about 673 BC and was succeeded by Partatua. The kingdom of the Scythians may well have been centred in the Mugan steppe of Azerbaijan, for this area served as a pasturage for the Il-khanid Mongols and other nomads of later times.

The centre of Kashtaritu's confederation was probably the area of Hamadan, the 'place of meeting', and he seems to have been closely related to Dayaukku. He was successful in forming a Median state and extending its authority over Parsua, and, according to Herodotus (I.102) even attacked Nineveh where he lost his life. It would seem however, that he was defeated rather by the Scythians and other Assyrian allies before reaching Assyria. The Scythians then dominated Media for twenty-eight years from circa 652-625 BC, when they were defeated by the son and successor of Kashtaritu, called Uvakshtra or Cyaxares [29] It is likely that Kashtaritu had already united the Medes in Central Iran, the task which Herodotus attributed to Deioces, but under Cyaxares the power of the Medes grew greater than ever before and the Persians, now in their final home of Persis, submitted to the Medes. They may have submitted to the father of Cyaxares, but we are certain of their inclusion in Cyaxares' empire. According to Herodotus (I.103) Cyaxares was the first ruler who arranged troops according to their weapons, such as archers, lance carriers and cavalry, and it is probable that he re-organised the Median army and state. Cyaxares learned well from the Scythians as well as the Assyrians, and he was now ready to strike at Nineveh.

Assyria, meanwhile, had become weak even though her troops had contributed mightily to the decline and fall of her traditional enemies Urartu and Elam. The peoples of the Near East were restless and the fall of the Assyrian empire was both desired and predicted, as we read in the Bible where the book of Nahum seems to be both a dirge and paean on the fall of Nineveh. The new Babylonian empire had asserted its freedom from Assyria and under Nabopolassar about 616 launched an attack on the Assyrians. This time, with Egyptian help, the Assyrians were able

79

to repulse the attack, but then the Medes marched forth to join the Babylonians and the end was near.

The Medes invaded Assyria in 614 and captured the important city of Ashur, after which Cyaxares met Nabopolassar and a treaty was made including the marriage of a Median princess with Nebuchadnezzar, son of Nabopolassar. Presumably a joint strategy was conceived by the two enemies of Assyria. It is unlikely that the siege of Nineveh lasted several years, though the events from 614 to 612 are uncertain.[30] After a few months' siege the city of Nineveh was carried by storm at the end of the summer of 612. The city was razed to the ground after which the Medes returned to their homeland with great booty. Although an Assyrian state continued to exist at Harran for several years the two allies destroyed this last centre of Assyrian resistance in 609. The Babylonians continued their expansion and with the defeat of an Egyptian army at Carchemish in North Syria in 605 they became rulers of the 'Fertile Crescent' and the real heirs of the Assyrians.

While the Babylonians were consolidating their power in the former Assyrian provinces in Syria Cyaxares had been advancing to the north through Anatolia. War between the Lydians and Medes led to no result and ended in a famous battle of the 'eclipse of the sun' in 585 when an armistice was secured with the Babylonians acting as mediators. The Halys river or present Kizil Irmak was made the boundary between the Lydian and Median empires. Part, if not all, of the old kingdom of Urartu was absorbed into the Median empire. That relations between the Medes and Babylonians became less friendly is evidenced by the great fortifications and the 'Median wall' which were built north of Babylon to defend the city against attack. Many indications in the sources attest to Babylonian fear of their northern and eastern neighbour, a fear voiced by Isaiah and Jeremiah. Presumably Cyaxares also devoted some efforts to his own northern and eastern frontiers, but we cannot determine the extent of Median power in those directions, not only because of the absence of records but also because of the loose nature of the extensive Median empire, a fact suggested by Herodotus (I.134). The Achaemenid idea of the 'king of kings' was surely also held by the Medes as formerly by the Urartians. The Median confederacy was at first composed primarily of Medes, Mannai and Scythians, but the development into an empire must have hastened the mixture of peoples. It would seem further that those eastern provinces of Assyria which were conquered by the Medes were absorbed into 'Media', for the territories of Parsua, Zamua and others were probably included in Ptolemy's designation Syromedia (*Geog.* VI.2, 6). North of the Araxes River in Azerbaijan, the border of Media, lived Caspians and Cadusians who, it seems, were not included in the Median state. The Medes themselves were a mixture of indigenous and Iranian peoples, for the six tribes of Herodotus (I.101), the Paretakenoi, Bousai, Stroukhates, Arizantoi, Boudioi and Magoi, seem to be a mixture of Iranian and non-Iranian names, in spite of attempts to explain all from Iranian.[31] The extent of Median rule eastward has been mentioned, but the assertion of Dyakonov that the Medes certainly ruled Parthia and Hyrcania, and most probably the Herat area too, is based on a tenuous argument that the Behistun inscriptions mention Parthian support of the rebel Phraortes who claimed to be a member of the Median royal house.[32] In any case, Median rule wherever it extended seems to have been rather loose.

It is not improbable that the satrapy system of the Achaemenids already existed under the Medes, for the very form of the title *khshathrapan-*, whence Greek *satrapes*, is Median rather than Persian (*khshassapavan*). The satrapies, however, are merely a development of the governorships (*pakhatu*) of the Assyrians and also of Urartu, although they are much larger and more important under the Achaemenids. So in political development the Medes follow an old tradition, as they did in general culture.

The Medes surely used writing as did the Mannai, but the question is when did Assyrian cease to be the written language of the Medes, and a change to Median occur? The answer to this question is bound up with another problem, the origin of the Old Persian cuneiform system of writing. Most scholars agree that Akkadian provided the prototype for the Old Persian system of writing, which can be characterised as a syllabary with a number of logograms or Akkadian symbols. Others emphasise the influence of scribes who wrote Aramaic, or a combination of those who wrote on clay and scribes who wrote on parchment. Some believe that the Old Persian form of writing is derived from a previous Median writing or Mannaean, both of which were influenced by Urartian. Other scholars assert that Darius 'invented' the Old Persian cuneiform for his own purposes. The arguments can be summarised briefly. Adherents of the Median origin of the Old Persian syllabary say that Old Persian inscriptions of Cyrus II, and even inscribed plates of the older Arsames and Ariaramnes, exist which would be unthinkable if their Median overlords did not already possess a writing of their own. Further, the Median words and style in Old Persian indicate a massive borrowing, although the Iranian words in Elamite are mostly Old Persian forms.[33] More significant is the obvious archaic nature of Old Persian, a language probably only in court use at the time it was written but presumably preserving an old tradition. Furthermore, the Behistun inscription was engraved on a cliff in the heart of Media and surely educated Medes as well as Persians could read the Old Persian version, otherwise one would expect a Median version as well as the other three. Adherents of the Darius school claim, however, that there is no real evidence that Old Persian existed before the great Achaemenid, for the Arsames and Ariaramnes inscriptions are later concoctions because of their broken-down language, while the Cyrus inscriptions are all from Paşargadai where Darius undertook extensive rebuilding and also had inscriptions regarding Cyrus erected.[34] The whole argument is somewhat exaggerated since Old Persian was apparently used only for imperial inscriptions and played a small role, even under the later Achaemenids, compared with Akkadian, Elamite and Aramaic. This would have been even more true before Darius, for certainly he used inscriptions in Old Persian far more than anyone else. The answer to the question of Median writing awaits the results of the excavation of the Median capital Hamadan or some other Median centre, but I suspect that the Medes used Akkadian for their records as did the Mannai.

The religion of the Medes has received considerable attention primarily because of the Magi. The Magi were known to the Greeks, principally after Alexander, as the priests of the Iranians, and later to Romans and Greeks as specifically Zoroastrian priests. Zoroaster was known as one of the Magi at least as early as Xanthos of Lydia in the fifth (?) century BC, but the Avesta does not know the word, rather using *āthravan* and other terms for 'priest'.[35] All of this would indicate that Herodotus was correct in calling the Magi a Median tribe, although there is evidence in Elamite tablets from Persepolis that *magu-* was in fact used in Achaemenid times for 'priest'. How can one reconcile this information? It is necessary to gather all of the information about them from Achaemenid or earlier times. From

82

the Elamite tablets of Persepolis and the Behistun inscription it would seem that the Magi were no strangers to the Persians. From Herodotus (I.107, etc.) we learn that the Magi were influential in the Median court as advisers and dream interpreters. We may assume then that the Magi were active among the Persians as well as the Medes, if not in eastern Iran as well. They sang theogonies at the time of sacrifice (Herodotus I.132), and we may presume that the Magi did this at least by the time of Median unity if not before. Further, we can say that their particular practices, such as exposure of bodies to birds and animals (Herodotus I.140), killing of obnoxious creatures, and the like, all conform to orthodox Zoroastrian practices as we know them much later. From this one cannot, of course, conclude that the Magi were followers of Zoroaster. It is important to remember that the conception of orthodoxy or a Zoroastrian church can hardly have existed so early. The difference between a *magu-* who followed Zoroaster and one who did not cannot have been that between the proponent of one religion and his opponent in another religion. I suggest that the teachings of Zoroaster had found receptive ears among Magi in Media and then in Persis. The eclectic nature of the Magi, however, is indicated by the later use of the word 'Magi' among classical authors, and the various connotations of magic and magician, especially applied to Mesopotamian priests. The origin of the word itself is unknown and no satisfactory etymology for it has been found.[36] One should not be led astray by the wide use of 'Magi' in Hellenistic and Roman times for priests of Mithraism and many other religions or sects. One may tentatively suggest that the Magi were a 'tribe' of the Medes who exercised sacerdotal functions. During the supremacy of the Medes they expanded over the Median empire as a priesthood since the priestly trade was kept, so to speak, 'in the family'. The theogonies they sung were the ancient hymns of the Aryan *Urzeit*, not well understood by Medes or Persians but impressive because of their antiquity. The problem of the relation of Zoroaster's Gathas to the 'Younger Avesta' of the Magi, if we may assume that the Magi at least favoured the 'Younger Avesta', is unclear. Following the simplest explanation, I suggest that many Magi did not see the conflict between the 'ideas' of Zoroaster and the 'rites', including the ancient hymns (Younger Avesta), of their faith. Perhaps both, in the course of time, underwent changes and adaptations until the final Zoroastrian religion of Sasanian times. Since the rites and practices of this Zoroastrianism can be, in some measure, traced back to the Median Magi, in one sense one can say that the Magi became Zoroastrian, of course, only from a certain view-point. Surely we cannot find Hinduism, as we know it later, in the Vedas. Then can we really find Zoroastrianism, as we know it later, in the Gathas? What would Christianity have been without the Church fathers, and what Zoroastrianism without the Magi? The process of the fusing of ancient, traditional beliefs and practices with the doctrine of the struggle between Good and Evil was probably long and gradual and not unexpected.

One problem has been the difficulty of accommodating the 'religion' of the Younger Avesta, which is more or less a continuation of the old Aryan beliefs, with the Gathas of Zoroaster. Why and how could the followers of the prophet accept the worship of Mithra, Anahita and other deities in their religion? This has perplexed many scholars but, in my opinion, the question has not been properly put. The question is not the integration of old Aryan beliefs into the religion of Zoroaster, but the reverse, the acceptance of the teachings of a little-known priest in a small principality in eastern Iran by the majority who followed priests of the old Aryan pantheon. The Magi accepted Zoroaster probably as they had absorbed other teachings, but Zoroaster became the founder and the prophet of the new syncretic religion which we call Zoroastrianism for all Iranians. This is the real problem to explain. The process of synthesis took place during the later Achaemenid empire after the Medes.

The Medes ruled a vast empire for over sixty years from the fall of Nineveh, and during this time they were the successors of the Assyrians in many respects. Unfortunately the architectural and art remains of the Median period are few and uncertain of identification, but there are indications that the syncretic art of the Achaemenids, based on Elamite, Mesopotamian and Urartian backgrounds, had its beginnings in the empire of the Medes. We have mentioned Median words, or rather Median forms in the Old Persian inscriptions, such as 'satrap', and others such as the word for king, *khshayathiya-*, which indicate the influence of Median concepts of the state and rule on the Achaemenids. It is not improbable that the Median empire was a cultural and religious centre which influenced all Iranians to the north, south and east. As evidence of influence outside the empire, the Greeks took a word from the Medes meaning 'royal pleasure or hunting garden' and passed it on to Europe as

84

'paradise'. Although many problems remain, the importance of the Median empire in the formation of many Persian institutions and traditions of which we learn later can hardly be underestimated. Undoubtedly the Median period was one of great changes and ferment, all of which underlines the great need for archaeological work in the territory of ancient Media.

The Rise of Persis

We know little of the last ruler of Media, Astyages, who ruled *circa* 585-549 BC, except in relation to the rise of Cyrus and the Persians. About Cyrus we have considerable information in Greek sources, some of which can be checked with Babylonian and Old Persian texts, but in this information we also have legends about the founder of the dynasty of the Achaemenids which must be used with caution as source material. We can distinguish between the 'external' history of the Persians and their rulers at this time and the 'internal' history of the Achaemenid royal family, which is exemplified by the use of Babylonian and Old Persian texts for the former and Greek sources for the latter.

The Babylonian chronicle of Nabonidus, the last Chaldean king, tells us that in the sixth year of Nabonidus (550-549 BC) King Ishtumegu (Astyages) 'called up his troops and marched against Cyrus, king of Anshan, in order to me(et him in battle). The army of Ishtumegu revolted against him and in fetters they de (livered him) to Cyrus. Cyrus (marched) against the country Agamtanu; the royal residence (he seized); silver, gold, (other) valuables . . . of the country Agamtanu he took as booty and brought (them) to Anshan.'[37] This general account is confirmed by Greek sources, one of which, the epitome of Ctesias by Nicholas of Damascus, says that Cyrus brought the booty to Pasargadai,[38] which raises the question of the identification with Anshan. The latter term is old, found in Akkadian texts as a place in Elam, but we are not concerned with the ancient uses of Anshan nor with the various spellings of the name. In the time of Cyrus and his father and grandfather Anshan for the Babylonians seems to have been eastern Elam including part of the later province of Persis with the site of Pasargadai. The equation of Anshan with Parsa is just as confusing as Umman-Manda and Medes in the Assyrian chronicles. The family of Cyrus had been ruling the Persians for generations, as Cyrus says in another Akkadian text, asserting that he was the 'son of Cambyses, great king, king of Anshan, grandson of Cyrus, great king, king of Anshan, descendant of Teispes, great king, king of Anshan, of a family (which) always (exercised) kingship'. [39] In Herodotus (VII.11) we find a genealogy of Xerxes also confirming the royal descent of Cyrus. The dynastic chart given in the appendix is generally accepted by scholars as genuine, while Achaemenes was considered the eponymous ancestor of the great kings. Although the chronology is uncertain, under his son (?) Teispes (OP Chishpish) the Persian domains may have been divided between his two sons: Cyrus, who would have ruled the western part extending to the plains, and Ariaramnes in the eastern portion including the area of Pasargadai. Speculation on the reasons for this, as well as the later course of their history is idle. Suffice it to say that Cyrus II probably united both parts of the Persian domain, putting an end to the rule of Arsames, son of Ariaramnes, but sometime later making Hystaspes, father of Darius, his satrap in Fars province. Evidence is lacking for further surmise.

When we turn to Herodotus, Xenophon and Ctesias we find considerable detail about the life of Cyrus II and his relation to the Median court; unfortunately the greater part of the information is legendary. Much has been written about the Cyrus legend, as it has been called, and it is impossible to discuss it in detail here. The story briefly, as given by Herodotus who says that there were three other less reliable stories about Cyrus (I.95 and 214), is as follows (I.107-130). Astyages, after a bad dream, gave his daughter to Cambyses, a Persian, to marry, because he feared to give her to a noble Mede who might try to dethrone him. Cyrus was born of this marriage, but another dream indicated to Astyages that Cyrus would replace him, so he ordered the baby killed. He ordered his chief adviser to kill the boy, but Harpagos gave Cyrus to a shepherd whose wife had given birth to a dead baby. The shepherd and his wife substituted their dead baby for Cyrus and Harpagos was satisfied. The name of the wife was Spako, which, Herodotus tells us, was the Median word for dog. This seems to be an echo of the widespread Romulus-Remus myth of a child suckled by a wolf or dog (I.122). When Cyrus was ten he was 'discovered' by Astyages but the Magi rationalised their interpretations of the dreams so that Astyages feared no more and sent Cyrus to his real parents in Persis. When Cyrus reached manhood he revolted and Harpagos was sent against him in command of the Median army, but part of the army with

Harpagos deserted to Cyrus and the rest fled. In a later battle Astyages was defeated and taken captive. There are more details, such as the reason for the desertion of Harpagos, but this story is repeated in part or with variations by some later classical authors.

The Herodotus story not only has parallels elsewhere, such as the baby Moses in the bulrushes and a similar motif in the childhood of Sargon of Akkad in the third millennium BC, but it is the first in a series of 'dynasty founder' stories in Persian history.[40] The story of the birth and youth of Ardashir, first of the Sasanians, is similar to that of Cyrus, for Ardashir had to be of royal stock yet had to undergo hardship, raised in secret by shepherds. Ardashir also has connections with the Parthian court as Cyrus with the Median; he also revolts and secures the rule. The motif of the founder of a dynasty being raised by shepherds or poor people who do not know, or who conceal the true royal descent of the child, becomes part of the charisma of Persian royalty repeated under the Safavids and other rulers in Persian history. I term it the West Iranian 'national' or 'royal' epic as compared with the East Iranian 'religious' or 'heroic' epic series.

Ctesias gives a different story, also with many details, preserved by Nicholas of Damascus and the Byzantine patriarch Photius.[41] This story has Cyrus the son of a Persian bandit of the Mardi tribe, Atradates, and a shepherdess, both with no relationship to Astyages. Cyrus secures a menial position at the Median court and begins his rise. He has a dream that he will become great, and when he is sent by Astyages as an envoy to the Cadusians he meets a Persian called Oibaras with whom he plans a revolt against Astyages. Astyages sends an army against the rebels who are besieged on a mountain at Pasargadai. The Persian women shame their men to deeds of valour and Cyrus defeats the Medes and captures Ekbatana. Why should Ctesias' story differ so much from that of Herodotus? The simplest explanation is that he was deliberately de-emphasising the royal blood of Cyrus. Ctesias' position as court physician of Artaxerxes II, who may have been seeking to discredit the name of Cyrus because of his own struggle with the younger 'Anabasis' Cyrus, could have been the reason for his story of the life of Cyrus. Xenophon in his Cyropaedia belonged to the opposing camp of the younger Cyrus and he flatly states that Cyrus the Elder was the son of Cambyses, king of the Persians and Mandane, daughter of Astyages. It would appear that Cyrus really was an Achaemenid prince who revolted and conquered the Median king by the aid of the Medes themselves,

87

for there are several indications that Astyages was cruel and disliked by his subjects (e.g. Diodorus Siculus IX.23).

It is unknown whether Nabonidus supported Cyrus in his uprising, but surely the Babylonian king cannot have been unhappy to see such a formidable opponent as Astyages in difficulty. Differences over the land of Cilicia and Median occupation of Harran, birthplace of Nabonidus, cannot have helped relations between them. During the Median-Persian hostilities Nabonidus occupied Harran probably in 553 BC. It is impossible to say whether Cyrus at this time was engaged in expeditions in eastern Iran or against the Armenians and other peoples south of the Caucasus for sources are not available, but it is not improbable that Cyrus had to consolidate his power and engage in some warfare on the plateau. Then he turned his attention to Lydia, probably in 547 BC after winning the allegiance of northern Assyria and Cilicia. Croesus the king of Lydia had taken advantage of the fall of the Median empire to enlarge his own domain and now Cyrus marched against him. Following an indecisive battle, Cyrus besieged Croesus in his capital at Sardis and after a short period took the city. Regarding the fate of Croesus, one must choose between a restoration of lacunae in the Akkadian chronicle of Nabonidus (column II, lines 16-18) that the king of (Lydia?) was killed, or the statement of Herodotus (I.88) that Cyrus treated Croesus in a friendly manner. One should, perhaps, trust the Greek historian unless he is proved wrong.

Herodotus (I.153) says that Cyrus organised Persian rule in Lydia and returned to Ekbatana to make plans for war against Bactria, Babylonia, the Sakas and Egypt, but a revolt immediately broke out in Sardis and Cyrus had to send a new army against the rebels. Herodotus tells us the general who conquered the Ionian cities was the same Mede Harpagos who betrayed Astyages and joined Cyrus. Since descendants of this Harpagos remained in Anatolia, Herodotus may have utlilised them as informants for material about Persia.[42] In conquering the Ionian cities and bringing them into the satrapy of Sardis or Sparda (Sephard-), the Persians learned how to divide and conquer the Greeks as well as the effectiveness of bribery.

The next conquest, of which we know, was Babylon, which was first threatened from the south by defections to the side of Cyrus. In Babylon the behaviour of Nabonidus had estranged the priests of Marduk and many others from him. The conquest by

Cyrus was swift as we learn from the Akkadian source, the so-called Nabonidus Chronicle. 'In the month of Tashritu, when Cyrus attacked the army of Akkad in Opis on the Tigris, the inhabitants of Akkad revolted, but he (Nabonidus) massacred the confused inhabitants. The fourteenth day Sippar was seized without battle. Nabonidus fled. The sixteenth day Gobryas (Ugbaru), the governor of Gutium and the army of Cyrus entered Babylon without battle. Afterwards Nabonidus was arrested in Babylon when he returned (there)'.[43] This was in October 539 BC, an important date in world history, for in a sense it marked the end of a long tradition in the land of Sumer and Akkad and the beginning of a new union of the Mesopotamian lowlands with the plateau which would continue for centuries. Cyrus himself, however, did not initiate any great changes. His attitude towards Babylon was not too dissimilar to that of the Assyrian kings in regard to the ancient city, one of awe and respect, but also as a protector. He used the ancient titles and protocol in Akkadian, such as, 'I am Cyrus, king of the world, great king, legitimate king, king of Babylon, king of Sumer and Akkad, king of the four rims (of the world)', and he further honoured Marduk and other gods. Although his inscriptions are in Akkadian for local consumption, one misses any mention of his own gods in them, so characteristic of older conquerors in the Near East. The freeing of the Jews from their Babylonian captivity is well known, while other peoples too profited from the generous religious politics of their first Achaemenid ruler. Former subjects of Babylon in Syria submitted to the new ruler and Cyrus joined the North Syrian districts to the satrapy of Babylonia and 'the other side of the (Euphrates) river' (Babili and Ebirnari) under Gubaru who, it would appear, is not to be confused with Ugbaru, the governor of Gutium in the Nabonidus Chronicle, since both names appear in the chronicle.[44] Cyrus' policy of mildness towards the erstwhile subject peoples of Babylonia, as we see in the Old Testament, must have helped greatly in the consolidation of Persian rule in Syria and Palestine. The book of Ezra is eloquent testimony to the actions of Cyrus in attempting to win support for Persian rule, and he was on the whole successful. The king, however, personally did not visit Syria but returned to Ekbatana leaving the work of consolidation to subordinates.

Ekbatana, the Median capital, became the centre of the far-flung empire of Cyrus for his first capital Pasargadai was not adequate to the task either in location or in size and prestige. We know next to nothing of Ekbatana buried under modern Hamadan but Pasargadai has been investigated. Herodotus (1.125) mentions the Pasargadai, together with the Maraphioi and the Maspioi, as the chief tribes of the Persians, while the Achaemenid family belonged to the Pasargadai. In the Cyrus story in Ctesias the name seems to refer to the mountain near the site or possibly to the district. The historians of Alexander the Great speak of Pasargadai as a town built by Cyrus, and one of them, Anaximenes of Lampsakos, gives an etymology of it 'camping ground of the Persians'.[45] It is, of course, possible that we have the assumption of an original tribal or district name as a city name and that all are the same, but this is not certain. A parallel might be Kirman province, Kirman city, and the Kirmani or Germani tribe. The etymology of the name Pasargadai as containing Parsa or 'Persian' in the first part and *gard-, or the like in the second, has been countered by Marquart who derives the name from a nearby mountain *pasārkadrish, 'behind (pasā) Mount Arkadrish', mentioned in the Behistun inscription.[46] Since tribal names are usually in origin totems or common words like 'the men', or heroic designations, the contention that the origin of the name of the people is from a small locality is dubious, while the reverse would be more probable. The consistent use of a plural ending in the name by classical authors, plus the lack of evidence that the river which flows through the plain was called Pasargadai would indicate an original tribal name. The Pasargadai are mentioned later as a tribe or people living in Carmania (Marciani Heracleensis, *Periplus Maris Exteri*, 1.28). There is also the possibility that we have two names, one for the city, another for the tribe.

It is not improbable that Cyrus II built a town on the site of Pasargadai (Quintus Curtius V.6, 10) and that the oldest ruins there do date from the time of the founder of the Achaemenid empire. The ruins of Pasargadai are located about 43 kilometres by air north of Persepolis, or almost double that distance by road, at an altitude of about 6,000 feet, the same as Hamadan, hence not a comfortable site for a capital in the winter. That the present ruins on the Murghab river are remains from Cyrus' city has been almost attested by the location, by the descriptions in classical sources, primarily the historians of Alexander, and finally by inscriptions from the site. The last are fragmentary but of some interest. One inscription says in Old Persian, Elamite and

Akkadian, in the usual form for imperial inscriptions, 'I am Cyrus the king, an Achaemenid', and it is located on pillars of a palace at Pasargadai repeated at least five times on five different columns. The inscription provides the chief argument for the contention that the Old Persian syllabary was in use before Darius. The argument is weakened, however, by the use of similar formulae on weights with the name of Darius, but undoubtedly in use later than Darius, as well as the general stereotype of Old Persian inscriptures indicating a very limited use of Old Persian cuneiform, surely predominantly by Darius if not invented under him. The demonstration that another inscription of Cyrus at Pasargadai was inscribed by Darius, both from new fragments of the inscription and from the patently later date of the remains of the building where the inscription was found, suggests that much of the construction at Psargadai was ordered by Darius rather than Cyrus.

In addition to remains of palaces and the 'tomb of Cyrus' at Pasargadai there are two objects of interest, because of copies elsewhere. One is a large terrace with huge, well-cut stones overlooking the plain and the other is the wall of a once large tower which was almost identical to a tower facing the tombs of the kings at Naqsh-i Rustam near Persepolis. The terrace of Pasargadai has been compared with a similar one at a site called Masjid-i Sulaiman in the present oil-fields of Khuzistan and with analogous cyclopean stone work in Urartu, all forerunners of the great terrace of Persepolis.[47] The further assertion, however, that these terraces clearly represent stages on the wanderings of the Persians from Lake Urmia to Persis is not really warranted. Certainly the use of large stones for building, especially in walls, is found in Urartu, though it is not unknown elsewhere on the Iranian plateau while naturally absent from Mesopotamia, but the idea of a raised platform or terrace is not unique to Iran. The prototype with bricks used for stone existed on the plains of Iraq. The white stone for the large blocks in Pasargadai and Persepolis came from quarries near the present village of Sivand south-west of Pasargadai, for cut and uncut stones have been found there.[48] The huge cut stones were probably floated down the river to the building sites, installed and then held together with iron clamps. The architecture at Pasargadai, as at Persepolis, is distinctive and original, a tribute to the genius of the Achaemenids. There is no space to discuss the origin of the columns in the oblong or square halls of the

Achaemenid palaces, although many of the elements of the style are from Ionia. Pasargadai seems to represent well early Achaemenid art and architecture while Persepolis is a more developed style of the same. Thus Pasargadai could be described as an example of the transition from the northern art and culture of the Medes, influenced by Urartu, to a southern Persian culture, influenced by Elam. Persepolis would be a representative of the latter.

The controversy among art historians concerning the relation of Greek to Achaemenid plastic art, and especially the question of the origin of the style of folds in the representation of garments on statues, has been more or less resolved in favour of the priority of the former. Pasargadai is our chief source for early Achaemenid art, but it seems clear that the use of folds in sculptured garments even here came to the Persians from the Ionian Greeks and furthermore early in the time of the Achaemenid Empire.[49] At Pasargadai as at Persepolis the ornamental purpose of the sculptured stone reliefs, unlike the Assyrian reliefs which give a pictorial narrative to be followed by the observer, is at sight obvious. Sculptures of animals in Achaemenid art recall those of Urartu as well as Assyria. Again we find that representation is subordinate to decoration as usual in Persian art throughout the ages. Unfortunately we have too little from early Achaemenid times, and until extensive excavations at Pasargadai and other Achaemenid sites distinguish between the work of Cyrus and that of later rulers, one must be cautious in developing theories of early Achaemenid art and architecture.

The consolidation of the empire of Cyrus possibly proceeded with the same policies by which the conqueror had united the tribes and peoples of Persis, both Aryans and the indigenous folk. It has been suggested that Cyrus may be a non-Iranian name.[50] More likely, however, is an Iranian origin related to *kur*, the word for 'son' in Kurdish and Luri dialects. The mixture of cultural elements from Aryans and indigenous peoples is also shown in the dress of the Persians pictured on reliefs from Persepolis, where they wear robes like the Elamites rather than trousers or boots as do the other Iranian peoples, including the Medes. Thus one characteristic of Cyrus' rule seems to have been a desire to learn from subject peoples, a respect for their religions and customs, and a desire to create a flexible empire. Another characteristic of the early Achaemenid empire was its continuation of the organisation and royal traditions of the previous state of the

Medes with only Cyrus replacing Astyages. For the empire of the Achaemenids to outsiders was the empire of the Medes and Persians. True the Persians held a privileged position but, although it was no Habsburg dual monarchy, the Medes did provide many high officials in the early Achaemenid state. The war against Croesus must have seemed a righteous cause to Cyrus, regaining land which had been occupied by the Lydians when Median forces had been withdrawn to fight himself. For Cyrus was the heir of Astyages and bound to uphold the traditions and boundaries of the Median state.

The victories of the Persians were not really greater or different from those of past conquerors, although military art had undoubtedly progressed with new tactics in the use of cavalry and otherwise. What was different was the new policy of conciliation and together with this the prime aim of Cyrus to establish a *pax Achaemenica*. For this Cyrus had to have the co-operation of the subject peoples, and to manage the far-flung empire the scribes of Mesopotamia and Syria provided the necessary bureaucracy. Just as in the art and culture of the Achaemenids, so in the government of the empire, the elements were present but the genius to weld these elements into a new synthesis was found in Cyrus and even more so in Darius. It is more than likely that the unity of the Achaemenid empire is the work of Darius rather than Cyrus, but the latter must have set the stage.

Cyrus had another task, the defence of the north-eastern frontier of his empire against nomadic invasions from Central Asia. We have already mentioned the unknown extent of Median rule eastward, but here also Cyrus probably found the ground prepared for him, although the areas of Bactria, Arachosia, etc., may have been conquered by the sword. Here also in his eastern conquests he may have followed the policy of attaching to himself lands which previously had owed allegiance to the Medes and now devolved upon him. Herodotus (I.205-215) gives a detailed story of Cyrus' expedition against the Massagetai east of the Caspian Sea. After war had started Cyrus sent his son and successor Cambyses back to Persis accompanied by Croesus, ex-king of Lydia. Then Cyrus dreamt that he saw the young Darius, eldest son of Hystaspes and grandson of Arsames, also an Achaemenid, with wings on his shoulders which overshadowed Asia and Europe. Since Darius was not yet twenty and was staying in Persis rather than with the army of Cyrus, the great king summoned Hystaspes and ordered him back to Persis to watch his son until the war was over, which Hystaspes did. In a first engagement Cyrus defeated the Massagetai and captured a son of Queen Tomyris who ruled the Massagetai. The son committed suicide and Cyrus was defeated and killed in the ensuing battle *circa* 530 BC after ruling twenty-nine years. This seems in general to be the most plausible story of the death of Cyrus, for other classical authors, including Ctesias, have similar tales, changing the opponents to Sakas, Derbikes or another nomadic people.

There exists an interesting indication of the extent of Cyrus' conquests in Central Asia, the city of Kyreskhata or Kyropolis, in Sogdiana, which was stormed and destroyed by Alexander the Great. The name has been explained as the 'city of Cyrus' (Sogdian: *kath*) and identified with a village Kurkath near the mediaeval city of Usrushana north-east of Samarkand.[51] This place name would pre-suppose the settlement of a garrison in a town founded by Cyrus to protect the frontier of his empire. Cyrus seems to have made a great impression on the Persians, and not only as the founder of an empire. Rivers or places as well as towns may have been named after him, at least in popular belief if not officially, while Herodotus (III.89) says the Persians remembered his mildness and called him father. We also have the 'Cyrus Saga' with variations, which was widely known among the people. All of this indicates the esteem and affection in which the founder of the dynasty was held by his people. It was not so with his son.

The Crisis of Empire

Cambyses has not had a good name in history perhaps undeservedly. We know more about him than about his father because of Babylonian documents and the circumstances attending his death, yet he still remains something of a mystery to posterity. Cambyses (OP Kambūjia) may carry a non-Iranian name, in spite of attempts to connect his name with the Kambojas, a people living in north-west India, meaning then 'king of the Kambojas', a throne name.[52] The possibility of a throne name as well as a personal name is attractive, but one problem is that neither the name Cyrus nor Cambyses can be satisfactorily explained as one or the other, and we really do not know. Cambyses was certainly closely associated with his father at least from the conquest of Babylonia. The exact significance of the occurrence of various titles dated from different years in Akkadian documents such as 'King of Babylon', or 'King of the Lands', or both, in the period 539-530 BC, is unclear. The province of Babylonia and 'beyond the River', as we have said, was governed by Gubaru, but Cambyses seems to have been the titular king of Babylonia while his ruling father Cyrus was 'King of the Lands' in Akkadian protocol. Problems in titulary go hand in hand with the chronology, and the 'accession year' of a king, which the Persians obtained from the Babylonians, has caused difficulties in the chronology. The accession year precedes the first official year of a king, for it includes those months remaining in the year in which the preceding king died. The first 'official' year of a king began in the month of Nisan of the following year, which month was always in the spring. News of Cyrus' death reached Babylon in late summer 530 for in September documents are already dated in the accession year of Cambyses 'King of the Lands'.[53] Plans to invade Egypt probably had been already made and Cambyses proceeded to the conquest of the land of the Nile.

Herodotus, as usual, is the chief source for Cambyses' conquest of Egypt. Greeks fought on both sides, for the Egyptians and for the Persians, a forecast of the nature of future armies and wars. Memphis and Thebes, the two principal Egyptian cities, were taken, garrisons were established and expeditions were sent south up the Nile river and westward to desert oases. None of these expeditions was really successful; it is said that the army sent to an oasis of Ammon was lost in a sandstorm. Cambyses is credited with many misdeeds in Egypt, such as the slaying of the sacred Apis bull, which, however, can be proved false from dated inscriptions on the sarcophagi of the succeeding bulls. Apparently, the measures of Cambyses to reduce the revenues of many temples raised the priesthood against him, and they spread false tales about him. Actually it seems Cambyses followed his father's policy of respect for local customs and religions, and some inscriptions attest to his quite normal policy in Egypt.

Finally we come to the crisis which shook the empire of the Achaemenids, and to the rise of Darius about whom much has been written. Some scholars insist that Darius was a usurper and a liar, others defend his integrity as the restorer of the Achaemenid house. There are both contemporary inscriptions and classical sources to tell us what happened, but do they tell the truth? In any case, the story of the Magian Gaumata and Darius' seizure of power is one of the greatest stories and scandals of ancient history.

The prime source for the events of the time is the Behistun inscription, also called Bisutun locally, from *Baga-stāna 'place of the god'(Ahura Mazda?), carved on a cliff high above the road which even today goes from the plains of Mesopotamia to Hamadan. One reason the relief and inscription has remained in a relatively good state of preservation is that Darius had the steps which led up to it smoothed away so no one could climb up to the relief. On the relief are pictured Darius seated and in front of him the rebels, with hands bound behind them, who were suppressed by the Achaemenid ruler. This was undoubtedly an important document for Darius since fragments of the text of the inscription in Aramaic were found in Egypt, and there is every reason to believe that Darius did make many copies and send them everywhere among the provinces, as he says (Behistun IV.88-92).[54] In this inscription he says the following (paragraph X, line 27):[55]

'This is what was done by me after I became king. (One) Cambyses by name, the son of Cyrus, of our family, was king here. There was a brother of that Cambyses called Bardiya, of the same mother and the same father as Cambyses. Afterwards Cambyses slew that Bardiya. When Cambyses slew Bardiya it was not known to the people that Bardiya had been slain. Afterwards Cambyses went to Egypt. When Cambyses had gone to Egypt, then the people became false and the Lie became multiplied in the land both in Persis and in Media and in other lands.

'Saith Darius the King: Afterwards there was a man, a Magian, Gaumata by name; he rebelled (fell out) from Pishiyahuvada. Fourteen days of the Month Viyakhna had passed when he rose up from the mountain Arakadri. He lied to the people thus: "I am Bardiya, the son of Cyrus, brother of Cambyses". Then all the people became allied (to him). From Cambyses both Persis and Media and the other lands went over to him. He seized the kingdom. Nine days of the month Garmapada were past; then he seized the kingdom. Afterwards Cambyses died naturally.[56]

'Saith Darius the King: This kingdom which Gaumata the Magian took from Cambyses, from early (times) this kingdom had belonged to our family. Afterwards Gaumata the Magian robbed Cambyses; he took for himself both Persis and Media and other lands. He made them his own possession. He became king.

'Saith Darius the King: There was not a man, neither a Persian nor a Mede nor anyone of our family, who could have taken the kingdom (from) Gaumata the Magian. The people feared him greatly that he might slay many who had previously known Bardiya. For this reason would he slay the people "lest they know me that I am not Bardiya the son of Cyrus". There was no one who dared say anything about Gaumata the Magian until I came. Then I prayed to Ahura Mazda. Ahura Mazda bore me aid. Ten days were past of the month Bagayadi, then I with a few men slew that Gaumata the Magian and those chief men who were his supporters. A fortress by name Sikayahuvati, a district by name Nisaya, in Media, there I slew him. I took the kingdom from him. By the grace of Ahura Mazda I became king. Ahura Mazda bestowed the kingdom upon me.

'Saith Darius the King: The kingdom which had been taken away from our family, that I put in (its) place. I re-established it on its foundation, as before. I rebuilt the temples which Gaumata the Magian had destroyed. I handed back to the people the chattel,[57] herds, household slaves, and houses which Gaumata the Magian had taken from them. I re-established the people on its foundations, (in) both Persis and Media and the other lands.'

Such is the story of Guamata as told by Darius. Herodotus who calls Cambyses' brother and the Magian both Smerdis (Greek *sm-* for *b-*), has more details but in its essential features the story is the same. Ctesias has much the same with significant variations in details such as the name of Cyrus' younger son Tanyoxarkes (Xenophon has Tanaoxares), which may be a 'nickname' meaning 'large bodied'. Much has been written about the details as well as the reliability of the Gaumata story and scholars are divided into two groups, those who believe that the Bardiya who revolted was the true younger brother of Cambyses and Darius revolted against him, inventing the story of the false Bardiya to justify his action to posterity. Others support the historicity of the story as related by Darius on his inscription. Both agree that there is only one story, the royal Persian version, which is the basis of the classical accounts. In general, I believe, one should accept inscriptions unless sufficient reason for doubting their veracity exists, for inscriptions are public and subject to continuing scrutiny. Most of the arguments on both sides are based on surmise and speculation, but it would be useful to present the argumentation of the two cases. The proponents of the mendacity of Darius present the following arguments, some of which are not accepted by various scholars, though others are. Aeschylus (*Persae*, 774) speaks of Mardos (Smerdis) as though he

97

were a legitimate ruler who was assassinated. Yet this passage does not really help us since it shows little knowledge of actual events. Further, it is argued, Cambyses had no son and successor and would not have killed his brother thus ending the line. Darius revolted against Bardiya, because in his inscription he emphasised Cambyses' 'natural death', and because he emphasised the lie calling all rebels liars, thus protesting too much.[58] Furthermore, Cyrus and Cambyses upheld Median interests while Darius restored Persian supremacy. Most reliance, however, is placed on two arguments, one that it is most unlikely that a usurper could deceive the people for a long time about his identity, and two that Darius lies in his own inscription about the chronology, when he repeats several times the assertion that he accomplished the suppression of rebels in one year. To discuss the latter point first, much has been written about the veracity of what Darius did in one and the same year (see note 53), and no conclusion has been reached acceptable to all concerned. One attempt, however, seems more reasonable than others by dividing the contents of the inscription into three sections, first (DB, paragraphs 16-20) the revolts in Elam and Babylonia, second (DB 21-48), the suppression of revolts in Elam, Media, Armenia and Sagartia (24-34), Parthia (35-37), Margiana (38), Persis (40-44), and Arachosia (45-48), third (DB 49-51) the second Babylonian revolt and its suppression. The chronology of the 'one year' of Darius would be from his accession year into his first 'official' year, from the first *dated* event, the battle for Babylonia in the first revolt to the last *dated* event, the end of the revolt of Frada in Margiana, one year less three days. This explanation by Hallock has been criticised by Shahbazi who showed that the 'one year' of Darius extended from the capture of the rebel Assina in November 522 until the execution of the last rebel Arakha in November 521.[59]

It is difficult to believe that a usurper could pass for long as a royal prince, but if a Magian called Gaumata could do it, then so could Vahyazdata later (DB, paragraph 40). The indications are that something was mysterious about Bardiya as Darius and the Greek authors tell. There is another factor to be mentioned regarding Darius' action after coming to power. If we follow classical sources (e.g. Herod. III.88) Darius married Atossa, sister of Cambyses and wife of Gaumata, as well as the daughter of the true Bardiya called Parmys, an unlikely act if Gaumata had really been the true Bardiya. Although the Behistun inscription bristles with difficulties and there are many points for discussion, the burden of proof for the falsity of the historical account must rest on those who seek to disprove it. They may be right but they have not proved their contention.

There are several questions to be raised in regard to the inscription at Behistun, one being the nature of Gaumata's revolt, assuming that Guamata was real and not a figment of Darius' imagination. First, however, a few words about chronology are relevant. Akkadian tablets, usually business documents, indicate that Bardiya had both an 'accession year' and an 'official year'. Some scholars have argued that Gaumata-Bardiya then ruled more than a year, but it is now apparent from the Akkadian sources that Darius (and Herodotus) was giving at least an accurate chronology of Gaumata. The accession year of Gaumata would be 523/522 BC and his first official year 522/521, but the former was also the seventh year of Cambyses and the latter the accession year of Darius. Matters were complicated, for the Babylonian scribes, not knowing how to date their documents, whether by continuing Cambyses' rule, by upholding Bardiya then by recognising the Babylonian rebel or finally Darius, must have been in a quandary not unusual for these confused times. The Akkadian clay tablets, however, have been indispensable for determining the chronology of the various reigns.

To return to the question of Gaumata the Magian, we should bring additional information to clarify the role of the rebel and other Magians. Herodotus (III. 79) tells us that when the Persians learned of the death of the rebels (in Herodotus there were two Magians who seized power) they drew their daggers and killed all of the Magians they could find, and from that time, in commemoration of the day the Persians have a holiday which they call *magophonia* or 'slaughter of the Magians'. The killing of the Magians is also suggested by the words of Josephus (*Jewish Antiquities*, XI.31) 'after the killing of the Magians' while Ctesias (note 41, p. 24) says that the celebration of *magophonia* is the anniversary of the killing of the Magian Sphendadates, his name for the usurper. More significant was the discovery of a Sogdian fragment with a word meaning a 'killing of the Magians', but here ascribed to Alexander the Great.[60] This would indicate the reliability of the two classical historians regarding the commemoration of the event of Gaumata's assassination. This, and the restoration of the destroyed '*āyadana*' has provoked much discussion about a Zoroastrian rising of the Magians or the opposite, a Zoroastrian Darius who suppressed the old, 'pagan' Magian religion. I believe the rebellion to have been provoked by Cambyses' long absence in Egypt which must have strained the resources of the empire. Gaumata the Magian seized power, or if one does not wish to believe the sources, the true Bardiya revolted against his brother Cambyses with the aid of some Magians. This revolt, if it may be designated as such, seems to have been accepted by most of the people, except for some Persians, including Darius. Darius killed the Magians supporting Gaumata and restored the *āyadana* which had been destroyed. What were the *āyadana*?

The identification of the *āyadana* has been connected with the religion of the Achaemenids, and the role of the religion of Zoroaster in western Iran. The explanation of the word *āyadana* as a place of worship, from the Old Persian form *yad-*, Median *yaz-*, Indian *yaj-* 'to worship', is generally accepted since the Elamite and Babylonian 'house of the gods' would support it, but what kind of a temple was it?[61] It has been suggested that the *āyadana* were sanctuaries dedicated particularly to the Achaemenid kings, but since Gaumata claimed to be an Achaemenid himself it is not likely that he would destroy the family shrines. On the other hand, the *āyadana* were in existence before and after Gaumata, and since there is no evidence that Gaumata left Iran or acted outside of Iran, we may suppose that the *āyadana* were proper to the Persians (and Medes). So the *āyadana* may have been local sanctuaries supported by Cyrus, Cambyses, and later Darius and his successors, probably destroyed by Gaumata for religious rather than dynastic reasons. Gaumata may have been a 'Zoroastrian', but need not necessarily have been to destroy local sanctuaries patronised by the Achaemenid rulers. It is too speculative to follow classical tradition that Gaumata's real name was Sphendadates, and further to accept his identification by later Magians with Spentadata son of Vishstaspa, a Zoroastrian martyr, thus making Gaumata a Zoroastrian hero against the Achaemenids, who consequently received no notice in Zoroastrian tradition.[62] One of the *āyadana* may be the structure at Naqsh-i Rustam facing the royal tombs called the Kaᶜbah of Zoroaster, but that is mere speculation with no evidence.

The religion of the Achaemenids has been much discussed with no generally accepted conclusions, and we have previously touched upon it. From Babylonian clay tablets, and an analysis of Cambyses' acts in Egypt, one may conclude that both Cyrus and Cambyses used religion as a political weapon to foster their own rule. Babylonian, Egyptian and Hebrew deities were honoured, so it would seem, by both monarchs, and there is no evidence that Darius displayed a great change from that previous policy. The *magophonia* could not have been directed against all Magians since we find them a few years after Darius' accession to the throne busy in Persepolis, as attested in Elamite tablets.[63] Whether the Magians before Darius held different beliefs from those permitted to function after Darius, is a question which cannot at present be answered, while the theory of several classes of Magians, priests and bureaucrats, is not improbable but also unproved.[64] It seems that the Magians were employed as *qādīs* (the religious leaders as well as judges and bureaucratic officials in Islamic times) and there may have been various 'classes' of Magians in ancient Iran. Among them were probably followers of Zoroaster but at the same time they could have recited the same hymns and theogonies, possibly relating to the origin of things, as did their brethren in eastern Iran. As Strabo said (XI. 532) 'the sacred rites of the Persians, one and all are held in honour by both the Medes and Armenians', and one might add by others as well.

The question of Ahura Mazda need only detain us briefly, for there is no question of an organised church with fixed dogmas under the early Achaemenids and men's beliefs are notoriously difficult to divine in history. One cannot say that Zoroaster himself 'invented' Ahura Mazda, even though the evidence of the names Assara Mazash in the list of gods from the time of the Assyrian king Assurbanipal is disputed.[65] Just as with Old Persian cuneiform writing, so with the god Ahura Mazda, it is under Darius that both appear in abundance. Ahura Mazda, however, is the god of the Aryans, as the Elamite version of the Behistun inscription (IV.62) says. And over Darius on his reliefs hovers the symbol of Ahura Mazda like the symbol of the god Assur of Assyria. Furthermore, Darius expressly declares himself to be a follower of Ahura Mazda (Behistun IV.44). Regarding other gods surely Ahura Mazda was like a 'king above all gods', perhaps already identified by many with Zeus and other such gods in other pantheons. Darius and a Magian could equally have been followers of Zoroaster irrespective of different burial customs or even different rites in sacrifice or worship, or one could have been 'more Zoroastrian' than the other. The practices and rites which later came to be identified as hallmarks of 'orthodox' Zoroastrianism must have accrued to a religion in formation gradually and from several sources. Certainly in this period it would be foolish to identify anyone as a 'true Zoroastrian' because of his use or non-use of *haoma* or the way he was buried. We must continually return to questions of religion for they were of supreme interest and importance in the Near East, something which modern secularists may find difficult to understand. Much has already been written about the religion of the Achaemenids which cannot be supported by any evidence.[66]

The One World of the Achaemenids. The Court and Bureaucracy

The empire of the Achaemenids was both the direct descendant of the Assyrian and Median states, as well as a new development in the history of the Near East. We have already mentioned important words in the Old Persian inscriptions which have a Median rather than Persian form, indicating a borrowing of the Achaemenids from the north. Strabo (XI.525) says:

'The Medes, however, are said to have been the originators of customs (of the Armenians) and also, still earlier, for the Persians, who were their masters and their successors in rule over Asia. For example, the "Persian" stole, as it is now called, and their (the Medes') zeal for archery and horsemanship, the service they render kings, their ornaments, and the divine reverence paid by subjects to kings, came 'to' the Persians from the Medes.'

He continues that the copying of the Medes by the Persians was especially true in dress, except in the south (?) where the Persians adopted the clothes of the conquered peoples (Elamites). There are many indications that much of the protocol of the Achaemenid kings had already evolved under the Medes. It is tempting to trace all the protocol, symbolism, and the concept of kingship in Iran back either to Indo-European prototypes or borrowings from Mesopotamia, but one must add a third possible source for concepts of kingship — those general ideas of kingship perhaps present in all societies and not distinctively Indo-European or ancient Near Eastern. In addition to these three view-points on the origins of the concept of kingship under the Achaemenids, we must not forget the many problems of disentangling additional beliefs which have become attached to original concepts throughout history, and which have also changed these fundamental concepts in many and subtle ways. Fortunately much of late has been written about the sacral and also the more secular character of Iranian kingship, and we may refer to a summary by Geo Widengren.[67] The points he raises can be briefly summarised. In ancient Iran, as among other Indo-European peoples, a king is elected from a certain family which has the charisma of kingship. The king is elected by the people or rather the warriors, the *kāra* of Old Persian, but in Achaemenid Iran he is king of many kings. His person is sacred and he is descended from the gods. The court ceremony expecially obeisance, *proskynesis*, reflects his divine status. He is also a priest and sacrificer, the chief participant in the New Year's festival which has many symbolic, cosmic associations. The day of the king's coronation is his birthday when he is 're-born' by assuming a new throne-name, and puts on a garment symbolising his position as a cosmic ruler. At his death his 'personal fire' is extinguished and mourning on the part of his family or servants sometimes takes extreme forms of suicide or mutilation.

Much of this can be inferred, though not proved, from scattered sources. Undoubtedly there was considerable symbolism, tradition and ritual connected with the office of kingship under the Achaemenids, but the cosmic significance of it is not at once so apparent. There exists apparently a contradiction between the position of the king of kings as one among many and the sacred, divine nature of any king. In an empire which kings or subrulers, if any, are meant to be sacred? Were all kings descended from the gods and thus sacred, or only the king of kings? In India kings were compared with gods but were not identified as gods, but in Iran the king in a sense became more important and the idea of legitimacy becomes paramount and, as we have mentioned is bound up with the 'kingly glory' or *hvarnah.*

It seems that the 'divinity' or 'sacredness' of kings was an ancient Near Eastern development, perhaps originally from Egypt, and not imported by the Aryan invaders, which would explain why the later Sasanian monarchs could place on their coins the phrase 'from the seed of the gods', while the early Achaemenids had not yet become fully assimilated to the Near Eastern milieu. Whether the early Achaemenids considered themselves 'brothers of the sun and moon' and thus 'sacred' is not attested, hence is dubious. Further, it would seem that for the Achaemenids even *proskynesis* did not signify the abject humility

103

before a god, but rather the sign of respect towards royalty, for the nobility a bow with the kissing of one's own hand as depicted on reliefs at Persepolis, or with knee bending, or even, in the case of supplication or requests, full prostration on the ground, especially for menials. In neither case was god worship intended.[68]

There are, of course, many details about the symbolism and acts of the king of kings, a discussion of which would engage far more space than available here. The coronation of a new king took place at Pasargadai, where according to Plutarch (Artaxerxes II.3) the new king was initiated by priests at a sanctuary of a militant goddess, probably Anahita, and then donned the robe of Cyrus after which he had a peasant's meal. This may have had an ancient, cosmic meaning, but it is doubtful if many Persians at that time knew or cared about it. By custom, but now by law, the firstborn son, born after the crowning of the king, became crown prince or heir apparent. In all of the institutions of kingship both sacred and profane interpretations of the kingly functions seem to apply, and scholars have devoted much labour to the mystical or symbolic interpretation of the characteristics of Persian kingship. Suffice it to say that under the Achaemenids principles of the institution of the 'king of kings' were fashioned from both ancient Near Eastern and Aryan concepts of rule, which with changes and additions have lasted down to the present.

The names of the Achaemenid kings after Darius, which have been preserved, were probably 'throne names' or appellations, perhaps taken at the time of accession. That Darius' personal name was Spentadata, hence connecting him with Zoroastrian tradition as son of Vishtaspa, patron of the prophet, is quite unproved. His 'throne name' may be explained as *dārayat* plus *vahush* 'having wealth (good things of life)'. It is odd that in the Aramaic documents of Egypt from the Achaemenid period, we find the shortest form of the name *drywš*, applied to Darius I, but later the name is longer *drywhwš*, as well as other forms. The name Xerxes probably means 'hero among rulers', Old Persian *khshaya-* plus *aršan-*, while Artaxerxes has nothing to do with *-xerxes*, rather it is a Greek explanation of Artakhshassa meaning something like 'having just rule', *arta-* and *khshassa-* (Old Persian form of *khshatra-*). To suppose from these names that the rulers who bore them must have been Zoroastrians because of a 'Zoroastrian' connotation of the words is both unwarranted and a rather futile task.

104

The royal family of the Achaemenids may well have been the leaders of the important Pasargadai clan, if not of all of the Persians during their migration to Persis. After their settlement it is probable that they intermarried not only among themselves but also with the local Elamite or other royalty or aristocracy. The harems of the Achaemenid rulers were large, for they contained not only the wives and concubines of the king but all of the women of the family, such as sisters, mother and others. Still we do not hear of an organised, institutionalised harem with many eunuchs until later, after Darius, though women certainly exerted a strong influence in court circles before his time. Many of the royal brides were non-Iranians, and pride in Aryan descent, as found in the Old Persian inscriptions, does not preclude an actual mixture of blood. Pride in being an Aryan or Iranian probably was not as strong as under the Sasanians.

The institution of the prime minister, the later Islamic *vizier*, does not seem to have existed under the Achaemenids, at least under the early kings. Certainly the king had his friends and confidants to whom he entrusted important missions, but there is no evidence for the existence of an institutionalised supreme representative of the king through whom the affairs of state were managed. The position of Mardonius in the army of Xerxes when he invaded Greece, as reported by Herodotus (VIII.67), does resemble that of a chief minister who was the contact between the king of kings and the subkings and rulers who were arranged in order of rank. But to assume that the Greek word *eisangeleus* signified more than the 'announcer', and rather was the office of prime minister, is reading too much into it.[69] Obviously the need for a spokesman of the king was ever present, and under the later Achaemenids, the *hazārapati-* 'thousand leader', a military officer it seems, assumed the duties of a prime minister. After Alexander we find the Greek title *khiliarkhos* (chiliarch), a translation of *hazārapati*, used by Hellenistic rulers for their second in command, a kind of prime minister.[70] From the name some may suppose that the commander of the king's bodyguard early assumed a role of importance at court, and he may be one of the figures pictured on reliefs at Persepolis standing before the king.

At the court were also to be found at various times local rulers and satraps, a growing court nobility which was based on local lords who came to live at court. The royal princes, the *visō puthra* of the Avesta and the *BR BYT* of the Aramaic documents

105

from Egypt, could be both officers at court and governors in provinces. Some were probably included among the table companions of the king, which was also a great honour conferred upon favourites (Herodotus V.24). Another title of honour reported by Herodotus (III.140; VIII.85) was that of 'well-doer' of the king, *orosangai* or *hu-varza-ka*(?). But these were honorary titles, and to return to the princes, it would seem that they increased greatly in number as the dynasty continued to rule. Their relation to the satraps, subkings and others would have been complicated by intermarriage, and the protocol of rank must have been rather involved at the court of the Achaemenids. The Median, Parthian and other Iranian chieftains must have retained considerable prestige and authority even under the empire, and they undoubtedly fitted into the satrapy system and the general political organisation of the empire. The famous 'six helpers of Darius' when he killed Gaumata were subsequently established in a special favoured position vis-à-vis the king, and their families and descendants shared in the privileges. Herodotus (III.70), and the Behistun inscription (IV.83) give the names of the helpers of Darius but they do not fully correspond. In Esther (1.14) the names of seven chiefs of the Persians and Medes who could view the face of the king are given, but from these names one can learn nothing about the families, and the names are neither those of Herodotus nor of Behistun. It has been proposed that the six families of Herodotus and Behistun plus the family of Darius himself, are the seven great families of Iran which is a tradition maintained throughout Parthian and Sasanian times. It seems clear that the seven are not to be equated with the principal kinglets or lords of vast estates in Achaemenid times, but one may suppose that they grew in power and established themselves more firmly because of their special relationship with Darius and then with his successors. Further, either the number seven became an actual, accepted number of the top aristocratic families, or the number seven for the aristocratic families became symbolic, or that which was proper in common belief. Such traditions are long-lived in Iran, and such an origin for the accepted 'ruling families' would not be unusual. In this domain, as in most others, Darius seems to be the great innovator, and one might well speak of Achaemenid history before Darius and after, with all of the features which we are describing coming after Darius in date.

The court of the Achaemenids was not fixed in one place, for the king had palaces in several localities according to Greek authors.[71] The main capital of the empire after Darius was the city of Susa, although Hamadan-Ekbatana must have maintained its ancient prestige as a former capital and an ideal summer resort for the court. There is no evidence that after Darius Ekbatana contained the royal archives as some scholars have interpreted a statement in Ezra 6, which says merely that search was made for a record in the archives at Babylon but the record was instead found in a palace (or castle) in Ekbatana. The great and ancient city of Babylon could hardly fail to be an important centre for Achaemenid rule though after a revolt in 482 BC, suppressed by Xerxes, Babylon lost some of its former glory. Excavations at Babylon, however, have not given us much of a picture of the Achaemenid city. Our knowledge of Achaemenid art and architecture comes from Susa, Persepolis, and to a lesser degree from the older Pasargadai. French archaeologists excavated the site of Susa for more than half a century and we have a mass of material from there, much of it, unfortunately, from the pre-World War I era when the methods of archaeologists were as yet unsystematised. Susa had fallen on evil days when Darius made it his capital, for there is no evidence that Susa was an Achaemenid capital before Darius; the notices of Herodotus (III.30, 70) reflect a projection backward of a later situation, since for the Greeks Susa is known only from later Achaemenid times. The Greeks reproduced the name of the city from the Old Persian form and not from Akkadian, Elamite or Aramaic. Cuneiform inscriptions from Susa tell of the building activities of Darius, Xerxes, Artaxerxes I, Darius II and Artaxerxes II, ample testimony of the interest of all the rulers in this their winter capital. The words for the buildings erected in Susa and also at Persepolis are not always clear. While many scholars translate the Old Persian words *hadish*, *āpadana* and *tachara* indiscriminately as 'palace', it seems clear from the contexts and etymologies that the first word is the general term for 'palace', or when used in a specific sense, the 'seat of authority' equivalent to the Sublime Porte of Ottoman days, the 'gate of the king' of the book of Esther. The *āpadana*, which is the prototype of the Islamic *aiwan*, was in both Persepolis and Susa the public area or the audience hall. It may have been a large open area where tents could be erected as one may infer from the book of Daniel (11.45), where incidentally the form is probably to be read *āppadana*. The word *tachara* is not clear in its origin, in

107

spite of attempts to explain it as originally 'race course' or 'stadium'. From its use in the Old Persian inscriptions, and especially the Elamite version of Artaxerxes II, Susa D (of R. Kent's classification) where the Old Persian *hadish* is given as *dasarum* or OP *tachara*, it would seem to be a little 'paradise' for the king during his lifetime.[72] So *tachara* would be the private palace of the ruler, perhaps managed by a *tacharapati-*, a chief eunuch (?).

Susa is the capital of the Achaemenids for the Greeks and in the Old Testament, and finds of objects from all over the empire indicate the cosmopolitan nature of the metropolis, perhaps rivalled in the various mixtures of peoples only by Babylon. Darius transplanted rebellious subjects from other parts of the empire to the province of Khuzistan (Herodotus VI.20, 119), and the many foreign workers on his buildings further mixed the population. A remarkable trilingual cuneiform inscription was found at Susa describing those who participated in the building of a *hadish*. The Babylonians made the bricks; cedar was brought from Lebanon and special wood from Kirman and Gandhara, gold from Sardis and Bactria. Precious stones such as lapis-lazuli came from Sogdiana and turquoise from Khwarezm, ivory from Ethiopia, Sind and Arachosia, and all of this was fashioned at Susa into various objects which adorned the palace. Stone-cutters were Ionians and Lydians, while the goldsmiths were Medes and Egyptians. Wood workers were Lydians and Egyptians while Medes and Egyptians adorned the walls. We have here probably the most cosmopolitan crew of workers ever assembled up to that time. Darius, however, wanted another palace, probably beginning about 520 BC, one which was to be located at a place of special symbolic importance, Persepolis.

Persepolis was virtually unknown to the Greeks before Alexander's conquests. The tombs of the later Achaemenid kings are hewn from the mountain behind the palace complex while Darius, Xerxes and two other kings are buried at Naqsh-i Rustam in the vicinity. From the Old Persian inscriptions and the Elamite clay tablets found at Persepolis it seems that this remarkable complex of palaces was not used for any governmental activities, or for the reception of foreign envoys. Nor was it a religious centre, for no temples or cult buildings have been excavated. Yet the ruins of Persepolis today proclaim it as a wonder of the ancient world. The countless tall columns which once stood in the halls must have been exceptionally impressive, expecially to the visitor approaching the platform on which the buildings were erected from across the plain now called Marv Dasht. The pillars and square buildings were the glory of Achaemenid architecture, the former more slender than Greek prototypes, and adorned with bull capitals. What was this impressive group of buildings on the plain of the tombs of the kings? One may speculate that the site was sacred or taboo to ordinary people, or that some event in the life of Darius made this area of special importance for him. It was likewise of some special significance for the Sasanian kings who carved rock reliefs in profusion at Naqsh-i Rustam and vicinity. One may aptly term the Persepolis area a dynastic home of the Persian kings in pre-Islamic times. Perhaps the whole area was a kind of national sanctuary where the religious archives or the paraphernalia for the crowning of the king were preserved in the building at Naqsh-i Rustam called the Ka'bah of Zoroaster. Perhaps Persepolis and vicinity played a role only for the New Year's festival, or solemn acts of the crowning or burial of kings. More likely is the interpretation that the function of Persepolis changed in time from a summer capital under Darius to a national, dynastic shrine under Artaxerxes II. We do not know whether one or all of these surmises was true, but we can say that Persepolis, or Parsa, Ba-ir-ša as it is called in the Elamite tablets, did have a special significance for the Achaemenid kings and for the Persians.

In any event, we can assume that Susa was the administrative capital of the Achaemenids and Persepolis was a dynastic, perhaps ritual, centre, while Ekbatana, Babylon and other cities maintained their importance as commercial or strategic cities or as provincial capitals.

To turn now to the centralised bureaucracy of the Achaemenids, the presumed special agents of the king have attracted considerable attention among contemporary scholars. Obviously, so the argument goes, the king of kings needed a corps of officers to keep him informed of events in his empire, and to keep watch over the many local kings and satraps. We do find references in Greek sources to the 'eye(s) of the king', and also more rarely to the 'ear(s) of the king', the two terms separated but their functions probably confused by Greek authors. Most of the Greek sources speak of one high official, 'the ear of the king', who was the emissary or representative of the king on missions, a kind of special internal ambassador. The Iranian sources have no title even similar to 'eye of the king', but in Aramaic papyri from

109

Egypt we find the term *gwshky* from Iranian **gaushaka* 'listener'. Here he seems to be an official who represented the central government in legal cases, perhaps a kind of state's attorney. This is all the firm evidence we have for these offices supposed from the Greek sources, although Aramaic sources give more offices. One may surmise from later practice in Parthian times and in Armenia that the official known as the *bitaxš*, represented an older Achaemenian office and title of **patyakhsh*, a vice-king, who might be identified as the 'eye of the king', and who might have supervised *inter alia* the many state prosecutors, or 'the ears of the king'.[73] Although espionage is age-old, and comparisons have been made with the thousand ears and eyes of the god Mithra and his ten thousand spies (Yasht 10.7 and 24), it would perhaps be more appropriate to compare the 'ears of the king' with the *adhyaksha* or 'inspector and overseer' of the king in ancient India.

The central administration did keep in close contact with provincial centres by developing the Assyrian tradition of an efficient 'postal service' over a network of roads, perhaps the most famous of which was the royal road from Sardis to Susa. Herodotus (VIII.98) describes the postal system, telling how Xerxes sent a message to Susa. 'Now there is nothing mortal that accomplishes a course more swiftly than do these messengers, by the Persians' skilful contrivance. It is said that as many days as there are in the whole journey, so many are the men and horses that stand along the road, each horse and man at the interval of a day's journey; and these are stayed neither by snow nor rain nor heat nor darkness from accomplishing their appointed course with all speed. The first rider delivers his charge to the second, the second to the third, and thence it passes on from hand to hand, even as in the Greek torch-bearers' race in honour of Hephaestus. The riding-post is called in Persia, *angareion*.'[74] The postal system was Mesopotamian in origin and for the most part limited to governmental communications. Since the later word for the postal service in Islamic times, *barīd*, can be traced back to Akkadian, it is probable that the Assyrians greatly extended the post in their far-flung empire and the Achaemenids were their heirs. Fire signals on towers were probably in wide use under the Achaemenids and remained so until the telegraph and telephone displaced them only a few decades ago. The roads of the Achaemenids were measured in *parasangs*, a measure usually said to be a little over three miles (about 6 kilometres), but probably really a measure of an hour's time travelling, shorter when the road was difficult and longer when easy. [75] This same method of measurement can be observed even today in parts of Afghanistan and Persia; in the former it is the distance a horse can travel in an hour. Since the roads were used for commerce, as well as by troops and private persons, they were patrolled, and the passage of letters or goods was subject to censorship or control.

The bureaucracy has been mentioned several times and something should be said about the remarkable chancellery which the Achaemenids fostered. Unfortunately we know too little about it. After the time of Xerxes Akkadian was all but a dead language used only by scribes and priests. Already under the Assyrians Aramaic, with its alphabet, had displaced Akkadian as the *lingua franca* of the Near East. The Achaemenids apparently supported the use of Aramaic as the general means of communication in their empire. Scribes were important people in antiquity and archives were also necessary. We know that Elamite was written on clay tablets at Persepolis to keep records of payments to workers, and Aramaic inscriptions on stone objects have also been found there. The Old Persian cuneiform inscriptions have already been discussed, but this writing apparently played no role in affairs of daily life, being only for royal use. From the Behistun inscription we learn, however, that the inscription was 'in Aryan (which formerly was not), and on clay tablets and on parchment it was composed', and 'it was inscribed and read off before me. Afterwards this inscription I sent off everywhere among the provinces. The people unitedly worked upon it. ' [76] From this we learn that the inscription may speak of the first writing down of Iranian (Old Persian) either in cuneiform writing or even in Aramaic letters, though possibly in both. The discovery of fragments of the Behistun inscription in Aramaic from Elephantine, Egypt and on a fragment of a clay tablet in Akkadian confirm the copying of the text of the inscription in various languages and the sending of them everywhere. The inscription was probably read to the king because he could not read himself. The process of disseminating the king's orders is given in Esther 3.12:

'Then the king's scribes were called on the thirteenth day of the first month, and an edict, according to all that Haman commanded, was written to the king's satraps and to the governors over all the provinces and to the rulers of all the peoples, to every province in its own script and every people in its own language; it was written in the name of King Ahasuerus (Xerxes) and sealed with the king's ring. Letters were sent by couriers to all the king's provinces.'

From Esther 8.8, and other indications, one can conclude that various officials of the king held his rings or seals, which were thus not personal objects but official. The discovery of an Aramaic-Greek bilingual rock inscription at Qandahar, Afghanistan, the Aramaic inscriptions at Taxila and Laghman in Afghanistan, show the widespread use of Aramaic. It is significant that archaic east Iranian words appear in the Prakrit words.[77] This would indicate that everywhere local words entered the Aramaic language used by the scribes, thus preparing the way for the development of the later Middle Iranian heterographic writing which will be discussed later.

The question of the legal organs of the empire is complicated for local legal systems were favoured by the early Achaemenids, although later some mixtures and consequent problems seem to have arisen. We know of the actions of Darius respecting decrees of Cyrus relevant to the Jews from the book of Ezra (6.1), and also his command to have the local laws of Egypt revised (Diod. I.95.4). Mesopotamia was a land long accustomed to law codes and Darius may well have been inspired by the traditions of Babylonian law, for we must explain the references in the Bible and in Akkadian documents to the law of the king. Every schoolboy has heard of the 'law of the Medes and Persians which changeth not', and stories of Persian justice in Greek authors attest the important position of law under the Achaemenids. A new word for 'law' appears in the Near East at this time, the Iranian dāta, which was borrowed by Armenian, Hebrew and Akkadian. The meaning of the Indo-European root is 'to arrange' or 'put in order', and one may presume that the basis of Achaemenid law was a development from the family or tribal law of the Aryan people. It would be natural to have a division between family or personal legal problems and those in which the state was concerned. Surely in the former local practices prevailed everywhere, while the central government took an interest in affairs of the latter category. There were what one might call 'social' tribunals for cases of the former and state or royal tribunals with the royal judges (OP *dātabara Aramaic dtbry) for the latter, as Greek sources and the Old Testament amply attest.

112

That Darius was greatly concerned with the law is evidenced by passages in his inscriptions (DB I.21): 'Within these countries the man who was accommodating, him I treated well; (him) who was false I punished well. By the favour of Ahura Mazda these countries showed respect for my law; as was said to them by me, thus was it done.' In another inscription (DNb 55) he exhorts his (Persian) followers[78] to believe what he has written and not to disobey the laws, while in still another place (DSe 30) he speaks of bringing justice, so that the strong do not harm the weak, through fear of his law.

Surely there was in ancient Iran a survival of widespread Indo-European concepts of trial by ordeal or oath, and, of course, the religious affiliations of law are present. The inscriptions hint at the importance of the oath when Darius says (DNb 21): 'If a man accuses (another) man, that does not convince me until he conforms to the oath of propriety'.[79] In Iran one probably swore by Ahura Mazda as done elsewhere 'by the gods'. The function of Mithra as the guardian of contracts in Aryan times has been mentioned, and it would seem that the sanctity of contracts occupies much of Persian law throughout history. The least ancient section of the Avesta called the Vendidad or Videvdat, which was probably finally compiled in Parthian times, is much concerned with various contracts as well as religious and ritualistic subjects, much of it a legacy from hoary antiquity.

In Akkadian and Aramaic sources we find a number of officials related to the courts, a discussion of which is here impractical, but a point of interest are the two words for judge in Akkadian documents, Semitic *dayyan* and Iranian *dāta-bar*, frequently used as synonyms, but perhaps originally designating the local and the royal judges respectively. The king was the chief judge for crimes against the state and Greek sources tell of the rigidity with which the rulers administered and conformed to the law. Praise of *arshta-* 'rectitude' and abhorrence of *drauga* 'the lie' were oft-quoted characteristics of the Persians according to the sources. Punishments were severe as they were generally in antiquity, impalement, mutilation and banishment being especially common. It would seem that a spirit of *jus talionis* generally prevailed, although family responsibility for the crimes of the condemned does not seem to have existed widely, since the reported instances are limited to rebels against the throne or particular crimes of high treason.

113

We have spoken primarily of matters concerning the central government, but the provincial administration was perhaps more of a departure from the past than the central organisation. The existence of provinces as well as vassal kingdoms under the Medes, as under the Assyrians, is certain, but under the Achaemenids the satrapal system is extended and the new satrapies are based on former political and national boundaries. The important title 'king of kings' is prominent with the Iranians for the Assyrians did not know it, although the Urartians did. Both Achaemenid princes and local rulers are found as satraps, and the administration of the satrapy was a model of the central government. The satrapy was divided into smaller units governed by Persians or local officials, but we know very little about local government which probably varied from province to province.

After the suppression of various revolts throughout the empire Darius made a new division of the satrapies, as various Greek sources state. Herodotus (III.89) gives a list of twenty satrapies probably based on a Greek geography or on a list of satrapies composed in his native Ionia. The list does not cover the entire empire, but only the satrapies which paid taxes, not the vassal states which sent tribute. The list, needless to say, is not completely reliable for the tax amounts are suspect. The new order of the provinces then continues the old tradition of satrapies as well as vassal kingdoms, but what is new is the stable tax system, each satrapy paying a fixed yearly amount in unminted gold or silver, and each vassal state paying a fixed tribute, usually in kind rather than precious metals. After Darius there were no new additions to the empire, but inside the empire there were rebellions which at various times severed satrapies from central control, as happened with Egypt on several occasions, and several redistributions of the existing satrapies did take place. Sometimes two or more satrapies were united under the control of one satrap, while other satrapies were divided; for example Caria was separated from Ionia about 400 BC. Generally speaking, one may say that the tendency was to reduce the size of the satrapies, so that there were more at the end of the reign of Darius than at the beginning and still more at the end of the empire than under Darius. The lack of information about the satraps and the sometimes confused nomenclature of high officials of the Achaemenid empire in the Greek sources, make it difficult to come to any conclusions about the development of the satrapies at the end of the empire. Furthermore, changes in the boundaries of

114

the satrapies did occur, some of which we know but most of which we do not.

The changing fortunes of the 'Fertile Crescent', the rich lands of Mesopotamia and Syria, need not detain us. It should be remarked that the use of geographical or ethnic designations such as Babylonia, Assyria and the like, do not always coincide with satrapal names. [80] Although the satraps were like minor kings with their courts and provincial organisation a model of the central government, the king of kings did maintain considerable authority in local matters. It has been mentioned that he was the supreme judge, a last court of appeal. He also maintained control through the army, although at the end of the Achaemenid period the union of military and civil authority in the hands of one person, the satrap, seems to have been a general rule. The satrap had to supervise the collection of taxes and administer the general economic, legal and political affairs of his satrapy. Of course, the empire was by no means uniform in its provincial divisions and generalisations are difficult to make, but the satrap everywhere seems to have been a powerful individual.

The Persians, as the ruling people, were exempt from paying tribute or imperial taxes, but they had to provide troops and were the backbone of Achaemenid power. Persians served far from their homeland, and Darius in his inscriptions relates with pride the achievements of the Persian soldiers. Small Persian colonies were to be found everywhere in the empire for Persian officers, troops, judges and other officials were sent to the farthest reaches of the state to serve the ruler. Persian names appear in the Aramaic papyri from Egypt, in Akkadian cuneiform tablets and in Greek sources attesting to the influence of the Persians everywhere in the empire. Estates of the royal family and the Persian nobility also were to be found all over the empire, and we have eloquent testimony of the practice of absentee landlordship in the Aramaic letters of Arsames, an Achaemenid prince, to various officials on his lands in Egypt. We have said that Achaemenid princes frequently were appointed to satrapies; other satrapies were hereditary in one family, an indication that high posts were by no means reserved exclusively for Persians. Indeed, the rulers of Cilicia, called Syennesis in Greek sources, for example, enjoyed for long a special position in the empire because of their early and continuous friendship and aid to the Achaemenids. The various city states of Phoenicia and Ionia remained almost independent save for the paying of taxes, for

115

they even issued their own coinage. Such diversity within the empire is not unexpected, not only because of the size of the empire but also the necessity for the conquering Persians to leave many affairs in the hands of their subjects, plus a feudal tendency to be discussed below.

The army was the means for control and order in the empire, but it too developed and changed during the reign of the Achaemenids. Under Cyrus the Persian army was composed of the fighting men of the Persian tribes which supported the rebellion against the Medes, and this is probably what the Old Persian *kāra* of the inscriptions means.[81] With the conquest of many other peoples the army system must have evolved to a complex military establishment, from a *kāra* to a professional army, a *spāda*. In Aryan times, as we learn from the Vedas and the cognate word in the Avesta, the charioteer was the epitome of the great warrior. While the chariot seems to have remained for long the foremost military arm in India, in western Iran the more flexible cavalry became more important. Chariots, of course, continued to be used by the Achaemenids to the end of the empire, but more as a small, special arm, while the *asabāra* 'cavalry' and *pasti-* 'footsoldiers' were the two main forces. The standing army in time of peace was primarily composed of Persians and Medes, as revealed by sculptures at Persepolis, while the royal cavalry guard and the 'Immortals' composed the core of this standing army. Much has been written about the 'Immortals', so called, according to Herodotus (VII.83) because they were always maintained at a strength of ten thousand, a new recruit immediately replacing a fallen member of the corps. They were probably in origin those Persian detachments which supported Darius in gaining the throne and were then constituted as an élite corps, a thousand of whom, commanded by a chiliarch, became the royal guard of the king. Whether the term 'Immortal' was a Greek designation, or more plausible, a mistranslation of an Old Persian word meaning 'follower' is not certain.[82] The Achaemenids soon made use of other troops, of course, and the army became a multi-national force, although usually with Persian commanders. The army units were divided according to the decimal system with commanders for tens, hundreds and thousands, and they were further arranged according to types—lancers, archers and cavalry. Inside these classifications soldiers were arranged according to nationality, all with distinctive armour, headdress or weapons, as described by

Herodotus (VII.61) and visible on reliefs at Persepolis. The mixture of nationality and type of weapon must have contributed to a certain lack of efficiency in the army, for among the cavalry were included camel riders. The Persian weapon *par excellence* was the bow, as pictured on Achaemenid coins, and a short sword called *akinakēs* (Sogdian *kyn'k*) by the Greeks. Other peoples carried their own distinctive weapons. Armour of various kinds was used and from Xenophon (*Anabasis* I.8.7) we learn that horses as well as men were covered with coats of mail. From numerous Iranian words relating to warfare, armour and the like, one can infer the great interest in matters of defence and conquest among the Persians.

In matters of tactics the Achaemenid forces were inferior to the Greeks, and at the end of the empire Greek mercenaries were perhaps the cream of the army next to the élite corps. We are not informed just how the various subject peoples performed their military service, or what the policy of the king was in this regard. There seem to have been a number of places of assembly throughout the empire where troops were assembled in time of war, and perhaps arsenals were also located there under continuous guard of Persian troops. This raises the question of garrisons and satrapal forces.

Garrisons were needed in many strategic centres of the empire to defend the frontiers or to maintain order, and we fortunately know about one such command from the island of Elephantine in the upper Nile river near the southern frontier with Nubia. The garrison here was primarily composed of Jews but with Iranian or Babylonian officers. One must be careful in making generalisations from this one garrison, for it would seem that these mercenaries were already settled in their fortress when Cambyses conquered Egypt and the Persians merely assumed the same relation to them as the previous government. Therefore the Elephantine garrison was perhaps more entrenched on the land than similar garrisons elsewhere. They were divided into 'standards' or *degel*, possibly detachments of a hundred fighting men who received rations. There was a commander of the garrison, and yet another officer of the district bearing an Iranian title *prtrk*, possibly a combined military-civil office similar to the Roman term *praetor*. The mercenaries at Elephantine were military colonists who were permanently settled on the land with families and possessions, participating in buying, selling and all sorts of legal transactions as did the civil population. There do seem to have been separate civil and military courts, but details of their respective jurisdictions are lacking. In fact there appears to have been some mixture of civil and military functions among the provincial officials although in theory we would expect a division between the civil and military authorities. Actually the satrap was responsible for the provincial troops as well as for those soldiers sent to serve in the central army in time of war. The satraps could also hire mercenaries if necessary, but in times of war we frequently find several generals in command of troops from various satrapies (e.g. Herodotus VII.82), which could be explained as a dual system of military control. We may assume that a new satrap appointed to a province brought his own bodyguard with him. He was in complete charge of the local, native forces, but not in full charge of the military garrisons of Persian and other foreign troops who were theoretically under the great king. We know that the Achaemenids practised the time-honoured custom of transferring populations. Herodotus alone tells us of Egyptians sent to Bactria (IV.204), Thracians to Asia (V.15), Ionians to Susa (VI.20) and Greeks in Khuzistan (VI.119), and further of the fear of the Ionian Greeks that they would be sent to Phoenicia while all of the Phoenicians would be settled in Ionia (VI.3). So the presence of foreign colonies all over the empire must have confused jurisdictions as well as the people themselves. Whether the empire later was divided into four huge military districts above the satraps is uncertain, but some military organisation above the satrap is not unlikely.[83]

To turn to another problem, the pay of the soldiers; we know that in the early reigns it was principally in *naturalia*, in meat, wine and grain, and the like, although rations and pay are sometimes difficult to distinguish. The satrap had to pay all troops stationed in his satrapy. The use of coins, discussed below, was very limited and seems to have been directed primarily for business with the Greeks including the hiring of mercenaries. When the imperial army passed through a province the people had to provide rations for the troops, usually a crushing burden. Soldiers and officers were rewarded for bravery or service with special titles or objects of rank, orders such as golden laurel leaves, robes of honour, special daggers of honour, bracelets, or similar things, as we learn from Xenophon in his *Anabasis*. This practice, of course, was already old, the Assyrian kings having given many such rewards to deserving officers. There were special offices too, such as lance bearer of the king or of certain high

118

officials. We also find in Achaemenid times the beginning of insignia or crests of families, so prominent in later Persian history, and special signs, such as the golden pomegranates on the spears of the 'Immortals'. Many features of later Persian 'feudalism' probably have their origin in Achaemenid times, but unfortunately our source material is so scanty we cannot find solid evidence for them.

The numbers of the armies were never very large and Greek sources usually exaggerate the size of the enemy forces. Certainly camp followers, womenfolk and servants, increased the unwieldiness of the Achaemenid army, while the various odd contingents made the army anything but unified and efficient. The Persian use of elephants and scythed chariots is well known, but nothing in the army could quite stand up to the well-disciplined Macedonian phalanx or even a well-knit corps of Greek hoplites, as the mercenary army in which Xenophon served amply revealed. The scorched earth policy in front of an advancing enemy was a normal Achaemenid tactic, but we do not know of other tactics specially employed by the Persians in their warfare. Soldiers, incidentally, did not begin service in the army before the age of twenty, and everyone knows of the training of boys in ancient Persia before they became soldiers, how they were taught to ride a horse, shoot a bow and speak the truth. Military service probably did not extend beyond the age of fifty-five.

The navy was primarily the domain of the Phoenicians and to some extent the Ionian Greeks, but Persians fought as marines on the ships and took an interest in naval affairs. Under Darius an Ionian admiral called Scylax sailed down the Indus river to the Indian Ocean and then to Egypt, a voyage of three months (Herodotus IV.44). It is not improbable that the Achaemenids sent other ships to explore the various seas and the coast of Africa, perhaps even circumnavigating Africa. Darius built a canal connecting the Mediterranean with the Red Sea, a forerunner of the Suez canal, and fragments of inscriptions commemorating this have been found. So the Achaemenids fostered trade and commerce by sea as well as by land. The Persians themselves, however, were never a seafaring people and it was left to their subjects to conquer the waves.

Economic Life

The main source of wealth in the Achaemenid empire was land, and all over the Near East from time immemorial water has been the key to life on the land. Irrigation was ever of great importance in the Fertile Crescent, on the Iranian plateau and wherever crops could be raised. It would seem that under the Achaemenids, as later under the Sasanians, *in theory* the king was considered the lord of all the land and people theoretically occupied it in fief. This did not mean, of course, that the ruler owned all of the land. The vast majority of land was held by private persons but a 'feudal' theory seems to have existed.

The use of the term feudalism, of course, must be quite wide since the mediaeval European social system, of course, was not identical to that in ancient Iran. Yet there are many features which recall what we understand by the word 'feudal'. It is true that the Achaemenid empire was a centralised power, but it was also a hierarchical empire, and something akin to feudalism would not be unexpected from a new people with pastoral traditions who conquered settled people. The theory that the king was above the laws, and able to grant gifts of land to his trusted followers who were again in theory all his slaves *(bandaka)*, would naturally lead to a system of feudalism. We have already mentioned royal domains, including hunting parks or 'paradises' in various parts of the empire, and also the *bg* or 'fief, domain' granted to royal officers, with absentee landlords. The Aramaic papyri from Egypt give a fascinating picture of the estates of Arsames, royal prince and governor *(MR²)* of Egypt, who spent much of his time in Susa or in Babylon but had agents to manage his Egyptian lands. Fiefs were granted usually to families, perhaps influenced by the old tradition of collective ownership in Mesopotamia. The Achaemenids, by establishing colonies of soldiers in conquered lands and by giving land to civil and military servants, favoured and promoted feudalism. From Akkadian records we hear of two terms in the feudal relationships, *ilku* and *qashtu*. The former was the old Baylonian fief or feudal service. But under the Achaemenids, and not attested before Cambyses, we find the word *qashtu*, originally meaning a 'bow' or 'division of land for the support of an archer', given to persons in return for military obligations to the ruler. It would appear that the institution of *qashtu* was introduced by the Persians, while the Babylonian *ilku* then becomes a monetary or silver obligation, and comes to mean 'ground tax' or simply 'tax'. The *qashtu*, given as fiefs to families, however, were subsumed under a *hatru*, which was primarily a tax-collecting institution with an important official called a *shaknu* over it. The *hatru* might be translated as 'canton' and in some cases may have been a collective of functionaries or soldiers. As the money economy grew and the empire became more stabilised under Darius II and succeeding rulers, the feudal military obligations were more and more taken over by feudal monetary obligations. This also went together with the policy of urbanisation favoured by the Achaemenids, as well as later by the Sasanians.

Since our sources are from Babylonia one may well ask whether conditions here were typical of the empire as a whole. If the situation were somewhat different elsewhere, none the less the influence of Babylonian custom must have been great everywhere. Darius I instituted a tax reform which broke with tradition and must have been general all over the empire. Previously taxes had varied considerably, so Darius sought to stabilise and fix the taxes. We know that long before the Achaemenids the Assyrians sold land not by acreage but by the amount of crops it yielded. Darius had the land surveyed and measured together with a record of past yields. Apparently before Darius in many cases taxes were assessed before the harvest which imposed hardships on the cultivators. For example, in Mesopotamia every year before the harvest a commission fixed the minimum yield of the date palms and even if the harvest was subsequently poor the tax had to be paid. Darius, on the basis of his survey, determined the fixed yearly land tax, on the basis of an average yield from the land, for each satrapy, taking into account, of course, the kind of cultivation as well as the average amount of the yield. The general word for 'tax' was Old Persian *bāji-*, and the tax collector was the **bājikara*, while Old Persian **harāka*, probably the Persian form of a Semitic word meaning 'to go on feudal service', came to be applied to monetary obligation from the land and is the ancestor of the Islamic *kharāj* or 'land tax', which was generally payment on the produce. Herodotus (III.97) speaks of the satrapies which paid taxes or tribute, giving the sums in *talents*, further of Parsa or Fars province which paid no tribute, and of other peoples in the empire who sent gifts instead of taxes. These 'gifts' probably had different appellations but after Darius' reform of the taxes one may suspect that he also fixed the sums of yearly 'gifts' from those not under the satrapy system. For example, the hereditary rulers of Cilicia probably contributed 'gifts' to the king regularly and in fixed amounts.

There was no difference between the king's private property

121

and state property; the ruler was the state and the central treasury was his household treasury. The satrap had to collect taxes and send the amount in precious metals to the central treasury, while supplementary taxes filled his own treasury, which actually was the same as the central treasury though perhaps somehow subdivided. To handle the large sums of money accountants (OP *hamārakara* Aramaic *hmrkr)* and treasurers *ganzabara* were needed and tax collecting could become rather involved. In Babylonia, for example, the banking house of Murashu and sons, with an establishment at Nippur, prospered in lending money and making tax collections. We have documents of the firm from *circa* 455-403 BC and a flourishing banking business is revealed by them. Murashu collected taxes from the fiefs *qashtu,* but paid the taxes to various *shaknu* of respective *hatru,* who in turn paid into the central treasury of the king.[84] The house of Murashu dealt with royal princes and common citizens as well, with much more of an interest, it would seem, in land than in commerce. The granting of land to another party by the king or by one of his ministers or officials might be characterised as sub-infeudation (in the latter case), and we learn of various kinds of sub-grants from our sources. For example, Arsames or Arsham, governor of Egypt, made a grant of land to an underling on condition that the latter pay the tax on the land to Arsham's estate.[85] Interest rates were high but the task of caring for feudal obligations and taxes undertaken by the Murashu firm was not easy. There were other banks and we learn much detail of business from the cuneiform archives, for example that slaves were juridical persons who themselves could own slaves in their own right.

Taxes, as usual, abounded in the Achaemenid empire. It seems there were harbour fees, market taxes, tolls on gates and roads and frontiers of various kinds, a tax on domestic animals, perhaps ten per cent, and other taxes as well. Gifts were received by the king on New Year's day, and when he travelled extra hardships were placed on the population. Most of these gifts, and sundry taxes, were mainly paid in kind rather than specie. *Corvée* labour, for roads, public buildings and the like, was employed extensively by satraps as well as the king. So life for the common person must have been at times oppressive. The local public works were probably financed by local taxes, while gold and silver streamed into the king's coffers. For we have not mentioned his own royal domains, mines and irrigation works, all of which yielded revenues. Most of the gold was used in war or as presents

122

by the king and we know the successful bribery practised on the Greeks by Persian satraps or kings. This brings us to the money, the famous gold *darics* with the figure of a kneeling archer on them.

Coinage had existed before the Achaemenids and the Lydians are generally credited with the introduction of coinage on a state scale. For the most part, gold and silver were melted and formed into ingots according to weight while coins were more or less limited, as we have said, to pay Greek mercenaries or for commerce with the Greeks, or in the Mediterranean coastal towns. Gold was rare and was hoarded by the king, while coined money was generally treated much as ingots to be weighed. Only the great king had the right to coin gold coins, the *stater* of Darius, as the Greek lexicographers explained the name *daric*. Some scholars say the name of the coin was derived from Old Persian *dari-* 'gold' and the Greeks simply made a play on words with the name of the king. Copper coins were minted by the satraps, as were silver coins, but the latter were also struck by generals for military purposes. Again the main reason for the coinage of silver was for military purposes. Autonomous cities such as Phoenician port towns, and local dynasts also struck silver and copper of a different form from the king's silver coins which had the same figure of a royal archer with bent knee as on the *darics*. A word in the Elamite Persepolis treasury tablets suggests an Old Persian *pasuka* or 'animal money' as an earlier basis of comparative values in Aryan times. Perhaps the unit of reckoning was one sheep which came to equal one *shekel* when coinage was introduced.[86] Gold coinage other than that of the great king was taken as the sign of rebellion, as in the case of a coalition of rebel satraps in Anatolia in the time of Artaxerxes II. The gold *daric* was 8·4 grams weight, while the silver *shekel*, the Greek *siglos*, was 5·6 grams. The relation of silver to gold was approximately 13⅓ : 1. The *talent*, in which the taxes were reckoned according to Herodotus, was not the same throughout the empire. Darius, however, brought order into the currency with his gold coins. So Darius, who according to Herodotus (III.89) was called a merchant by his subjects, created a new system of coinage which was recognised throughout the empire. Greek coins may have been more popular than the Achaemenid coins in some parts of the empire, but we may suppose that payment in kind was the rule except possibly in Asia Minor, Lebanon, Egypt and India for various reasons. [87] In India, which had a gold surplus, the ratio to silver was lower than the royal 13⅓ : 1 and more *shekels* than *darics* have been found there. That other local coinage existed in the vast empire, especially towards the end of it, is amply attested by the various coin types in the great collections of London, New York, Paris and elsewhere.

We have mentioned above that slaves in the Achaemenid empire were juridicial persons. Whether this was universally true all over the empire is uncertain, but from various sources it appears that many slaves were in an even more favoured position than free workers. Since the slaves on royal estates were state property, so to speak, there must have been an incentive to take care of property which was of value. One should not overestimate the condition of slaves, however, and one study which claims that slaves working at Persepolis were better paid than free workers is unproved and unlikely. [88]

Religion under the later Achaemenids

We return to the question of the religious beliefs of the Achaemenid kings which we discussed above. The determination of the personal faith of a Persian monarch in this period would be very difficult, especially when we consider that there is no evidence for the existence of an organised church or orthodox tenets and creeds under Darius. But surely by the time of Darius followers of Zoroaster existed in many if not all parts of Iran, though we know very little of their religion. Can we analyse, even in conjecture, the religious situation in Iran under the later Achaemenids, from sparse and not unequivocal information? We can hardly do more than give general, tentative suggestions.

If we turn to the very general division of religion into belief or creed, on the one hand, and ritual on the other, we can surmise that adherents of the old Aryan religion were more rites-centred and the adherents of Zoroaster, perhaps to be designated as Aryan reformers, more belief-centred. One should not categorically assign belief-centredness to pastoralists and rites-centredness to settled folk, even though there is probably good reason to do so in some cases. This division, one would assume, would be more evident in eastern Iran than in western Iran. In the latter Near Eastern elements, including the Magians, probably concerned both with ritual and belief, complicated the picture. The Magians, for general purposes of classification, are to be subsumed under Near Eastern influences because they seem to have been the agents of Aryan-Near Eastern syncretism, or at least not opposed to it. One might guess that the process of

124

amalgamation between the western Iranians, principally the Medes and the Persians, and the indigenous population, evidenced by the breakdown of the Old Persian language in western Iran, was paralleled by a similar process of amalgamation of religious beliefs and practices. Since this seems already to have been the temper of the times, if not the outright policy of the Achaemenid empire, and the Magians do emerge as the priesthood of Iran, then the Magians must have fostered what one could generally designate the process of 'syncretism'. Surely the teachings of Zoroaster from the eastern homeland of the Iranians would find a welcome reception among many persons in western Iran. Even among the Magians, who were admittedly very 'rites conscious', the beliefs of Zoroaster would probably have found some support, especially if Darius and the royal family adhered to the teachings of the prophet. We can say that Darius, and undoubtedly many others, recognised Ahura Mazda as the 'god of the Aryans' (i.e. Iranians). This does not mean that he was the only god, but rather the one whom the Iranians should worship, and both Zoroaster and Darius adhered to this point of view. But we can hardly speak of a Zoroastrian 'religion' in the time of Darius, if we mean by Zoroastrianism the religion and 'church' of late Sasanian times. In the Gathas of Zoroaster as well as in the inscriptions of Darius we find emphasis on truth and hate of the lie, and both the prophet and the king are Mazdayasnians 'Mazda worshippers'. Now the Magians were active in the vicinity of Persepolis as we learn from the Elamite Fortification tablets. Were these Magians Mazdayasnians or worshippers of the old pantheon? Was there a religious struggle between Darius, partisan of Zoroaster and Ahura Mazda and the Magian followers of the Aryan pantheon? We do not know, but in the absence of contrary information we may assume that even from pre-Darius times there were some Magians who accepted Zoroaster's teachings without abandoning completely the old pantheon, while others had not heard of, or would not listen to the message of the prophet.

The Mithra Yasht which is commonly dated in the fifth century BC, but which undoubtedly contains older elements, may be a creation of the Mazdayasnian Magians. The fact that the Yasht is written in an eastern Iranian language with an eastern Iranian geographical horizon, is no positive proof that it must have been written there. After all, Christian hymns and poems in Latin, or even Hebrew, were written in western Europe for

125

centuries concerned with Palestine. The Achaemenids, if not already the Medes, had brought eastern Iran, the spiritual as well as actual homeland of the Iranians, into contact with western Iran where the process of amalgamation and syncretism of culture was well under way. This process over a long period of time led to the Zoroastrian 'church' of Sasanian times, and was a sort of inexorable historical process not to be halted even by the personal beliefs of a king.

There is no reason why the Mazdayasnian Magians could not have sponsored, if not actually written, the rest of the Avesta. Surely they could have written the legalistic, ritualistic part, the Vendidad, for they were in sympathy with the minute and monotonous regulations for purification and ritual which we find in the book. The answer to the question: why did they not compose in Old Persian or Median, is found in many parallels in Judaism, Christianity, and most religions with a written religious tradition; the vernaculars were not used for such purposes. In short, I believe that the development of Zoroastrianism runs parallel with the cultural and social development of the Achaemenid empire and need not be a tortuous, involved process. There are certain problems, however, which must be mentioned.

Just as today in the mountains of Kurdistan several religions or sects can be found, so in antiquity in western Iran there probably existed various religious practices and beliefs, from which one could explain the sometimes conflicting evidence in classical sources about the religion of 'the Persians'. Achaemenid religious policy generally was to respect the faith and practices of the non-Iranian subject peoples. Whether they had a different attitude towards the non-Iranian or partly Iranicised peoples of western Iran is unknown but unlikely. There is very little evidence for religious struggles or persecution among the Iranians, for example the Magians versus the followers of Zoroaster. Differences undoubtedly existed but one cannot spell them out, especially in neat systems of orthodox and heretical sects. There are, however, a few lights in the darkness of our knowledge about the religious history of the Achaemenids which we should note and assess.

The first matter to be discussed is the so-called trilingual *Daiva* inscription of King Xerxes carved on stone tablets from Persepolis. The passage of importance to us (lines 35-41) reads: 'Among these countries (submitted to Xerxes) was (one) where previously *daivas* were worshipped. Then, by the favour of Ahura

Mazda, I destroyed that *daiva* place, and I had proclaimed, the *daivas* shall not be worshipped. Where previously the *daivas* were worshipped, there I worshipped Ahura Mazda properly with the Law (*arta*)'.[89] It is generally agreed that the *daiva* worshippers were not Babylonians or Egyptians but rather Iranians, or at least Aryans. One may ask whether the Indians living within the Achaemenid empire, who worshipped the old gods, may have been regarded as *daiva* worshippers. More likely the *daiva* worshippers were those Iranians who did not worship Ahura Mazda. Whether Ahura Mazda worship and the proscription of *daiva* worship is to be ascribed to the followers of Zoroaster, and to *them alone*, is unknown, but since at least we can put the general label on them, we may conclude that Xerxes was acting in a general 'Zoroastrian' spirit. The identity of the *daivas* has been much disputed, but it would seem that we can turn to only two sources, as usual, to ancient India or to later Iran. For the former, the *devas*, the Indian cognate of the Iranian *daivas*, were the Aryan gods, including the troublesome one for our problem, Mithra. For later Iran the *devs* are just evil spirits; but we should examine these sources more closely since I believe that continuity in Iran is more significant than deviation from India.

In the Middle Persian inscriptions of Kartir, the organiser of early Sasanian Zoroastrian orthodoxy, we find a passage remarkably similar to the passage in the Xerxes inscription. After speaking of the attack on various religions such as Buddhism, Christianity and Judaism in the empire, Kartir says, 'and the idols were destroyed and the lairs of the *devs* were uprooted and (in them?) the places and seats of the god(s) were erected'.[90] Here Kartir is opposed to the adherence of Iranians to foreign religions in the empire, which attitude of the Zoroastrians we also learn from the acts of Christian martyrs in Persia. Can we assume that Xerxes is also opposed to the adherence of Iranians to foreign religions in Iran? If so, then where is the line drawn between the 'religion of the Aryans' and foreign religions? The 'religion of the Aryans', as we have seen, is Mazda worship; therefore non-Mazda worship can be equated with *daiva* or *foreign* worship. When Darius in Behistun V. 16 says the Elamites did not worship Ahura Mazda, it is as if this was an explanation for their revolt, and perhaps worse, that these people who live with or near the Persians should be required to worship the Iranian god. But presumably Mazda worship *plus* 'the other gods that are', as Behistun IV. 61 has it, would be acceptable.[91] In other words, we

127

may see the process of the formation of later Zoroastrianism already in this period.

If the god Mithra was considered a *daiva*, he should have been chased from Iran, but apparently he was strong enough or popular enough to win royal approval under Artaxerxes II (404—359 BC). Furthermore, he has a Yasht dedicated to him in the Avesta. So we are possibly faced with the anomaly of either a Mithra who refuses to be subordinate to Ahura Mazda and is thus considered a *daiva* by the Mazdayasnians, or a Mithra who recognises the supremacy of Ahura Mazda and is accepted into the fold. Can we postulate then a conflict between the Mazdayasnian Magians and the Magians of Mithra as well as other deities? The evidence for the acceptance of Mithra by Mazda worshippers, or even the acceptance of Ahura Mazda by Mithra worshippers, is strong. First, we have the inscriptions of Artaxerxes II, where he calls on Anahita and Mithra, *after* Ahura Mazda, to protect him. Second, we have the statement of Berossos that Artaxerxes was the first Persian king who erected statues of Aphrodite or Anahita in Babylon, Susa, Ekbatana, Bactria, among others, plus the mention of a warlike goddess who had an important sanctuary at Pasargadai in Plutarch's life of Artaxerxes II.[92] Finally, we have the 'so-called Zoroastrian calendar', probably introduced in 441 BC before Artaxerxes II on an Egyptian model, with the month names coinciding with month names of the Younger Avesta. The month names contain names of Aryan gods, Mithra among them. Much has been written about the calendar which cannot be discussed here.[93] but we may say that the process of development in Zoroastrianism had probably reached a point similar to the Old Persian language — no break with the past, but rapid development toward Middle Iranian times.

About the time of Artaxerxes II one may suppose that Zoroaster's name becomes prominent in Magian circles of western Iran and thus known to the Greeks. Other cults or even religions undoubtedly existed in Iran, but the Magian-Zoroastrian-Achaemenid fusion would have been accomplished. The further development of what came to be known as Mithraism in the Roman empire need not concern us here for the entire subject of Mithra has been amply discussed by others.[94]

Questions of ritual, and the mode of burial are very difficult to trace. In my opinion the importance of the mode of burial has been exaggerated. Reasoning from burial, for example, could be fallacious, such as exposure of the dead to birds and animals, said to exist among the Magians (Herodotus I.140) and among the Bactrians (Strabo XI.517). Thus a northern Aryan custom, both in Media and in Bactria, would be compared with later Zoroastrian practice and contrasted with the rock-hewn tombs of the Achaemenid kings at Persepolis and Naqsh-i Rustam and unwarranted conclusions about the original Zoroastrianism of the Magians and the paganism of all the Achaemenids might emerge. Actually the royal practice of encasing the king's body in wax was probably an ancient Near Eastern practice, and the principle of keeping the body from polluting the soil, a Zoroastrian belief found later, could be maintained in many ways.

Next-of-kin marriage, prominent among Iranians later, may have been restricted to the royalty and aristocracy, as in the courts of Europe, and it may have been also of ancient Near Eastern origin, passed to the Persians by the Elamites. Many of the features of the goddess Anahita, identified by the Greeks with Aphrodite or Artemis may be traced to the substratum of peoples on the Iranian plateau before the coming of the Iranians. Anahita can be taken as an example of the combination of Near Eastern and Iranian features in the religious domain. The name *anahita*, probably meaning 'immaculate', is in origin an appellation of the goddess Ardvi of the Avesta associated with water. In western Iran and Mesopotamia it seems she was associated with the goddess Nana, and undoubtedly also with other female deities or mother goddesses.[95]

The Fall of the Achaemenids

The main events of Achaemenid political history are generally known from the Greek sources, and it has been the fashion of late to minimise the importance of the Greeks and the defeats of the Persians at Marathon, Salamis and Plataia. The loss of all the European conquests of Darius, the challenge to Achaemenid hegemony in western Anatolia, and above all the loss of prestige throughout the empire, however, cannot have failed to worry the Achaemenids. For the great empire which had expanded under Cyrus, Cambyses and Darius was now on the defensive and at times hard put to maintain order. It would be desirable to survey the fortunes of the empire from Darius to the conquest of Alexander the Great, an important turning point in history.

Darius, after the suppression of many revolts at the beginning of his reign, undertook many reforms which we have mentioned. He also extended the boundaries of the empire eastward and westward. In the Behistun inscription India (*Hindu-*) is not included among the lands which obeyed or came to Darius; so one may assume that the eastern extent of the empire of Cyrus was Gandhara. The Greek admiral Scylax of Caryanda who explored the Indus river set out from Persian domains in Gandhara. He sailed *circa* 516—512 BC down the river to the Indian Ocean and then to Egypt, a long voyage. After this trip Darius conquered the Indians of the Indus valley and opened trade by sea. The satrapy of India, primarily the wealthy Punjab, paid the largest tax of all the provinces, 360 talents of gold dust (Herodotus III.94), an important addition to the empire. The influence of the Achaemenids in India must have been great, a striking example being the rock edicts of the later Indian ruler Aśoka. The protocol employed, 'thus speaks the king . . .' is reminiscent of Achaemenid usage, while the very idea of royal inscriptions on stone may have come to India from Persia. In Central Asia the Scythians were pacified and undoubtedly cther peoples submitted to Darius, but his most spectacular and best known expedition was against the Scythians of south Russia.

Apart from the lengthy account of Darius' expedition against the Scythians of south Russia in Herodotus (IV.83 foll.) about the year 510 BC, we have two interesting pieces of evidence for the Achaemenid struggle with the nomads. One is the inscription at the rock-hewn tomb of Darius at Naqsh-i Rustam where the 'Saka who are across the sea' are mentioned, together with the Skudra or Thracians, as tributary to the great king. In the inscription of Xerxes at Persepolis the Skudra are still mentioned as subjects but not the Sakas of south Russia, which would coincide with the account of Herodotus. Another evidence of Darius' famous campaign is a fragment of a clay tablet with an Old Persian cuneiform text found in Roumania.[96] While this inscription may have been brought to the Roumanian or properly Transylvanian site by Roman soldiers in a later period, it was probably made as a foundation document of a building somewhere in the Balkans, hence proof of an occupation by the Persians, the westernmost extension of Achaemenid rule. Furthermore, Herodotus (IV.91) tells us of inscriptions on pillars, erected by Darius on his expedition. The expedition led to nothing since the Scythians followed a scorched earth policy before the advancing Achaemenid army and Darius was lucky to escape only with moderate losses, and not the loss of his whole army.

The story of the wars with Greece begun by Darius and ended in a débâcle by Xerxes should be known to every schoolboy. The military superiority of the Greeks in the face of superior forces, but not as many as the Greek sources would have us believe, is undeniable. In 478 BC after the final defeat of the Achaemenid forces it might have seemed as though the Greeks had all of Anatolia open for their conquest of at least part of the great empire. The Persians, however, though defeated in battle now exercised their skill at bribery with the great funds of wealth at their disposal. The resulting quarrels and wars between the city states of Greece and the leagues of city states is part of Greek history. For the Persians it meant that the empire was safe from Greek attack, but not from an ever-growing Greek influence, especially in Anatolia, at the expense of local languages and customs. The Hellenised Oriental rulers of Anatolia were instruments of Greek cultural penetration in the empire before Alexander.

Xerxes seems to have followed a less tolerant policy towards the subject peoples of the empire than his father. Egypt had revolted at the end of Darius' life and Xerxes, two years after his accession, reconquered the land of the Nile and was much harsher towards the people than his predecessor (Herodotus VII.7). The Persian monarch no longer pretended to be the successor of the pharaohs, nor were native customs or religious practices particularly respected. Similar treatment was meted out to Babylon when that great city revolted, and one may conjecture that these actions attest to the decline of Babylonian and Egyptian cultural predominance in the Near East. After the defeats in Greece Xerxes devoted himself to the building of Persepolis and to the harem which came to occupy a dominant position in imperial affairs. Xerxes was assassinated in 465, a bad omen for the future.

Artaxerxes came to power by assassination and intrigue, which came to be almost an established pattern. Egypt revolted again with Greek aid in 460, and only by great exertion could the Persians in 455 led by one Arsames, possibly the same as mentioned in Aramaic papyri, reconquer the land. The influence of Queen-mother Amestris at the court, which can only be described as baneful, also set a precedent for the future. Artaxerxes I probably abandoned residency at Persepolis at the

131

end of his reign and in this he was followed by his successors. After the death of Artaxerxes I there was civil war and more assassinations which ended in the accession of Darius II called Ochus, son of Artaxerxes and a Babylonian concubine. Darius II was much under the influence of his wife and half-sister, Parysatis, an able but cruel woman. Although the empire suffered from the rebellions of various satraps the Greeks, engaged in the Peloponnesian war, were unable to profit from Persian weakness; rather Persian gold proved far more effective than the troops of Xerxes.

Darius II died in 404 and was succeeded by Artaxerxes II whom we have met previously. The expected troubles at the beginning of a new reign were not slow in developing, but for this civil war we are fortunate in having Xenophon's *Anabasis* describing the attempt of Cyrus the Younger, brother of the king, to secure the throne. At the same time, Egypt again seized the opportunity to become independent. The story of the retreat of the 10,000 Greek mercenaries after the death of their patron, Cyrus, at the battle of Cunaxa in 401, is not only a Greek classic but also a source of information about the Achaemenid empire. The story of intrigues, revolts and assassinations in Persian-Greek relations, especially concerned with Ionia, is somewhat monotonous, but it also reveals the ability of the Achaemenids to sow dissension among Greek rivals to their own advantage. Egypt proved too strong to be reconquered and remained free from Persian rule under a native dynasty. Furthermore, with satraps in Anatolia revolting against the central power, it seemed as if the empire were on the verge of collapse. The accession of an able though blood-thirsty monarch, Artaxerxes III, in 359 saved the empire for a few years. Various satraps who had revolted and issued their own coinage were won back to Achaemenid allegiance, but then some of the Phoenician city states revolted. In fact, it is quite difficult to follow the varying fortunes and allegiances of the satraps of Asia Minor and the rulers of the coast of the eastern Mediterranean Sea, always with Greek mercenaries and Greek interests involved. The process of the Hellenisation of Asia, which was to be accelerated by Alexander the Great, was already well under way in the last reigns of the Achaemenid house.

Already a new power was being felt in Greece, that of Macedonia, even as Artaxerxes III prepared to reconquer Egypt. He first had to subdue Phoenicia in 345. Sidon was captured and burned, and the captives sent as slaves to Babylon and Susa. The way to Egypt was open and in the ensuing fighting it was more a struggle of Greek mercenary against Greek mercenary than Persian versus Egyptian. Lower Egypt was restored to Persian rule although the native Egyptian dynasty continued to rule in most of upper Egypt. None the less, it seemed as though under Artaxerxes III the Achaemenid empire had received a new impetus and was regaining past power and glory.

The intrigues of Philip of Macedon, Athens and the Persians fill the period of the last years of Artaxerxes III. History might have been different if Artaxerxes had not been poisoned at about the same time (*circa* 338 BC) that Philip was uniting the Greeks behind him by conquering them at the battle of Chaeronea. The threat of a united Greece had now materialised and it marked the death knell of the Achaemenid empire. Achaemenid troops had not proved a match for well-trained Greek soldiers in the past and the martial qualities of the Greeks were now abetted by the even more warlike Macedonians.

The murderer of Artaxerxes was a capable but unscrupulous eunuch called Bagoas, who could not, however, ascend the throne himself. Instead, after almost exterminating the Achaemenid royal family, he gave the throne to a distant member of the family who is known as Darius III Codommanus. He was able to take the reins of power in his own hands and reconquer Egypt, but he was unable to arrest the decay of the empire. Alexander, justly designated the Great, was determined to conquer the Achaemenid empire and in a short space of time he did so.

If one were to assess the achievements of the Achaemenid Persians, surely the concept of 'One World', the fusion of peoples and cultures in one *'oecumene'*, was one of the important legacies to Alexander and the Romans. The Achaemenid monarch thought of himself as a king of kings over many peoples with their various rulers. Hand in hand with the idea of empire went the process of mixture and syncretism; members of distant tribes and nations were brought into contact with each other under the umbrella of the Persian peace and there must have been much give and take. One should not exaggerate the ease of communication because it was surely arduous and not as frequent as might be supposed. On the other hand, the appearance of a Khwarezmian in a garrison of upper Egypt attests to contacts between the extreme frontiers of the empire.[97] Our view of the Achaemenid empire and its achievements is, of course, somewhat

133

distorted by the brilliant light of Greece. But have we not perhaps asked the wrong question of the Orient in antiquity, as we still do today? One asked why the Orient remained behind the Greeks, as we ask why the Orient today remains under-developed. Is it not more appropriate to ask instead why the Greeks developed as they did, or why the Renaissance and the Industrial Revolution made the Occident what it is now? In other words, perhaps we should explain why the West is abnormal while Asia and Africa have developed as expected in the course of history. Then the West today would be over-developed rather than the East under-developed. These may appear to be glib words, but if we change our perspective, perhaps we can understand some things better in the present as well as in the past.

The Achaemenid bureaucracy and army, as well as merchants, were the main agents for the spreading of ideas and practices throughout the empire. The Achaemenid rulers were themselves of mixed blood and were, it would seem, cosmopolitan in their outlook. Greek doctors, Phoenician explorers and Babylonian astronomers were welcome at the court of the king of kings, and if we believe Greek sources, the Persian monarchs sought to lure, usually unsuccessfully, numbers of prominent Greek scientists or thinkers to their courts with promises of great rewards. The question of Plato and his relation to and influence on the Orient cannot be discussed here. We have already mentioned the artisans of all nations who worked on Persian palaces with the resulting imperial architecture. For the art and architecture of the Achaemenids is imperial, monumental in size and impressive in detail. Perhaps the most characteristic feature of the architecture is not the height of the pillars or the intricate design with inlay and colouring of the bas-reliefs, but rather the use of space. A contribution of the Persians to architecture was the design of great vaults and the use of wide spaces to great effect. The employment of the great cedars of Lebanon in building and the best artisans of the empire, plus enormous wealth, enabled the Persians to build on an 'imperial' scale, and they did so in an appropriate manner. The pointed arch and squinch are later developments in Persia, but the early concern with larger rooms and ceilings inspired later features of architecture.

The Achaemenid empire was not only *the* empire and the Persian king the *king*, for the Greeks but also, one may conjecture, for the Indians. We have already noted the influence of Achaemenid protocol and practice on the Maurya dynasty and its greatest ruler, Aśoka. Further, the Kharoshthi alphabet which became widespread in northwest India owed its origin to Aramaic, the *lingua franca* of the Achaemenid empire, likewise the Brahmi alphabet which spread much farther in India than did the Kharoshthi alphabet. Maurya art, too, little though we know of it, shows Persian influence in the capitals of columns like inverted bells or with animals. So Indian contacts with the West undoubtedly existed before Alexander the Great.

Persian influence in the western part of the empire was also important. Especially significant, and also apparent, was this influence on Armenia and Cappadocia. It would not be too much amiss to say that the Armenians were Iranised in the Achaemenid and later in the Parthian period. Their religion and rites were the same as the Medes and Persians, and especially Mithra and Anahita were honoured (Strabo XI.532). The great borrowing of Iranian words into Armenian is well known. While most of them show borrowings from Parthian or Middle Iranian dialects, others show an older stage of borrowing, such as *t'agawor* 'king' and *partēz* 'garden', but in the archaic tendency of Parthian in much of its vocabulary makes a determination of Achaemenid influence in the Armenian language difficult.[98] In Cappadocia the influence is seen mainly after the fall of the Achaemenids in names of rulers and in religious practices reported by classical authors. Cappadocia was a meeting ground of Greek and Persian culture, and also later a great centre of Christian thought, but this was true to a lesser degree of most of Anatolia. Anatolia of the fourth century BC has been characterised as the pathway of Hellenism to the Orient.

The Jews and Israel have not received much attention for they were mostly quiet under Achaemenid rule though not un-influenced by the Persians. After all Cyrus freed them from their Babylonian captivity and allowed them to go home to rebuild their temple which was finished about 515 BC. It was under Persian rule that the Torah was established as the law of Israel, probably at the same time and in much the same manner in which Egyptian laws and the laws of other peoples were codified or revised. In the Biblical books of Ezra and Nehemiah we find much evidence of contact with the Achaemenid court. Some scholars have dated the rise of modern Judaism from this period when observance of the Law was instituted with imperial approval. The question of the Persian religious influence on

135

Judaism and Christianity has many rumifications, but one may postulate a mutual sympathy, if not direct influence, in many aspects of religious thought. Such concepts as 'the holy spirit' and 'the angel of wisdom' appear in post-exilic Judaism and may be influenced by Iranian angelology or the attributes of Ahura Mazda. This is perhaps most striking in the dualism of good angels and bad which again comes to the fore in the Judaism of the Achaemenid period. Some books of the Apocrypha appear to be more influenced by Iran than parts of the Old Testament, and the concept of Satan himself could well be borrowed from Iran. Further speculation on influences in eschatology, time speculation and other similar topics is interesting but not very fruitful in proving historical borrowing. The people of the Dead Sea scrolls are later and present many problems.

There is one aspect of Persian rule which must be mentioned, especially in consideration of any comparison with the Greeks. It is perhaps best expressed in an answer which several Spartans gave to Hydarnes, a satrap in western Anatolia, who complained to them for not accepting service with the great king (Herodotus VII.135).

'Hydarnes, the counsels which you give us are short-sighted. You know only that which you recommend, not that which you urge us to leave. You understand how to be a slave, but you know nothing of freedom, whether it be sweet or bitter. If you had but tasted it you would counsel us to fight for it not only with spears but with axes.' A further necessary qualification of this freedom of the Greeks was given to Xerxes by the former Spartan king, Demaratos, who had fled to the great king and joined him in his campaign against Greece. In describing the bravery and ability of the Spartans he adds (Herodotus VII.104): 'Even though they are free, still they are not fully free. Their master is the law, which they fear far more than thy people fear thee.' Thus we have an inkling of those qualities which made Greece great.

NOTES

1 G. Cameron, *Histoire de l'Iran antique* (Paris, 1937), 40, and W. Hinz, *Das Reich Elam* (Stuttgart, 1964), 74-76.

2 Attempts to identify the Guti with the Albanians of the Caucasus (Udi) have not been proved by Yampolskii; cf. I. M. Dyakonov, *Istoriya Midii* (Moscow, 1956), 110.

3 The ready availability of the bronzes is such that I omit an extensive pictorial representation of them in this book.

4 E. H. Minns, *The Art of the Northern Nomads* (London, 1942), 25, and R. Ghirshman, *Iran* (London, 1954), 105.

136

5 A. Godard, 'Les bronzes du Luristan', Orientalia Romana (Rome, 1958), 51-72.

6 Ghirshman, loc. cit.

7 E. Herzfeld, Archaeological History of Iran (London, 1935), 2, also his The Persian Empire (Wiesbaden, 1968), 191-200.

8 I. M. Dyakonov, Istoriya Midii, 282, note.

9 The earlier dating is by A. Godard, Le trésor de Ziwiyè (Haarlem, 1950), 12; the later and more likely one is put about 625 BC when Sakkiz, the capital of the Scythians, who ruled in this area from about 625 to 653, fell. Godard's declaration that in Sakkiz we have the name of the Saka-Scythians is difficult to accept from the outset since the town is named from the river and not likely to be called after a people. Cf. R. Ghirshman, 'Notes Iraniennes IV', Artibus Asiae 13 (1950), 201.

10 Cf. G. A. Melikishvili, Nekotorye voprosy istorii maneiskogo tsarstva', Vestnik Drevnei Istorii, 1949 (1), 57.

11 Cf. G. A. Melikishvili, Nairi-Urartu (Tiflis, 1954), 19.

12 I. M. Dyakonov, 'Poslednie gody Urartskogo gosudarstva', Vestnik Drevnei Istorii, 1951 (no. 2), 30.

13 B. B. Piotrovskii, Vanskoe Tsarstvo (Moscow, 1959), 116, 241.

14 Ibid., 124.

15 G. Kapantsyan, Istoriko-lingvisticheskie ratboty (Erevan, 1956), pp. 1-259.

16 Piotrovskii, Karmir Blur, 1 (Erevan, 1950), 77, fig. 48.

17 R. Ghirshman, Iran (London, 1954), 123.

18 K. L. Oganesian, Karmir-Blur, 4 (Erevan, 1955), 7-8, 107. A general discussion of the architecture may be found here.

19 H. Frankfort, The Art and Architecture of the Ancient Orient (London, 1958), 189.

20 G. A. Melikishvili, Urartskie klinoobraznye nadpisi (Moscow, 1960), 33.

21 Frankfort, op. cit., 202.

22 F. W. König, Älteste Geschichte der Meder und Perser (Leipzig, 1934), 8. Cf. E. A. Grantovskii, Rannyaya istoriya iranskikh plemen Peredner Azii (Moscow, 1970).

23 König, 10, and Grantovskii, 67.

24 König, op. cit., 20-21.

25 The Iranian origin of the Cimmerians, and the meaning of their name as 'hero' (Georgian gmiri) has been discussed by Dyakonov, op. cit., 239-241, who also suggests they were a tribe or a part of the 'Scythian' peoples of the steppes, using 'Scythian' in its widest sense but still predominantly Iranian.

26 D. J. Wiseman, 'The Vassal-Treaties of Esarhaddon', Iraq, 20 (1958), 10.

27 The terms for the nomadic invaders are sometimes misleading. It would seem that the Assyrians and Babylonians used the name 'Cimmerian' for all of the nomads from South Russia and Central Asia, as the Greeks used 'Scythian' and the Persians 'Saka', but Dyakonov's suggestion that all three terms should be equated cannot be wholly valid.

28 Wiseman, op. cit., 13. The name Phraortes is probably to be derived from fravarti-. Khshathrita would seem to be a 'throne name', as among the

Achaemenids (discussed later). The Babylonian form Kashtaritu has variants for the Iranian original.

29 The Akkadian form of his name was U-ak-sa-tar with variants; cf. the discussion by W. Eilers in *ZDMG*, 90 (1936), 174.

30 For the chronicle of events see D. J. Wiseman, *Chronicles of Chaldaean Kings* (London, 1956), 15.

31 Herzfeld, *Zoroaster*, 724.

32 Dyakonov, *op. cit.*, 349. On p. 358 he brings Sogdiana under Median hegemony.

33 There are a number of examples of this such as Elamite *ba-ak-shi-ish* for Bactria, which Elamite form is derived from Old Persian * Bakshi- where the Old Persian inscriptions themselves have Bākhtrish.

34 R. Borger and W. Hinz, *'Eine Dareios - Inschrift aus Pasargadae'*, *ZDMG*, 109 (1959), 127. The supporters of the Darius invention of Old Persian cuneiform, such as Weissbach and Hinz, stress the fact that Old Persian is artificial in that it is only used for royal inscriptions, since Elamite and Aramaic were the written languages used at Persepolis, the heart of Persis. Cf. M. Mayrhofer, *'Das Altpersische seit 1964'*, *W. B. Henning Memorial Volume* (London, 1970), 277-80.

35 I do not believe in bringing the term *maga-* 'brotherhood, etc.' or other unclear words (Yasna 65.7) into the argument, for we are looking for the clear word *magu-* as 'priest'.

36 Etymologies are summarised in E. Benveniste, *Les Mages dans l'ancien Iran* (Paris, 1938), 20.

37 Translation of A. Leo Oppenheim in J. B. Pritchard, *Ancient Near Eastern Texts* (Princeton, 1950), 305. The name Ishtumegu is to be read Ishtuvegu, but the Iranian etymology 'lance brandisher' of Herzfeld, *Archaeologische Mitteilungen aus Iran*, 7 (1934), 128, is unconvincing. Cf. Dyakonov, *Istoriya Midii*, 414-5, note 3.

38 C. Müller, *Fragmenta Historicorum Graecorum*, 3 (Paris, 1828), 406.

39 Cf. Pritchard (note 37), 316.

40 For a comparison of the Cyrus saga with Roman, German, etc., stories, see A. Bauer, *'Die Kyros-Sage und Verwandtes'*, *Sitzungsber. der Akad.* (Vienna, 1882). G. Hüsing, *Beiträge zur Kyros-Sage* (Berlin, 1906), is difficult to understand.

41 Note 38, pp. 398-406, and R. Henry, *Ctésias, les sommaires de Photius* (Brussels, 1947), 12 foll.

42 Cf. Dyakonov, *op. cit.*, 17, 424, with references.

43 Pritchard (note 37), 306. Gutium is old Babylonian usage for the land between Assyria and Media, east of the Tigris.

44 See the discussion in O. Leuze, *'Die Satrapieneinteilung in Syrien und im Zweistromlande'*, *Schriften der Königsberger Gelehrten Gesell.*, 11 (Halle, 1935), 182.

45 Anaximenes, in Stephan of Byzantium *sub* Passargadai. References to all sources are in E. Herzfeld, *'Pasargadae'*, *Kilo*, 8 (1908), 10 foll.

46 *'Untersuchungen zur Geschichte von Eran'*, *Philologus*, Supplement-band 10 (Leipzig, 1905), 154. For a summary of various etymologies see Ali Sami, *Pasargadae* (Shiraz, 1956), 16-18 (in English).

46a Cf. Cameron, 'An Inscription of Darius from Pasargadae', 5 (Iran, 1967), 7-10.

47 R. Ghirshman, Iran (London, 1954), 123.

48 Ali Sami (note 46), 42-43.

49 Survey of the discussion in K. Erdmann, 'Griechische und achaemenidische Plastik', Forschungen und Fortschritte, 26 (1950), 150-153.

50 In 1903 F. C. Andreas first proposed that the Elamite form of his name, Kurash, was the original rather than the Old Persian Kurush. For ancient and modern etymologies see F. Weissbach, article 'Kyros', in Pauly-Wissowa Realencyclopädie, Supplementband 4 (Stuttgart, 1924), 1128. See David Stronach, Excavations at Pasargadae (Oxford, 1976).

51 E. Benveniste, 'La ville de Cyreschata', Journal Asiatique (1943-1945), 163.

52 J. Charpentier, 'Der Name Kambyses', Zeitschrift für Indologie und Iranistik, 2 (1923), 148, and K. Hoffmann, 'Vedische Namen', Wörter und Sachen, 21 (1940), 146.

53 See the discussions of chronology in A. Poebel, 'The Reign of Smerdis and Others', American Journal of Semitic Languages, 56 (1939), 121-145, and R. Parker, 'Persian and Egyptian Chronology', ibid., 58 (1941), 285-299.

54 For the Aramaic version see A. Cowley, Aramaic Papryi of the Fifth Century B.C. (Oxford, 1923), 248-271. It is probable that the Old Persian version is the original while the Akkadian may have been the basis for some other versions.

55 Mainly based on R. Kent, Old Persian (New Haven, 1950). The Babylonian and Elamite versions have not been consulted.

56 The expression * huvāmarshiyush has caused trouble. Kent translates 'died by his own hand', i.e. suicide, p. 177. In Baluchi we have wadh = way miri 'self dying', i.e. natural death, according to M. Longworth Dames, Popular Poetry of the Baloches, 2 (London, 1907), 200. Parallels in other Indo-European languages would support the view of a natural death. Cf. J. Markwart in Caucasica, 6, Part 2 (1930), 66, note 3, and J. P. Asmussen, 'The Death of Cambyses' Bulletin of the Iranian Cultural Foundation, 1 (Tehran, 1969), 21-7.

57 Or goods: compare New Persian afzār 'instrument, goods'. Kent has 'pastures'. The Elamite version is different but not clear. Compare also Skt. abhicarah- 'servant'.

58 Herodotus III.72, makes Darius give a defence of lying. Stories of pretenders to the throne abound in Persian history; for example, a parallel to the false Smerdis may be found in the story of Ismaᶜīl Mirzā, son of Shāh Tahmasp, in Safavid times.

59 R. T. Hallock, 'The "One Year" of Darius I', Journal of Near Eastern Studies, 19 (1960), 36-39, and A. Shapur Shahbazi, 'The One year of Darius re-examined', BSOAS, 35 (1973), 609-14.

60 W. B. Henning, 'The Murder of the Magi', Journal of the Royal Asiatic Society (1943), 135.

61 A parallel with Sanskrit āyatana 'the place to which one returned, stronghold', synonym of pur 'fort', hence a family abode is not likely.

62 J. Marquart, Fundamente israelitischer Geschichte (Göttingen, 1896),

48. Darius is the Spentadata of Zoroastrian tradition according to Herzfeld (*Zoroaster*, 95) and others.

63 R. Hallock, *Persepolis Fortification Tablets* (Chicago, 1969), 723, *sub Makuš.*

64 The characterisation of the pre-Darius Magians as Chaldaean priests, and the post-Darius Magians as Zoroastrians, as König proposes, is unproved. Cf. F. W. König, *Der falsche Bardiya* (Vienna, 1938), 95, and 180, for the Magians.

65 *Ibid.*, 87 for reference.

66 A word should be said here to refute the contention of Geo Widengren of Uppsala (in *Numen*, 2, 1955, 81 and elsewhere) that the name of the Iranian time god Zurvan (Chronos) appears in ancient cuneiform tables from Nuzi. E. A. Speiser in *Annual of the American Schools of Oriental Research*, 16 (1936), 99, nos. 47 and 48, notes that this name should be read Zarwa[n], a Hurrian goddess, probably a deified place name, and with no hint of time speculation or any connection with Zurvan.

67 '*The Sacral Kingship of Iran*', *Numen*, Supplement, 4 (Leiden, 1959), 242-257.

68 See Feodora Prinzessin von Sachsen-Meiningen *apud* F. Althiem, *Geschichte der Hunnen*, 2 (Berlin, 1960), 125-167.

69 The Old Persian form of *eisangeleus* was rather ⋆*azdākara*, a word attested also in Sogdian and elsewhere. Cf. A. Meillet and E. Benveniste, *Grammaire du vieux perse* (Paris, 1931), 150.

70 Diodorus Siculus XVIII.39.7, and XLVIII.4.49. In Armenian sources we find the term *hazarapet dran Ariats* '*chiliarch* of the gates of the Persians', obviously a later 'prime minister' in function. See also E. Benveniste, *Titres et noms en iranien ancien* (Paris, 1966), 67-71.

71 In Gabai (Isfahan) and Taoke (somewhere in southern Fars province) according to Strabo XV.728, Arrian *Indica*, XXXIX.3, and others.

72 W. Eilers, '*Die Ausgrabungen in Persepolis*', *Zeitschrift für Assyriologie*, 53 (1959), 249 note. On the word for 'paradise' see E. Benveniste in *Journal Asiatique* (1954), 309.

73 See A. Pagliaro, '*Riflessi di etimologie iraniche nella tradizione storiografica greca*', *Rendiconti della Accademia Nazionale dei Lincei*, 9 (Rome, 1954), 135 foll. The etymology is more likely *pati-āxš* 'to watch over'.

74 Translation by A. D. Godley in the *Loeb Classical Series* (London, 1924), 97. The word *angaros* has been explained as Akkadian *egirtu*, Iranian *⋆hangar*, or otherwise. Since it appears in Aramaic, Syriac and possibly in Demotic Egyptian, with related forms meaning *corvée*, it would seem that the Babylonians had a better claim to the word than the Persians. The word in Plutarch, *Alexander* 18, *astandes*, 'royal courier' may not mean 'courier', for Darius was not a courier before becoming king.

75 The etymology of *parasang*, New Persian *farsakh*, is not related to 'stone' Old Persian *thanga*, but rather to the root *sah-* 'to announce', as Marquart proposed; cf. also Schaeder in *Ungarische Jahrbücher*, 15 (1935), 563. Compare the second part of the word *orosanges* (Herodotus VIII.85), unless this word is from ⋆ *huvarzaka-* 'good doer'. The *stathmoi* of Seleucid times were probably based on the Achaemenid road system.

76 Translation of R. Kent, *Old Persian*, 132. The phrase 'which formerly was not' appears only in the Elamite version. Cf. I. M. Dyakonov, '*On the*

140

interpretation of para. 70 of the Bisutun Inscription Acta Antiqua, 17 (Budapest, 1969), 105-7.

77 For the Taxila inscription see F. C. Andreas in the *Nachrichten der Gesellshaft der Wissenschaften zu Göttingen,* 1931. The Aramaic-Greek bilingual has been published by D. Schlumberger and others in the *Journal Asiatique,* 1958, while the Laghman inscription by W. B. Henning may be found in the *Bulletin of the School of Oriental and African Studies,* 13 (1949), 80 foll. Another Aramaic inscription was found in Qandahan; see E. Benveniste, *et al., 'Une inscription indo-araméenne d'Aśoka provenant de Kandahar', JA,* 253, (Paris, 1966), 437-70.

78 Rather than 'menial' as Kent translates for **maryaka.* Cf. above and note 78 of chapter 2.

79 I follow Benveniste in *Bulletin de la Société de Linguistique,* 47 (Paris, 1951), 37 in taking *ha(n)duga* in the sense of 'affirmation' or 'attestation' rather than as a physical inscription.

80 See G. Cameron, *The Persian Satrapies and Related Matters,* JNES, 32 (Chicago, 1973), 47-56.

81 Cognates are found in Lithuanian *karas,* and German *Heer,* probably an Indo-European collective designation of the warriors of the tribe.

82 Proposed by Pagliaro (note 73), 149.

83 E. Meyer, *Geschichte des Altertumus,* 4 (Stuttgart, 1939), 70.

84 G. Cardascia, *Les archives des Murashu* (Paris, 1951), 7 foll. See also his *'Le fief dans la Babylonie achéménide, Receuils de la Société Jean Bodin* 1, (1958), 55-8.

85 Letter 8 of G. R. Driver, *Aramaic Documents* (Oxford, 1957), 31.

86 J. Harmatta, *'Elamica I', Acta Linguistica,* 4 (Budapest,1954), 302 foll.

87 On general questions of coinage cf. E. Meyer, *op. cit.,* 74, and for a Greek hoard from Achaemenid times found in Afghanistan see D. Schlumberger, *Trésors monétaires d'Afghanistan, Mémoires de la délégation arch. franç. en Afghanistan* (Paris, 1953), 24-30.

88 F. Altheim and R. Stiehl, *Die aramäische Sprache unter den Achaimeniden* (Frankfurt, 1961), 173.

89 The literature on this is vast; see Kent, *Old Persian,* 112, where a bibliography is given. Kent's translation of the last phrase. 'I worshipped Ahura Mazda and Arta reverent(ly)', while grammatically correct is misleading, for the meaning is more that the king worshipped Ahura Mazda as one should,' not perhaps as some *daiva* worshippers regarded Ahura Mazda.

90 To be found in line 10 of the 'Ka' bah of Zoroaster' inscription and line 14 of Sar Mashhad (with gaps). The third or Naqsh-i Rustam inscription is too destroyed to use the traces. Cf. P. Gignoux, *L'inscription de Kartir à Sar Mašhad,* JA, 256 (Paris, 1969), 395, 414.

91 I personally believe that Mithra and Anahita were always respected by the Achaemenid royal house, for the expressions 'Ahura Mazda together with the gods of the royal house (*vithaibish*)', and 'Ahura Mazda, greatest of the gods' (in Darius Persepolis d 24 and h 9 respectively) can hardly refer to Mesopotamian or non-Iranian deities. Cf. M. Boyce, *'On Mithra's part in Zoroastrianism', BSOAS,* 22 (1969), 10-34.

92 Berossos in Jacoby, *Fragmente Gr. Hist.* (Leiden, 1958), Dritter Theil C, p. 391, 680, F 11.

93 Cf. S. H. Taqizadeh, *The Old Iranian Calendars Again'*, *BSOAS*, 14 (1952), 603.

94 Gershevitch, *The Avesta Hymn to Mithra*, 61 foll. and J. Hinnells, ed. *Mithraic Studies*, 2 vols (Manchester U. Press, 1975).

95 References to Ardvi Sura Anahita are gathered by L. Gray, *Foundations of the Iranian Religions* (Bombay, 1927), 55 foll.

96 J. Harmatta, *'A recently discovered Old Persian inscription'*, *Acta Antiqua*, 2 (Budapest, 1954), 1-14.

97 The form *ḥrzmy* is found in letter 6, line 2, and *ḥrzmy* ' in letter 8, line 23, pp. 16 and 22 of Cowley (note 54). One would have expected a *waw* after the *ḥ*.

98 Cf. R. N. Frye, *'Continuing Iranian Influences on Aramaian'*, *Yad nāme-ye Irānī-ye*. Minorsky (Tehran, 1969), 80-90.

99 See Frye, *'Iran and Israel'*, *Festschrift für W. Eilers* (Wiesbaden, 1967) 74-84.

4 L'IRAN EXTÉRIEUR

Alexander the Great and his Legacy

The conquest of the Achaemenid empire by Alexander and the subsequent establishment of Hellenistic states, is the most important event in the history of the ancient Near East. In a sense it marks the end of that ancient history and the beginning of a new era, an era of an oecumenical culture generally called Hellenism. Of course Hellenism itself is also a transitional period to the world of Rome. Hellenism properly belongs to Greek history, but with its world-wide influence we must consider the consequences of Alexander's conquest of Iran in the framework of the legacy of that country. For Iran, Alexander meant the end of a period of greatness and a new era of foreign rule and disunity. Unfortunately the centuries between Alexander the Great and the rise of the Sasanians are little known and the sources are few, almost all of them in Greek. None the less, changes did occur which were significant in the history of the country and an attempt to reconstruct them should be made.

So much has been written about Alexander that a survey of his campaign is unnecessary here, but several remarks about his remarkable achievements are of interest to our subject. The expedition against the Achaemenid empire had been planned by Philip long before his assassination and it was only natural that his son should carry out these plans. The army which was to realise the dream of Alexander was composed primarily of two elements, Macedonians and the Greeks of the League of Corinth. The latter had been created by Philip by force of arms and Alexander maintained the league as his instrument of control in Greece, hence the war against the Persians was presented as a pan-Hellenic cause. The army of Alexander might be compared to the one which Napoleon led to Egypt, for both had historians, scientists and *littérateurs* as well as engineers, surveyors and soldiers. Camp followers were numerous as with most ancient armies, and their numbers must have increased with Alexander's victories. The combat troops, however, were experienced, well trained and led by competent officers. Furthermore, the Macedonian phalanx was probably the finest military organisation of the time, for those heavily armed foot soldiers were the backbone of the army, and at this period they were more flexible than the later tightly massed phalanxes with their very long spears. Alexander early saw the importance and need for cavalry on the plains of Asia, and he steadily increased the number of horsemen in his army. Still this was one part of the army which did not surpass, if it really even equalled, the Persian cavalry. In his fighting in eastern Iran Alexander did not hesitate to enrol local contingents of cavalry in his army, and on the whole they served him well.

The picture in the West of Alexander and the last Darius has been traditionally that of David and Goliath, but the actual situation must have been quite different. Because of the common practice of the Greek city states to banish wrong-doers or political opponents there was continually a large number of Greeks in exile. Perhaps similar to the French Foreign Legion, many of these exiles became mercenaries, and in a real sense they provided the bulk of the fighting forces of the ancient world. The Persian forces were much fewer than they had been, for since the end of Achaemenid expansion under Xerxes the empire had enjoyed comparative peace for a long time and had become militarily weak. In the three battles of the Persians against Alexander, the Granicus river crossing, Issus and Gaugamela. Greek mercenaries played important roles in the armies of Darius, for the prowess of the Greek hoplites was known and feared in Asia. It is reported that Persian troops, during one of their campaigns in Egypt, fled from Egyptian troops wearing Greek armour while they fought well against Greeks wearing Egyptian garb [1] When Alexander led a combined Macedonian-Greek army against the Achaemenid empire, it was not as foolhardy as might appear at first glance. Most of the Greek sources, of course, exaggerate the numbers of the enemy and the small losses of Alexander, thus enhancing his accomplishments. The unreliability of the figures given by Alexander's historians is generally known and is confirmed in one case by the great disparity between the wounded and dead of Alexander's army after a battle which cannot be accurate. [2] It might be closer to

144

the truth to say that at the Granicus Alexander outnumbered the enemy, at Issus the armies were almost equal while at Gaugamela Darius probably held a considerable superiority. In all of them, however, the difference between the army of Alexander, which was an excellent disciplined fighting machine, and the unwieldy, variegated forces of Darius must have been striking. The use of scythed chariots by Darius at Gaugamela possibly was a sign of weakness, like an act of desperation, to try everything and anything to stop the conqueror. As it was, the fine Achaemenid cavalry almost won the day for Darius, but his foot soldiers could not oppose the phalanx and other units of Alexander's army. This is neither to detract from the genius of Alexander nor from the ability of his capable lieutenants, but the one-sided picture of the conquests of Alexander which we obtain from the Greeks should be corrected. If a king other than Darius had been on the throne history might have been different, but history, just like an individual's life, is full of many 'ifs'.

One may conjecture that the Achaemenid dynasty had lost its hold on the people, if not actually or politically, then symbolically. One may doubt if the Achaemenids really ever held the same place in the hearts of the Persians as did later dynasties. The solidarity complex of 'Aryanism', however potent it may have been, cannot have been the same as later 'Iranian nationalism' with such loyalties implied by the concept of nationalism. The legitimacy of kingship may have been supported without much further allegiance to state or nation, although the foreign invasion at least roused some eastern Iranians. Darius, however, by his flights from the battle-fields of Issus and Gaugamela cannot have endeared himself to most Iranians, and he was finally assassinated by his own followers fleeing before Alexander. Inasmuch as the satrap of Bactria, Bessus, who had turned against Darius, now considered himself the successor of Darius and assumed the Achaemenid throne-name, Artaxerxes, one might conjecture that Darius was about to surrender to Alexander and Bessus and his friends were opposed to this.

With the death of Darius, Alexander became his successor as king of Asia and all who did not recognise him were automatically rebels against their rightful sovereign. We know of many Persian notables who joined Alexander after the battle of Gaugamela and certainly the conqueror's welcome and his generosity helped to reconcile many to a new order. For Alexander did bring a new order to the world, not only for the Orientals but also for the

Greeks. The main actors in the attempt to fuse the Greek and Oriental worlds were the Greeks and the Persians, for the scarcity of non-Iranian names among the enemy in the histories of Alexander indicates the degree by which Iranians had dominated the upper bureaucracy, and such posts as satrap and general, all over the Achaemenid empire. So the first purpose of Alexander was to bring the Greeks and the Persians together, and he sought to accomplish this by appointing both Persians and Greeks to govern his satrapies. Atropates, a Persian, was appointed satrap of Media and his name gave the name to the province of Atropatene, while Phrataphernes, satrap of Parthia and Hyrcania, who remained true to Darius until the latter's death, was reinstated in his satrapy by the conqueror. At the same time Macedonians were also installed as satraps, so the plan for the fusion of peoples, often attributed to Alexander, had in fact a basis in his actions. Large areas of the Achaemenid empire, however, remained outside Alexander's control; for example, we find a certain Orontes ruler of Armenia both under Darius and later under Alexander, even though Alexander appointed as new satrap of Armenia the Persian governor of Susa, Mithrenes, who obviously could not secure his new post. Alexander's conquests extended only the length of his campaign in Asia, but after all, he went far and covered an enormous territory. Wherever he had the authority, however, Alexander fostered the idea of a fusion of Greeks and Persians, or better, it should be said, Hellenes and Iranians. For the Greek-Macedonian rivalry, although a problem for Alexander, must have been insignificant for the Iranians to whom both peoples must have appeared as one folk, albeit with family quarrels.

The idea of a Graeco-Iranian union was probably no startling new discovery of Alexander, for it must be remembered that Greeks had served in both armies, and after his victory at Gaugamela Alexander was prepared to accept Iranians in his army. A certain amount of fusion must have existed already before Alexander. His marriage with Roxane, daughter of a Sogdian lord, and the mass marriage of his troops with Iranian women at Susa after his return from India, were steps towards a union of peoples.

It is the aftermath of Alexander's conquests, what he established that survived his death, which is more important for the history of Iran than his actual deeds, and we must consider the intangibles as well as his specific changes or reforms, beginning with the latter.

Finances were important to Alexander but he had not time to survey and change the system of taxation even if he had wished to change it. Some abuses, especially those of the middlemen between the peasant and the treasury, were rectified. In many instances new tax assessors or supervisors were appointed but elsewhere the system continued much as before Alexander. After all, in some areas there was little he could do as, for example, in Ionia where the Greek cities were his free allies. Those cities continued to mint coins and pay taxes as they had done under Achaemenid rule. It was formerly thought that Alexander tried to bring uniformity in the coinage of his empire by adapting the Attic standard to both gold and silver. He would have fixed the gold stater (in place of the *daric*) equal to twenty silver *drachmae*, but with the gold to silver ratio a more realistic 10:1 rather than the traditional 13⅓:1 of the Achaemenid empire. This traditional view has been challenged for it would seem that Alexander did not and could not enforce any such monetary unity in his empire. [3] The old mints continued in service as before, most of them in the western part of the empire. The ruler's treasury and the state treasury remained the same as it was under the Achaemenids, while corruption and dishonesty among officials, unfortunately, was not ended with a new ruler.

One may detect the direction of several reforms which Alexander might have carried out had he lived. The desire for a tripartite division of authority in the provinces or satrapies between civil, military and financial officials probably came into existence in his time in a few cases, but Alexander did not systematically institute this reform throughout the empire. Even under the Achaemenids a division of authority in the satrapies frequently appeared so this was not a completely new idea of the conqueror. There is not enough definite information to come to any conclusion about Alexander's activities in reorganising the provincial bureaucracies, for he died too young to carry out any overall plans he may have had.

A word should be said about Alexander's officers, surely as capable a group of lieutenants as any commander of an army ever had. As Alexander's conquests continued the old generals of Philip yielded the stage to equally capable younger men, companions of Alexander. We know best the generals who later became famous in their own right, such as Ptolemy, Antigonos and Seleucus, but there were many others. They were worthy

147

followers of a brilliant commander, working together for a common goal, but as soon as Alexander was dead each sought to exalt his own star to the detriment of the others.

Much has been said about the significance of Alexander the Great in history, some writers exalting him as the epitome of Greek freedom and democracy opposed to Oriental despotism or tyranny. It is true for example, that Alexander in general supported the democratic factions of the Greek city states of Asia Minor against the tyrants who were for the most part partisans of the Persians, but one should not forget that in the eyes of many Greeks Alexander himself was the arch-tyrant, the real enemy of Greek democracy. While one might argue for Alexander's real belief in democracy for the Greeks, an extension of this to include the peoples of the Orient is most unlikely. Even Alexander's support of democracy among Greeks can be explained on the grounds of political expediency, and one can hardly bring Aristotle, Alexander's teacher, to support a learned appreciation of democracy in his pupil. One may ascribe this belief in an antithesis between Alexander and the Orient, explained as a symbolic manifestation of the antithesis of democracy and tyranny, to the fancies of later writers.

The idea of a fusion of peoples in one world may be more safely attributed to Alexander, for we have mentioned his policy of inter-marriage and appointment of Orientals to positions of authority. The related concept of the brotherhood of man is not so obvious, although Tarn (p. 434) has prepared arguments for this belief of Alexander's, thus making him far ahead of his time. Whether Alexander, not only by his deeds but also by his ideas, influenced several philosophers so that he is to be considered the real originator of the ideal world state of Zeno's Stoicism, cannot be proved. At least the very extent of his conquests must have greatly impressed not only his contemporaries but also future thinkers.

Alexander founded cities, the most famous of which was Alexandria in Egypt, and in these cities lived a mixed population. Yet the cities were basically Greek, ruled by Greek laws, and no matter what Alexander may have intended there was hardly an equality between Greeks and natives. There was indeed a community of culture on a Greek model, much as that of the Occident today which sets the pace everywhere in the world. We hear of Iranian youths trained in Greek fashion and, of course, natives were admitted into the army, but no one should mistake

148

Persepolis: 1 (*left*) The entrance to the Palace grounds; 2 (*below*) Shah's tented camp, which was used for anniversary celebrations

3 Lion and bull motif at Persepolis. This panel, showing a lion killing a bull, may represent some cosmic event, or allude to royal power

4 A rock-relief at Naqsh-i Rustam showing the investiture of the founder of the Sasanian Empire, Ardashir I, by the god Anura Mazda, who is represented in human shape. The Sasanians revived Zoroastrianism after its long eclipse

5 The captive Roman Emperor Valerian kneels before Shapur I

6 An Assyrian lion hunt

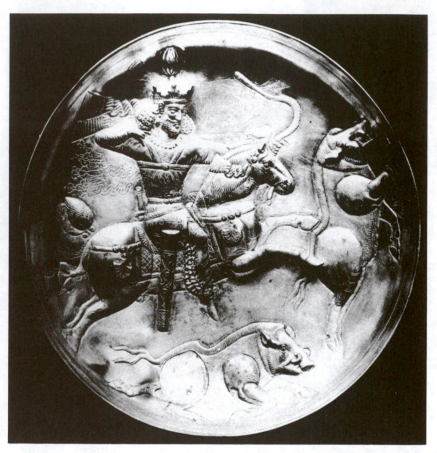

7 A silver plate of diameter 24 cm, showing King Perez hunting boars

8 Fragments from a Sasanian Palace: a stucco panel showing a boar hunt

9 The large Buddha at Bamiyan

the reality which was that Greece and its culture had conquered the world.

Most of Alexander's new cities were called Alexandria, but the former native names or new nicknames were in use to distinguish among them. Most of the cities, it seems, were in eastern Iran, but their number, as given by classical historians, is greatly exaggerated. Likewise the belief that towns did not exist in eastern Iran before Alexander must be discarded in view of Soviet archaeological excavations. Since Alexander had to fight more in eastern Iran than elsewhere the towns he founded were probably purely military centres for the control of strategic routes and they may have been based on Achaemenid garrison towns. The foundation of a real Greek *polis* took much time and Alexander was probably not the founder of many cities later attributed to him.

Hellenism, which has so many parallels with Westernisation in the Orient today, was thus begun by Alexander but carried out by his successors. The interplay of the forces of innovation and of traditional society are veiled in obscurity but they must have been in operation shortly after the death of Alexander in 323 B.C.

Seleucid Centralism

With the fall of the Achaemenid empire the Iranians lost the reality as well as the symbols, traditions and organisation of their central authority. Foreigners had become the arbiters of the royal destiny and the Persians turned to the local authorities for guidance and gave their allegiance to them. It seems as though the lower units of society, the extended family, the clan, and the tribe reasserted their influence after the collapse of the empire and nation. So the new foreign central authority based on professional, mercenary armies was faced with tribal or clan units of power and authority which, however, never seriously threatened the central government since they had no imperial pretensions. Only when the central government was weak and *its own provinces* prepared for independence, hence with royal or imperial claims, was the authority of the Seleucid king shaken. The Parthians, or rather the Parni as we shall see, however, can be described as a fortunate combination of both tribal and satrapal aspirations to imperial power which eventually succeeded in creating a new state on the remains of the Seleucid kingdom.

149

During the wars of the Diadochi some Greeks and Macedonians must have remained in both eastern and western Iran, guarding the trade routes and assuring some continuity to Alexander's conquests. Perdikkas, the successor of Alexander in authority, sought to maintain the unity of the empire as did Antigonos, 'the one-eyed', who brooked no opposition to his attempt to restore the empire under his own rule. At the death of Alexander we hear of two satraps: Peukestas, a Macedonian who adopted Persian customs and learned the Persian language, in Persis and Pithon in Media. They quarrelled and fought among themselves but the appearance of Antigonos on the scene ended not only any dispute but also both satraps. We find first an Iranian as successor to Pithon and later Nikanor, while a certain Euager served Antigonos as satrap of Persis. The situation changed again with the appearance of Seleucus whose entry into Babylon in 312 BC marks the beginning of the Seleucid era of reckoning.

From 311 to 302 BC Seleucus was able to destroy opposition and to lay the basis of loyalty to himself and his family in Babylonia and in Iran. He did well, for loyalty to the house of Seleucus remained strong among the Hellenes of the Orient even when the kings of the dynasty were busy in the west and in Syria, the real centre of their kingdom. We have no detailed information, but it was probably in this first decade of rule that Seleucus created a system of military colonies, including refounding centres which had declined and lost their importance, such as Ekbatana (Pliny VI.17) and Hecatompylos (Appian, *Syriake*, 57). Probably about 306 BC Seleucus secured the allegiance of Bactria and the eastern regions after a struggle, as one might guess from an incomplete phrase in Justin (XV.4, 'Bactrianos expugnavi'). That Seleucus did much fighting to secure the allegiance of the Macedonian satraps or local rulers is implied by a sentence in Appian (*Syriake*, 55) that after he acquired Media by killing Antigonos' satrap he 'fought many battles with Macedonians and barbarians'. About 305 BC Seleucus crossed the Indus river and met the new Maurya ruler of a united western India, Chandragupta (in Greek Sandrokottos). We do not know the course of events save that a truce was made between the two rulers after which Seleucus turned his attention to western opponents.

The most colourful account of the hostilities is given by Plutarch in his life of Demetrius, son of Antigonos, where he cites

150

the elephants which Seleucus had secured from Chandragupta as the deciding factor at the battle of Ipsus in 301 which ended the life of Antigonos and secured Seleucid rule in Syria and parts of Anatolia. Previous to this Antigonos had assumed the title of king, followed by Ptolemy and Seleucus, thus ending any pretence of the unity of Alexander's empire. Seleucus officially became king in 305/304 BC and ruled for twenty-five years when he was assassinated in Greece in September, 281.[4]

Seleucus had placed his son Antiochus, whose mother was an Iranian noblewoman, in charge of the provinces east of the Euphrates river (Appian, *Syriake,* 62), and it was probably more the initiative of Antiochus than that of his father which was responsible for the consolidation of Seleucid rule in the east. We hear that Antiochus rebuilt a city in the Merv oasis or Margiana called Antiochia, and he enclosed the oasis with a long wall to defend it against attacks primarily of nomads.[5] In addition he rebuilt two Alexandrias in Central Asia at Khodjent and Termez, and others as part of the Seleucid policy of colonisation which we shall examine briefly.

The Assyrians had favoured urbanisation while the Achaemenids were less known for this activity. Under the Seleucids and later the Sasanians, as we shall see, the founding of cities was an important function of the ruler. There was no fixed pattern of city founding by the Seleucids, but their purpose was primarily military and political, to ensure Seleucid rule by the establishment of Greek colonies in Asia where the colonists would owe their rights and security to the person of the king. Obviously there were not enough Greeks and Macedonians to control all of Asia by their settlements, especially since Ptolemy in Egypt, and other Hellenistic rulers, sought to obtain colonists themselves. For the Seleucids Syria with the capital Antioch, and the principal arsenal Apamea, and Babylonia with the eastern capital Seleucia on the Tigris, were the two centres of their power and interest. The third area of importance was western Anatolia, principally Ionia, the source of most of the colonists in Iran. Both western and eastern Iran were less important in the empire, although Media remained a valuable source of horses needed for the cavalry. The main routes of conquest and trade in Iran were secured by the settlements and the Seleucids effectively ruled only where settlements could ensure control; this was really much the same as under the Achaemenids. Many institutions of the Achaemenids, such as the road and postal system, were preserved virtually unchanged. The main feature which distinguished Seleucid from previous rulers was perhaps the system of colonisation by which the new rulers scattered Greek settlements throughout their empire.

It must be emphasised from the outset that there seem to have been no official or standard practices in the colonisation but rather varying policies according to conditions in the different lands and satrapies comprising the empire. We have a problem here for we must deduce a probable situation in Iran from sources dealing with Asia Minor or Syria. Much has been written about the Seleucid colonisation, but there is disagreement on the usage of various terms. In the eastern part of the Seleucid world the term *katoikiai* probably meant rural military settlements, the predominant form of Greek colonies. A *katoikia* was something less than a Greek city *(polis)* with all of its institutions and privileges. Unfortunately ancient Greek political theory does not apply to the Hellenistic age. For the ancient Greeks there was only the city and the village *(komē)*, while such forms of organisation as the *katoikia* or classical *politeuma* 'corporation' are not found.

In the Seleucid military settlements the colonists received their land from the king (*klēros* 'a lot') and their tenure on the land became hereditary. For this grant they were subject to military service, or rather the *klēros* had attached to it a military obligation which remained even if the land were sold. The colonists owed allegiance to the king and their fate in a sense was bound to his. Colonies, however, could become cities as, for example, Susa which became a *polis* with new rights and privileges almost making it independent of the king. The old military obligations in the *klēroi* of Susa, however, continued as the land remained in fief to the king.⁶ As Tarn has indicated, it was hard work to found a new *polis*, for the city needed an organisation, a division into 'tribes', and a council chosen from the tribes. Further, a subdivision into *demes*, a charter and, of course, a gymnasium were all necessary features of a city. The number of full-fledged Greek cities on the Iranian plateau was probably quite small; Raga-Europos near present Tehran, Baktra and Alexandria in Asia (Herat) may have been among them.

Since almost all of the Seleucids died on the field of battle the military character of the state must have been strong. Our literary sources are concerned mainly with the wars of the

152

Seleucids against the Ptolemies and other Hellenistic rulers. A remark of Strabo is singularly appropriate for all of Iran when he says in regard to Hyrcania, the land to the east of the Caspian Sea, that 'the Macedonians ruled over the country for a short time, but they were so occupied with wars that they could not attend to their remote possessions' (XI.509). We can investigate certain generalisations about the Seleucid empire as a whole, accepted by most scholars, which may be of some aid in guessing how the Seleucids ruled in Iran.

There was, of course, no national Seleucid state as we understand it today, but only subjects of King Seleucus. The king was the supreme judge, general and legislator of the realm and for many of his subjects he assumed super-human qualities. The question of the deification of Hellenistic kings has been much discussed and disputed, but it would seem that the adoption of various appellatives by early Seleucid kings such as *sōtēr* or *nikatōr* by Seleucus I and *theos* by Antiochus II, and others, should be understood on the whole as honours bestowed on them by grateful subjects as the result of a victory or a great service rendered to a city, province or a tribe by the king. Certain titles held by a king might be current in one part of the realm and not in another, or they may have been either in restricted or in widespread use. The question of the 'divinisation' of the kings should not be exaggerated especially for the early Seleucids, although later, with new religious and soteriological ideas rampant, the matter assumes a somewhat different significance. [8]

Of course the kings had various official titles and protocols, but we have no evidence of a dynastic cult of the ruler for the whole empire before Antiochus III (223-187 BC). This cult, in any case, applied primarily to the army, the court and the central institutions of the state, and it should not be confused with local honours of divinity conferred upon a king from the time of the first Seleucus.

The nerve-centre of the empire was the court where we find the old Achaemenid institution of the 'house of the king' *(oikos)* plus the 'friends of the king' *(philoi)*, which group was so prominent under Alexander the Great. The court was important since the rule of the Seleucids was highly personal. The court was large since the 'house of the king' included his relatives with their families, slaves, servants, altogether a great number of people. The office of prime minister, as usual, causes difficulties since under the active early rulers we do not hear of one. Under

153

Antiochus III a kind of vice-king does appear in a certain Hermias who is in charge of 'works', but who may have been a military as well as a civil officer.[9] There must have been a large chancellery, as under the Achaemenids, and we hear of the office of *epistolographos*, perhaps the head of the scribes. The organisation of the royal guard, the mercenary army and other central government institutions, however, is not our concern and we must turn rather to the local administration.

There was a political theory in Hellenistic times applied to the Seleucid empire, dividing the subjects of the empire into four categories: vassal kings, vassal dynasts, cities and peoples *(ethnē)*, the last represented, for example, by the Galatians in Asia Minor and by semi-nomadic tribes in Iran.[10] Whether this division was believed by the Seleucids and acted upon is uncertain; but surely all of the categories existed. There were tribes or peoples in the empire which were ruled by their own chiefs owing only nominal allegiance to the Seleucid king. We have no information about the Seleucid cities of Iran, but one can assume that in general they did not have the same independence or internal autonomy as did many of the cities of Asia Minor. Some of the Anatolian city states were really allies of the Seleucids with representatives at the court. It is doubtful if any of the cities in Iran were simply allies of the king, especially under the early Seleucids, although later we have the example of Seleucia on the Tigris which was practically independent. The local dynasts were local rulers who held sway over their domains as vassals of the Seleucid king. Such were the princes of Armenia, Media and others who held in their hands both civil and military power and acted as independent minor kings with courts like the Seleucid court.[11] The distinction between a satrap of the Seleucid king and a minor dynast was frequently very slight. Likewise the difference between a minor dynast and a vassal king is difficult to determine. Perhaps a ruler who was more independent or more powerful would be considered a king rather than a dynast in Hellenistic terms, unless there was really only one king, the Seleucid ruler, as one category among the rest, as has been argued by some scholars. The changing nomenclature and boundaries of satrapies and kingdoms throughout Seleucid rule makes the later Islamic designation of this period of history as that of the era of many local kings quite apt.

Tarn has shown that east of the Euphrates river there was a three-fold division of satrapy, eparchy and hyparchy, corresponding to the Egyptian *nomos, topos,* and village although it was much looser than in the Ptolemaic organisation.[12]

The eparchy was the most important subdivision of the Seleucid empire and when the latter began to disintegrate many eparchies became independent. The terminology, however, is again unclear; for example, Susa seems to have been an eparchy of the satrapy of Fars at least for a certain time, and the title of *stratēgos* given to the governor of that eparchy is frequently equated elsewhere with satrap.[13] Perhaps *stratēgos* 'general' was a purely military title of one in charge of a group of soldiers, and the title might or might not have been carried by a satrap and an eparch, or by one without any civil functions. In practice, probably, the functions of satrap and *stratēgos* were united in one person. The old Achaemenid satrapies of Bactria, Parthia, Arachosia, Media and Persis are mentioned as Seleucid satrapies in the sources but there were changes in them in the course of the empire.[14] The ambiguity of civil and military powers points, I believe, to the basically military nature of Seleucid rule, for the confusion of military and civil functions would apply to a time of wars and conquests and to a military-oriented state.

Taxes, as usual, were complicated, but in all probability again basically the Achaemenid system was adopted with few changes. The Seleucid satraps had to collect the land taxes from the landlords, and this tax was fixed as Darius had fixed the tribute on the various provinces. In the satrapies the assigned tax was divided among the communes rather than placed on individuals. Later the Romans replaced this fixed tax in the western part of the Seleucid empire by a *decima* or percentage of the harvest.[15] Other taxes, however, were collected by royal officials rather than by the satraps as had been the case under the Achaemenids. The central treasury had agents in the provinces to collect the customs tolls, salt tax, tax on slaves, etc., but here again practices must have differed widely not only between provinces but between cities, colonies and villages in the same satrapy. The cities would seem to have collected their own taxes for remittance to the central treasury. Local taxes and special levies for war also existed, while revenues from mines and royal factories were substantial. Booty from war and confiscations are known from the sources and both were important sources of wealth. Antiochus III lost his life when he tried to plunder a temple in Khuzistan, and such confiscations became more common as the dynasty declined and the rulers sought more

155

revenue.[16] Again, conditions in Anatolia or Mesopotamia may have been different from elsewhere; the sources show no uniformity.

The great innovation of the Seleucids in Iran concerned the city. Now in general terms the Greek concept of the *polis* was wedded to the ancient Oriental tradition of empire which finally produced the political syncretism of the later Hellenistic states. The growth of city state mentality, however, is a key to understanding what happened in Iran (and elsewhere) under the Seleucids. If we examine the basis of the theory of land ownership under the Achaemenids and under the Seleucids the change becomes apparent. Theoretically, the western conquerors found two kinds of land in the Achaemenid empire when they conquered it, king's land and temple land or 'land of the gods'. The king's land was subdivided into direct royal lands, which really meant state property such as mines, forests and royal estates, and what we may call 'feudal' land. The last was the vast majority of the lands and consisted first, of land occupied by local rulers or tribes over whom the king of kings had little effective control, and second, of estates of large landowners who held the land 'in fief' from the Achaemenid ruler. The peasants who tilled the land were usually attached to it as serfs who could not leave their domicile without permission of the landlord or state official. Temple land was owned by a temple and the peasants on that land paid taxes to the priest or high priest, who then remitted the taxes to the central treasury. Sometimes the temples were freed from paying taxes for various reasons. All types of land holding may have existed in a satrapy, although again conditions surely varied considerably from satrapy to satrapy.

In this matter the Seleucid kings assumed the role of the Achaemenid ruler, although perhaps in theory the temple land was considered another kind of royal land granted to the temple. Some of the old estates were given to Greek friends of the new king; others were broken up and distributed, while still others were preserved with the original Persian or other landlord. But the new factor was the grant of land to cities or to military colonies founded by the Seleucids. Land grants to cities came from royal land, either land formerly belonging to landlords or directly to the monarch, or even in a few cases from temple land, although on the whole the Seleucids did not molest the temples.[17]

The establishment of a Greek *polis* must have had a great influence on the surrounding country for the growth of city life is an undeniable feature of Seleucid rule. Even though there were few genuine Greek cities there were many imitations of the full-fledged *polis*. We have mentioned the military colony or *katoikia* (with *klēroi*) which was usually established beside a native village like the cantonments of British India. In time the native village and the settlement fused and a new Hellenistic *politeuma* came into being. Rather one should say a new collection of *politeuma*, for the *politeuma* was usually a community or a quarter of the city as, for example, the Jewish community in a quarter of Seleucia on the Tigris which was a *polis*. There must have been a great attraction among the natives to become Hellenic in culture and in time, of course, the Greek and Oriental elements did fuse. In the early Seleucid period the Greeks seem to have been jealous of their prerogatives as citizens of a *polis* or even as inhabitants of a military settlement, perhaps admitting only selected natives into the ranks of citizens, while the majority of natives were admitted into the city as part of a *politeuma*.[18] This situation gradually changed so that by Parthian times the citizens of the various cities were predominantly native everywhere in the east.

When a city acquired land with serfs the condition of the latter in many instances improved for many serfs became free, hereditary settlers paying taxes to the city. This may be considered the main basis for the social and economic changes which occurred under Hellenism, comparable to the later changes under Islam and to Westernisation at the present time. The Greeks who settled in Asia with their ideas of government, culture and art were the catalysts for change and change there was.

We have already noted that the Greeks did not try to Hellenise anyone; rather they taught by example. With supreme confidence that their way of life was the best in the world and superior to all others, the Greeks were not only tolerant, but actually fostered local cultures. Again a parallel with the British in India may be instructive. In Babylonia under the Seleucids there was a revival of cuneiform learning as we learn from the great number of clay tablets from this period dealing with astronomy, business transactions and above all with ancient hymns and rituals. The last cuneiform documents date from shortly before the birth of Christ. Together with this went a religious revival for the Seleucid kings patronised various temples.[19] Surely one of the factors which gave the Seleucids popularity among their subjects was their tolerance of native religions and the fostering of local cults, and one may assume that the situation in Iran was little different from Babylonia. Before turning to Iran, however, we should summarise the achievements of the Seleucids.

The influence of Hellenism, and of the Seleucids, in the East is perhaps most clearly seen in the spread of the Greek language and of Greek law. Many scholars have denied any appreciable Greek influence on Iran, and certainly it was far less strong there than in Syria or in Mesopotamia, but the discovery of Greek inscriptions and the recovery of the history of the Bactrian Greeks, for example, make a revision of this point of view desirable. Perhaps more significant than the discovery of a Greek inscription from Qandahar, Afghanistan, which will be discussed when speaking of the Bactrian kingdom, are the Greek inscriptions from Transcaucasia and the parchments from Avroman, Kurdistan. One is not surprised to find Greek inscriptions in Susa (Seleucia on the Eulaios) and Nihavend (Laodicea) where Greeks lived, but the legal documents in Greek from Kurdistan in which not a Greek name occurs, and the inscriptions from Armenia and Georgia where there were few if any Greeks, attest to the prestige and influence of the Greek language in Asia. It is true most of these inscriptions, as the Avroman documents, date from the Parthian period, but this would indicate the persistence of Greek which is even more impressive. [20] The same documents attest the popularity of Greek law which undoubtedly had a great influence all over the Seleucid empire.

Apart from the influence of language and law and such benefits of city culture as perhaps a systematic administration and even taxation, the Seleucids achieved a uniform currency, weights and measures, and a calendar. Only the king could issue coins, although cities could also issue special coins with his permission and in his name. We find gold, silver and copper (bronze) coins based on the Attic unit of weight which was 4.30 grams in the *drachme*. Because the Ptolemies, however, adopted a Phoenician standard of *circa* 3.60 grams, there were two mutually exclusive systems in the Hellenistic world. Gold coins for circulation were only struck under the early Seleucids; they may have been intended perhaps just for trade with India which trade later became difficult. Commemorative issues in gold are another matter and are found also under the later Seleucids, struck in honour of a victory or the like. Coin types are sometimes misleading. For example, coins with Alexander's portrait were

158

struck by various Hellenistic rulers long after Alexander, and Antiochus I began striking coins in Baktra for his father *circa* 290 BC, and he continued this practice into his own reign. [21] The usual reverse of early Seleucid coins was a seated Apollo, Zeus, or an elephant. Until the time of Antiochus IV the coins carry the simple legend 'of king n.n'. but afterwards epithets such as *epiphanēs, theos* and others appear.

Some Seleucid coins have been found with overstrikes by certain cities showing the independence of the city, because certain cities had special signs on their copper coins for local circulation, for example, the fortune of the city of Seleucia on the Tigris. [22] The Attic system of weights and measures was spread throughout the empire although it did not displace the local systems, but was used side by side with them. The Seleucid era system of dating from a fixed year is well known and needs no further elaboration except to say that it too did not displace other methods of reckoning but was supplementary. We may now turn to Iran to gather the fragmentary evidence of Seleucid rule there.

The sources for our reconstruction of Seleucid Iran are a few references in classical works, usually from a later period, coins and scattered archaeological data, a meagre collection. The geographical extent of the eastern part of the empire under Seleucus I may be outlined briefly. The cities founded by Seleucus or Antiochus I can give a general indication of where the early Seleucids ruled. Azerbaijan is singularly absent from any notice of the extent of Seleucid rule and Strabo (XIII.523) tells us that the satrap Atropates prevented the northern part of the land of Media, called Media Minor, from becoming subject to the Seleucids. Strabo further says that the capital was at Gazaka, identified by some scholars as the present site of Takht-i Sulaiman which, according to a recent archaeological survey, may have been a 'sacred place' as early as Median or even pre-Median times, while later, under the Sasanians, it seems to have had a dynastic and religious significance. [23] That Azerbaijan was not under direct Seleucid rule, though at times tributary, is further indicated by a remark of Polybius (X.27) that Alexander founded a ring of Greek cities on the borders of Media to protect it from the neighbouring barbarians.

We may assume likewise that the Caspian coastal lands of Gilan and Mazanderan were not under Seleucid rule. Armenia, to the west of Azerbaijan and closer to the Seleucid heartland, though also independent, was probably more subject to Seleucid

159

influence and at times also tributary. Hyrcania to the east and south-east of the Caspian was subject to Seleucus I (Appian, *Syriake* 55) but with the rise of the Parthians not long after his death it was lost to the Seleucids. Khurasan was also lost to the Parthians and to the Bactrian Greeks, while Bactria was a special problem. To the south the Seleucids held on to Khuzistan, but they probably lost control in much of Persis after Seleucus' death. Kirman, the Makran areas and beyond were hardly under Seleucid control. What then did the Greeks rule?

It seems clear from the list of cities founded by the Seleucids that they were concerned with the route of communications and trade to their outpost in the farthest east, Bactria. We know that many cities were founded in Mesopotamia especially around the Persian Gulf, but in Iran, save for the exceptions mentioned below, the cities follow the road from Seleucia on the Tigris to Baktra. Pliny (VI. 116) says the city of Laodicea founded by an Antiochus was on the extreme limit (of Persis?), and he notes also an Alexandria somewhere in Kirman. Several other names in Ammianus Marcellinus and Ptolemy, because they sound Greek, have been designated as cities founded by the Seleucids although there is no firm evidence.[24] There probably were a number of military settlements of the Seleucids in Persis, for we hear of a satrap of Persis as late as Antiochus III, but numismatic evidence, however, would lead us to believe that Seleucid rule was not firm but rather existed side by side with or near a local dynasty.

Evidence of a prolonged and actual Seleucid occupation comes from Nihavend, where inscriptions of Antiochus III and artistic remains have been found.[25] Ekbatana, Behistun and other sites on the road from Seleucia are also attested as Seleucid centres. Likewise we have a number of cities of Greater Media collected by Tscherikower. Few of these cities can be identified with present towns, but the striking impression one gains from a list of Seleucid cities is that they were indeed strung out along the road to Bactria with the greatest concentration of them in the farther east. One comes to the conclusion that Isidore of Charax in his *Parthian Stations* is not only following the post road to the east but also the line of Seleucid settlements. This means that northern and southern Persia were separated by the Seleucid line of cantonments to the east. One may assume that the different local traditions of the once unified empire of the Medes and Persians would develop independently under the aegis of the now

160

dominant culture of Hellenism with perhaps a nominal suzerainty of the Seleucids as well. The future history of the Parthians may be interpreted in the light of this Greek wedge between north and south. When Antiochus VII in 130 BC tried to restore Seleucid rule in Iran it was to Ekbatana, the chief city of Media that he went to establish his base, for this is where support for the Greeks could be found. Unfortunately he alienated the people who supported him and Seleucid rule was permanently ended not only in Iran but in Mesopotamia as well.

The Hellenistic Heritage

At the time of Alexander's conquest Aramaic was still the *lingua franca* and the language of bureaucracy in western Asia, but Greek had already made inroads on it. From what we have said above it would be natural to assume that the old tradition would have continued in those areas of Iran not subject to direct Seleucid rule while Greek would have become dominant in the areas of Greek colonisation. In support of this we have the few Greek inscriptions from central Iran and a lack of any other literary evidence in the pre-Christian era. On the other hand we have interesting evidence for the coexistence of both Greek and Aramaic in the farther east. The important bilingual inscription of Aśoka from Qandahar implies that even in a part of the Maurya empire where presumably Greeks and Iranians were settled, Aramaic served as the means of writing for the Iranians.[26] Fortunately, all the material on the use of Aramaic in Iran and the development of Middle Iranian languages and scripts has been assembled, from which one may draw historical conclusions about writing in Iran in this period.[27]

In my opinion, the historical process of the use of writing in Iran under the Seleucids can be reconstructed somewhat in the following manner. The Seleucids, as we know, retained Persians and others, as did Alexander, in the government of their empire. The process of creating a Greek chancellery and bureaucracy for the empire must have taken some time, and it would seem that a dual 'bureaucracy' existed at least in the eastern part of the empire, in Greek and in Aramaic, the legacy of the Achaemenids. In order to communicate with their subjects the Seleucids needed some form of writing, and this was naturally Aramaic. When Aśoka wished to write an inscription for the inhabitants of the Qandahar area he had to write it in Greek and Aramaic, since the local spoken Iranian language obviously was not written. I

161

suggest that this imperial bilingual inscription, as well as the bilingual of Mtskheta in Georgia, reflects the reality of this duality of the bureaucracy and not just a desire to write in two classical languages. In Mesopotamia where presumably Aramaic dialects were spoken in this period we find seals, bullae and tablets reflecting this duality. The two names, native and Greek, used by Hellenised Babylonians again attest the duality. Undoubtedly there were Aramaic-speaking scribes, both of Mesopotamian and of local origin in Iran, but presumably they followed the old Achaemenid system of 'reading off' the Aramaic inscriptions or documents in the local language to the local people.

The problem then is when did the system of writing of Aramaic with Iranian loan words change to a system of Iranian with Aramaic ideograms? It must be emphasised that the interpretation of the document or inscription was the same in both cases; it was read aloud in the local dialect. One may argue for a long and gradual development from the Aramaic of the Taxila and Qandahar inscriptions to the inscriptions of the early Sasanian kings where the system of ideograms or heterograms is well established. The Aramaic inscription of Aśoka from Pul-i Darunta or Laghman in Afghanistan with its Prakrit vocabulary of more than just a few 'loan words' would indicate a possibly early transition to the ideographic system of Middle Iranian, but in this case we are dealing with the Indian border-lands and a Prakrit tongue. The development of Kharoshthi writing from the Aramaic script in north-west India would raise a natural question why the Iranians did not follow suit and write their language alphabetically. The answer may well lie in the retention and support of the Achaemenid Aramaic chancellery by the Seleucids. I suspect that the normal development of writing in Iran was retarded by the policy of the Greeks, or rather one should better say that the support of the old system by the Greeks kept the use of 'bureaucratic' Aramaic side by side with Greek.

The next question is the time when we definitely have the end of Aramaic and the writing of Iranian with ideograms. This is, of course, difficult to answer but one may hazard a guess that in Afghanistan Aramaic writing vanished with the spread of Kharoshthi together with Greek. The coins of the later Bactrian Greeks are in Greek and Kharoshthi, not Aramaic. A rough guess for the disappearance of Aramaic in the farther east would be *circa* 200 BC. Probably the Iranian reaction, on the other hand, is later here than in the west, for the use of Greek letters to write Iranian in Bactria may well have been started by the Kushans, and probably by order of King Kanishka, at the end of the first or beginning of the second century AD. On the other hand, the Iranian reaction would be earlier in the Parthian homeland than in Bactria since the ostraca from Nisa near Ashkabad in Turkmenistan are in Aramaic but to be read surely in Parthian, mainly dating from the first century BC when Hellenism already is being weakened by a strong Iranian cultural movement.[28] There is no evidence that the Seleucids attacked native tradition in favour of Hellenism, but rather the contrary, and the decline of Aramaic and the rise of local systems of writing may parallel the decline of the Seleucids and the lack of a centralised imperial bureaucracy where the old Achaemenid tradition could be preserved. The local rulers went their various ways in the matter of bureaucracy and writing, and some of them probably more conservative than others.

Something more should be said about the Seleucid bureaucracy, and especially in some detail about the seals and bullae used by officials. Seleucid seals and seal impressions have been found in the excavations of Seleucia on the Tigris, in Uruk. and elsewhere, and various studies of them have been made.[29] Rostovtzeff described the two systems of sealing documents in Seleucid Babylonia, corresponding to the two bureaucracies there. One was the old Babylonian method of clay tablet and 'envelope' with the seals of individuals, witnesses or others, impressed on it. The other was the Greek system of sealing a rolled or folded parchment or papyrus with clay on which seals were impressed. There was, however, a third system already used under the Achaemenids which combined cuneiform clay writing with parchment Aramaic writing. The cuneiform clay tablet was apparently attached by string to a copy of the same document on parchment or papyrus in Aramaic. This, we remember, may have been the form of the records in Persepolis, in Elamite and Aramaic. Under the later Seleucids a modified form of this last system of writing finally dominated the other two systems, although the cuneiform system declined together with the cuneiform writing itself. The document, written probably on parchment rather than on Ptolemaic papyrus, was bound with a string and a lump of mud was pressed into the string around the document giving a napkin holder effect. The seals of witnesses, the owner, or others were impressed on the clay and the document

163

was deposited in the archives. By the time of the Sasanians this method of sealing documents is further modified so that instead of a napkin ring around the document, the ends of the string pass through a flat lump of clay which then hangs from the document as did many seals in Western Europe until recent times. Incidentally, the anchor seems to have been a sign or symbol of the Seleucid dynasty as revealed on many impressions.

Further discussion of the fascinating and informative subject of seals would lead us into much detail, but a few more words about them would indicate their value as sources for economic and art history. The Greeks used a man's profile, an animal or pictorial design on their private seals, and as far as we know, never exclusively writing, as did, of course, later the Muslims.[30] The Seleucids followed this tradition but they added a new feature that only their official seals had exclusively writing or monograms.[31] Later, probably following Oriental practice, one finds pious ejaculations on Greek seals with figures from Seleucid times, but there was a rather clear division between private and official seals, although some official seals too were uninscribed, being differentiated from private seals by style, size or figure represented.[32] This tradition continued into Sasanian times when the bullae and seals with writing alone represented are official seals, frequently of great value for the topography and the history of the period. These seals will be met with later, but their study indicates the continuity of much bureaucratic practice from Achaemenid times through the Sasanians.

We may assume that the influence of Greek law also increased the need for an expanded bureaucracy, while the almost constant warfare of the Seleucid rulers ever brought about new taxes and levies. For example, taxes on the import and sale of slaves may be an innovation of Antiochus I, who seems to have been the real organiser of the Seleucid administrative system.[33] A salt tax and various other taxes served to fill the coffers of the government, local as well as central, and presumably such taxes applied to Iran as well as to Mesopotamia and the rest of the empire.

Polybius wrote:
'I ask you, do you think that fifty years (sic) ago either the Persians and the Persian ruler or the Macedonians and their king, if some god had foretold the future to them, would ever have believed that at the time when we live (circa 160 BC), the very name of the Persians would have perished utterly — those who were masters of almost the

164

whole world — and that the Macedonians, whose name was formerly almost unknown, would now be lords of all.'[34]

So it must have seemed to the classical world, but to the Orient memories were longer. It was not only in Persis, the homeland of the Achaemenids, that ancient traditions were preserved, but also in the various satrapies where in the time of the king of kings the local courts had aped the imperial splendour of Susa or Persepolis.

After the Macedonian conquest no doubt many of the local rulers continued much as they had existed before Alexander. Perhaps the best known example of the continuing Persian traditions was in the court of the small dynasty of Commagene. At the site of Nimrud Dagh, shortly before the time of Christ, the kings Mithradates Callinicus and Antiochus, his son, proclaimed their descent from the great Darius in a series of colossal ancestor statues and inscriptions.[35] At the same time the syncretism of the religious beliefs is revealed in the reliefs showing various Oriental deities identified with Greek counterparts. For example, on one famous relief Zeus is identified with a Semitic Bel and an Iranian 'Religion of the Mazdayasnians', perhaps a euphemism for Ahura Mazda. We know that Iranian influences were strong also in Pontus and Cappadocia; then how much more they must have been in the homeland. These were local, provincial courts away from the centres of Hellenism, yet they must have been influential enough to preserve ancient traditions which would revive after Greek rule had ended.

The life of the majority of people in the Seleucid empire, especially the peasants, was little affected by the passage of armies or the life of the Hellenistic cities. It is probable that the Greeks learned more about agriculture, new fruits and crops, from the Orient than vice versa. We know that the Greeks called the peach by the name 'Persian apple', while the 'Medic apple' was used for the citron; and Medic grass was alfalfa. These and other borrowings were probably made during the Hellenistic age when contacts were close. We know much more about the Ptolemies than the Seleucids, but presumably the latter like the former were great patrons of learning, of inventions and material progress. At this time one such invention, the water wheel, may have spread from the western Iranian plateau.[36] Surely the Seleucids, as the Ptolemies, did much to promote irrigation and agriculture in their domains. The widespread use of cotton in the

165

Mediterranean area is probably the result of the aftermath of Alexander's conquests, while real Chinese silk also came into the Near East on a large scale at this time.[37] Procopius *(Persian Wars,* I.20) tells us that the silk was called Medikon by the Greeks of old, which at present, that is the time of Procopius, was called Seric. Undoubtedly the spread of Hellenism both eastward and westward opened new markets for international trade, exemplified by the great expansion of the cosmetics, dye and perfume trade, and the diversification of wine-making. In all of this activity the Iranians must have participated.[38]

At the same time that the native Iranian 'cultural' traditions were maintained, one may say that the influence of the Greek cities and settlements was not completely lacking in the countryside. In an age when Stoicism and other philosophies were popular, and ideas of utopias or the ideal state were in the air, we cannot dismiss the possibility that certain of the Seleucid rulers thought of themselves as great civilisers or law bringers to the whole world. Perhaps the great literary activities of such scholars as Euclid, Manetho, Eratosthenes in Alexandria, or Berossos, Megasthenes, and Diogenes the Stoic philosopher and Seleucus the geographer, both called Babylonian, in Seleucia on the Tigris, had but faint echoes outside the Greek intelligentsia, but one suspects that their influence was more than we know. Merely the external forms of life such as the gymnasia, the city government, the Greek way of life, must have impressed all who came in contact with them.

One matter of interest is the question of slavery in the Near East which was different from slavery in the Roman empire or in the pre-Civil War United States. Soviet authors have written a great deal about slavery in the ancient Orient, but attempts to find slave revolts and mass movements of slaves on the whole have not been successful. The reason is not difficult to find. The free tenant farmer or share cropper has been the basis of Near Eastern agriculture throughout its history, while the free artisan or skilled worker has dominated the crafts and industry.[39] The great latifundia of Roman Italy were not a feature of Near Eastern lands. When we survey the ancient history of the Near East, Iran included, we find that the economic basis of life remained surprisingly constant, and slavery was taken for granted. Unlike the slaves in the southern United States, however, the majority of the slaves in the Near East were of the same race and speech as their masters. Slavery was frequently the result of poverty and the transition from a slave to a free status and vice versa was not overly difficult. A man could sell himself or members of his family into slavery to raise money for indebtedness. Of course, there were many forms of slavery with a complex of obligations, rights and the like, and the cuneiform documents of Mesopotamia are full of legal provisions for slaves, including guarantees against escape or contingencies in case of death. A slave could be adopted, manumitted, or could buy his freedom, for slavery was primarily a monetary affair; the slaves were chattel and could be used as money, barter or as security in the case of loans. Although the majority of the slaves were domestics, the line between a household slave, and one who tilled the soil, or for that matter between the slave and the freeman, was not sharply drawn. By Achaemenid times we find slaves who own real estate, who possess their own slaves, have their own seals, or who are legal personages paying a head tax to their masters in lieu of service, or paying a percentage of profit made in a business. The price of slaves rose through Achaemenid and Seleucid times to such an extent that free hired labour became cheaper. Slave labour on estates could not compete with tenant farming, and likewise free, skilled labour was more economical than slave, skilled labour. So by Seleucid times the proportion of the slave population to the free population of the empire was probably less than before, save for temple slaves and state slaves.

In the Seleucid empire it would seem that temple slavery and state slavery became more important than the third type, domestic slavery. There always had been dedication of children or domestic slaves to slave service in a temple and consequently Alexander the Great found many large and important temple estates with many slaves who worked on the fields or who served the priests in one capacity or another. Again the conditions of temple slavery varied considerably and legal problems abounded. Dedication to a god sometimes served as a safeguard for treatment of a domestic slave in that after a certain length of service for a private master the slave would go to the temple, which in any case considered the slave as temple property even when first leased to a private master.[40] We know from classical sources that prisoners of war were frequently dedicated to the service of a temple, but in general war captives became state slaves or the property of the king.

Slaves for the king could be purchased on the market, but state projects such as road building were usually carried out by

167

corvée labour, as well as by prisoners of war. Private slaves, of course, as well as the free population, were subject to *corvée* labour, and in Seleucid times in cases of the sale of private slaves we frequently find stipulated in the contract that the slave had already performed the state *corvée* demanded of him.[41] One important industry in which slave labour was extensively used was mining, where conditions of work were hard and dangerous. Here many prisoners of war were used.

Although the proliferation of temples in the Seleucid empire increased temple slavery, it would appear that private slavery declined otherwise. The new philosophies and religions seem to have been more humane and manumissions on the part of owners became more frequent. Furthermore, in regard to Iran, it seems that slavery was never as widespread or as important as elsewhere in the Near East. Of course, slavery continued to exist in Iran, but we rarely find masses of slaves as on the Roman estates.

To turn to the domain of fine arts, in Seleucid art and architecture we can trace native traditions, pure Greek forms and the hybrid of both. This is not the place to detail the characteristics of and differences between Greek art and Oriental art, the former perhaps more concerned with natural representation, the latter with illusion and symbols.[42] A reconstruction of the course of art history in Iran may supplement our picture of political and social development in this period. Since Greek artists were known at Achaemenid Susa and Persepolis, influences surely existed before Alexander. Achaemenid art, as we know it, was a royal art, the style of the court, which in many ways summed up the various ancient traditions of the Near East, just as the Achaemenid empire encompassed so many different subject-peoples. Greek art, on the other hand, had no imperial background but could be termed 'popular', concerned with the mythology of the people and with cult practices. At the same time in the Achaemenid empire the Semitic peoples and the Egyptians had flourishing local arts which also were concerned with myth and rites, whereas a 'cult art' seems to have been lacking among the Iranians. With Greek replacing Persian rule, we find in Egypt a native Egyptian art and culture flourishing in the temples and in the countryside while in Alexandria Greek culture was dominant. The same was true in Mesopotamia where, for example, Uruk, a centre of old Babylonian astrology and religions, flourished side by side with Greek Seleucia. In Iran, however, the situation was somewhat different for the Persians

168

with their imperial art had been the masters and now the Greeks became the rulers and had to create a new, imperial style. Hellenistic art is different from classical Greek art with its strict conventions. It has been suggested by some scholars that classical Greek art was more concerned with naturalism, with telling a story, or even with religious symbolism, while Hellenistic art is more concerned with creating an illusion.[43] It may be true that art takes a course parallel with the development of religion and politics, and that much of what in Hellenistic art is different from classical Greek art is not just the result of external Oriental influence, but of internal changes in Greek society. Consequently, at the beginning of Seleucid rule we may have had a new Greek art side by side with old Oriental arts in various parts of the old Achaemenid empire.

Because Iran possessed the imperial traditions, the process of fusion of old Oriental, primarily Iranian, elements and new Greek elements into still another hybrid style of art probably took place sooner in Iran than in Syria or Mesopotamia. But other elements were added to this fusion in the first century BC, both in Iran and in the eastern Mediterranean. In Iran it was the introduction of new cultural traditions from Central Asia, principally Parthian, which created a new court art in the service of new Iranian kings.[44] In the West it was, of course, the Romans who brought about the development of a new Graeco-Roman art. Both marked the end of the Hellenistic age.

As in art, so in religion one may distinguish between old Oriental beliefs, new Greek cults and the syncretistic mixture. But just as in art, the syncretism in religion was ended in the eastern Mediterranean by Rome and by Christianity and in Iran by a revival of Zoroastrianism under the Parthians and Sasanians. We have already mentioned Seleucid encouragement of ancient Babylonian religious rites and beliefs. Presumably the same applied elsewhere in the empire, including Iran, except again for the fact that the Persians had been the previous rulers and now new masters were on the scene. In many cases this changed status favoured a co-operation between the two and led perhaps to more of a synthesis than elsewhere in the former Achaemenid empire. The parallel with the later Arab conquest of Iran is instructive, for in both cases the Persians were more apt to join the conquerors to share in the rule than other peoples who held more tenaciously to their customs. This characteristic adaptability of the Persians has been noted by many ancient and modern writers.

Because of this, and other factors, one may assume that Zoroastrianism, whatever its influence or status may have been at the end of the Achaemenid empire, declined under early Seleucid rule. Later Parsi tradition calls this a black period in the history of the good religion and it probably was so. It would seem that Zoroastrianism in some form continued in Fars province and elsewhere, but soon the Graeco-Iranian syncretism overshadowed everything as a kind of *Zeitgeist*. The Parthians, however, probably put religious matters into a harmony with the changed times leading up to the Sasanian state church of later times.

In discussing the syncretism of the Hellenistic age, again we are not concerned with inner Greek developments, but the focus of interest will remain on Iran. As has been mentioned in our discussion of religion under the Achaemenids, we can hardly speak of a particular 'Iranian' religion as we speak of the ancient Egyptian religion or even classical Greek religion. For the Achaemenids had been too much under the general influence of the indigenous non-Aryan people of western Iran and Mesopotamian culture to escape their religious influences. For example, the cult of the ancient Mesopotamian goddess Nanai had probably already coalesced with the Iranian Anahita in later Achaemenid times to spread far and wide.[45] The Anahita-Nanai relationship is not clear, and the problem is not helped by the simultaneous use of both names, probably considered as two goddesses. The spread of the Anahita-Nanai cult was far and wide, for we hear of a Sogdian called 'the slave of Nanai' in Chinese Turkestan in the early fourth century AD, as well as of an estate of the temple of Nanai in Nisa, Parthia from the second century BC.[46] The importance of the cult of Anahita in Armenia and western Iran is well known, while that of Nane, as she is called in Armenian, is more obscure. It would seem that in Armenia, probably in the late Seleucid period, Nane and Anahita both were identified with Artemis, but Agathangelos, in considering the beginning of the fourth century AD, still distinguishes between temples of Anahita and of Nane.[47]

Another cult which was widespread in the Seleucid domain was that of Heracles, as evidenced by the number of statues of him found. In Armenia he was identified with Vahagn, the national hero, prototype of the Iranian Verethragna, later Bahram. In Bactria he seems to have been identified with Śiva, at

170

least by certain worshippers there. [48] There was also a connection between Heracles the hero-god and the cult of the divinised Alexander, and, of course, Heracles was the patron of gymnastics. The Ptolemies of Egypt, in their religious propaganda, traced their origin to Heracles as the Seleucids did to Apollo, The role of Heracles as a kind of dynastic patron, however, is not clear. It would seem that Heracles was especially popular among the masses as a kind of power symbol, but as wars increased, prices rose and poverty increased, gods of healing and salvation came to the fore [49]

Among the Greeks of the Hellenistic age one might trace the growing popularity of saviour religions to the decline of that expression of Greek genius — the city. For in classical Greece the *polis* was more than a political entity; religion was a civic affair and exile from the city meant moral and religious as well as a political exile. Hence to be exiled from one's city was a great tragedy. In Hellenistic times, even though most of the rulers sought to maintain and foster the old Greek institution of the city, none the less the individual became more and more detached from his group, which comprised the citizens of a *polis*, and his allegiance in matters religious turned to 'individualistic' cults. This is a feature of late Hellenistic and early Roman-Parthian times, and Christianity was only one of many soteriological religions of the age.

The cult of the ruler also assumed a more religious significance at the end of the Hellenistic period when epithets such as *sōtēr* and *epiphanēs* appear frequently in the titles of rulers. Since the city gods had lost their importance, the kings took their place. Probably it began with the divinisation of the ruler who had founded the city. The divinisation of the rulers was now not just an honour, or a juridical aspect of the rights of the king over citizens of a *polis*, but an assumption of the position of the god in a city, though now in an empire. Divinised rulers were placed in the pantheon with other gods, but in a sense they were the immediate forerunners of the saviours and messiahs of new cults.

In Iran a similar development of religion must have transpired among the Greeks settled there. Likewise the growing belief in *'Tyche'* 'fortune', as well as increased belief in demons, must have obtained, and a corresponding development among the native peoples can be assumed. The early part of Hellenism is characterised by a separation of Oriental and Greek cultures,

171

while later Hellenism is syncretistic. Just as the religion was syncretic, so also was literature with such productions as the fantastic Alexander romances, the book of Enoch, and the like. An allegorical and even mystical interpretation of old texts comes into vogue and Berossos interprets old myths in allegorical form. Furthermore, the old gods now become humanised. Oracles, books of magic and zodiacs abound, while theosophy takes the place of philosophy. The early philosophers had been interested in science and cosmology, but by the first century BC, they turn to the fate of the soul and man's relation to the gods. The interest in magic and numbers is well illustrated by neo-Pythagoreanism, where numerology becomes a means of controlling the fate which controls man's fortunes. Perhaps one may generalise on a large scale and say that the later Hellenistic period is one of pessimism, a world where the bankruptcy of both the rationalism of the Greeks and the ancient institutionalised authoritarian religions of the Orient is manifest. And the way out of the dilemma for both is a saviour who is above reason and who abolishes the law. Saviour cults abounded, and among them only Christianity finally triumphed.

All of these developments were surely not limited to the Greeks, but applied to the native peoples as well. Similar trends in religion can be found in cuneiform tablets from Babylonia, but unfortunately elsewhere in the Seleucid realm literary evidence is lacking. In Iran, that part of the Avesta called the Vendidad reflects this age, although the text itself cannot be dated except approximately by the system of measurements in it related to Graeco-Roman measurements. [50] The history of the development of the text of the Avesta cannot be traced with certainty but we may presume that in the Seleucid and early Parthian period no fixed canon of the text existed, rather that various Yashts were being brought together by various communities in the syncretistic spirit of the age. The background for the spread of Mithraism in the Roman empire may be sought in this period. For the western Mithras, of course, was an Iranian god by origin although not one Mithras temple has been found on Iranian soil, nor is one ever likely to be found.

It is probable, as a detailed study has indicated, that the western Mithras had its roots in a *daevic* cult of the god as practised in Mesopotamia and Anatolia, and not in the cult of the Zoroastrianised Mithra in Iran.[51] The western Mithras is a saviour god in an era of saviour gods. There may have been

172

echoes of this western Mithras saviour cult in Iran, but we have found no traces of it and it cannot have played any significant role in Iranian religious history. On the other hand, neither can we assume that from the time of Zoroaster we have a Zoroastrian religion which evolves in a straight line, without changes, into the state faith of Sasanian times. Hellenistic syncretism, as well as other Iranian cults and Mesopotamian religions, must have influenced the development of the religion which we call Zoroastrianism. Fortunately, Mithra and the history of Zoroastrian doctrines have been discussed in some detail by Zaehner and others and need not detain us here.[52] In conclusion one may suggest that the religious situation in Hellenistic times in Iran ran parallel to the social and political situation which is only to be expected.

The Extended Cultural Area

Tarn has said that we should revise our concept of the term Diadochi, usually taken as referring to the four main Hellenistic kingdoms of the Seleucids, Ptolemies, Attalids and Antigonids, to include a fifth, the Euthydemids of Bactria.[53] He might have added a sixth, the Spartocids of south Russia, or more precisely the kingdom of the Cimmerian Bosporus. The Greeks in the Crimea and south Russia can be compared to the Bactrian Greeks in many ways, but primarily by their similar relationship to the Iranians, principally nomads, among whom their city states were erected. For the early Middle Ages in Europe, the south Russian background of the Goths, Vandals and other Germanic tribes is certainly important, and the Iranian influence on them was very strong. One must not forget, however, that the Greeks in south Russia had not been under Alexander's rule, and furthermore Hellenism had taken roots there long before Alexander. In spite of these and other formal differences from other Hellenistic states, the Cimmerian Bosporus was not isolated from the general spirit of the Hellenistic age.

The Greeks had established trading colonies in the Black Sea area from early times and their power and influence steadily grew. About 437 BC a certain Spartok established a dynasty of tyrants in Panticapaeum, capital of the Bosporan state. The Spartocids were probably of Thracian origin, for the local population was composed of Thracians as well as other peoples.[54] The dynasty lasted down to the time of Mithradates Eupator of

173

Pontus, who fled to the Bosporan kingdom after his last defeat by Rome. The Bosporan kingdom continued to exist, however, to the fourth century AD when it succumbed to barbarian pressure. There were, however, other Greek cities and states on the northern shores of the Black Sea and their history is a fascinating episode in the Hellenistic-Roman period, while their influence on the Scythians, Sarmatians and then the Germans should not be under-estimated. The story of the migrations of the Visigoths and Ostrogoths to Italy, Spain and North Africa, bringing with them Alans and other Iranian tribes with their art and culture, however, cannot be discussed. We are concerned only with the Iranians in south Russia, and even their long history cannot be detailed.

The vast Eurasian steppes from the Carpathian mountains to the Altai undoubtedly contained many tribes and different ethnic groups. If the Ural area is considered the homeland of the Indo-Europeans, one must consider Finno-Ugrian peoples to the north west and Turko-Mongolians to the east all in an unrecorded past. From classical and Chinese sources come many names and it is very difficult to link any of them with the archaeological remains which have been brought to light in recent years by the many Soviet excavations. On the other hand, there is a cultural unity to the steppes which have been likened to an enormous sea over which people may travel long distances. The discipline required for a nomadic existence and the rather complex pattern of such a life have made nomads the most formidable and feared enemies of all settled folk, while the migrations of tribes were probably better organised than the movements of the regular armies of the settled peoples in ancient times. The movement of tribes on the steppes has been usually from east to west, especially because the western steppe lands of south Russia were and are more fertile than those of Siberia and Central Asia.

To the settled people on the peripheries the steppes must have seemed as terrifying as the ocean appeared to mariners before Columbus. Information about the far reaches of the nomads was little and confused to the Greek, Chinese and Near Eastern peoples. All of these settled cultures influenced the inhabitants of the steppes, but the culture of the various peoples of Central Asia, Siberia and south Russia remained surprisingly uniform. The most characteristic feature of the art of the peoples of the steppes is the 'animal style' which, in objects from the graves of nomads in the Ordos region of North China, shows

174

strong Chinese influence, just as the objects from Scythian *kurgans* in south Russia reveal many Greek patterns. Also, just as the Gandharan art of north-west India may be divided into an earlier stone era and a later stucco period, so the steppe art of south Russia may be divided into an earlier monochrome 'Scythian' and a later polychrome Sarmatian style. The overall unity of style through space and time, however, remains; it is an art, or rather *the* art of the steppes. Let us briefly consider the history of the western steppes before turning to the eastern.

We cannot reconstruct the early history of the North Caucasus, the Kuban area, and South Russia except in broad statements of probability, although the continuing extensive archaeological work may make some surmises more likely than others. When the Iranian Scythians came from the east into south Russia in the eighth-seventh century BC they found the Cimmerians and other peoples in the area. Classical sources speak of the Sindi and Maeotic people living in the Kuban and Taman peninsula. Whether they were related to the Thracians or were Caucasian language speakers we do not know. Other than the linguistic, their ethnic or racial identification is difficult, for the Scythians themselves were ethnically mixed. [55] In later times we know of an extraordinary confusion of languages, tribes and peoples such as the Avars and pseudo-Avars, various Huns, and the Mongols of the Golden Horde in which state a Turkic dialect was used as the official language. In earlier periods we may assume the same confusion. If there was a settled Sindo-Maeotic state in the sixth century BC, the peoples of it must have been greatly influenced by the nomads who brought new weapons and a new culture on the scene. [56]

As mentioned before, the nomads of the Eurasian steppes were called Scythians or Sakas. It would seem that they were the first full horse-riding nomads whom we know in the steppes. They were mounted archers with short swords, and Herodotus, in his fourth book, tells much about them. In the seventh century BC they are already in south Russia between the Don and Dnieper rivers. We cannot discuss the interesting information about the religion of the Scythians, their elaborate burials with many slain horses interred with the warrior in his *kurgan*, and other customs told by Herodotus. Suffice it to say that archaeology has confirmed many of his stories. The art of the Scythians has also received much attention, and here again the Iranian feature of the predominance of decoration is apparent. Both Ionian and

Achaemenid Persian art influenced the Scythians, but since Bosporan Greek artists made many of the objects found in graves in South Russia for Scythians, the Greek influence on the animal style is the strongest. The very size of the Scythian gold objects in the Hermitage Museum in Leningrad is striking, a reminder that size was also a love of the inhabitants of Russia long before the expansion of the Slavs. In the fourth century BC there was apparently a movement of the Scythians westwards and northwards up the Dnieper and also into the Crimea. They were blocked by the Thracians, Celts and finally by the migrating Germans. From the east came a new Iranian people, the Sarmatians.

The Sarmatians are first heard of in Polybius (*circa* 160 BC) as occupying the area between the Don and the Dnieper. Great confusion regarding the Sarmatians has been caused by the name Sauromatians, mentioned by Herodotus (IV.21, 117) as an autochthonous non-Scythian people who spoke the Scythian language. Although the two peoples are not identical, it would seem that the Sauromatians were a mixed local and Scythian tribe who gave their name to the later Sarmatians.[57] The identity of the names Sauromat and Sarmat is likely, although the Ossetic etymology 'dark arm' proposed by Abaev is questionable.[58] In any case, the general term 'Sarmatian' covers the various particular tribes or confederations of tribes called Alans, As, Roxolani, and others who seemingly came to south Russia from Central Asia at different times. The written evidence for Sarmatian history in classical authors is so fragmentary and at times equivocal that we can be sure of very little.

One tradition of steppe or nomadic organisation of rule which may be mentioned is the 'royal' tribe or clan, leader of the others. This feature of a ruling group among the steppe tribes may be found in the 'Royal Scythians', in the position of the Kushans in the tribal confederation which invaded and ruled the Graeco-Bactrian kingdom, and among the Turks and the Mongols. It was probably also true of the Sarmatians, but we cannot say which tribe provided the 'royal' Sarmatian leadership. We should postulate several waves of Sarmatian migration from Central Asia to South Russia, and most scholars have sought to connect events in the west with the movement of peoples on the Chinese frontiers mentioned in Chinese sources. Before turning to the Far East, however, Sarmatian culture and history in the west may be briefly summarised.

176

It may be true that the first Sarmatian invaders of Europe were the Iazyges who lived farthest to the west about the Bug and Dniester rivers, but the geographical position of nomadic tribes can sometimes be misleading. The Iazyges later moved into Hungary. The Roxolani, whose name has been explained as 'light or shining Alans', may have been later migrants. [59] A Sarmatian centralised state was probably created about 125 BC which lasted some sixty-odd years, as Harmatta has convincingly described, and after the time of Mithradates the state probably fell to pieces. [60] Various Sarmatian tribes, speaking different Iranian dialects, came from the area east of the Don, and by the time of Ptolemy the whole of South Russia is called Sarmatia, European Sarmatia to the west of the Don and Asiatic Sarmatia to the east. [61]

The wars of the Roman emperors Vespasian, Domitian, Trajan and Marcus Aurelius, although they led to the annexation of Dacia, were primarily defensive actions against the Sarmatians and the Goths. Long before this, Pompey had fought against Alans in the Mithradatic wars while Josephus mentions them trying to invade Transcaucasia in AD 35. The Alans probably became the leading Sarmatian tribe and they are mentioned many times as invaders of Armenia and neighbouring regions in the second and third centuries AD. The later history of the Alano-Gothic migration to Italy, Spain, and even to North Africa with the Vandals, is well known. Less information exists about the relation of the Sarmatians with the Greek cities of the Black Sea such as Olbia, Chersonesos and the cities of the Bosporan kingdom. That these relations were close and important is attested by many items including the office of 'chief translator of the Alans' for the Greeks, found in an inscription from Taman and dated AD 208. [62] The relations of the Greek city states with Rome, the Scythians in the Crimea, the Sarmatians and the Goths is not our concern, but this was an important avenue of the exchange of ideas as well as wares, and the Iranians had a great influence on Europe, much of it through south Russia.

The Sarmatians, we are told, were armed in a different manner from the Scythians. The latter were light horsemen, primarily mounted archers, while the Sarmatians were knights in armour with the long sword, rather than the bow as their principal weapon. Because of the mounted Sarmatian knights, it has been suggested that the Sarmatians invented the stirrup, for its history cannot be traced before them, but it may be later in

177

origin.[63] The Sarmatian burials were far simpler than the huge Scythian *kurgans*, and the Sarmatians seem to have become more Hellenised than had been the Scythians. We find an interesting feature of Sarmatian society in the use of monograms or signs, later called *tamgas* by the Turko-Mongols. From the first to the fourth century AD we find a proliferation of these signs on all sorts of objects of silver, stone or other. [64] It would seem that these monograms were both personal (family) and tribal (or clan) marks, as were the well known Turko-Mongol *tamgas*. Each king or ruler in South Russia had his own monogram, a feature found also among the Kushans. One might conjecture, from the dates of their use and the area where they have been found in numbers, that the widespread use of monograms was brought into south Russia by the Alans and kindred tribes while related peoples brought them to Afghanistan and India. [65] This in no way means that the Sarmatians invented the monograms since a study of ancient monograms in general would have to account for Greek and ancient Near Eastern examples.

Because of archaeological finds and the lack of written materials, the art of the Sarmatians perhaps more than anything else has received attention from scholars. As has been mentioned, Sarmatian art differs from Scythian primarily in the use of polychrome techniques. Here again, polychromy is no invention of the Sarmatians, but a revival of styles and techniques which had never really died out in eastern Iran and Central Asia. The widespread animal style changed and ornament now reigns supreme, whereas in the Scythian animal style, more accurately one should say 'earlier animal style', there is some naturalism present. [66] Sarmatian art abounds in jewel-encrusted silver more than gold objects, with techniques the influences of which can be found in Germanic and western European art of the early Middle Ages. [67] Relations with the art of China, Siberia and north-west India about the time of Christ cannot be discussed here. Before turning to the Altai and the Graeco-Bactrian state a word must be said about the Alan-Ossete relationship.

It was long ago proposed that the contemporary Iranian-speaking Ossetes of the north Caucasus were descendants of the Alans. Generally speaking the Ossetes, who today speak two dialects, Digor and Iron, with a third dialect spoken in the recent past, should be descended from Iranians who lived in the North Caucasus area. Since the surrounding settled people have always designated all of the people of the steppes by a generic name at

178

various periods of history, first Scythian-Saka, then Sarmatian-Alan, then Huns, Turks and Mongols, one cannot say definitely that ancient Ossetic was the language of the Alans, but if one uses Alan in the widest sense then most probably modern Ossetic is descended from an Alanic tongue. Questions of the relations of the Alans with Khwarezm or Sogdiana cannot be definitely answered, while the etymologies of the words Iron, Digor, Ossete, have a large and controversial literature.[68]

Iranians were not only active in south Russia and the northern Caucasus, but also in Siberia, the Altai, Chinese and Russian Turkestan. In the Minusinsk area extensive archaeological work has revealed a series of strata showing long occupation by different cultures. Kiselev has studied the sequence of the Afanasiev culture on the Yenisei river in the third millennium BC, the Andronova epoch of the sixteenth to twelfth centuries BC, the Karasuk era 1200—700 BC, and the Tagar culture of 700—100 BC.[69] The last is characterised by the animal style in bronze and in bone. Although there are differences between the Minusinsk and the south Russian animal styles, local individuality can explain them, for the presence in the graves of a predominantly European population with a small mixture of Mongoloids, corresponds to the Scythian graves of south Russia.[70]

Perhaps the most spectacular discoveries in recent times in this area were made at the *kurgans* of Pazyryk, in the Gorno-Altai region of southern Siberia where rich, frozen tombs were uncovered. The oldest known carpet in the world with Achaemenian motifs (found in *kurgan* five), and many other objects of art, may indicate a flourishing trade with Iran, probably as early as Achaemenid times.[71] It is possible that there were not only extensive trade contacts but also that Iranians existed among the population of Pazyryk. The problems of the relations between the steppe-dwellers and the forest-dwellers of the Altai mountains have not been resolved, but Kiselev suspects that the Saka-Massagetai taught nomadism to the Altaic peoples of southern Siberia.[72] While we are not authorised to claim certain archaeological remains for Sarmatians, Alans or Massagetai, the excavations are filling in the abysmal gaps in our knowledge of Central Asia, and it would seem that the entire area from the Altai, or indeed the wall of China to Transylvania and Hungary had a kind of unity, and that Iranians played a most important role in this vast area for at least a millennium until the Hunnic

179

expansion of the early centuries of our era.

Trade has been mentioned and certainly the extensive trade routes across Central Asia in ancient times account for much influence between the Near East, south Russia and China, not forgetting the forests of Siberia and the steppes themselves. Rostovtzeff has studied the silver horse trappings or *phalerae* of this period and concluded that north-west India and south Russia had contacts, while literary sources confirm a lively trade between south Russia and India.[73] Furthermore, Bosporan coins of the Roman period have been found in graves in the Altai.[74] Chinese relations with the western countries have fascinated scholars for a long time, and while certain cultural phenomena indicate early contacts, we do not know of direct Chinese-Near Eastern trade contacts through Central Asia before the period of the Graeco-Bactrian kingdom in the second century BC. That Iranian peoples lived on the western borders of China is known from Chinese sources as well as from the literary remains of the Sakas from Chinese Turkestan. This brings us to the notorious 'Tokharian problem' and the Indo-European peoples of the western Chinese borderlands.

The 'Tokharian problem' cannot be discussed in detail for it is buried in a morass of conflicting data. After the decades since the discovery of the Centum Indo-European language named 'Tokharian', with several dialects, from the oases of the northern Tarim basin, can we come to any general historical probabilities about the people who spoke 'Tokharian' and their relations to the Iranians? No matter what the precise linguistic position of 'Tokharian' may be, related to the Celtic or Thracian group of Indo-European tongues or to other groups, we may assume that 'Tokharian' was most probably a very early intrusion into Chinese Turkestan before the Iranian expansion of the first half of the first millennium BC, rather than a late 'mediaeval' intrusion into the territory. In other words the 'Tokharians' were probably there before the Saka-Scythian expansion. To identify the 'Tokharians' with the Chinese Wu-sun and the Issedones of Herodotus is a conjecture based on purely circumstantial grounds, but tempting none the less.[75] There is really no need to account for any other Indo-Europeans besides 'Tokharian' speakers and Sakas in Chinese Turkestan before the Christian era; Sogdian traders and other Iranians from the west come later. One basic difficulty with Central Asia in the sources is that the Chinese writings are full and clear when dealing with Chinese Turkestan but beyond that are confused, while classical sources can help us a bit in West Turkestan but to the east are unreliable. If the Chinese and classical sources only could be correlated so that identifications could be made we might be able to reconstruct some of the early history of Central Asia.

From Chinese sources we learn that the expansion of the early Han empire caused a people called the Hsiung-nu on their frontiers to exert pressure on their western neighbours. The oft-quoted passage in the early Chinese historical work, the *Shih-chi* ch.123, tells us how the Hsiung-nu attacked the Yüeh-chih, killing their king, after which the Yüeh-chih migrated westwards and conquered the Sai. There the Wu-sun, vassals of the Hsiung-nu, attacked the Yüeh-chih again driving them to Ferghana and Bactria which they conquered.[76] It is difficult to identify the names and to place them in history, but we can assume that the Chinese sources (the *Shih-chi* and the annals of the Han dynasty as well) are reporting an historical event. Haloun sensibly dates the first migration *circa* 174-160 and the second 133-129 BC.[77] The Sai have been identified long ago with the Saka, while the Wu-sun, as mentioned above, may be the 'Tokharian' speakers, the Issedones of Herodotus. Possibly some of the Wu-sun were the Asianoi who were among the invaders of the Bactrian kingdom.[78] The problems of the later forms of words such as *tugr, arsin,* and the like, in Uighur and Sogdian documents, have been explained satisfactorily by Henning.[79] What language the Yüeh-chih spoke can hardly be decided; all we have are Saka and 'Tokharian' dialects in Chinese Turkestan, plus the indigenous Iranian language of Bactria (and Tokharistan). The various splinters or ethnic-linguistic fragments brought into settled lands by any and all migrations from Central Asia are common phenomena difficult to disentangle.

For our purposes it is clear that Iranians were active in Central Asia and Siberia, and that Iranian cultural influence in these areas was strong. With the Hunnic expansion, especially in the third and fourth centuries of our era, the pendulum begins to shift in favour of Altaic peoples and later to an overwhelming Turkish influence, not only in Chinese and Russian Turkestan but in south Russia, Azerbaijan and Anatolia. We should also not forget the Dardic or Indian dialects which may have extended into Central Asia in ancient times. Iranian-speaking peoples, however, seem to have been the dominant force all over Central Asia in the pre-Turkish period.

We are not authorised to reconstruct life in Bactria before Alexander on the basis of the Avesta. The latter might, however, be used as a check or corroboration of archaeological and historical data. Now that the dominant language of Bactria in the time of the Kushans has presumably been revealed from inscriptions, a new page in the history of eastern Iran has been opened. [80] The earlier period, however, awaits the work of archaeologists, and undoubtedly much can be expected in the future.

We have noted that Bactria was the central province for control of eastern Iran in the Achaemenid empire. This is also true during the Greek and later, incidentally, the Arab periods. Ionian Greeks may have been exiled to Bactria by the Achaemenid kings, but there is no evidence of a large Greek settlement there before Alexander. On the other hand Greek culture and certainly Greek coins were not unknown before Alexander and the invaders cannot have been regarded as strangers from another world. [81] It is clear that Alexander, after his extensive campaigns in Sogdiana, considered Bactria a necessary strong point or military centre of his empire in the east. The Graeco-Macedonian garrisons could well have been substantially greater here than elsewhere in eastern Iran. Since we do not hear of satraps or *stratēgoi* anywhere in Transoxiana under the Seleucids, we may assume that the governor of Bactria was the main representative of Seleucid power in dealings with the local princelings. The actual extent of Seleucid rule in Central Asia is unknown, but Sogdiana was probably subject to Seleucus I and his son Antiochus, for Pliny (VI.49) says that Demodamas, a Seleucid general, crossed the Syr Darya on a campaign. [82] With the well-known embassy of Megasthenes in India, the exploratory voyage of Patrocles on the Caspian Sea, and other indications, we may surmise that Seleucus and Antiochus were much interested in eastern Iran and ruled most of what Alexander had conquered. Most probably Bactria received new garrisons and especially families of colonists, the Greeks coming principally from Ionia.

The story of the formation of the Bactrian kingdom has received considerable attention, one might even say over-elaboration, of late. [83] The sources for the history of the Bactrian kingdom are a few short passages in Justin, Polybius, Strabo and Pliny, all much later than the formation of the kingdom, plus a remarkable series of coins. We have coins of almost forty Greek rulers in Bactria or north-west India, and some of the earliest are considered the finest specimens of Greek numismatic art. From the coins a comprehensive history of the dynasties and kings of the Greeks has been reconstructed. Unfortunately numismatists have been over-zealous in interpreting the complete dynastic relationships on the basis of undoubtedly valuable coins, but which are none the less limited in the information they have to give. This is not to say that the work of the numismatists is unreliable or unimportant. On the contrary, the coins are contemporary evidence and the work of the numismatists has proceeded on systematic principles with cautious deductions, but because of the extreme paucity of literary sources, their reconstructions can only be regarded as very tentative. For example, from the large number of rulers it has been generally thought that the Graeco-Bactrians had a system of sub-kings with their own courts rather than satraps like the Seleucids. There is no evidence, however, that the Greeks in Bactria departed from the usual practice of the other Diadochi, and while we have many examples of joint kingship reflected in the coins, we know of no system of sub-kings elsewhere. Furthermore, there is no reason to suspect that the Greeks of Bactria were any less warlike or quarrelsome than those in other Hellenistic kingdoms.[84] So it is likely that there were rival rulers issuing their own coins in the Bactrian area and that rivalries were common. Indeed, Justin (XLI.6.3) says that the Bactrians were weakened from having fought many wars, undoubtedly many among themselves as well as against local native rulers. It must be admitted, however, that one striking difference between the Bactrian Greeks and other Hellenistic kings is the number and variety of names of the Graeco-Bactrian rulers. There are very few similar names on the Bactrian Greek coins comparable to the frequent Seleucus, Antiochus and Ptolemy royal names. The work which has been done by the historian in this field can be compared to Avestan studies with their many keys towards understanding the text. Tarn arranges the Bactrian coins in some measure according to facial resemblances of the coin portraits, along with other factors, while Narain concentrates on the reverse types of the coins. If he finds Pallas Athena on the reverses of the coins of different rulers then they should be somehow related. Simonetta classifies the monograms on the coins and draws his conclusions primarily from them. The results are not the same but Narain and Simonetta, the numismatists, see more eye to eye than Tarn, and one feels that some progress is being made. We are not concerned here with whether there was one Apollodotus or two (probably two), or with disputed points of the temporal or geographic placement of names. [85] The two main problems of the Bactrian Greeks have been the chronology plus the geography, a matter for the numismatists, and their art and culture, the domain of the archaeologists and art historians.

It is generally agreed that the Graeco-Bactrians ruling north of the Hindu Kush mountains problaimed their independence of Seleucid rule under Diodotus I at about the same time as the Parthians did, possibly *circa* 246 BC. Now Diodotus may have been independent *de facto* long before this date but we do not know. Indications in classical sources would lead us to diametrically opposite conclusions: that the Bactrians revolted before the Parthians, or just the reverse. [86] It would be a reasonable guess that most of eastern Iran broke away from the Seleucids at the beginning of the reign of Seleucus II, who had great difficulties in the west with Ptolemy. It is probable that the satrap of the province of Parthia, to be identified with the Andragoras who struck coins, also revolted against Seleucid rule. [87] He did not last long, however, but succumbed to Arsaces, whom we will discuss below in dealing with the rise of the Parthians.

The real founder of the Graeco-Bactrian kingdom was one Euthydemus, who seized power, presumably after killing the successor of Diodotus I some time between 235 and 230 BC. Euthydemus was still king in 208 when Antiochus III marched against him and unsuccessfully besieged him in his capital of Baktra (Polybius X.49; XXIX.12.8). Peace was made and Antiochus retired over the Hindu Kush mountains where he met an Indian king, Sophagasenus, in the Kabul valley and made peace with him before returning to Syria.

Euthydemus probably ruled over some of the oases of Central Asia principally in Sogdiana, but we have no conclusive evidence how far the Graeco-Bactrian state extended northwards. There is a possibility that he led expeditions as far as Kashgar in Chinese Turkestan but rule beyond the Ferghana valley, if it included that, is unlikely. [88] Presumably Euthydemus ruled the Herat area and other oases, but again evidence is lacking.

After the death of Euthydemus, possibly *circa* 200 BC, our troubles begin, for the plethora of names on various coins makes the reconstruction of relationships and genealogies like a jig-saw puzzle. There were undoubtedly several ruling families and the geographical extension of Graeco-Bactrian power reaches south of the Hindu Kush mountains, probably beginning with Demetrius I and Antimachus I, successors of Euthydemus. We learn of a rebel who was successful against Demetrius II *circa*

184

171 BC, one Eucratides, who established himself and his successors as rulers of Bactria.[89] Other Greeks, presumably of the family of Euthydemus, ruled south of the Hindu Kush mountains or in Gandhara. Antimachus was the first king to strike square coins on an Indian model, while Demetrius II was the first to have Kharoshthi as well as Greek legends, indications of Indian connections.[90]

The real conqueror of India, however, was probably Menander who is the best known of the kings. His coins are the most plentiful and have the widest geographical range of all the Bactrians. Strabo (XI.516) says that 'more tribes were subdued by (the Graeco-Bactrians) than by Alexander, mostly by Menander'. Furthermore Buddhist tradition gives him an important role, especially in the *Milindapanha* which is supposed to be about him. He conquered Gandhara, including Taxila, and then extended his sway beyond to Swat, where an inscription relating to him has been found, and further into the Punjab, even raiding to Pataliputra.[91] This event may have occurred in the vicinity of 130 BC, but this is only an approximate dating. The Greeks seem never to have ruled east of the Ravi river in India, but minor dynasts lasted long in north-west India and maybe longer in the Hindu Kush.

I have suggested that there is no evidence for a system of sub-kings among the Bactrian Greeks, but there is evidence for satraps or *stratēgoi* and subdivisions under *meridarchs*.[92] The *stratēgoi* were probably as prone to rebel at signs of royal weakness as were their counterparts in the Seleucid realm, but it is more likely that after Eucratides, if not before, there were a number of 'Graeco-Bactrian' kingdoms in Afghanistan or north-west India. Menander was most probably a Buddhist and we should speak of him and other Greek rulers more properly as Indo-Greeks rather than Bactrian Greeks.[93]

The atomisation of Greek rule after Menander makes any reliable reconstruction well-nigh impossible. Eucratides had lost the western districts of Tapuria and Traxiane *circa* 160 BC to the powerful Mithradates I of Parthia.[94] The main blow to the Bactrian Greeks, however, came from Central Asian nomads, the Yüeh-chih of the Chinese sources. Before the Yüeh-chih, however, the Sakas were active and this has caused much confusion and trouble. It is now generally accepted that we are not to identify the Yüeh-chih with the Sakas even though unions of tribes or peoples were common in nomadic migrations. One vexing problem was how to reconcile the Chinese sources on the migrations of the Sakas with the brief classical notices on the

185

invasion of Bactria and with the coins. Narain gives a summary of a position which, I believe, solves more of the inconsistencies and problems than any other, and it is this position which we mostly follow here. [95]

According to Chinese sources, as noted above, the first migration of the Yüeh-chih took place *circa* 160 BC when they arrived in the Ili-Lake Issyk Kul region displacing the Sakas. Some of the latter went south to Kashgar, Gilgit and eventually to Swat and north-west India. The contention that geographical barriers made this route impassable to a large group of nomads is now considered untenable. So the Sakas, who appeared in north-west India and split the Greek kingdoms, probably came by this route rather than by any long western route. [96] On the other hand, it took almost a century for them to establish a kingdom in Udyana (Swat), for Maues, the first Saka king to issue coins in north-west India, is probably to be dated in the first half of the first century BC. The route followed by these Sakas is unknown although several suggestions have been made. [97] Other Sakas moved westwards and eventually came into the Herat and Seistan areas. These Sakas (using the term generically) caused trouble for the Parthian kings Phraates II and Artabanus II, *circa* 138-123 BC, both of whom were killed in fighting against the nomads. But we must return to the Yüeh-chih and the Bactrian Greeks.

The Chinese sources tell us further that the Yüeh-chih were attacked again in their new home in the Ili valley by the Wu-sun, after which they moved southwards and occupied Ta-hsia. Here a Chinese envoy, Ch'ang Ch'ien, visited them to secure an alliance against the Hsiung-nu, but he failed. Most of the Chinese information about the western lands probably stems from the embassy of Ch'ang Ch'ien to be dated *circa* 129 BC. The Sakas, as we have seen, had dispersed in two directions, to the south (and east) and to the west. Parts of the former group trickled down to north-west India while the main body, it would seem, remained in the Pamirs or in Kashgar and Khotan. The documents in Khotanese Saka, and in another Saka dialect from Tumshuq and Murtuq in Chinese Turkestan may be considered the remains of the ruling Sakas, while the modern Pamir tongues of Yidgha, Munjani and Roshnani show many Saka affinities. [98] It is most likely that the ancient Iranian language of Bactria was related to Saka, or at least underwent strong influences from Saka tongues, while the Saka invaders of India both from the north and the west most probably spoke Saka dialects. Therefore, we may conclude that Saka dialects were dominant in Iran *extérieur*, and that the Yüeh-chih probably played the same role vis-à-vis the Saka as, say, the Mongols did with the Turks in south Russia in the Golden Horde.

To return to the Chinese sources, Ta-hsia usually has been identified with Bactria, whatever the transcription or the meaning of the characters may be.[99] The Yüeh-chih then occupied Bactria, moving southward from north of the Oxus, and this occupation may be roughly estimated at *circa* 120-100 BC. Various Saka tribes had preceded them, some of them further occupying the Herat area, Seistan, Arachosia and India, but their story is connected with the Parthians. In Bactria one of the tribes of the Yueh-chih, the Kushans, succeeded in conquering the other four major divisions of the people and setting up a dynasty.[100] The Chinese sources are specific in their information about the Yüeh-chih since they had been former neighbours in Kansu and the Chinese evidently kept track of them and knew more about them than they did about other peoples in the west.

There are always problems of identification in Chinese sources, because the designations sometimes change and the same name may refer to another locality at another date, but in the case of the Yüeh-chih the later *Han-shu* (official history of the Han dynasty) says that the Yüeh-chih, or the Kushans as other people now called them, invaded An-hsi, which has been identified with Parthia (*an-siək* = *aršak)*, and then took Kao-fu, which on the basis of later identifications rather than phonetics has been identified with the Kabul valley.[101] Later the same source says that Kao-fu never before belonged to the Kushans, and the history of the former Han dynasty was in error when it put Kao-fu under the five Yüeh-chih tribes. Later Kao-fu fell under An-hsi, and when the Yüeh-chih defeated the An-hsi they took Koa-fu for the first time. This would indicate generally speaking, as Narain has seen, that the Graeco-Bactrians lost to the Kushans north of the Hindu Kush mountains and to the Parthians south of the mountains, while in India their domains were absorbed by the Sakas. This, of course, did not happen all at once. The Greeks north of the Hindu Kush may have been in some sort of tributary or vassal relationship to the Yüeh-chih when the latter ruled north of the Oxus river, while the situation in India between Greeks and Sakas is extraordinarily complicated if one tries to follow the coins. The key to an understanding of the sequence of rulers in north-west India is Taxila where extensive excavations have provided strata in which coins have been found, thus giving a basis for a rough chronology.[102] The first Saka king of Taxila was a certain Maues who seems to have come from Udyana. He was probably followed by two

187

Greek rulers Apollodotus and Hippostratos, then Azes, a Saka. [103] The dates, of course, must be conjectured, and perhaps Maues conquered Taxila *circa* 80 BC, and a few decades later Greek rule in India would be over. Whether some Greeks managed to rule afterwards in enclaves east of the Jhelum river is dubious, for the field was then open to other western invaders, western Sakas and Parthians, the Pahlavas of the Indian tradition. In the Hindu Kush, the Paropanisadai of the classical authors, the picture of the last Greek kings is also unclear. Hermaeus is usually considered the last king and his dates must be pushed to the vicinity of 100 BC. [104] A puzzling matter is the extent and variety of the Hermaeus coins, and the prevailing opinion now is that many imitations of his coins were made by later rulers using his name. [105] This would explain the coins issued in the name of Hermaeus and the Kushan ruler Kujula Kadphises; they were not contemporaries as hitherto assumed, and one can postulate an appreciable time lag between the two. In fact we may have to revise some of our conceptions of Saka-Pahlava coinage as a result.

Among the coins of the successors of the Greeks south of the Hindu Kush, we find a number struck with two names, for example Vonones and Spalahora, Vonones and Spalagadama, Spalyris with Spalagadama son of Spalahora, Spalirises with Azes, Azes with Azilises, Azilises with Azes. [106] In each case the former name is in Greek on the obverse while the latter name is in a northwest Prakrit tongue in Kharoshthi script on the reverse, similar to the coins of Hermaeus together with Kujula Kadphises. It has been assumed automatically that the ruler on the reverse followed the one on the obverse, but now we must hesitate. Obviously this matter needs further study and new material is necessary before one can reconstruct safely the genealogies or sequences of the rulers. Another problem, hitherto neglected, is the popularity of the coins of the Greek ruler Heliocles, for his coin types were imitated by probably non-Greek rulers north of the Oxus, [107] as well as by a group of Pahlava-Saka rulers south of the Hindu Kush. [108] All of this indicates the strong influence which Greek numismatic tradition had in the east, and as a corollary the long lasting influence of Greek art and culture in north-west India, Afghanistan and Central Asia.

It would seem that the Sakas in north-west India shared the fate of the Greeks, and the dynasty of Maues, Azes and Azilises was replaced by a new series of kings, the most prominent of whom was Gondophares; or possibly he was the founder of a new Pahlava or Indo-Parthian dynasty. Gondophares is a king known to Christian tradition in the *Acts of St. Thomas*, and he has been identified with Caspar of the Biblical three kings. [109] Consequently we are in the early Christian era with the Pahlava kings, and Gondophares must have ruled about the middle of the first century AD. This brings us to Indian history and complicated matters of different eras in inscriptions, something beyond the scope of the present book. There is no question, however, that Iranian influences were strong in north-west India and every invasion or migration from Central Asia brought new Iranians into the plains of the sub-continent.

In north-west India, in this late 'Hellenistic' period, there were three primary cultural and perhaps ethnic influences, Greek, Iranian and Indian. All three 'cultures' were seemingly strong and it is perhaps more possible to recognise them in the art of north-west India, the early and the late 'Gandhara' style, than in other fields.

Gandhara and Western Influences

Gandharan art is, generally speaking, the art of north-west India during the Kushan and later periods. The primary inspiration of this art is from Greece or the west although the art may be described as syncretic, a fusion of many influences. There are two major problems connected with the art of Gandhara, one more or less restricted to India while the other is also concerned with Eurasia. The former, put briefly, is the question of the prime western influence on the art of Gandhara, both the early stone (Kushan) and the later plaster and stucco (Hephthalite) style. One school maintains that Gandharan art is primarily the result of a provincial Roman style influencing Indian art. This view has gained currency with interesting comparisons between the art of Palmyra and Gandhara. [110] Others contend that the Bactrian Greeks provided the main 'Western' influence in Gandharan art. The work of the French archaeological mission to Afghanistan at Surkh Kotal and especially at the Greek city today called Ay Khanum on the Oxus and Kokcha rivers, has tipped the balance in favour of the Bactrian Greeks. The followers of the Roman-Buddhist thesis, as Schlumberger calls it, have pointed to the gap in time between the end of Greek rule and objects of the Gandharan school. There is certainly no clear evidence of continuity. On the other hand, Schlumberger protests (*op. cit.* p. 150) that the coinage, and especially the use of the Greek alphabet by the Kushans, does point to continuity and it would be absurd to think that the remarkable coins of the Greeks had no counterparts in art. Both sides make sense, but both have had to broaden their perspectives and enlist the aid of Mesopotamia, south Russia and even China to support their theories. We have already touched upon Scytho-Sarmatian art and the 'animal style'.

The Eurasian problem is concerned with linking the art of the Central Asian nomads with the settled people of the Near East and with the Greeks. Since the neighbour of both the Kushans in the east and the Seleucid-Romans in the west was Parthia, attention turned to the art of the Parthians, themselves connected with Central Asia, as a possible missing link in the problem. We have mentioned the profound changes in philosophy and religion which can be observed at the end of the Hellenistic age, the first century BC. These can be matched with changes in art. In an aesthetic vein, the result of the change has been designated as the 'expressionist' style, in contrast to the straightforwardness and explicitness which were the hallmarks of both classical Greek and Achaemenid art.[112] Specifically, two features appear in the art of the 'Parthian' period, frontality in human representation and activity exemplified in the 'flying gallop' motif in reliefs and wall paintings.

Rostovtzeff coined a term, Neo-Persian, for this art, and said: 'Neo-Persian art was certainly the leading art of Iranian Asia and Europe in late Hellenistic times.'[113] He further traced features of this art to Han China, Siberia and south Russia, claiming that frontality appears first in south Russia with the Sarmatians (p. 239). In an interesting fashion he tried to demonstrate that the Neo-Persian style drew its inspiration from northern Mesopotamia, from the Assyrians through the Achaemenids and hence is a revival and not influenced by Greece. He further showed, in a convincing manner, that it was the Parthians who started an Iranian renaissance and not the Sasanians, who instead fostered a short-lived Greek influence under Shapur I. The old traditions in art, of the hunt, war and banquet motifs, as well as the ancient use of polychromy, were revived under the Parthians but should not be attributed solely to them, for both the settled folk and the nomads of Central Asia with their animal style, and minor dynasts of Anatolia, such as Commagene, participated in the Neo-Persian movement.

The theory of Rostovtzeff was modified by Schlumberger, who pointed out that frontality, although it is more striking in Parthian art than elsewhere, is also found in Greece in an earlier period. For him it was the Greeks who started the art revolution in the Hellenistic age by introducing frontality and three-quarter profiles in human representations, with the purpose of capturing an illusion, which was symptomatic of the time. [114] Schlumberger claims that the Greeks themselves abolished the old classical convention of frontality in statues and profile in the graphic arts. Both the Greek and traditional Oriental styles fell before the new Hellenistic-Oriental art of the first century BC, which was a court art in the service of an Iranian king replacing the city art of the Greeks and the temple art in the service of the old gods (p. 280). Parthian art for him is a mixture of Greek art (the old as well as the new art, I presume) and two Iranian influences, the old Achaemenid tradition plus the new nomadic tradition from Central Asia. Schlumberger returns to Gandhara and suggests that Gandharan art is to be explained as the mixture of this (new) Graeco-Iranian art with (older) Graeco-Indian traditions.

It should be clear now that the art picture is indeed complicated, but this is what one would expect in an age of cross cultures, movements of peoples over vast areas and syncretism. Certainly many problems remain, but if we believe that a people's art reflects both its way of life and its religious outlook, and if we remember that nomads can hardly bring certain features of architecture and art with them just because they are nomads, then the historical realities probably provide the best guide to the art problems. The Greeks did occupy Bactria for over two centuries; they did extend to India; their wonderful coins do exist, and their influences lived after them. [115] On the other hand, the Greeks must have been absorbed by the native population and the invaders from Central Asia, both having their own traditions. So Gandharan art must owe something to the Graeco-Bactrian background, probably more than the partisans of the Roman-Buddhist thesis allow and less than the supporters of the Graeco-Bactrian theory assert. Part of the answer to the problem lies in Ay Khanum and other similar sites. But certain continuity from the Bactrian Greeks through the Kushans can only be demonstrated by new excavations in Afghanistan and Soviet Central Asia.

NOTES

1 See A. T. Olmstead, *History of the Persian Empire* (Chicago, 1948), 433.

2 Discussion in W. W. Tarn, *Alexander the Great,* 2 (Cambridge, 1948), 137. I subscribe to most of Tarn's conclusions about the army and battles of Alexander.

3 The traditional view is given by B. Head, *Historia Numorum* (Oxford, 1911), 224. The question of Alexander's monetary policy is confused, but in a letter of 6 April 1962 A. R. Bellinger suggests that Alexander arranged his

currency to meet his own needs in an area affected by Philip's gold and Attic silver, and that the ratio 10:1 was the result of the exploitation of the Pangaean mines hence a phenomenon of Philip's reign. Alexander made a simple system by using *drachmae* of equal weight, making one *stater* equal to five *tetradrachmae*. But he did not try to revise the Achaemenid ratio of 13⅓:1.

4 According to Babylonian custom the year in which a king died was counted as the last full year of his reign. Seleucus became king in the year seven of the Seleucid era. Cf. A. J. Sachs and D. J. Wiseman, '*A Babylonian Kinglist of the Hellenistic period*', *Iraq*, 16 (1954), 202.

5 According to Strabo XI. 516 the wall was 1,500 stadia in length, while Pliny VI. 18 says the circumference of the city was 70 stadia.

6 For information on the colonisation of the Seleucids see M. I. Rostovtzeff, *The Social and Economic History of the Ancient World*, 1 (Oxford, 1941), 501; E. Bikerman, *Institutions des Séleucides* (Paris, 1938), 79, 87, 100, and W. Tarn, *The Greeks in Bactria and India* (Cambridge, 1951), 5-12, with differing views.

7 Tarn, *loc. cit.*, 6, 9.

8 In this on the whole I follow Bikerman, *op. cit.*, 256.

9 Bikerman, 197, Rostovtzeff, 518.

10 This 'political theory', which is evidenced by inscriptions, lasted into Roman times. Cf. E. Meyer, *Blüte und Niedergang des Hellenismus in Asien* (Berlin, 1925), 43, and Rostovtzeff, 3, 1439. The interpretation of this theory in regard to Asia Minor would certainly be different from that in Iran, and *ethnē* in one case might be completely different in another area.

11 Bikerman, 167.

12 W. Tarn, *Hellenistic Civilisation* (London, 1952), 130.

13 Bikerman, 199.

14 *Ibid.*, 201-202.

15 *Ibid.*, 107. I find no evidence for Tarn's assertion (*Hellenistic Civilisation*, 142) that, according to Appian, *Civil Wars*, V.4.18, when Marc Antony boasted of the justice of the Roman tax of ten per cent of the harvest to the citizens of Ephesus in the kingdom of Pergamon he was following Seleucid rather than Ptolemaic practice.

16 References to sources in E. Bevan, *The House of Seleucus*, 2 (London, 1902), 120.

17 Bikerman, 123, Tarn, *Hellenistic Civilisation*, 155, Rostovtzeff, 506.

18 Tarn, *Hell. Civ.*, 156.

19 Rostovtzeff, 3, 1427. Antiochus I ruined the city of Babylon by transferring its population to Seleucia, but Babylonian learning continued.

20 For the Avroman documents in Greek see E. H. Minns, '*Parchments of the Parthian Period from Avroman*', *Journal of Hellenic Studies*, 35 ((1915), 22. For the Transcaucasian inscriptions see the convenient collection in K. V. Trever, *Ocherki po istorii kultury drevnei Armenii* (Moscow, 1953), 162 foll. and the report of excavations at *Mtskheta* 1 (Tiflis, 1958), 70, *et passim*.

21 E. T. Newell, *The Coinage of the Eastern Seleucid Mints* (New York, 1938), 230.

22 Bikerman, 226.

23 Strabo's text is unclear at this point. Whether the fortress of Ouera

192

which he mentions here is the citadel of Gazaka (Ganzak) as J. Marquart, *Ērānšahr*, 108, believed, is questionable. The evidence of the sources (Stephan of Byzantium, Dio Cass, etc.) indicates that there were two cities Ganzak and Fraaspa, and Ouera is not necessarily to be identified with the latter. The location of both of the cities in Takht-i Sulaiman given in *Pauly-Wissowa* only confuses the matter. V. Minorsky, *'Roman and Byzantine Campaigns in Atropatene'*, BSOAS, 11 (1944), 263, places Fraaspa or Phraata in Maragha.

24 V. Tscherikower, *Die hellenistischen Städtegründungen* (Leipzig, 1927), 99.

25 On the inscription of 193 BC of Antiochus III on behalf of the cult of his queen, and a possible inscription of Seleucus IV from the same site see L. Robert, *Hellenica*, 7 (1949), 1-30.

26 D. Schlumberger, *et al.*, *'Une bilingue gréco-araméenne d'Aśoka'*, *Journal Asiatique* (1958), 1 foll. Cf. E. Benveniste, *et. al.*, *'Une inscription Indo-Araméenne d'Aśoka'*, *JA* (1966), 438-70. Also S. Shaked, *'Notes on the new Aśoka Inscription from Kandahar'*, *JRAS* (1969) 118-22.

27 W. B. Henning, *'Mitteliranisch'* in B. Spuler, *Handbuch der Orientalistik* (Leiden, 1958).

28 The appearance of Iranian writing on Parthian coins comes, however, a century later, first under Vologeses I *circa* AD 55, when the Iranian revival is in full swing.

29 The best general studies of Seleucid seals are R. H. McDowell, *Stamped and Inscribed Objects from Seleucia on the Tigris* (Ann Arbor, 1935) and M. I. Rostovzett, *'Seleucid Babylonia: Bullae and Seals'*, *Yale Classical Studies*, 3 (1932).

30 G. M. Richter, *Catalogue of Engraved Gems of the Classical Style* (New York, Metropolitan Museum, 1920), xxi.

31 McDowell, *op. cit.*, 27-29.

32 Rostovtzeff, *op. cit.*, 19 foll.

33 McDowell, 179.

34 Polybius, *Histories*, XXIX. 21. The Loeb series translation by W. R. Paton has been used here.

35 Bibliography in Rostovtzeff, *Social and Economic History*, 3, 1533, 1536. They fostered their relationship with the Seleucids as well.

36 R. J. Forbes, *Studies in Ancient Technology*, 2 (Leiden, 1955), 87.

37 *Ibid.*, 4, 46-55.

38 *Ibid.*, 3, 25, 113.

39 Most of the information here used may be found in the book by I. Mendelsohn, *Slavery in the Ancient Near East* (New York, 1949).

40 *Ibid.*, 100-106.

41 *Ibid.*, 99.

42 For a concise summary see G. Contenau, *Arts et Styles de l'Asie Antérieur* (Paris, 1948), 18, and K. Erdmann, *'Griechische und achaemenidische Plastik'*, *Forschungen und Fortschritte*, 26 (1950), 150.

43 Cf. D. Schulmberger, *'Descendants non-méditerranéens de l'Art grec'*, *Syria*, 37 (1960), 261.

44 It is the merit of Rostovtzeff to have first elaborated this thesis; cf. his

'Some New Aspects of Iranian Art', Seminarium Kondakovianum, 6 (Prague, 1933), 161, 'L'art gréco-iranien', Revue des Arts asiatiques (Paris, 1933), 202, and other publications. Some of his views, of course, now need to be modified. For example, when he wrote the nomadic character of Central Asia was taken for granted. Now we know much more about settled life there, thanks to Soviet excavations.

45 On the Mesopotamian Nana see K. Tallqvist, *Akkadische Götter-epitheta* (Helsinki, 1938), 385. On Anahita see the convenient summary in L. Gray, *Foundations of the Iranian Religions* (Bombay, 1927), 57. Some scholars claim that Anahita is non-Iranian in origin and derived from Nana.

46 For references to the Tun Huang Sogdian letters cf. W. B. Henning in *BSOAS*, 12 (1948), 603, and for the Nisa ostraca I. M. Dyakonov and V. A. Livshits in the *Sbornik v chest I. A. Orbeli* (Moscow, 1960), 329.

47 Tiflis ed. (1909), 409-410. For the Greek edition see V. Langlois, *Collection des historiens de l'Arménie*, I (Paris, 1880), 168. A good survey of the spread of Nana ~ Nanai ~ Nane may be found in H. Ingholt, *Parthian Sculptures from Hatra* (New Haven, 1954), 12.

48 K. Fischer, 'Neue Funde zur indischen Kunst', Arch. Anzeiger des Deutschen Archäologischen Instituts (1957), 418. His further identification of the figure with Buddha is not convincing.

49 The many terra-cottas of Heracles from Seleucia on the Tigris attest to the popular base of the cult. Cf. W. von Ingen, *Figurines from Seleucia on the Tigris* (Ann Arbor, 1939), 106-108, plate XVIII.

50 Cf. W. B. Henning, 'An Astronomical Chapter of the Bundahishn', JRAS (1942), 235.

51 I. Gershevitch, *The Avestan Hymn to Mithra* (London, 1959), 66, et passim.

52 R. C. Zaehner, *The Dawn and Twilight of Zoroastrianism* (Weidenfeld & Nicholson, London, 1961), and J. Hinnells, ed. *Mithraic Studies* (Manchester, 1974).

53 *The Greeks in Bactria and India* xx.

54 Cf. V. F. Gaidukevitch, *Bosporskoe Tsarstvo* (Moscow, 1949), 57. There is a vast literature on the Greeks in South Russia in Russian but little in Western European languages.

55 S. I. Rudenko, *Gornoaltaiskie Nakhodki i Skify* (Moscow, 1952), 20.

56 For conflicting views on the Sindi and Maeotians see *Voprosy Skifo-Sarmatskoi Arkheologii* (Moscow, 1952), 20, 34, article of N. N. Pogrebova.

57 E. I. Krupnov, *Drevnyaya Istoriya Severnogo Kavkaza* (Moscow, 1960), 68.

58 V. I. Abaev, *Osetinskii Yazyk i Folklor* (Moscow, 1949), 37. The relation of Sauromat-Sarmat-Avestan Sairima has been much disputed, but a double (*u* and *i*) epenthesis would be odd. Too much etymological play can be misleading. Cf. F. Altheim, *Geschichte der Hunnen*, I (Berlin, 1959), 70.

59 Abaev, *ibid.*, 178, and L. Zgusta, *Die Personennamen griechischer Städte der nördlichen Schwarzmeerküste* (Prague, 1955), 265. The assertion of J. Junge, *Saka-Studien* (Leipzig, 1939), 79, that the name should be rather Roxonaloi cannot be accepted.

60 J. Harmatta, *Studies on the History of the Sarmatians* (Budapest, 1950), 35.

61 Harmatta, *Studies in the Language of the Iranian Tribes in South Russia* (Budapest, 1952).

62 V. F. Gaidukevitch, *op. cit.*, 345.

63 A. D. H. Bivar, *'The Stirrup and its Origins'*, *Oriental Art*, n.s.1 (1955), 65, may be right in giving the Avars in the fifth century AD credit for spreading the use of the stirrup. There may have been an earlier use of stirrups, however, indicated by a toe ring stirrup on a relief from the second stupa of Sanchi from the second century BC; see J. Marshall and A. Foucher, *The Monuments of Sanchi* (Calcutta, 1940), 40b, plate 82.

64 Gaidukevitch, 430. M. Rostovtzeff, *Iranians and Greeks in South Russia* (Oxford, 1922), 167, thought that these signs were the first stages in the development of Sarmatian writing, but this is unlikely since similar signs continued to flourish among the Turks long after they knew writing.

65 E. I. Solomonik, *Sarmatskie Znaki Severnogo Prichernomorya* (Kiev, 1959), 17, where the Sarmatian origin of the South Russian signs and the dating in the Christian era is defended. The relations between such signs found in South Russia, Khwarezm, and Siberia is also expounded.

66 For a survey of Scythian-Sarmatian art and bibliography see T. T. Rice, *The Scythians* (London, 1957), and many publications of Rostovtzeff.

67 Rostovtzeff, *Iranians and Greeks*, 198 foll., believes the 'animal style' originated in the Altai mountains and spread both to China of the Chou dynasty and to South Russia with the Scythian migration.

68 Cf. Abaev, *Istoriko-Etimologicheskii Slovar Osetinskogo Yazyka*, I (Moscow, 1958), 47, *sub Allon;* I. Gershevitch, *'Word and Spirit in Ossetic'*, *BSOAS*, 17 (1955), 486; H. W. Bailey, *'Iranian Arya- and Daha-'*, *Transactions of the Philological Society* (1959), 98.

69 S. V. Kiselev, *Drevnyaya Istoriya Yuzhnoi Sibiri* (Moscow, 1951) *passim*.

70 *Ibid.*, 249-250.

71 The basic publication is by S. I. Rudenko, *Kultura Naseleniya Tsentralnogo Altaya v Skifskoe Vremya* (Moscow, 1960); cf. also M. Griaznov, *L'art ancien de l'Altai* (Leningrad, 1958).

72 Kiselev, *op. cit.*, 315, 357.

73 Cf. Harmatta, *Studies*, 34, for references. A good survey of Near Eastern-Siberian relations can be found in M. P. Gryaznov, *'Svyazi Kochevnikov Yuzhnoi Sibirii so Srednei Aziei, etc.'*, in *Materialy Vtorogo Soveshchaniya Arkheologov Srednei Azii* (Moscow, 1959), 136.

74 Gaidukevitch, 374.

75 Cf. W. Samolin, *'Historical Ethnography of the Tarim Basin before the Turks'*, *Paleologia*, 4 (Tokyo, 1955), 39, and his *'The Archaeology of the Tarim Basin'*, *Central Asiatic Journal*, 4 (1958), 66, for references. The Wu-sun have been identified with the As-Alans by many scholars, but both linguistic and historical problems arise. Cf. most recently Altheim, *Geschichte der Hunnen*, I, 63, who also notes the Alan-Massagetai identification in Ammianus Marcellinus.

76 See bibliography and references in the valuable article by G. Haloun, *'Zur Ue-tsi-Frage'*, *ZDMG*, 91 (1937), 245, note 7. The identification of the

Hsiung-nu with the Huns may not be provable, but as an *overall* nomenclature it can be accepted. For an explanation of the name Yüeh-chih = ★ *togara*, 'Tokharian' cf. Bailey, *'Ariaca', BSOAS,* 15 (1953), 536.

77 Haloun, 248-249; cf. O. Maenchen-Helfen, *'The Yüeh-chih Problem Re-examined', JAOS,* 65 (1945), 71-82.

78 The ancient Chinese pronunciation of Sai can be reconstructed as ★ Sak-. It is difficult to identify the Issedones (var. Essed-) either with the Wu-Sun or the Arsi, or with the Asiana, or with the As-Alans, though any or all may be possible. In any case whatever the linguistic identification of Yüen-chid, whether Scythian as Haloun thought, or more probably = Tokhar as Henning, note 79 (below) proposed, the *historical* identification of Yüeh-chih = 'Tokharians', and Kushans, etc. is now generally accepted. Cf. Bailey, *'Ariaca', loc. cit.*

79 *'Argi and the Tokharians', BSOS,* 9 (1938), 563.

80 A. Maricq, *'La grande inscription de Kanishka', Journal Asiatique,* 246 (1958), 345-440, and W. B. Henning in *BSOAS,* 23 (1960), 45-55. The attempt of H. Humbach, *Die Kanishka-Inschrift von Surkh-Kotal* (Wiesbaden, 1960), to interpret the main inscription on the basis of Avestan as a hymn to Mithra is not convincing.

81 R. Curiel et D. Schlumberger, *Trésors monétaires d'Afghanistan* (Paris, 1953), 1-6.

82 Pliny (*ibid.*) says that the Scythians called the Jaxartes river Silis, which has been recently etymologised as derived from *Sir-ob* 'abundance of water'; by S. G. Kljashtornij, *'Iaxartes — Sir-Darya', Central Asiatic Journal,* 6 (1961), 24. K. compares NP *ser* 'full' and Sogdian *šyr,* but he neglects to distinguish the two words 'good' and 'very' in Sogdian, plus the Middle Persian form *sgry.* This renders his interpretation suspect.

83 Principally W. Tarn, *The Greeks in Bactria and India* (Cambridge, 1938, 2nd ed., 1951); F. Altheim, *Weltgeschichte Asiens,* 2 vols. (Halle, 1948); A. K. Narain, *The Indo-Greeks* (Oxford, 1957), A. M. Simonetta, *'A New Essay on the Indo-Greeks', East and West,* 9 (1958), 154 foll.

84 When the author of the *Periplus Maris Erythraei,* para. 47 ed. C. Müller, *Geographi Graeci Minores,* I (Paris, 1855), 293 speaks to the very warlike nation of the Bactrians he is referring to the Greeks. The absence of any evidence for a system or political theory of sub-kings does not mean that there were no vassal 'rulers' who were permitted to strike coins. Some numismatic evidence would point to a vassal or treaty relationship. It should be noted that the title of king in Greek is not found among the Bactrian rulers, or for that matter among the Seleucids. The great number of coins would indicate a long rule for the Graeco-Bactrians, as well as several dynasties.

85 The geographical distribution of coin finds can be tricky for Bactrian coins have been found in Ardabil and Kirmanshah, evidence of trade but not of Bactrian rule in western Iran. The whole question of the classification of the Greek coins has not been resolved. Sometimes they are classified as Graeco-Bactrian (those with Attic weights) and Indo-Bactrian (lighter, Indian weight). Another classification is based on the legends, including the script (Greek alone, or with Kharoshthi), or by style, or by deities on the reverses, or by monograms.

86 See the study by J. Wolski, *'L'effondrement de la domination des Séleucides en Iran au IIIe siècle av. J. C.',* *Bulletin international de l'académie polonaise des sciences et des lettres,* 5 (Cracow, 1947), esp. 15-17. He concludes (p.40) that Diodotus proclaimed his independence in 239 BC, while Narain, p. 14, places the revolt of Diodotus in 256 BC.

87 Wolski, *'Le problème d'Andragoras',* *Mélanges G. Kazarow* (Sofia, 1949), 113.

88 Narain, 25, 170, quoting Strabo XI. 516.

89 *Ibid.,* 53, with summaries of Justin and Strabo.

90 *Ibid.,* 48.

91 *Ibid.,* 80-86.

92 Tarn, 242.

93 Narain, 98.

94 The identification of these small satrapies was made by Tarn, *'Seleucid-Parthian Studies',* *Proceedings of the British Academy,* 16 (London, 1930), 20-24. The form Tapuria is secured from a correction of the Turiva of Strabo's text (XI.517), while Traxiane still presents a problem. Tapuria, however, does not mean the later Tabaristan; it was rather a district on the Murghab river or near Mashhad.

95 Narain, 128-164, with translations of relevant sources.

96 Narain, 137, discusses this point in detail.

97 Cf. A. M. Mandelshtam, *Materialy k istoriko-geograficheskomu obzoru Pamira i pripamirskikh oblastei* (Stalinabad, 1957), 79 *et passim.*

98 The best information may be found in the writings of H. W. Bailey; cf. esp. his *'Languages of the Saka',* in *Handbuch der Orientalistik, 4,* erste Abteilung, ed. B. Spuler (Leiden, 1958), 132 and *Khotanese Texts,* IV (Cambridge, 1961), 17.

99 Tarn, *The Greeks in Bactria and India,* 296-297, surveys the problem and concludes that Ta-hsia is the name of a mythical western land in Chinese tradition later given to Bactria.

100 See below, and Narain, 131, with a translation of the relevant part of the annals of the later Han dynasty.

101 Cf. E. Chavannes, *'Les pays d'Occident d'après le Heou Han chou',* *T'oung Pao,* part 2, 8 (1907), 191 foll.

102 J. Marshall, *Taxila,* 2 (Cambridge, 1951), 764, 768.

103 G. K. Jenkins, *'Indo-Scythic Mints',* *Journal of the Numismatic Society of India,* 17, part 2, (1955), 16. Neither the question of the various conquests of Taxila by Azes nor the inscriptions of Maues-Moa-Moga, and the 'Saka era' can be discussed here. Cf. Narain, 142.

104 A. D. H. Bivar, *'The Bactrian Treasure of Qunduz',* JNSI, 17 (1955), 43; Jenkins *op. cit.,* 21.

105 Marshall, *Taxila,* 2, 764, and his article *'Greeks and Sakas in India',* JRAS (1947), 25.

106 See the valuable survey by Jenkins and Narain, *'The Coin Types of the Saka-Pahlava Kings of India, JNSI, Notes and Monographs,* 4 (1957).

107 V. M. Masson, *'Drevnebaktriiskie monety, chekanennye po tipu tetradraxm Geliokla',* *Epigrafika Vostoka,* 11 (1956), 63 foll. esp. 73-75, where the author proposes that the imitations are early Yüeh-chih coinage and related to the enigmatic Heraya, early Kushan, coins. See also his

'*K voprosu o chekane Yuechzhiiskoi Baktrii*', *Izvestiya otd. obsh. Nauk, Akademiya Nauk Tadzhikskoi SSR*, 14 (Stalinabad, 1957), 109-114, where he gives the date of Heliocles as 140-130 BC, and calls him the last Greek king of Bactria proper.

108 Marshall, '*Greeks and Sakas in India*', 19. The ruler should be Narain's Heliocles II (p. 109) but he is surely more important than Narain believes.

109 Cf. material assembled by S. Konow, *Corpus Inscriptionum Indicarum*, II, part I, *Kharoshthi Inscriptions* (Calcutta, 1929) xliv foll., and the good discussion in L. de La Vallée-Poussin, *L'Inde aux temps des Mauryas* (Paris, 1930), 276.

110 The partisans of the Roman school are H. Ingholt, *Gandharan Art in Pakistan* (New York, 1957); B. Rowland, *The Art and Architecture of India* (London, 1953); H. Buchthal, '*The Western Aspects of Gandhara Sculpture*', *Proceedings of the British Academy*, 31 (1948), and others.

111 This is the view of A. Foucher and the '*French School*'. Both positions have been summarised concisely by D. Schlumberger, '*Descendants non-méditerranéens de l'Art grec*', *Syria*, 37 (1960), esp. 136-142.

112 T. T. Rice, '*The Expressionist Style in Early Iranian Art*', *Ars Islamica*, 5 (1938), 219.

113 '*Dura and the Problem of Parthian Art*', *Yale Classical Studies*, 5 (1935), 270.

114 *Op. cit.*, 261. See p. 169, under Hellenistic art.

115 Andhra coins in Central and South India had Greek as well as Brahmi and Kharoshthi legends, E. J. Rapson, *Catalogue of the Coins of the Andhra Dynasty* (London, 1908), cxci. On Greek words in Central Asia cf. Bailey, *Khotanese Texts, IV*, 10. The Greek sculptures and other objects from Parthian Nisa, dated to the first century BC, would indicate a continuation of such influences in the East. The Greek artist (Agesilaos) whose name was found by Konow on the reliquary made for Kanishka (CII note 109), p. 137) has now disappeared since T. Burrow read the word as derived from *agniśālā* 'hall of fire', in *Journal of the Greater India Society*, 11 (1944), 13-16.

5 THE ADAPTABLE ARSACIDS

A Forgotten Dynasty

We have already said that during the rule of the Parthians great changes occurred in Iran in the realms of art, religion and literature. While one should not attribute these changes merely to innovations of the Parthians, none the less they did leave a lasting imprint on the history of the land. It is during their rule that the history of Iran perhaps can be characterised as a transition from an ancient to a mediaeval era, which is the difference between early Parthian rule and the later Parthians. We know much less about them than about their predecessors the Achaemenids and the Greeks or their successors the Sasanians, but here and there we can find indications of Parthian contributions to the legacy and culture of Persia.

A prevalent view of the Parthians as degenerate Greeks, as phil-Hellenes under whom Iran experienced its 'Dark Ages', is surely unjustified. As we learn more about this period of history from new inscriptions and excavations it is becoming clear that the Parthian period of history was one of great development in many areas. Parthian architecture, with its liwans and squinches, is by no means degraded Greek in inspiration, but rather an art with many new ideas. The Parthians in a sense preserved the Zoroastrian religion, giving it the basis of a canon which passed to the Sasanians and down to the present day. The heroic lays of Persia's poets stem in great measure from Parthian bards who sang to their nobles about the heroes or *pahlavāns* of the national epic. In short the Parthian period of Iran's history has been not only neglected but even maligned, and we should endeavour to set the record aright.

The Parthians, however, have not suffered as much from contemporary students as from their immediate successors the Sasanians. Firdosi exemplified the prevailing view in Persia when

199

he said at the end of the few lines he devoted to the Parthians in his *Book of Kings;* 'since their roots and branches were short one cannot say that their past was illustrious. I have heard nought but their names and have not seen them in the chronicle of kings.' Why were they forgotten?

Islamic authors reflect Sasanian tradition on the Parthians, and there is a curious reduction of the time span between Alexander and the rise of the Sasanians which can be found in many Islamic sources. The great scholar al-Bīrūnī knew of this blunder by many of the historians, and, following Ḥamza al-Iṣfahānī, he gives the various false chronologies current in his time, as well as several almost correct tables.[1] Masʿūdī says that the Sasanians deliberately falsified the chronology between Alexander and Ardashir, the Sasanian ruler who overthrew the Parthians, by reducing a period of 510 years approximately to half of that period. This was done, according to him, because of the millenary eschatology of the Zoroastrian religion, according to which the empire of the Persians would perish a thousand years after Zoroaster. The prophet flourished some 300 years before Alexander, according to Zoroastrian tradition, and the end of the millennium then was drawing near under the Sasanians. Thus the Sasanian *mobads, herbads* and government officials are supposed to have perpetuated this chronological fraud to cheat fate.[2] Other sources substantiate this difference in the chronology between the Persians and other peoples. The Zoroastrian tradition, as contained in the *Bundahishn* (Ch. 34 on 'time reckoning'), gives the length of Parthian rule as 284 years which does not correspond to any of the tables of al-Bīrūnī yet does show that the post-Sasanian Zoroastrians too followed a false chronology. It is possible that Masʿūdī is correct in explaining the false chronology on religious grounds since the Persians hardly can have been completely unacquainted with Greek and other versions of the length of Parthian rule. It does indicate, however, the importance of a strong, centralised state in maintaining historical records and traditions, a condition which did not exist, it seems, under Parthian rule. Our lack of knowledge cannot be just the result of the efforts of Sasanian kings to extirpate the Parthian nobility and their history, no matter how much Ardashir and his successors may have derogated the achievements of their predecessors.

The Parthians were able to assimilate much of Hellenism, and yet they also maintained Iranian traditions. While one might characterise early Parthian times as phil-Hellenic and the later period as an Iranian reaction, we have no real evidence for a 'reaction', but rather a transition from a world in which Greece was dominant to a new world in which Hellenism was swallowed up by the Orient, but not at one instant. The parallel of the rise of Parthia with the rise of Rome out of Hellenism may be instructive, but this is neither unexpected nor was the process sudden.

Origins

The origins of the Parthians have been much studied, and while many details and questions of dating are uncertain, a probable reconstruction of events can be made.[3] The Parthians are known from Achaemenid times living roughly in the modern Persian province of Khurasan. After the death of Alexander the Great there was a movement of tribes in Russian Turkestan resulting in the destruction of some Greek outposts in Central Asia, but Seleucus I and his son Antiochus rebuilt the towns and established Seleucid rule. It is possible that among those tribes were the Parni. Strabo (XI.508 and 515) called the Parni a part of the larger Dahi confederation. It is possible, as Markwart proposed,[4] that the Parni-Aparni were called in an Iranian tongue the Aparnak, who gave their name to Aparshahr or the Nishapur region, although the term Aparshahr/Abar is probably derived from an ancient designation of 'the upper countries' of Achaemenid or 'upper satrapies' of Seleucid times.[5] The Parni were probably the leading tribe which occupied the settled area of Parthia and certain words in Armenian and Manichaean Parthian texts have been described as Parni words brought into Parthian by the conquerors.[6] For it appears that the newcomers adopted the tongue of the settled people and spread it beyond its original confines.

The chronology of the rise of the Parthians is bound up with that of the Bactrian Greeks. There is a tradition that Arsaces, the first Parthian ruler, was a governor of the Bactrian Greeks who revolted and fled westwards to establish his own rule.[7] This cannot be verified, but it would seem that the satrap of Parthia, perhaps the Andragoras of coins, revolted about the same time as the Bactrians, and he in turn was defeated by the Parni led by Arsaces after a few years' rule. This may be dated approximately

238 BC [8] if one must have a date for the beginning of Parthian rule in Iran.

The dynasty of the Parthians, as it is known in western sources, was probably named at home after its founder Arsaces and as such it is known in Oriental sources. The question of the historicity of the first Arsaces now seems settled by an ostracon from Nisa, a Parthian centre in Turkmenistan, where a descendant of the nephew of Arshak I is mentioned. [9] The name Arshak, by which the dynasty was known, was used by the succeeding kings on their coins making precise identifications difficult. It has been explained as a clan name from *araša* — (Avestan) — 'bear' a totem, or as 'man, hero' from *aršan-*, which is more probable. The Arsacids traced their genealogy back to the Achaemenid Artaxerxes II, and this was probably taken seriously since from Nisa we have the royal name Artakhsharakan applied to a vineyard, which name probably referred to Artaxerxes II. [10] What is believed, of course, may be quite different from what was true, and here we seem to have the required traditional elements in the founder of an Iranian dynasty, royal descent from the previous Iranian dynasty, plus flight or exile (from the Bactrian Greeks). Arrian *(Parthica* 17.2) further says there were five nobles, plus his brother, who raised Arsaces I to be king, together making seven, similar to the case of Darius. Thus does Arsaces I conform to the 'legend' of the founder of a dynasty in Iran.

Later, after the Parthians were established, they adopted an era of time reckoning, probably copied from the Seleucid era, which combined some important event with the first year 247 BC. To speculate on that event is at present idle. Arsaces I was succeeded, probably, by his brother Tiridates, which kind of succession seems to have been not abnormal. We know from the coins of the Indo-Parthians that succession apparently sometimes went from the king to his brother to his brother's son, which was, in my opinion, a feature of Central Asian steppe and nomadic society. [11] The Parthians began their expansion with the annexation of Hyrcania. Now the rise of the Parthians probably was regarded by the Seleucids as a revolt similar to those of Andragoras and Diodotus, for we know that the Seleucids had many revolts in their eastern provinces. [12] The expansion of the Parthian realm was relatively slow and there were several setbacks. One occurred at the beginning when Seleucus II finally moved against the Parthians about 228 BC, but was forced to

202

return to Antioch because of internal troubles, leaving the Parthians free.

Antiochus III led an expedition against the Parthians after suppressing the revolt of Molon and his brother Alexander, and after securing the allegiance of Artabazanes, ruler of Median Atropatene (Azerbaijan) and regulating affairs in Armenia.[13]

The date of the beginning of the expedition was about 209 BC and lasted several years. Antiochus fought a number of engagements with the Parthians, the final result of which seems to have been a peace treaty with the Parthians recognising Seleucid supremacy. Next Antiochus fought against Euthydemus and succeeded again in obtaining a recognition of Seleucid suzerainty. It may well be that both Parthia and the Bactrian state maintained their allegiance to Antiochus, at least until his defeat by the Romans at Magnesia in 189 BC. Possibly the interval from 209 to 189 saw a revival of Greek influence in Iran, but we have no information from the sources.

We hear again of the Parthians about 171 when the real founder of the empire, Mithradates I, ascended the throne. We do not know the date of his accession but he was regarded as a contemporary of Eucratides of Bactria and of Antiochus IV.[14] Tarn believed that Parthia remained small and relatively impotent in the face of a Seleucid revival in the person of Antiochus IV and his relative Eucratides. There is no evidence for a family relationship between the two Greek rulers and still less for a powerful entente between the two, because Bactria and the Seleucid state hardly had common frontiers at this time. For the governor of the Seleucid eastern provinces, Timarchus, did not even rule the area of present-day Tehran, which was in Parthian hands when Antiochus IV started his expedition into Iran.[15] The attempt of Antiochus IV Epiphanes to restore Seleucid losses in the east was not a success although he seems to have done something to restore the Greek position in western Iran, so that Ekbatana-Hamadan was renamed Epiphaneia in his honour (Stephan of Byzantium, *sub Agbatana*). The death of Antiochus in 164 opened the way for further Parthian conquests.

There is, of course, no clear distinction between Parthia with its original geographical boundaries (as in Ptolemy), and the later greater Parthia extending over Khurasan and then even beyond, but we can follow the progress of the Parthians in their successive capitals.[16] The earliest capital was probably at the town called Dara by Justin, the site of which, near Abivard, has been

203

identified by M. E. Masson.[17] The town of Nisa or Parthaunisa, as Isidore (paragraph 7) calls it, was the necropolis of the early Parthian kings and this is the place where fruitful excavations have been conducted since World War II.

About 18 km. north-west of Ashkabad two towns, Old Nisa and New Nisa, were excavated. It is possible that Nisa was really the first capital, or at least the home town of Arsaces I. The size and splendour of the excavated halls attest to the wealth of the Parthian rulers. It is not known whether the original Parthian name of Old Nisa was Mithradatkirt, or whether this was a renaming (and rebuilding) of the old site by Mithradates I or more likely Mithradates II.[18] A large square hall (60 m. a side) contained a treasure of ivory objects, primarily some rhytons with bands with scenes of Greek mythology around the rims (fig. 115), eloquent testimony of the flourishing Oriental Greek art in eastern Iran.[19] The necropolis and the artistic remains, including fragments of greater than life-sized statues, lead one to suppose there was a cult of the dead Arsacid kings. The discovery of fragments of similar statues in Toprak Kale in Khwarezm, in the Kushan sanctuary of Surkh Kotal, as well as the well-known statues of Nimrud Dagh and the large Parthian bronze statue of Shami attest the widespread popularity of what may be called a cult of the heroicised dead king.[20]

The most informative remains from Old Nisa were over two thousand ostraca found in a wine cellar. They represented documents of registration rather than tax receipts as was first thought by the scholars who worked on the inscriptions. In spite much controversy, it is almost certain that the inscriptions in black ink on the ostraca are in heterographic Parthian rather than in Aramaic for reasons which have been given elsewhere. [21]
These important sources of information give us great help in regard to many phases of the culture and history of the early Arsacids. Many of the place-names of the ostraca have been identified with contemporary villages and all of the personal names are Iranian, with the majority even Zoroastrian in character, as, for example, 'hwrmzdyk (*Ohrmazdik) 'rtwyhshtk (*Artavahishtak). spndrmtk (*Spandarmatak) dynmzdk (*Denmazdak), prnbg (*Farnbag) and others.[22] At the same time there is no evidence of a flourishing Zoroastrian cult in Nisa. The documents were dated by the Arsacid era with Zoroastrian months and the oldest was *circa* 100 BC, while the latest were *circa* AD 13. Many other details of interest, such as the burial of

bones in *astodans* (receptacles for the bones of the dead), and evidence of a Greek theatre, have come from the excavations. They have cast a new light on the early history of the Parthians.

The next capital of the Parthians was the fabled Hecatompylos located at Qumis, a site 32 km. west of present Damghan. Hecatompylos is mentioned as the royal city of the Parthians by Strabo, Pliny, Ptolemy and other classical authors, but we do not know when it became the capital. [23] Isidore (paragraph 11) does not mention it, but he does say that in the city of Asaak (for Ashak), Arsaces was first proclaimed king and an eternal fire was kept there. Finally the city of Rayy, called Arsakia, for a short time may have been a summer capital of the Parthians. So we find a number of towns located in modern Khurasan which were important in the early history of the Arsacids.

The Road Westwards

The conquests of Mithradates I brought the Parthians into western Iran and Mesopotamia and established the kingdom of the Arsacids as a world power rather than a provincial principality. In Media the Seleucid satrap Timarchus had proclaimed his independence and Mithradates had to fight against him. We do not know the chronology of events but it would seem that Mithradates did not kill Timarchus; more probably Demetrius I Soter the Seleucid finally crushed him. [24] In any case the ultimate victor was Mithradates who occupied Media perhaps about 155 BC. Afterwards Mithradates may have been called to his eastern frontiers to defend them against invaders. We have noted already (p. 185) that he took two provinces from Eucratides, though their exact location cannot be determined. There are several indications that he campaigned in Arachosia to the borders of India but we have no details. It is probable that Herat, Seistan, Gedrosia, and other districts in eastern Iran had long before Mithradates passed from Greek to native rule. The use of the term Ariane by Eratosthenes and later authors for most of eastern Iran save Bactria would indicate that the term was used for the non-Greek lands. The term some time later may have been applied to the Parthian empire but again evidence is not definite. [25] There is no reason to deny campaigns and conquests of Mithradates eastwards as some classical authors claim. [26] Mithradates earned the title of 'great king' which is found on his coins.

205

In the west, Mithradates entered Seleucia on the Tigris in the summer of 141 BC. Tarn's interesting theory that the Seleucid king Demetrius II Nikator and Heliocles of Bactria joined forces to fight Mithradates on two fronts is intriguing. He says that Mithradates defeated Heliocles in December 141 and then returned to Babylonia to defeat and capture Demetrius in 140 or 139. [27] With the Seleucid king a prisoner Mithradates could have regarded himself as the successor of the Achaemenids and of Alexander. Most of western Iran as well as Mesopotamia must have been in his hands, for records show Parthian rule in Susa and elsewhere. [28] The Parthians then were masters of the Iranian plateau.

In the reign of Phraates, son and successor of Mithradates, Antiochus VII led a Seleucid army for the last time to try to recover Iran. He reconquered Mesopotamia and invaded Media, but was defeated and slain whereupon Phraates reoccupied Mesopotamia. But the eastern frontier was threatened by the Saka migration from Central Asia and Phraates lost his life in a battle against the invaders about 128 BC. Phraates was probably still a young man when he perished, for it was his uncle Artabanus who ascended the throne. Artabanus too lost his life in the east, probably fighting the Yüeh-chih, and it would seem that the extensive territory in the east won by Mithradates was now lost. At the same time most of Mesopotamia was wrested from the Parthian governors by Hyspaosines, ruler of the new state of Characene, the capital of which, Spasinu Charax, had been renamed from Alexandria — Antioch. Fortunately for the Parthians their new king was a worthy namesake of the first Mithradates, and Mesopotamia was recovered, evidence of which is found in coins of Hyspaosines overstruck with the portrait and titles of Mithradates II. The dynasty of Characene, however, continued to reign over southern Mesopotamia as vassals of the Parthians down to the time of Trajan's conquests in AD 116. [29] Mithradates II, it would seem, was the first Parthian ruler to use the title 'king of kings' on his coinage, while the various types and great number of his coins found suggest an extensive and flourishing reign. On some of his coins he wears a tall cap or helmet with jewels on the edges and a star in the middle. This headgear was to become the most fashionable of Parthian royal crowns copied by the kings or Edessa (Abgar), Elymais, by certain Indo-Parthian rules and by Ardashir, the first Sasanian. [30]

In the east Mithradates II re-established Parthian rule,

206

settling the Sakas and probably receiving their nominal allegiance. The boundaries of the Parthians extended to the frontiers of India, including present day Qandahar, as we learn from Isidore (paragraph 19). In spite of the ingenious reconstruction of the history of the Parthian feudal house of Suren in Seistan by Herzfeld, with the supposition that the Suren Gondophares broke away from Parthia when Artabanus III succeeded Vonones I to the throne, we in fact know nothing about Parthian-Saka relations in the east.[31] His identification of Vonones I of Parthia with the Vonones of the Indo-Parthian coins is possible but quite unproved. We have already said that at times the succession among the Sakas and Indo-Parthians was from the king to his brother to his nephew, perhaps on a matrilineal basis as Herzfeld proposes.[32] But the matter is perhaps more complicated than scholars have hitherto thought since, for example, one of the Indo-Parthian kings, Sanabares, may have been primarily the ruler of Merv in Central Asia according to the extensive finds of his coins there.[33] Indian sources imply that the Sakas and Pahlavas were allies in their Indian conquests and this would seem to be corroborated by the coins with both Saka and Parthian names. The adoption of the title 'king of kings' by Gondophares, Orthagnes and Pakores would imply that these Indo-Parthian kings were completely independent of the Parthian rulers, and it is unlikely that they were concerned with affairs in Persia. The problem of the eastern relations of the Parthians in Arachosia and the western boundaries of the Indo-Parthians cannot be solved, but the separation of the Indian and Iranian kingdoms should be maintained.

It has long been proposed that Seistan and the Sakas provided a large part of the national epic, and especially the epic cycle of Rustam. Because of the discovery of fragments of the story of Rustam in Sogdian in Chinese Turkestan, the Saka origin of much of the lore about Rustam in the *Shahname* is probable. It is perhaps too romantic to identify Rustam with Gondophares, and the home castle of Caspar who followed the star to Bethlehem with Kuh-i Khwaja, the plateau in the middle of the Hamun Lake in Seistan.[34] The identification of the Sakas or Kushans with the Turanians of the national epic, is also intriguing, especially since there was a Turan east of Seistan, and a religious antagonism between the two peoples might have existed with the Parthians as defenders of Zoroastrianism. Yet these questions will not be solved by names and etymologies and learned constructions; we need rather new archaeological remains and inscriptions.

Towards the end of his reign (Justin XLII.2.7) Mithradates II also exterted his influence in Great Armenia where a certain Artavasdes was king, probably of the same family as Artaxias (Armenian: Artashēs) who had been confirmed by Antiochus III as king or as satrap.[35] Mithradates obtained some territory from Armenia and, as a hostage, a young prince who was later to become Tigranes the Great of Armenia. Parthia was soon to face Rome in many disputes over Armenia, but finally the Arsacids obtained the throne in Armenia which remained in Arsacid hands long into the period of Sasanian rule.

Parthia and Rome

Until the battle of Carrhae in 53 BC the Romans had not considered the Parthians as the main power in the east, but afterwards the world was divided between Rome and Parthia according to Greek and Latin authors.[36] The population of the easternmost dominions of Rome sometimes looked upon the Parthians as potential deliverers from the Roman yoke, while the westernmost subjects of the Parthians frequently entertained hopes of Roman support in their defections. The period of almost three centuries from Carrhae to the fall of the Parthians is filled with the varying fortunes of war in Syria, on the Euphrates, in Mesopotamia and Armenia. The Parthian wars of Marc Antony, Octavian, Tiberius, Nero, Trajan and Septimius Severus are relatively well known from Roman authors. They resulted in the building of a Roman *limes* in Syria and a series of frontier posts analogous to the Rhine and Danube fortifications. The buffer states and small principalities behind the *limes* were changed into provinces of the Roman Empire, but what happened in Parthia?

The centre of interest of the Parthians definitely shifted to western Iran and Mesopotamia after Mithradates II, but the eastern frontier still occupied them even when a greater danger came from the west. The weakness of the Parthians lay in their lack of centralisation and the many 'vassal' princes who were at least nominally under Arsacid rule. If we survey the Parthian empire and neighbouring states about the time of Christ we find a large array of sub-states.

In Transcaucasia a kingdom of Georgia or Iberia (Parthian *wyršn*) existed, which in the first century (*circa* AD 30-60) was ruled by an active king Farsman (Pharasmanes) with his capital at Mtskheta north-west of present Tiflis.[37] The Georgians and the Albanians were generally friendly to Rome and Roman culture; and at times they were even under nominal Roman suzerainty but there is no evidence that they were ever under the Parthians. Other princelings existed in Transcaucasia but we do not hear of them in Parthian history. The Alans, as we learn from Josephus, raided across the Caucasus as far south as Parthian domains. The kingdoms of Great Armenia and Media Atropatene have been mentioned. The former had its capital at Artaxata, though for a time under Tigranes the Great at Tigranocerta on the upper Euphrates. The country was a source of conflict between the Romans and Parthians, though the Armenians were more often against the Romans than were the Georgians, especially after AD 54 when the Arsacid prince Tiridates started a new dynasty. Media Atropatene had its own dynasty in Parthian times, and after Marc Antony retreated from Media and Armenia, the king of Atropatene made an alliance with the Romans against this Parthian suzerain (Dio Cass. XLIX.33 and 44), and Roman-Median collaboration continued under Octavian (*ibid.* LI.16).

The mountainous area south of Lake Van, called Korduene or Gorduene (Beth Qardu in Syriac sources), probably had its own chiefs with nominal submission to the Parthian throne. The kingdom of Adiabene or Hadhaiyab, with its most famous town Arbela, was ruled by a certain Izates I shortly after the Christian era, and his daughter and grandson Izates II were converted to Judaism (Josephus, *Ant.* XX.17-37). Arbela also was said to be the burial place of the later Parthian kings (Dio Cass. LXXVIII.1), but more likely this is a mistake for the kings of Adiabene rather than the Parthian rulers. Farther north-west following the Tigris River were the districts of Zabdicene, Arzanene, Nisibis on the Khabur River called Beth Arbaya in Syriac, Sophene or modern Diarbakr, and Edessa or Osroene, modern Urfa, ruled by the Arab kings of the Abgar family. In the first century the boundaries of the Abgarids seem to have included most of the areas on the Tigris mentioned above, for Pliny (VI.31, 129) says that the Arab tribes of the Orroei and Adiabeni bordered each other. If the area later called Beth Nohadre in Syriac sources is the same as Adiabene, or the western part of it, then we may see the title *nakhodar* 'prefect or governor' as the Parthian designation of the king of Adiabene.[38]

In the desert between the Tigris and Euphrates stood the strongly fortified city of Hatra, which successfully defeated several Roman attempts to conquer it. Ardashir the first Sasanian at first failed to take it, but at last Hatra succumbed to him and his son Shapur in 139 AD, after whose conquest it was abandoned. Hatra, as Edessa, as ruled by Arabs, for desert tribes had occupied it in the first century BC.[39] The most famous king of Hatra was called Sanatruq whose name lived long in Arab traditions. Hatra's prosperity, like that of Palmyra, seems to have been based on the overland trade and the excavations of the site have provided important artistic remains from the Parthian period.

The country between the Tigris and the Iranian plateau north-east of Ctesiphon carried the name Beth Garme in Syriac, with the present city of Kirkuk as its centre. We hear of a king of Kirkuk who joined Ardashir in his revolt against the Parthians, but we know nothing more about a kingdom in this area.[40] It is possible that Marquart is correct in connecting a dynasty ruling here with the family of Izates ruling Adiabene but such speculation has really little firm basis.[41]

The last capital of the Parthians, which was probably merely their winter capital, was Ctesiphon across the Tigris from Seleucia, which had gradually grown since the Parthian occupation until it was the equal of Seleucia.[42] Vologeses I built a new capital, Vologesokerta, farther north on the river, but as a capital it hardly survived his reign. It is probable that the land near the capital was under direct royal rule since we hear of no local rulers.

In southern Mesopotamia the principality of Characene or Mesene has been mentioned. It not only extended over the mouth of the Tigris-Euphrates, but also at times extended northwards.[43] One may suppose that here, as frequently in the history of the area, local chieftains maintained an independent existence. To the east in Khuzistan was the little kingdom of Elymais in the foothills of the Zagros beyond Susa, which city was governed by a satrap for the Parthian king. The number and chronology of the kings of Elymais are uncertain since the only sources are their coins, but inscriptions from Tang-i Sarwak reveal that the population was Aramaic-speaking.[44]

In Fars province ruled the *frataraka (princes), who counted themselves the successors of the Achaemenids to judge from their names, Darius and Artaxerxes, on the coins.[45] From the coins it

210

would seem that a local dynasty or dynasties ruled Fars from perhaps the middle of the third century BC to the rise of the Sasanians (see below). They were thus ruling Fars when Alexander, the brother of Molon, was satrap of Fars at the time of his revolt against Antiochus III. This would indicate either a joint rule of the *frataraka and the Seleucid satraps, or a division of rule between them in the province. One may doubt whether the Seleucids ever controlled much of Fars, save a few cities or military colonies. In any case, under Parthian rule the province was in the hands of a native dynasty which issued coins. Part of Kirman probably belonged to Fars and to the east and south independent tribes roamed freely much as during most of the history of Gedrosia, which is later known as Baluchistan.

To the north conditions in Gilan and Mazanderan are absolutely unknown but again, on the analogy of later times, it is probable that the Parthian kings had little if any jurisdiction over the lands north of the Elburz Mountains. East of the Caspian Sea was Hyrcania next to the Parthian homeland and one of the earliest conquests of the Parthians. The appearance of Hyrcanian ambassadors in Rome on several occasions in the first century AD has led some scholars to suppose that Hyrcania became a separate kingdom.[46] Since there are no Hyrcanian coins and no other evidence for this, we may suspect this theory, noting, however, that satraps frequently revolted in the Parthian state and even long periods of independence were possible. Eastern Iran in Parthian times was far from contact with the Greeks and Romans who left us their writings and we know next to nothing about conditions there.

Undoubtedly the first century AD was a time of great trouble for the Parthians (Tacitus XV.1). It was also a period of change. It is not possible to attribute the changes to a native reaction against the Romanophile king Vonones, or to an eastern Iranian (Hyrcanian) reaction against the pro-Hellenistic culture of the kings before Artabanus III.[47] Certainly in the first century changes are apparent such as the appearance of Aramaic-Parthian legends on the coins instead of Greek from the time of Vologeses I. The native names of cities, at least in eastern Iran, appear in place of the Greek names, for example Merv instead of Antiochia Margiane.[48] A process of decentralisation had occurred, such that Pliny (VI.112) could say that the Parthians had eighteen kingdoms, eleven called upper and seven called the lower kingdoms. It is particularly the last two centuries of

Parthian rule which provided the later characterisation of the history of the Parthians as the period of the 'tribal kings'.

The Romans took Ctesiphon three times, once under Trajan in 116, under Marcus Aurelius *circa* 164, and Septimius Severus in 198. The last century of Parthian rule seems like one continuous war with the Romans and Parthia was greatly weakened. It was perhaps inevitable that one of the revolts of the vassal kings or satraps would succeed, and success came to the ruler of Persis, the old homeland of the Achaemenids.

The Government and Bureaucracy of the Empire

We have mentioned various kingdoms within the Parthian empire as well as satrapies. The relations of both to the central power are by no means clear, especially since circumstances changed frequently in the many struggles for the throne of the Arsacids. The Parthian monarchy has been described many times as feudal, and the minor kings and even satraps have been termed vassals of the great king but such terms, borrowed from Western Europe, can be misleading. The Parni were nomads with nomadic traditions of rule who invaded settled lands which retained Achaemenid features of government as well as the more recent Seleucid. At first Greek culture and Greek ideas were dominant, which is what one would expect with a tribe taking power from a Hellenistic monarchy, a tribe, moreover, insecure in its position until Mithradates I or even Mithradates II. The nomadic background was still very prominent with the early Parthian kings, and after the state was firmly established a series of internal crises, plus a two front war with the Romans to the west and with the Kushans to the east reduced the strength of the central government in favour of the aristocracy.

One may plausibly assume that the Parthians borrowed most of their ideas of the king and kingship from the Seleucids or the Graeco-Bactrians. The early Arsacid state in its organisation and ideology must have been much like the Seleucid state, or any other Hellenistic monarchy. There were, however, some features which differentiated the Parthian king from a Hellenistic monarch. We have already mentioned the existence of an odd law of succession found among the Indo-Parthians, and though we have no sources for this feature among the Parthians themselves, perhaps an echo of it may be found in the accession of Mithradates I, successor and brother of Phraates I, as well as later cases of brother succession. This type of succession of the

212

eldest or most important person of the extended family or clan is found among various nomadic states of Central Asia, and this is its origin, I believe, rather than a matriarchate or a matrimonial custom of succession.[49] This is not to deny, of course, the important role of queens in the Parthian state, as well as in most monarchies, but there is no evidence of their preponderant role in the Parthian succession.

The progressive 'feudalisation' of the Parthian kingdom is revealed in many minor details such as the proliferation of coats-of-arms or insignia after Mithradates II.[50] Indeed after the reign of Mithradates II, when the direct line of kings from the founder died out, the role of the nobility with their *synedrion* or council (Strabo XI.515) increased in importance such that the nobles ratified the accession of, and at times even appointed, the king of kings. The lack of central authority is reflected in the apparent absence of strict rules or legal processes governing the accession and succession of a monarch and the lack of precision in ranks and offices, of which there were many. How did the nobles become so strong?

When the Parthians conquered Seleucid territory under direct Greek rule they found the cities *(polis)* and the towns which had been military colonies. In addition they found the old Achaemenid satrapal system which had somewhat broken down, and under the satrap probably the eparchy and further the hyparchy. Many eparchies had become the equivalent of satrapies. The early Parthians favoured the cities and Hellenistic culture, probably maintaining the old Seleucid organisations in those areas where they had survived. We hear, for example, of a certain Bacasis put in charge of Media by Mithradates I (Justin XLI.6.7), and Himerus over Mesopotamia (*Ibid.* XLII.1.3). Further the title 'satrap of satraps', on the analogy of 'kings of kings' is found on a Greek inscription of Mithradates II at Behistun.[51] Otherwise the office of satrap seems to have lost its significance although, of course, the word appears frequently in classical sources.[52] One may surmise that the reason for the strength of the nobility lay in the granting of 'feudal' domains by the great king to his relatives and followers principally in the territory through which the old road from Seleucia on the Tigris to Bactria and Arachosia passed. In time this land, once royal domain, became little different from the land ruled by the rulers of Armenia, Adiabene, and the like, while intermarriages further mixed the Parthian with the local aristocracy.

Meanwhile Iranian ideas of society and kingship, as developed under the Achaemenids, had continued through Seleucid into Parthian times. The fiction of the seven great families appears again in the Parthian age, although it is unlikely that there were exactly seven leading noble families. We know the names of some of the families, and can even locate their *principal* fiefs, although they probably owned land in various parts of the kingdom. From Arabic sources and occasional notices in classical texts, we may suppose that the Karen family had its headquarters in Nihavend Media, the Suren family in Seistan, and the Mihran near Rayy (near Tehran). This last family may be connected in some way with another family name from Rayy, Spandiyad.[53] Other names of noble families are mentioned in the sources but we know nothing about them, such as the family of Spahpat in Gurgan (?), perhaps replacing the house of Gev, or the family of Zek in Atropatene replacing the local dynasty in the later part of Parthian rule.[54] These feudal princelings apparently had their own armies, such as the force which the Suren led in the battle of Carrhae, according to Plutarch in his life of Crassus. The assembly of these great lords undoubtedly was of prime importance in the last half of Arsacid rule.

According to Plutarch and Justin (XLI.2.5) the Parthians were divided into a small number of freemen and a vast number of slaves. By freemen they meant the nobility or *āzātān*, plus the great families and officials of the kingdom, the *vazurkān (RB'n)* of the Middle Persian inscriptions. These last, one may assume, occupied leading positions at the court and in the army, with special ranks and privileges. All indications point to the development of forms of protocol, an extensive titulary and other forms of 'feudal' society in the Arsacid period. The proliferation of titles and offices makes it very difficult to put an order or hierarchy into the bureaucratic organisation of the Parthian state. Furthermore, conditions in Mesopotamia were surely different from those obtaining in Khurasan or elsewhere, and certain titles undoubtedly came into existence and flourished in some areas or died in others. We can only say that there is no apparent fixed order in either the Parthian bureaucracy, or even in the titles given to nobles. If we restrict ourselves only to the Parthian period, and do not consider the later Sasanian inscriptions, Arabic or Armenian sources, we actually find very little information.

The excavations of Dura-Europos, on the Euphrates River in

214

present-day Syria near the border with Iraq, have provided much information about the Roman-Parthian borderlands. For a time the Parthians ruled this city founded by Seleucus I, and we have from Dura Parthian as well as Greek, Latin, Aramaic and Middle Persian inscriptions. The Greek inscriptions are the most numerous and several give interesting data about Parthian titulary. Probably the most important of the Greek documents for our purpose is a loan contract on parchment which gives a number of Parthian titles, honorifics and personal names. It is sometimes difficult to distinguish between these three categories of proper 'names' in Iranian history, and foreign observers from the time of Herodotus to the present frequently confused them.

In the parchment loan contract from Dura we have the creditor, a certain 'Phraates, the eunuch, *arkapatēs*, one of the people of Manesus son of Phraates, who is of the *batēsa*, and of the "Freemen", tax collector and *stratēgos* of Mesopotamia and Parapotamia and *arkhos* of the Arabs'.[55] The various titles of both men indicate the complexity of a noble's position, undoubtedly paralleled in Parthian territory elsewhere. In *arkapatēs* we have either a rank or a specific office, probably the former meaning just 'vassal lord'.[56] Phraates stood in a subordinate position to another Iranian, Manech, son of another Phraates, who was probably a member of one of the few great feudal families. The *batēsa* must mean something like 'grandees' or *āzātān* which, however, is the next word, 'Freemen' in Greek. Could the two be complementary, i.e. he belonged to the Iranian class of *āzātān* and to the Mesopotamian class of *batēsa*?[57] In any case his office was tax collector and governor of Mesopotamia and Parapotamia plus an added charge, ruler of the Arabs, which causes no difficulty. The document was signed in the presence of the military officer who was commander of the garrison and belonged to the order of the honoured friends and body-guards (of the king), a rank known from Seleucid times.

The distinction between rank and position can be observed elsewhere in Parthian territory. In the inscription of Kal-i Janggāh near Birjand in eastern Iran a certain Gari-Ardashir had his name scratched beside a rock carving showing a man (presumably himself) killing a lion with his bare hands.[58] He is there called *nḥwdr* and *ḥštrp*, the latter the Parthian form of 'satrap', at this time probably the ruler of a city district as in the inscription of Shapur on the Ka'bah of Zoroaster at Naqsh-i Rustam. The rank or title of *nohodar*, 'holder of first place', is

215

found in Armenian as *naxarar* 'feudal chief', here again a rank name rather than an office.[59] The Byzantine historian Theophylactus Simocatta (I.9) remarked that Persians would rather use honorary titles than their own names, a feature no doubt of Parthian as well as more recent times, but which complicates our understanding of the feudal and the bureaucratic structure of the Parthian state.

Satraps none the less seem to have been the backbone of the Parthian administration, but, of course, on a very reduced scale compared to their position in Achaemenid times. In Nisa it appears that the *marzbān* 'margrave' was above the satrap, while below the satrap was the *dyzpty* the head of a 'fortified village'. The *marzbān* might be another name for *patikōspān*, 'margrave', attested from Sasanian times.[60] How far this pattern extended is unknown, but possibly only over Persia.

From the Transcaucasus region we find frequently the term *bitaxš*, *pitiaxši*, *vitaxa*, Armenian *bdeašx*, which was, as we have mentioned in note 57, identified with the Dura *batēsa*. I would also compare *bitaxš* with *nohodar* 'first place man', and interpret *bitaxš* as 'second place (ruler?)'.[61] Whether this title was limited to the north-western part of the Parthian domains is uncertain, but it is definitely and plentifully attested there, while not localised elsewhere. It must be emphasised again that bearers of these titles occupied various offices which have confused the issues especially when one tries to assign a particular function to a title. The military characteristics of the Seleucid state were strengthened, it would seem, under the Parthians, but any attempt to reconstruct a feudal system of vassalage under the Arsacids would be highly conjectural because of lack of sources and ambiguities in words and etymologies. Since material relating to Parthian times is so fragmentary we will find many Parthian survivals when we discuss the organisation of the Sasanian empire.

The position and influence of the Greek cities in the western part of the Parthian state later declined in favour of royal and provincial authority, for this is clearly revealed by the coinage. We can follow the economic history of the Roman Empire thanks to many sources and studies, but it would be hazardous to attribute anything more than the general trends of the Roman development to the economic situation of the Parthians. The debasement of Roman coins in the second and especially third centuries AD is well known, and this general tendency, though

216

not so clearly, can also be observed in the Parthian coinage especially after Vologeses I. The tetradrachme, popular under the Seleucids and especially the Bactrian Greeks, had given way to the drachme by the first century BC. Prices probably continued to rise until economic conditions were bad at the end of Parthian rule. The institution of slavery, uneconomical as it was, declined, however, as in the later Roman empire, while serfs, if one may so call the indebted peasants, increased in importance. The question of kinds of slavery and bondage in Parthian times is very difficult to resolve because of the lack of sources, but if one may use later Sasanian materials as a reflection of conditions in earlier times, one would expect a distinction between foreign slaves captured in warfare (the *anšahrik* or 'non-subjects' of Parthia), and those natives who sold themselves or were made slaves by debt *(bandak?)*. [63] One may suspect that the Roman colonate, the tenant estates, also influenced the Parthians towards the end of their rule. As in earlier times, it may be doubted whether large latifundia with huge numbers of slaves ever flourished in the Parthian state, although Mesopotamia would have been a more appropriate field for them than the Iranian plateau. Plutarch (*Crassus* 21) may refer to a kind of serf when he speaks of the mass of the Parthian army composed of *pelatae* or 'clients, mercenaries'. [64] One may postulate absentee landlordship as an important cause for the economic troubles of Parthia as it was in the Roman Empire, and the luxury of the Arsacid court was repeated in the courts of the nobility and minor kings, all to the detriment of the peasantry.

We know little about taxes in the Parthian state and probably they differed in various parts of it. If we can rely on later information, primarily the Talmud, then we can reconstruct some of the taxes in Parthian Mesopotamia. There apparently was a land tax called *tasqā* in the Talmud, and *keraga* or poll tax, which latter word can be compared to the later Islamic land tax. [65] It would seem that in Mesopotamia, as in Palestine, once a person paid a tax in a town he was considered a citizen of that town or village and was registered there for tax purposes. [66] If one could not pay his taxes then his property would revert to the king, for all land was in theory owned by the king; but a person, of course, could sell himself or his family into slavery to one who paid his taxes. The poll tax was not paid by the nobles, soldiers, priests or members of the bureaucracy, but there were many other taxes including a *corvée* on government projects called *angarya* in

217

the Talmud.[67] Duties on river transportation, on salt, on the import and on the sale of slaves are known and the list undoubtedly could be lengthened. [68]

Much has been written about the Parthian army which the Romans knew well. It was probably Mithradates II who organised the Parthian army and made the cavalry more important than it had been in Seleucid times. The cavalry seems to have been divided into light cavalry, primarily archers whom the Romans feared, and heavy armoured cavalry, the *clibanarii* with heavy lances and the *cataphracti*.[69] The tactics of attacking and then riding away to lure the foe, while employing the *clibanarii* as a psychological shock more than a basic force, at first upset the Romans. Later, possibly under Artabanus III, a royal body-guard and mercenaries are more important than they were previously.

Trade developed greatly under the Parthians for many Parthian coins have been found on the Volga, in the Caucasus, in Chinese Turkestan and elsewhere, especially from the first half of the first century AD.[70] The discovery of the monsoon by the Romans in the first century BC brought the spice and luxury trade of the Indies and the Far East closer to the Roman Empire. At the same time Parthian-Chinese contacts overland are attested in Chinese sources. The aggressive Han dynasty extended its sway throughout Chinese Turkestan on several occasions and undoubtedly merchants penetrated to lands beyond the attainments of the armies. With the decline of both Chinese and Parthian power in the second century AD the Kushans became the heirs of both as the dominant power in Central Asia. The settlement of some 10,000 Roman prisoners in Merv by the Parthians according to Plutarch has led to some interesting speculation about direct Roman-Chinese contacts in Turkestan.[71]

Literature and Culture

Although we have no literary remains of the Parthians from their own time, we may postulate something about literature under the Arsacids. Greek, of course, served as an official written language on the coins and elsewhere, and surely there were many educated Parthians who knew Greek. We know that Greek drama was cultivated, not only from classical sources, but from excavations of theatres and a form or mould for making a comedy mask from Nisa.[72] In Mesopotamia Semitic languages were in use, and as we know from the documents of Nisa and Avroman, Parthian was written heterographically with Aramaic words as well as letters. From this awkward way of writing one would not expect an extensive written literature in Parthian, but there was a flourishing oral literature at the courts of nobles and rulers in Parthian times.

There is evidence that the Parthians gave the Iranian national epic the basic form in which the Sasanians recorded it and passed it on to Firdosi. Parthian poet-musicians *(gōsān)* not only created many of the heroic-feudal characteristics of the epic, but they probably preserved the old legends of the Kavis of eastern Iran, the Kayanians of the epic who were the ancestors of Vishtaspa, patron of Zoroaster.[73] These lays of ancient Iran, if one may call them that, were secular rather than religious in content, although the Zoroastrian priests may have later contributed to their preservation. In the course of Parthian rule many new elements entered the tales, such as the labours of Heracles, which the Parthians surely heard about from the Greek population, and which may have provided a prototype for the heroic deeds of Rustam. We have already mentioned that the Rustam cycle of stories was probably brought into the Iranian national epic by the Sakas from Central Asia. Undoubtedly the minstrels in Parthian times wove many strands together in their stories of heroism in ancient Iran.

The north-eastern origin of most of the tales in the epic, attested by the mingling of Kayanian, Saka and Parthian traditions, has been convincingly proposed.[74] The decline of the widespread tradition of minstrel-poems, it would seem, began in Sasanian times, but the loss of such poetry later came primarily, we may conjecture, in the change of society, in the influence of Arabic after the conquest of Iran by the Arabs, and in more sophisticated and new forms of poetic expression. But under the Parthians the minstrels flourished and, one might say, dominated the scene as far as literature was concerned.

Parthian art was mentioned when speaking of the Sarmatians and the animal style. The former view of Parthian art as degenerate Greek art must be revised, and, although there is continuity, Parthian art is also different from Sasanian art. Certainly Greek influences were very strong among the early Parthians as we learn from Nisa, but the Parthians returned to old Iranion traditions in art as in other domains; scenes of the hunt, the banquet scene, war and sacrifices come to the fore in later Parthian art. The resurgence of polychromy in decoration is a feature of Parthian minor arts as of Sarmatian art. In architecture one can see Hellenistic forms, but the decoration and many new features are Oriental. Whatever the origin of these features, they certainly are found as leading characteristics of Parthian architecture. They include the dome on squinches, the central importance of the liwan, and mural decoration as sculptured tapestry. The 'expressionism' of this art already has been noted.[75] In speaking of the Parthian art, of course, we are using a very general term, for undoubtedly in this domain, and especially in architecture, there were local differences. Architecture is an especially complicated subject for this period and we cannot discuss it here.

The nomadic background of the Parthians may be seen in some equestrian features of dress, such as leggings *cum* boots with tucked-in trousers, which were popular all over the Near East in the first two centuries of our era.[76] The social life, the art, oral literature and political organisation of the Parthians, such as we know them, all testify to the heroic quality of the Parthian way of life, and appropriately they have left their name in modern Persian as *pahlavān* 'hero, brave man'.

Foundations of Zoroastrianism

More has been written about the religion of the ancient Persians than about any other phase of their life because of the texts, the Avesta and the Pahlavi religious books. Furthermore, religion dominated the lives of the ancients far more than of contemporary man. With the Parthians, however, we lack sources for this as for other aspects of their history. Speculation about the religious situation in Iran between the Achaemenids and the Sasanians has usually been based on the syncretism of the Seleucid period, which seems to have lasted into Arsacid times. There is much evidence in classical sources, including inscriptions, to suggest that cults based on the identification of Greek deities with their Oriental counterparts, together with the new messianic features, were dominant in Near Eastern religious life. What happened in Iran in this period, and how did Zoroastrianism develop?

We may suspect that the Magi, in various parts of Iran, upheld the worship of Ahura Mazda and/or other old Aryan gods in varying forms and degrees of piety. That there existed a 'Zoroastrian orthodoxy' in this period is difficult to believe, but one may perhaps assume a generic relationship among the forms

220

of worship among the Iranians, which might be called the Mazdayasnian faith. The Sasanians might have denied the adherence of the Arsacids to any form of the Mazdayasnian faith, but Zoroastrianism as we later know it must have been taking shape under the Parthians. The Pahlavi *Denkart* speaks of the restoration of the good religion (Zoroastrianism) under the Sasanians after its long eclipse after Alexander the Great, which only conforms to the general pattern of later Iranian views of the Parthians.

Undoubtedly the Parthians were more tolerant and less concerned about religion than the Sasanians; at least we hear of no great persecutions of adherents of foreign faiths by the former. The position of Jews, for example, was better under the Parthians than under the Sasanians, and from the Talmud *(Baba Kamma* 117a) we learn that Ardashir I deprived the Jews of the right of inflicting capital punishment on members of their own faith which they had held under the Parthians. Various religious bodies maintained a separate existence under their own leaders, as usual in the Orient, down to the *milets* of the Ottoman empire. Undoubtedly many sects and cults existed in the Near East, but to disentangle them in the sources is a most difficult task. If we speak of the religion of the Iranians, as do the classical sources, we will find many contradictions and problems, but if we speak of a general Mazdayasnian religious predominance or 'atmosphere' with a latitude perhaps similar to 'the religion of the Romans', then we may expect many sub-divisions and even aberrations. One might distinguish between the religions of the Indo-Parthians, the Kushans, the Sakas, the Sogdians, the Parthians, the Armenians, the Persians, and the Iranicised population of Pontus, Cappadocia and Commagene, not to mention syncretic cults of Mesopotamia and elsewhere. When one speaks, however, of Iranian elements in the pantheon of the Kushans, presumably we interpret this as meaning descendants of old Aryan gods or peculiarly Iranian practices such as the exposure of the dead or reverence for fire. Also when Bardesanes, for example, speaks of consanguineous marriages among the *Magousai* of Asia Minor, we think of a Zoroastrian practice even though the Ptolemies practised it and its origin may be sought elsewhere.[77]

The Magians are frequently singled out in classical sources as the representatives of 'the religion of the Persians', *par excellence,* and it would not be amiss to suppose that their influence was very strong. Origen *(Against Celsus.* VI.80,693) said that the word magic derives from their name, and as magicians and sorcerers they were known in the West. We may suppose that in Iran they were the priests who took care of any rites of marriage, burial and the like, and that they served various deities, the most important of whom, after Ahura Mazda or Ohrmizd, being Mithra and Anahita.

It is impossible to discuss here certain practices such as the sacrifice of horses, apparently an old Aryan custom, mentioned by Tacitus (VI.37), Philostratus (*Life of Apollonius*, I.31) and others, as practised by the Parthians, or certain interesting survivals such as the god Assur in Mesopotamia, or the Aramaic inscription relating to 'the goddess Nanai the king' (masculine!), and her relation to Anahita.[78] Problems are many but certain solutions are few. A few items, however, may be of interest and importance.

An Armenian historian, writing about Yazdagird II in the fifth century AD, speaks of the *pahlavik* and the *parskaden*, presumably the Parthian and Persian religions which have been interpreted as a northern Parthian and a southern Persian school of Magi, or two sects.[79] That this is a cogent explanation may be inferred from the theomorphic names from the documents of Nisa which, as we have seen, are good Zoroastrian names. Together with the use of the Zoroastrian calendar, they would indicate that the inhabitants of Nisa were Zoroastrians.[80] It should be added that many names also have in them the God Mithra, such as Mihrbozan, Mihrdatak, Mihrfarn, showing the popularity of the 'sun god' in the Parthian homeland. Of special note is the estate at Nisa called ’*yzn nnystnkn*, the *ayazan* (OP *āyadana*) or the 'temple of Nanai', an indication that probably here Nanai is to be identified with Anahita, whose name does not occur. Since the documents from Nisa are from the second and first centuries BC, perhaps the attribution of a gathering of the Avestan fragments together by a king Valakhsh in the *Denkart* should be referred to the Arsacid king Vologeses I. One may accept this tradition if we remember the 'orientalisation' of the Parthian state which can be connected especially with the reign of Vologeses I.

From archaeology and brief remarks in classical sources one may suppose that the Seleucid cult of the ruler continued under the Parthians, and homage to ancestors was also prominent [81] From the remarks of Strabo, Pliny and others, it would seem that many of the tedious observances as described in the

Vendidad, such as prohibitions and even taboos and charms, were in vogue in Parthian times. The mysteries of Mithra, as mentioned above, although Iranian in instigation, had practices and features which may be traced to Mesopotamia or Asia Minor, while *daevic* or Ahrimanic connections have been ably discussed by others. [82]

The Kushans and the East

We have spoken of the conquest of Bactria by the Kushans, but it would not be amiss to quote the well-known passage of the later *Han-shu* relating to this:

'Formerly, when the Yüeh-chih were attacked by the Hsiung-nu, they migrated to Ta-hsia and divided the country among the five *hsi-hou*, that is to say, Hsiu-mi, Shuang-mi, Kuei-shuang, Pat-tun and Tu-mi. More than one hundred years had passed after Chi'u-chiu-ch'üeh, *hsi-hou* of Kuei-shuang, having attacked and destroyed (the other) four *hsi-hou*, became independent and set himself on the throne. (His) kingdom was called Kuei-shuang-wang.' [83]

We can accept this account as reliable and assume that the Yüeh-chih were united under the chief of the Kushan tribe. The term *hsi-hou* generally has been recognised as the Chinese equivalent of the title which appears on the coins of Kujula Kadphises, the first great Kushan ruler, in Kharoshthi script as *yavuga*. This in turn has been equated with the early Turkic title *yabghu*, but since the Turks probably borrowed their titulary from Iranians, one may assume that *yavuga* is Iranian. [84] Since Kuei-shuang also is clearly Kushan, the name of the leader Chi'u-chiu-ch'üeh (Ancient Chinese *k'ieu dz'ieu k'iak*) represents Kujula Kadphises, the etymology of which is most uncertain. [85]

His son Vima Kadphises succeeded him, apparently after having made extensive conquests in India. Under Vima, the exact form of whose name is uncertain, Kushan power extended northwards across the Oxus river. The extent of his realm into Sogdiana and westwards at the expense of the Parthians cannot be determined and coin finds in Central Asia are uncertain indices of actual control. [86] The approximate dating of Kujula and Vima in the latter part of the first century AD seems assured by the imitation of the coins of the early Roman Empire by Kujula.

It is under the next kings, Kanishka and Huvishka, however,

223

that Kushan power reaches it apogee. Kanishka is well known in Buddhist writings as a great defender and propagator of the faith, while his inscriptions and those of succeeding rulers have caused great quantities of ink to flow in trying to answer a hotly disputed question on the date of Kanishka. At least two international symposia on Kanishka's date have been held in the past sixty years, but no conclusive decision has been reached. The problem lies with the inscriptions dated according to a Kanishka era. Some scholars maintain that this era is in fact the so-called 'Saka era' of Indian history, and should begin AD 78. Others claim that Kanishka had his own era which is not the same as the Saka era, and his date should be *circa* AD 124-144. Recently some documents found in Khwarezm, and dating from the eighth-ninth centuries AD according to archaeological remains, contain dates from the year 658 to 753 of an era which should have begun shortly after the Christian era. Thus the Khwarezmian era parallels various Indian eras, as well as the Seleucid and Parthian eras.[86a] Future epigraphical discoveries may solve some of the problems of the eastern Iranian cultural area. The main actors in this domain seem to have been the Kushans.

There are some matters on which most scholars agree, one of which is the syncretic culture of the Kushan realm which was even more variegated than that of the Parthian state. This may be seen most clearly in the art objects found by archaeologists at Begram, Afghanistan north of Kabul. Plaster plaques with Greek profiles on them, Chinese lacquer, Indian carved ivories and Egyptian glassware attest the widespread contacts of the Kushans[87] Similar observations may be made of the coins where Hellenistic or Roman deities, such as Heracles, Hephaestus, Serapis, are pictured as well as Iranian gods and goddesses such as Mithra, Ardoxsho, Atar and Verethragna.

To these are added Indian deities such as Siva (Oesho), Mahasena and Buddha. Indeed here too the Kushan empire seems remarkably similar to the Roman with its various cults and foreign influences. The coinage of the Kushans is notable for the many gold issues beginning with Vima, based on the Roman gold *denarius* of about 8 grams, and the lack of any silver issues, in contrast to the Parthians. The gold coinage, more than anything else, indicates the separation of the Kushans from the Parthians with their silver, traditionally the money of the steppes, the preference of nomads. The Kushans perhaps felt themselves the heirs of the Greeks of Bactria, for it probably was Kanishka who adapted the Greek alphabet to record the Iranian language used in the Kushan kingdom. At the same time trade connections with the Roman empire were many and ideas, art and culture passed between the two as well as objects of trade.

After Kanishka came Huvishka who had a long reign to judge from his manifold and abundant coinage. It was probably under this king that the Bactrian inscription of the temple sanctuary of Surkh Kotal, dated in the year 31 (after Kanishka), was written telling of the restoration of the sanctuary. [88] It must be emphasised again that we do not know the dates or the circumstances of succession or rule of the various kings. From the style and legends of the coins one may make reasonable guesses, but they are no more. The practice of collateral succession among the Kushans, similar to the Indo-Parthians, makes the reconstruction of a table of succession of the Kushans highly speculative. [89]

After Huvishka the coins of a King Vasudeva have been found in considerable number, but after him a repetition of coin types similar to the proliferation of the coinage of the Graeco-Bactrian kings seems to occur. Can we assume that the immense empire of the Kushans extending from Mathura in India to the Oxus and beyond, in Central Asia, split into two or more parts? It would seem that the Kushans held the greatest territory when their neighbours were weak, while with the rise of the Sasanians in Persia, if not before, and the Guptas in India at the beginning of the fourth century, Kushan power is ended even though minor Kushan dynasts did continue to rule. Under Shapur I the Kushans were tributary to the Sasanians but presumably not under their direct rule, while later in the time of Shapur II the Sasanians had governors at least in Bactria. The question of Kushan rule in Central Asia cannot be solved without new archaeological material, particularly inscriptions, for the few finds of Kushan coins in the excavations of S. P. Tolstov in Khwarezm can be explained as the result of trade. From Chinese sources, as well as from archaeological indications, one might assume that the Kushans did control Kashgar, Sogdiana and the Ferghana valley at least under Kanishka. How far to the west, north and east they went cannot be determined, but the Kushans established a reputation and a new dynastic legitimacy in eastern Iran and north-west India so that their successors the Hephthalites and the Shahi kings of Kabul, before the Islamic conquest, claimed descent from the Kushans. In Buddhist tradition Kanishka looms large and the extent and influence of the Gandharan art school already has been mentioned. The Kushans not only brought Central Asian and Chinese influences into eastern Iran and India, but they also contributed to the Iranisation of north-west India, which make them worthy of our attention.

The Traditions of Persis

Under the Seleucids and the Parthians the province of Persis, the homeland of the Achaemenids, maintained some of the old imperial traditions. At the side of the rock-cut tomb of Darius at Naqsh-i Rustam there is a much weathered and almost totally illegible inscription in the Aramaic script, but in the Old Persian language, as evidenced by at least two words *hšyty wzrk* 'great king' (line 20), while other readings are less clear. If this inscription is to be dated in Seleucid times, it would be a surprising document perhaps written by Persians under Greek rule to preserve the memory of their illustrious kings.[90] More certain is the series of coins minted by the *frataraka* presumably under Seleucid overlordship (Strabo XV.736), although one may surmise that the *frataraka* simply continued a provincial office of the late Achamenid empire which the Seleucids accepted. It is significant, I believe, that the obverses of the early coins resemble Achaemenid satrapal issues, while some reverses have the ruler in adoration before a structure resembling the so-called Ka'bah of Zoroaster at Naqsh-i Rustam over which, on a few coins, the Achaemenid winged figure of Ahura Mazda is placed.[91]

After the Parthian conquest of western Iran the coins change to resemble Parthian prototypes and the title *MLK'*, 'king' appears. It would be interesting if the assumption of the title 'king' by the rulers of Persis coincided with the use of the title 'king of kings' by the Parthian great king, but one cannot date the coins of Persis. At the same time as the title 'king', the language on the coins changes from Aramaic to heterographic Middle Persian, as evidenced by the word *BRH*, 'son', literally 'his son' in Aramaic, which appears on the coins of a certain *D'ryw*, 'Darius' son of Autophradates, perhaps to be dated in the first century B.C. The coins have been divided into three series, extending down to the Sasanians and the earliest have been dated *circa* 220 BC, while none of them have Greek legends.[92] This is further evidence for the continuity of Achaemenid traditions in Persis, and the names of the rulers, Darius and Artaxerxes support this belief.

Other than the coins there is little information about Persis before the Sasanians. Strabo (XV.736) would have the local princes without any real power and subject to the Parthians. Pliny (VI.152) says that Numenius the governor of Mesene, appointed by Antiochus (IV?), won a battle against the Persians first with his fleet and then his cavalry on the coast of the Persian Gulf, which tells us little. Lucian (*Macrobius*, ch. 15) quotes from an unknown work by Isidore of Charax saying: 'Artaxerxes, another king of the Persians, whom Isidore of Charax the author says ruled in the time of his parents, after living ninety-three years, was treacherously murdered through a plot of his brother Gochihr.' Unfortunately this ruler cannot be definitely identified with any king of the coin series.

The religion of the princes of Persis was important to them since fire altars appear on the later coins and on the earliest coins *prtrk' ZY 'LHY'*, 'governor (by grace?) of the gods' (rather than 'divine *frataraka*), which would indicate a religious sanction of rule. Further speculation on the significance of this, to make a dynasty of Zoroastrian priest-kings may be plausible but should be avoided until more source material is at hand.

The existence of a temple or sanctuary of Anahita near Persepolis from the time of the Achaemenid Artaxerxes II to Ardashir the Sasanian seems attested by a number of sources.[93] It would appear that the goddess was especially venerated in Persis, not exclusively but together with Ahura Mazda and Mithra. Islamic sources tell us that a certain Sasan was in charge of the temple of Anahita at Istakhr (near Persepolis) at the same time that a king called Gochihr from a family called Bazrangi was ruling in Persis.[94] If this tradition is reliable Gochihr should be a ruler who issued coins in the series of the rulers of Persis, but no coins of his have been found. This name, however, is not unexpected, any more than that of Sasan, whose name is also found among the coins of the Indo-Parthians.[95] One story has it that Sasan married a daughter of Gochihr and his son Papak revolted against Gochihr and killed him. Thus the foundation of the Sasanian dynasty was laid.

The rise of Ardashir is shrouded in similar, but even more, legendary lore to that of Cyrus and the first Arsacid ruler. It is quite probable that by the time of Ardashir Parthian, or rather eastern Iranian, epic tales had long since penetrated Persis and were sung by minstrels perhaps together with local lays. The

227

priesthood in Persis had been accommodating various facets of rites and worship to each other and forming the background of what was to be the basis of the new Zoroastrian state church. After the Sasanians were well established the legitimacy of the dynasty as the lineal descendants of the vague great empire of the past had to be propagated. The priests who could write were interested in other matters and it fell to the minstrels to take up the task of weaving the story of the rise of the Sasanians into the national epic. Since the pre-Sasanian era was one of heroic epics rather than of sober, written history, this was not a difficult task. After Ardashir history begins in Iran, even in the epic, and one might also say life becomes more prosaic and more ordered. Although much of the feudal, heroic culture of the Parthians continues we are in a new epoch; a new national consciousness comes into being. Yet still the legacy continues showing the remarkable continuity of Iranian traditions.

NOTES

1 E. Sachau (trans.) *The Chronology of Ancient Nations* (London, 1879), 116 fol. Hamza knew that information about the Parthians was confused, but he also knew the true state of the chronology; cf. U. M. Daudpota (trans.), *The Annals of Ḥamzah al-Isfahānī* (Bombay, 1932), 9, 13.

2 *Kitāb al-tanbih* ed. M. de Goeje (Leiden, 1894), 97, and trans. B. Carra de Vaux (Paris, 1896), 140.

3 Many of the results of many years' study on early Parthian history, published in numerous articles, by J. Wolski are generally accepted by most scholars. See his '*The Decay of the Iranian Empire of the Seleucids and the Chronology of Parthian Beginnings*', *Berytus,* 12 (1956-1957), 35-52. The booklet by B. P. Lozinski, *The Original Homeland of the Parthians* (The Hague, 1959) cannot be used except for its bibliography.

4 J. Markwart, *A Catalogue of the Provincial Capitals of Eranshahr* (Rome, 1931), 52. The upper countries and upper satrapies are mentioned by Polybius V.40. The thesis of H. W. Haussig, '*Theophylakts Exkurs über die skythischen Völker*', *Byzantion,* 23 (1953), 329 foll., that the name Aparni is to be connected with Avar, and other tribal names, is to be regarded with scepticism.

5 References and discussion in Henning, *Handbuch der Orientalistik, op. cit.,* 95.

6 *Ibid.,* 93.

7 N. Debevoise, *A Political History of Parthia* (Chicago, 1938), 10.

8 Wolski, *op. cit.,* 47.

9 I. M. Dyakonov i V. A. Livshits, *Dokumenty iz Nisy* (Moscow, 1960), 20, Ostraca no. 1760, dated in the Arsacid year 157/91 BC. Here, fortunately personal royal names were used rather than the dynastic Arshak, but the first ruler apparently was called Arshak as his personal name.

228

10 *Loc. cit.* On the mythical Kavi Arshan, archer and eponymous ancestor of the Arsacids see R. von Stackleberg, *'Iranica' ZDMG*, 45 (1891), 620. There was also, apparently a tradition that the Parthians were descended from Gushtasp or Vishtaspa, patron of Zoroaster (Ṭabarī I, 708). Descent from Artaxerxes is noted by Arrian, a later author.

11 Cf. Jenkins and Narain, note 106 of Ch. 4, *passim.* J. Wolski, *'Arsace II', Eos,* 41 (Warsaw, 1946), 160, concluded that Tiridates was legendary and Arsaces I ruled over thirty years, but a royal Tyrydt seems assured by the Nisa Ostraca, although it might be Tiridates II.

12 For example, in Media alone we know of several rebels, Molon under Antiochus III and Timarchus under Demetrius I.

13 See Polybius V.55, who correctly says Azerbaijan had not submitted to Alexander. Regarding Armenia there is confusion about the ruler and exactly what happened. Cf. A Bouché-Leclercq, *Histoire des Séleucids,* 2 (Paris, 1914), 569. After Magnesia we hear of an independent dynasty. Perhaps the rulers of the two main parts of the country, confirmed by Antiochus III, simply went their own ways.

14 Justin XLI.6.

15 *Ibid.,* XLI.5, where the brother and predecessor of Mithradates, Phraates by name, is said to have subdued and resettled the Mardi in the region of Tehran; also Isidore of Charax, *Parthian Stations,* 7.

16 K. Mannert, *Geographie der Griechen und Römer,* 5 (Leipzig, 1829), 69-78 is still valuable as a survey of the classical views on Parthia. On Ptolemy see W. Kubitschek, *'Studien zur Geographie des Ptolemäus I', Sitzungsberichte der- Akad. der Wiss.,* 215 (Vienna, 1934), III, and his introduction.

17 *'Novye dannye po istorii Parfii', VDI* (1950), 3, 43

18 'Mtrdtkrt BYRT᾽', 'the city-fortress of Mithradatkirt', occurs on ostracon, 1693; cf. Dyakonov i Livshits (note 9), 22.

19 M. E. Masson i G. A. Pugachenkova, *Parfyanskie Ritony Nisy* (Moscow, 1956) with 120 magnificent plates.

20 For Nisa cf. L. I. Rempel, *'Terrakoty Merva i glinyanye statui Nisy', Trudy Yuzhno-Turkmenistanskoi arkh. ekspeditsii,* I (Ashkabad, 1949), 360, and M. E. Masson in *Trudy, etc.,* 5 (Ashkabad, 1955), 64. For Toprak Kale see M. A. Orlov, *'Rekonstruktsiya zala Voinov dvorsta Toprak-Kala', Trudy Khorezmskoi Arkh. Ekspeditsii,* I (M., 1952), 47 foll. For Surkh Kotal D. Schlumberger, *'Le temple de Surkh Kotal, 3', JA* (1955), 275.

21 Dyakonov i Livshits (note 9), 9, and their *'Parfyanskoe Tsarskoe Khozyaistvo v Nise', VDI* (1960), 2, 15. The alternative theories are described there in sufficient detail.

22 *Ibid.,* 24, and their *'Iz materialov Parfyanskoi Kantselyarii staroi Nisy', Sbornik v chest I. A. Orbeli* (Moscow, 1960), 332.

23 The classical sources are quoted and discussed by A. D. Mordtmann, *'Hekatompylos', Sitzungsber. der bayer. Akad. der Wiss.* (Munich, 1869), 512-526. Hecatompylos may have become a capital before the campaign of Antiochus III, but it was prominent only after his fall. Cf. J. Hansman and D. Stronach, *'Excavations at Shahr-i Qumis 1967', JRAS* (1970), 29-62.

24 Pompeius Trogus, *Prologue,* 34, 13, and Bevan, *The House of Seleucus,* II, 195.

25 See the discussion in E. Herzfeld, *'Sakastan', Archaeologische Mitteilungen aus Iran,* 4 (Berlin, 1931), 36.

26 Diodorus Siculus XXXIII. 18, Paulus Orosius V.4. 16, Justin XLI.6.8.

27 Tarn, *The Greeks in Bactria and India,* 273.

28 Debevoise, 26.

29 Cf. G. Le Rider, *'Monnaies de Characène'*, *Syria*, 36 (1959), 251-252. A bibliography of previous studies may be found in the notes to Le Rider's article.

30 E. T. Newell, *'The Coinage of the Parthians'*, in *A Survey of Persian Art*, ed. A. U. Pope, I (London, 1938), 480. I have been unable to locate the coins of Artabanus, father of Mithradates II, with the legend 'king of kings', according to J. de Morgan, *Manuel de Numismatique orientale* (Paris, 1923-1930), 132, 147. It is possible, of course, that the title was used before Mithradates since the rulers of Elymais, Persis and elsewhere probably used the title of king after the Parthian conquest and before Mithradates II.

31 E. Herzfeld, *'Sakastan'* (note 25), 101.

32 *Ibid.*, 94.

33 From a conversation with M. E. Masson in Tashkent, July, 1955, and observation of the coins. This is contrary to the usual opinion, but I confess to scepticism on the various arrangements of Indo-Parthian kings which do not distinguish between the all Greek and the Greek-Kharoshthi legends. The monogram on the Sanabares coins is found on the coins of Pakores I and Phraates IV of Parthia and not on Indo-Parthian or Saka coins. All of this indicates a closer connection between Merv, Herat and Seistan than hitherto assumed. Indeed geographically communications would be easier between these areas than between Seistan and India. Cf. A. Simonetta, *'An Essay on the so-called "Indo-Greek"-Coinage'*, *East and West*, 8 (Rome 1957), 50, for information on the coins of Sanabares, and M. Masson, *'Vostochno-parfyanskii pravitel Sanabar'*, *Trudy Gos Istor, Muzei*, 26 (Moscow, 1957), 32-42.

34 Herzfeld (note 25), 116. This surmise would conflict with the equally speculative assertion that both the king and the Holy Grail originated from Shiz or Takht-i Sulaiman in Azerbijan. Cf. L. I. Ringbom, *Graltempel und Paradies* (Stockholm, 1951), and his *Paradisus Terrestris* (Helsingfors, 1958).

35 The history of these early rulers of Great (eastern) Armenia, as well as that of Little (western) Armenia and Sophene, is little known. The discovery of at least three Aramaic 'milestones' or marker stones near lake Sevan tell us Artaxias was the son of a Zariadres, ʾrtḫ̌š̌ MLK BR ZY zrytr rwndkn. Cf. I. M. Dyakonov i K. B. Starkova, *'Nadpisi Artaksiya'*, *VDI*, 2 (1955), 168, and *'Novonaidennaya nadpis Artashesa'*, *VDI*, (1959), I, 88-90.

36 The lack of any fear of the Parthians or even regard for them on the part of the Romans before Carrhae has been shown in detail by J. Dobiaš, *'Les premiers rapports des Romains avec les Parthes'*, *Archiv Orientálni*, 3 (Prague, 1931), 215-256.

37 *Mtskheta* (Tiflis, 1958), 71. The notorious Armazi inscriptions (one Greek bilingual) have produced an extensive literature. Cf. A recent article with bibliography P. Grelot, *'Remarques sur le bilingue Grec-Araméen d'Armazi'* *Semitica*, 8 (1958), 11. The question whether the Armazi inscriptions are written in ungrammatical Aramaic or in heterographic ancient Georgian or an Iranian tongue is not resolved. Whereas the inscriptions in Armenia over two centuries earlier were written in Aramaic, in the first and second centuries AD one could expect heterographic writing. It is unlikely that the people of Mtskheta were trilingual at that late time, using Greek (as the *lingua franca* of the time), Aramaic and their own native tongue.

38 Differently in J. Marquart, *Ēransahr* (Göttingen, 1901), 23. On the Parthian title *naxwadar*, see Henning in *Journal of the Royal Asiatic Society* (1953), 135-136, and A. Maricq, *'Hatra de Sanatrouq'*, *Syria*, 32 (1956), 278.

39 A. Caquot, *'Nouvelles inscriptions araméennes de Hatra'*, *Syria, 29*. (1952), 112.

40 E. Sachau, *'Die Chronik von Arbela'*, *Abhandlungen der preuss. Akad. der Wiss.* (Berlin, 1915), 60.

41 Marquart, *Erānšahr*, 22.

42 Seleucia was destroyed by the Romans in AD 165 after which Ctesiphon remained the main city of the Parthians. Cf. M. Streck, *Seleucia und Ktesiphon* (Leipzig, 1917), 24.

43 On the names Mesene and Characene see the discussion in U. Kahrstedt, *Artabanos III* (Bern, 1950), 53. See also G. Le Rider, *Suse sous les Séleucides et les Parthes* (Paris, 1965).

44 Henning, *'The Monuments and Inscriptions of Tang-i Sarvak'*, *Asia Major*, 2 (London, 1952), 177.

45 The meaning of the title rather than name, *prtrk*ʾ, which has been read by some scholars as *prdtr*ʾ 'fire keeper', is uncertain. I prefer the explanation of Andreas, who compared the Old Persian title *prtrk*ʾ 'governor' in the Elphantine papyri, See W. Eilers, *Iranische Beamtennamen* (Leipzig, 1940), 119.

46 Kahrstedt. *op. cit.*, 47, 83. He believes that Artabanus III, before becoming Parthian king, was the ruler of a 'greater Hyrcania' including Herat and Kirman to the Persian Gulf and the Indian Ocean. This surmise may be correct but it is only a surmise. The same is true of his further conjectures (p.83) that Hyrcania after AD 62 became Kushan territory and was no more Parthian land, or (p.47) that Gondophares declared his independence from Parthia at the succession of Artabanus III. Artabanus then placed his relatives on the thrones of Artopatene, Elymais and Persis who lost their thrones after the death of Artabanus III. The attempt of V. Minorsky, *'Vis u Ramin I' BSOAS* (1946), 32-35, to connect the story of Vis and Ramin with the house of Hyrcania is unsupported by any real evidence. The period is confusing.

47 M. E. Masson, *'Novye dannye po istorii Parfii'*, *VDI* (1950), 3, 49, would date what he calls the phil-Hellenic period of Parthian history to AD 10 when the anti-Hellenic period begins. This is based primarily on the excavations at Nisa, where the early 'Greek culture' of rhyta and statues is replaced by a 'native Parthian' culture. The reign of Vologeses I in the second half of the first century would be a better division.

48 *Ibid.*, 50, for a discussion of the city names.

49 As proposed by J. Wolski, *'Remarques sur les institutions des Arsacides'*, *Eos*, 46 (Wroclaw, 1954), 64-65. The question of the brother-in-law in the succession in Seistan (Herzfeld, *'Sakastan'*) is unclear and by no means sure.

50 Rostovtzeff, *'Dura and the Problem of Parthian Art'* (note 113 of Ch. 4), 175.

51 E. Herzfeld, *Am Tor von Asien* (Berlin, 1920), 39.

52 One must be careful in interpreting Greek or Latin designations of Iranian titles, not only because of the persistence of old terms, as found in Herodotus and others, but also because of the difficulty in defining Parthian ranks and offices. See the various notices of satraps by Rostovzeff and C. B. Welles, *'A Parchment Contract'*, *Yale Classical Studies* 2 (1931), 46, where it is correctly stated that satrapy was not the proper designation for 'province' (in the Achaemenid sense) in the Parthian kingdom.

53 See especially Marquart, *'Beiträge zur Geschichte und Sage von Eran'*, *ZDMG*, 49 (1895), 635.

54 Herzfeld, *'Sakastan'*, 57-58, 68. Frequently these family names were

mistaken by Greek or Roman authors for titles, e.g. Mihran in Procopius I.13.16 and II.30,7; and Aspāhpat, *ibid.*, I.9.24.

55 *The Excavations at Dura-Europos*, V, part I, *The Parchments and Papyri*, ec. C. B. Welles (New Haven, 1959), 115.

56 The word has a large bibliography; cf. Henning, *'Mitteliranisch'* in *Handbuch der Orientalistik*, 41, and Herzfeld, *Zoroaster*, 128, note 22. My observations in the Dura volume (preceding note p. III, note 15) should be corrected by the following remarks. The sense of *ark/hark* may well be similar to Akkadian *ilku* 'corvée, feudal service', hence possibly already in Achaemenid times ★*haraka pati* 'lord of tribute', or perhaps really the local tax farmer rather than the official tax collector (the *hamārakar?*). Cf. the University of Chicago Assyrian Dictionary, 7 (Chicago, 1960), 80. H. W. Bailey in *Asia Major*, 7 (1959), 18, however, proposes an Iranian origin ★*hrāka* for Arabic *kharāj*. Also compare Greek *xopxyix*, P. Schwarz in *Der Islam*, 6 (1916), 98.

With the rise of the Parthians the rank or honorary character of the title may have come to the fore, so that it becomes more of a social or class distinction. This would account for the use of the title in Palmyra and in the Syriac acts of the martyrs, such as the 'eunuch who according to his rank was *arzabed'*; O. Braun, *Ausgewählte Akten persischer Märtyrer* (Munich, 1915), 5, 22, and the expression 'of the house of the *Argabet'* in J. Chabot, *Synodicon Orientale* (Paris, 1902), 21. Several problems remain: (1) the form in *arz-*, either a misspelling or a confusion with the word for 'land, earth', usually *'rq'*, (2) the New Persian word, *arg* 'citadel', which may be explained either as a secondary derivation from Middle Persian *harg* 'service', as the place where the *arkpat* or lord lived, or less likely as a derivation from Latin *arx*. The various functions or offices of an *arkapatēs* at Palmyra or in the Sasanian court would not be dependent on his rank. The possibility, however, of several words and offices being confused in the various forms of *arkapatēs, arzabed*, etc., should not be dismissed. Cf. my article *'Some Iranian Titles'* in *Oriens*, 15 (1962) 352-9.

57 The term *batesa* is usually identified with the title *bitaxš*, which latter has been called an Iranian predecessor of New Persian *padishāh*. Cf. Rostovzeff amd Welles, *'A Parchment Contract'*, *Yale Classical Studies*, 2 (1931), 52. The Dura term would seem to be an honorary title while the Iranian evidence would indicate a high office such as 'sub-king' or 'margrave'. Perhaps *batesa* is not Iranian but Semitic, a form of Akkadian *paḫatu*, for in the Babylonian Talmud *pḫwt'* means 'grandees. noble ones'. The form *p't'* is also found but the difficulty with the ending *-sa* remains. Of course Aramaic *PḤT'* was used in the Parthian documents from Nisa for 'satrap', but this need not conflict with a different development of the word in Mesopotamia.

58 A photograph and reading of the inscription may be found in Henning, *'A New Parthian Inscription'*, *JRAS*, 1953. As I ascertained from people of the village of Khusf and on the spot the site is called Kal-i Janggāh 'battlefield', rather than *Jangal* 'jungle'. The name Gari-Ardashir has a parallel in the Nisa documents, Garifarn.

59 Contrary to G. Widengren, *Iranisch-semitische Kulturbegegnung in parthischer Zeit* (Cologne, 1960), 33 note, who considers the word both a feudal title and an office.

60 Dyakonov i Livshits (note 9), 18. This threefold division in the Nisa documents might reflect the Seleucid division of satrapy, eparchy and hyparchy, wherein the Parthian satrapy = Seleucid eparchy. The *marzbān* of the frontier against the Kushans in northeastern Persia was called the *kanārang*, presumably a Kushan title by origin.

61 H. S. Nyberg, *'Inscriptions antiques en Géorgie'*, *Eranos*, 44 (Göteborg, 1946), 237, note 2, proposed *bitiya* < *dvitīya* 'second', for the first part of the compound. Less likely is a connection with New Persian *padishāh*.

62 The title of the crown prince, or heir to the throne, ★*pc 'gryw*, appears in several sources. Cf. I. Gershevitch in *JRAS* (1954), 125, and Widengren (note 59), 29, for further references.

63 A. G. Perikhanian, *'K voprosu o rabovladenii i zemlevadenii v Irane Parfyanskogo Vremeni'*, *VDI* (Moscow, 1952), 4, 15. There are many other writings on slavery by Soviet authors, but many conclusions are based on insufficient evidence.

64 *Ibid.*, 21.

65 Yu. A. Solodukho, *'Podati i povinnosti v Irake v III-Vvv'*, *Sovetskoe Vostokovedenie*, 5 (M, 1948), 56, where a discussion of problems and a bibliography may be found. The terms used in the Talmud are not free from ambiguity as shown by I. Hahn, *'Sassanidische und spätrömische Besteuerung'*, *Acta Antiqua*, 7, (Budapest, 1959), especially 155. Cf. J. Newman, *The Agricultural Life of the Jews in Babylonia* (London, 1932), 161 foll., and S. Kraus, *Persia and Rome in the Talmud and Midrash* (Jerusalem, 1948), 269-274 (in Hebrew).

66 Solodukho, 64. The case of Mary and Joseph under King Herod illustrates this. Some taxes were paid in kind as well as coin.

67 *Ibid.*, 69 where a Persian original *angāre* is proposed. It would be easy to find an Iranian etymology but see note 74, chapter 3. The confusion, if it really exists, between 'couriers' and 'corvée' is seen in S. Funk, *Die Juden in Babylonien* (Berlin, 1908), 65.

68 R. McDowell, *Stamped and Inscribed Objects from Seleucia* (Ann Arbor, 1935), 172, 176, 179.

69 F. Rundgren, *'Iranische Lehnwörter im Lateinischen und Griechischen'*, *Orientalia Suecana*, 6 (1957), 50, derived the word *'clibanarius'* from Iranian *griv-pan* 'armour' rather than from Latin *clibanus* 'oven' but a play on words by the Roman soldiers cannot be excluded for the Latin texts. The term *clibanarii* is found later than *cataphracti*, which Polybius (31.3.9) uses for Seleucid times. The *Historia Augusti*, (56.5) says: *'cataphractarios quos illi [Persae] clibinarii vocant'*.

70 References in M. E. Masson in *Trudy Yuzhno-Turkmenistanskoi Ekspeditsii*, 5 (Ashkabad, 1955), 33-35. Parthian art objects were found in Olbia and other sites in South Russia indicating an extensive trade.

71 H. H. Dubs, *'A Military Contact between Chinese and Romans in 36 BC'*, *T'oung Pao*, 36 (Leiden, 1940), 64-80'

72 M. E. Masson in *Izvestiya Akad. Nauk Turkenskoi·SSR*, I (Ashkabad, 1951), 93.

73 M. Boyce, *'Some Remarks on the Transmission of the Kayanian Heroic Cycle'*, *Serta Cantabrigiensia* (Wiesbaden, 1954), 49-51, and her interesting summary of the literary scene in *'The Parthian gōsān and Iranian Minstrel Tradition'*, *JRAS* (1957), 10-45, where she convincingly shows the existence of a two-fold literary culture (written and oral) from earliest times down to the Arab conquest (p. 35).

74 Boyce, *'Zariadres and Zarēr'*, *BSOAS*, 17 (1955), 476.

75 Notes 43, 44, 110, 111, of Chapter 4. Vaults on squinches and domes on squinches were probably brought from eastern Iran to Mesopotamia by the Parthians. Cf. O. Reuther, *'Parthian Architecture'*, in A. U. Pope ed., *Survey of Persian Art*, I (London, 1938), 427.

76 G. Widengren, *'Some Remarks on Riding Costume among Iranian*

Peoples in Antiquity, 11 (Uppsala, 1956), 241 foll.

77 In Eusebius, *Praeparatio Evangelica*, VI.10.16. The classic work on the Magusians, the Magi of Asia Minor, is by J. Bidez and F. Cumont, *Les mages hellénisés*, 2 vols. (Paris, 1938).

78 Jensen in W. Andrae, *Die Partherstadt Assur* (Leipzig, 1933), 89, and W. Andrae, *Das Wiedererstandene Assur* (Leipzig, 1938), 180.

79 Eghishe, *On Vardan and the Armenian War*, ed. E. Ter-Minasean (Erevan, 1957), 144, and R. Zaehner, *Zurvan* (Oxford, 1955), 29. Whether this division corresponds to the 'northern mobads' and the 'southern herbads' of S. Wikander, *Feuerpriester in Kleinasien und Iran* (Lund, 1946), 140 *et passim*, is difficult to determine, to say the least.

80 Dyakonov (note 9), 24.

81 Attested by the remains of ancestorial statues in Nisa and remarks of Ammianus Marcellinus. Cf. J. M. Unvala, *Observations on the Religion of the Parthians* (Bombay, 1925), 26.

82 Gershevitch, *Mithra*, 61-72, and literature in footnotes. Cf. J. Hinnells, ed. *Mithraic Studies* (Manchester, 1974).

83 Translation of K. Enoki in Narain, *The Indo-Greeks*, 131.

84 Later in one Middle Iranian text both of the forms, with initial *y-* and initial ž- occur, in F. W. K. Müller, *'Ein Doppelblatt'*, Abhandlungen der Preuss. Akad. der Wiss. (Berlin, 1912), lines 77 and 93. This would correspond to Parthian *ymg* 'leader' of a Manichaean congregation, for the b/m alternation is widespread. A form of the same word appears in the language of Bukhara, *jamuk*, meaning 'Noble, leader', cf. *JAOS*, 71 (1951) n 142. It should be noted that an Altaic origin for *yabghu/yavgu* has been proposed by G. Clauson in *Asia Major*, 8 (London, 1960), 115, with a form ★*davgu*, which to me seems unacceptable.

85 An attempt to find an Iranian etymology was made by H. W. Bailey, *'Irano-Indica* III', *BSOAS*, 13 (1950), 397. Cf. the discussion in Marquart, *Eransahr*, 209.

86 B. Ya 'Staviskii', *'O severnykh granitsakh Kushanskogo gosudarstva'*, *VDI* (1961), 1, 108-114. Cf. the extensive bibliography in B. Ya. Staviskii, B. I. Vainberg, *et. al.*, *Sovetskaya arkheologiya Srednei Azii i kushanskaya problema*, 1 (Moscow, 1968), 62-8.

86a. W. B. Henning, *'The Choresmian Documents'*, Asia Major, 11 (London, 1965), 168, and V. A. Livshits, *'The Khwarezmian Calendar'*, Acta Antiqua, 16 (Budapest, 1968), 440.

87 J. Hackin, *Nouvelles recherches archéologiques à Begram* (Paris, 1954), *passim*.

88 A. Maricq in *JA*, 1958, 345 foll., and W. B. Henning in *BSOAS*, 23 (1960), 48.

89 Cf. A. L. Basham, 'The Succession of the Line of Kanishka', *BSOAS*, 20 (1957), 77-88. and E. V. Zeimal, *Kushanskaya khronologiya* (Moscow, 1968).

90 W. B. Henning, *Handbuch* (note 56), 24, reads one word *slwk* = Seleucus. This reading, however, is neither absolute nor if the name Seleucus is really meant, is an identification with Seleucus I obligatory.

91 Especially the coins of Autophradates; cf. G. F. Hill, *Catalogue of the Greek Coins of Arabia*, etc. (London, 1922) and de Morgan (note 30), 279. I cannot accept Wikander's assertion in *Feuerpriester in Kleinasien und Iran* (Lund, 1946), 16 that the title ★*frataraka* in the Aramaic papyri from Elphantine was an insignificant office. The holder of this title Vidrang was actually a prominent Persian who was commander of the garrison at Syene and *hpthpt'* before he became ★*frataraka* of Yeb, which was a higher

position. The title *hpth* plus *pt*' would seem to be a combination of a Semitic and an Iranian word, perhaps meaning 'in charge of supplies' or 'in charge of the treasury'. The etymology of ★*frataraka* is uncertain, for we have *hratarak* in Armenian which means an announcer and in modern parlance a publisher (see note 45). For an attempted etymology see H. Acharean, *Hayerēn Armatakan Baṛaran,* 4 (Everan, 1932-), 431. In any case ★*frataraka* is elsewhere attested as a title; ★*fratadara* is not.

92 The dating of the coinage to *circa* 280 BC by Newell, *The Eastern Seleucid Mints* (New York, 1938), 161, was based on a hoard from Persepolis which included a coin of Seleucus I and nine local coins of Bagdat, Oborzos and Autophradates. Since the hoard was very small, however, no conclusion can be drawn. R. Stiehl, in F. Althiem, *Geschichte der Hunnen* 1 (Berlin, 1959), 376, following G. F. Hill, convincingly identified the name Oborzos in Polyaenus (7.40) with the *wḥwbrz* of the coins. Connecting the independence and minting of coins of the ★*frataraka* (rather than *fratadara* as she calls them) with the same in Elymais, she dates the beginning of the independence of Persis *circa* 187 BC and the end of it *circa* 140 BC when the Parthians imposed their rule on both Persis and Elymais, which is attested by the coins. This reconstruction is satisfactory but by no means proved. Her reading of the end of the coin legends as *pr(s) br (t')*: 'fortress of Persis' = Persepolis or rather Istakhr, however, is unacceptable.

93 The source material has been conveniently assembled by M. L. Chaumont, *'Le culte d'Anahita à Stakhr', Revue de l'histoire des religions* (Avril-Juin, 1958), 154-175. Cf. K. V. Trever, *'K voprosu o khramakh bogini Anakhity v sasanidskom Irane', Trudy Gos. Ermitazha,* 10, (Leningrad, 1969), 48-54.

94 Tabarī, translated by T. Noeldeke, *Geschichte der Perser* (Leiden, 1879), 4, and the Persian Tabari translated H. Zotenberg, 2 (Paris, 1874), 67. The suggestion of Wikander, *Der Arische Männerbund* (Lund, 1938), 105, that ★ *vazrang* was a title with the same ending as *kanārang* (see note 60) 'margrave' is not convincing, since we would have something like 'holder or preserver of *vaz*' which does not make good sense. A personal name, like the *wydrng* of the Aramaic documents from Elphantine. is more likely. It may be mentioned in passing that a Kurdish tribe in Fars the Ram Bazinjan considers itself descended from a Bazrang.

95 Cf. A. Simonetta in *East and West,* 8 (Rome, 1957), 49; the final letters are not absolutely clear, Sasou (?) in Greek, Sasasa (?) in Kharoshthi. The attempt of Herzfeld to explain the name as a military title *sastar* is not convincing; cf. *Arch. Mitt. aus Iran,* 8 (1936), 23, note 3.

6 HEIRS OF THE ACHAEMENIDS

Ardashir and the Cycle of History

For the Persians solid history begins with the Sasanians. What transpired before Ardashir is vague and legendary, a heroic age; but this does not mean that after Ardashir we escape myth and uncertainty, for what happened and what people believe should have happened are frequently confused even in that portion of Iran's history which is related by many different sources. The story of the founding of the Sasanian dynasty is not unlike the story of Cyrus or even Arsaces, both of which generally conform to epic norms.

In one Pahlavi source, the *Kar Namak of Ardashir,* or his 'book of deeds', which we may call the 'epic' account, it is related that Sasan was a shepherd of King Papak who ruled in the city of Istakhr near Persepolis. Sasan was a descendant of the Achaemenids, but he kept this a secret until Papak had a dream which was interpreted that the son of Sasan would one day rule the world. So Papak gave his daughter to Sasan and from this union Ardashir was born. This story is repeated by Firdosi in the national epic and it was evidently widely believed since Agathias (*Historia* II.27), living in the sixth century, gave a somewhat garbled version of the story, stating that Papak was an astrologer and Sasan a soldier who was a guest in his house. Recognising signs of greatness in Sasan Papak gave him his wife and Ardashir was born. Much later when Ardashir was king a quarrel between the two old men broke out, which was settled by calling Ardashir the son of Papak though descended from Sasan.

Another tradition found in Ibn al-Athir (ed. Tornberg I.272), in Eutychius (ed. Cheikho, foll. 65v) and others, has Sasan a princelet in Fars, Papak his son, and Ardashir his grandson. This is the position adopted by most scholars today, especially after the discovery of the famous trilingual inscription

236

of Shapur I on the Ka'bah of Zoroaster which is the Sasanian counterpart of the OP Behistun inscription.[1] This inscription, however, merely names Sasan with a title 'the lord' possibly as an ancestor, while Papak is here and elsewhere specifically called the grandfather of Shapur. The mother of Papak is given as Denak, but it is not stated whether she was married to Sasan who is never named as Ardashir's grandfather, although this is a general assumption. Therefore an obscurity does exist, even in the inscriptions, about the exact relationship between Sasan and Papak. One possible explanation would have Sasan the real father of Ardashir married to Papak's daughter, as in the epic account, but Sasan died shortly after his son's birth, whereupon Papak adopted Ardashir and then made him his heir after the death of his own son Shapur.

In the Syriac chronicle of Arbela, we read that in the time of Vologeses IV (*circa* AD 191-207) the Parthians fought against the Persians, and later the same chronicle says: 'In earlier times the Persians tried to unseat the Parthians; many times they exerted themselves in war but were defeated.'[2] The chronicle further says that later the Persians and Medes made an alliance with the kings of Adiabene and Kirkuk and that together they overthrew the Parthians. The date and circumstances of the defeat and death of Artabanus V, the opponent of Ardashir, are not clear; the usual dates have been given as either AD 224 or 226. The coins of the last Arsacids, however, confuse the matter, so much that a long joint rule of Vologeses V (207-227?) and Artabanus V (213-224?) has been proposed with the son of Artabanus, Artavasdes, ruling one year 226-227.[3] Inasmuch, however, as Arsacid resistance did not end with the death of Artabanus one might suppose that coins of the last Arsacids were minted in his name even after the victory of Ardashir which may be dated from various sources probably as April 224.

In the titulary of the royal Sasanian inscriptions one may see the expansion of the state. Sasan, as noted, is referred to merely as 'lord' while Papak is 'king', Ardashir is 'king of kings of Iran' and Shapur is 'king of kings of Iran and non-Iran'. An indication of how one might be misled in interpreting an inscription, is the appellation 'god' (*bgy*) for Papak in SKZ, but 'Mazda worshipping god' for Ardashir and Shapur. This might induce one to assume that Papak held a different position in faith or religion from his son and grandson. Yet the same formula appears on later inscriptions in Taq-i Bustan, and one cannot

237

conclude anything from the practice of omitting '*mazdayasnian* from the name of a grandfather. The phrase 'whose seed (or origin) is from the gods', however, is a continuation of a Seleucid if not Achaemenid formula while the term 'god' applied to the ruler had probably by this time assumed the significance of 'your majesty' in protocol.

For the dating we fortunately have an inscription written in the Parthian and Sasanian Middle Persian languages on a pillar in Bishapur. The text says: 'In the month of Fravardin of the year 58, forty years of the fire of Ardashir, twenty-four years of the fire of Shapur, (which fire is) the king of fires'.[4] On the reverses of Sasanian coins we have Aramaic *NWR'ZY* 'fire of-' until Shapur II; then we have the Iranian *'twr y* until Yazdagird II (439-457) after whom it disappears. Each king apparently had his own fire, lighted at the beginning of his reign, and this fire was on a portable fire altar similar to those on the coins, as one would gather from Sebeos the Armenian writer, from Ammianus Marcellinus and from others. Shapur's fire was called the king of fires possibly because it was identified with the Gushnasp fire of the warriors, which was later designated 'the victorious king of fires' (*Kar Namak*, X.16, but the text is not clear), or maybe the king's fire was called the king of fires simply as a manner of speaking.[5] The date of accession and the date of the crowning of a king have usually differed in the ancient Orient, and these dates are not precisely known in regard to Ardashir and Shapur. From the inscription of Bishapur we would have three dates, the beginning of the Sasanian era, the accession of Ardashir and the accession of Shapur. Great controversy has raged over the date of Shapur's accession and crowning, but his first year must begin either at the end of 239 or 241.[6] A Greek codex on the early life of Mani at first promised to solve this problem when it reported, 'When I (Mani) became twenty-four years old, in the year in which the Persian king Dari-Ardashir conquered the city of Hatra, and in which King Shapur, his son, put on the greatest diadem (was crowned).' This should have been the year 239-240 AD, but the question remains whether this date meant the crowning of Shapur as sole ruler, or as co-regent with his father. It would seem that one coronation was sufficient for Shapur, and the earlier chronology should be adopted.[7]

If Papak had been the director of the Anahita shrine at Istakhr before he became king, afterwards he and especially his son were busy with other affairs, even though both may have

238

retained the dignity as head of the temple. Papak had a small court, the most prominent members of which are named in Shapur's great trilingual inscription. There is only one title, the *major domo ('dnyk)*, mentioned and no religious designations, so one should assume that Papak's court was that of a small principality with no bureaucratic tradition. After Ardashir became the king of kings of Iran, the successor of the Parthians, the situation changed. Ardashir inherited the feudal organisation of the Arsacids which is clearly seen in the inscription. At the new court we find an order of protocol beginning with four powerful eastern kings, three of whom oddly have the same name as Ardashir. The first on the list is the king of Khurasan, the upper country and homeland of the defeated Parthians, while the second is the king of Merv who is called Ardashir. It would be natural to suppose that relatives or close friends of Ardashir were appointed to offices in the new empire, especially in the important posts in eastern Iran, but we do not know the relationship of these rulers to the king of kings. The next two kings, of Seistan and Kirman, are also both called Ardashir, the latter, according to Tabari, being a son of the king of kings. One may further assume that these 'kingdoms' were won by force of arms, and hence were free to be assigned to favourites, while rulers who submitted to the Sasanian monarch probably retained their principalities in a feudal relationship.

The inscription continues with three queens, probably the king's mother, grandmother and sister, the 'queen of queens'.[8] Then follows an Ardashir the *bitaxš* and a Papak the *chiliarch (hazārpat)*. From their names and high rank both were presumably members of the Sasanian family. The former was probably almost like an assistant to the king since the title as used earlier in Georgia implies that there the *pitiaxši* was second to the king in rank and importance.[9] At the Sasanian court this rank may have declined somewhat, so that the *bitaxš* and the *chiliarch* divided the civil and military direction of the affairs of the empire between them.

The heads of the great Parthian feudal families are next in the list, first the Varaz family which is new. The Varaz may have been essentially a northern Iranian family since the name appears frequently in connection with Armenia or Azerbaijan.[10] Second in rank of the feudal families is a representative of the famous Suren family, while third comes the lord of Andegan, also called Indegan, presumably another feudal appanage.[11] Two members

239

of the well-known Karen family are followed by a name known elsewhere, Apursam, who bears the honorific 'glory of Ardashir', followed by the lord of the area around Mt. Demavend and a member of the Spahpat family which ends the list of families. [12]

The chief of the scribes, chief of the armoury and other officials, as well as prominent persons with no offices named, complete the list of people in Ardashir's court who were honoured by having sacrifices performed in their names at the fires established by Shapur I at Naqsh-i Rustam. [13] The court of Ardashir shows the same features of an unfixed central state and bureaucracy which also would have been characteristic of the Parthian court, and everything points to a continuity from the past. The early coins of Ardashir too are probably copies of those of Mithradates II, but the traditions of iconography of the various crowns worn by the early Sasanian kings are by no means clear. [14] One must resist the temptation to see cultic or religious significance in *every* feature of ancient art and archaeology even though such ideas must have been frequently present.

Later Sasanian tradition, reported mainly in Arabic sources, traces the beginnings of all institutions of church and state back to Ardashir. He is the ruler who reinstated or resurrected the old Persian empire with its various institutions as well as the religion of Zoroaster which had been in eclipse under the Hellenistic kings and the Parthians. Apursam, the confidant of Ardashir, was credited with holding the office of prime minister *(vuzurg framadar)* while Tansar (probably a misreading of the name Tosar since it appears in a patronymic SKZ: Line 59 Middle Persian *Mtrky ZY twsrk'n*) was the first chief *mobad according to* Arabic sources. The purpose of the later Sasanians in attributing an early origin for many offices was probably that they wished to seek authority for new developments by claiming that these were in fact not new, but dated from the beginning of the empire although they had fallen into decay. The antiquarian renaissance of the time of Chosroes I is well known and will be discussed below, and this was probably the period when the reference of institutions back to Ardashir was made. A writer in Arabic Masʿūdī, for example, attributed not only the founding of certain offices to Ardashir but also the ordering of society into classes which, however, could not be the work of one king, Ardashir I. [15]

From Shapur's inscription we can also infer the extent of Ardashir's empire. From Islamic and other sources scholars have proposed that Ardashir re-established the Achaemenid empire in the east including the Punjab and did well in advancing the frontier against the Romans in the west. The same sources, however, tell us that Ardashir had much fighting to do to consolidate his rule, especially in Armenia where resistance was strong. The fact that in inscriptions Ardashir is called the king of kings of Iran but not of non-Iran, would imply that he did not appreciably advance his boundaries outside of *Eranshahr* which, of course, included Mesopotamia but not Armenia (according to the Paikuli inscription, line 8) and probably not the Kushan empire in the east. On the other hand Ṭabarī (trans. Noeldeke 17) says that the kings of the Kushans, of Turan and Makran came to Ardashir, after his victories in the east, and offered their submission. It is possible that under Ardashir they stood only in a vassal relationship to him while under Shapur the Kushan kingdom and other areas were really included in the empire. This further implies wars by Shapur of which we have no evidence. The hegemony of Ardashir may have been light, based on a few victories over the allies of the Arsacids rather than actual conquest afterwards.

The Imperialism of Shapur

In addition to extensive irrigation the Sasanian kings greatly favoured urbanism, a trait not in such evidence among their predecessors. The first two sovereigns of the house of Sasan were the greatest city founders of the line and most of the cities with royal names (see map at end) in them were founded or renamed by Ardashir or Shapur. The confusion of ancient native, Hellenistic, and Sasanian names given to cities frequently makes identifications of the cities difficult.

While their neighbours must have realised that the change of dynasties in Iran was not particularly to their interest, the Sasanians were soon to show the Romans and Kushans that a new Iranian nationalism and imperialism was a distinct peril to the peace. The Romans had won many victories in the last century of Parthian rule, so Ardashir was somewhat of a change while Shapur's conquests turned the balance of power in favour of Iran. We know much about his wars with the Romans because they were spectacular as well as victorious campaigns. His inscription of the Kaʿbah of Zoroaster is both an important record and a paean of victory regarding his wars with Rome. Some scholars have accepted every word of his record of the struggle with the

241

Romans as true, but have denied any other conquests of Shapur since they are not mentioned. Another inscription on the same structure, written by the order of an important religious figure Kartir, however, does tell of campaigns in Transcaucasia. We may also assume that victories in eastern Iran extended the empire to India, although we cannot exclude the possibility that some of these campaigns occurred towards the end of Ardashir's reign.

Shapur's inscription of KZ tells of three campaigns against the Romans, first at the beginning of his reign when Gordian marched against Shapur but was defeated and killed, whereupon Philip the Arab succeeded him as Roman emperor and made peace with Shapur. The second campaign resulted in the destruction of a Roman army of 60,000 men, after which the Persians ravaged Syria and Cappadocia, capturing Antioch on the Orontes as well as many other cities. In the third campaign the Emperor Valerian was defeated and captured after which Shapur again raided Syria and eastern Anatolia. Other sources tell us that in the third campaign King Odenath of Palmyra attacked and defeated the Persians, seizing much of their booty while they were on the homeward march. The first and third campaigns of Shapur can be dated in 243-244 and 259-260 and can be followed in literary sources. The second campaign presents problems in dating and identification because of the excavations at Dura-Europos. The evidence from Dura suggests that this Roman outpost on the Euphrates was captured by the Persians in 253 who held it for a few months and then again in 256 when the city was stormed and destroyed by Shapur. The question arises, which of the dates belong to Shapur's second campaign. Generally speaking a 'campaign' in the Near East from ancient times has meant an expedition of one year. It is possible, however, that the second expedition of Shapur lasted a number of years, including 253 and 256, as I have suggested elsewhere. [16] More study has inclined me to think that this is unlikely and that 256 is the date of the second campaign while 253 was a minor raiding expedition not mentioned in KZ.

The capture of Valerian was an unparalleled event in history and Shapur made certain that the world knew about it through his inscription and rock reliefs at Bishapur and Naqsh-i Rustam. Although the interpretation of these reliefs is varied and disputed it may be true that they are a kind of counterpart in pictures of the inscription and the three Romans at Bishapur represent the three Roman emperors mentioned in the inscription, Gordian, Philip and Valerian.[17] The prisoners captured by Shapur in his wars with the Romans included many technicians and from Antioch the bishop of the city who, with many of his flock, was settled in Khuzistan. The city of Gundeshapur ('the better Antioch of Shapur') was settled with Roman prisoners and the Caesar's dam at Shustar was one of their constructions. Prisoners were settled in Fars, Parthia, Khuzistan and elsewhere (according to KZ, line 16 of the Parthian version) and they probably provided the basis of the later Christian communities in Iran.

Although the fortress town of Hatra, which had repulsed the Romans on various occasions, as we have mentioned, fell to Ardashir, one may also tentatively assign the ruin and abandonment of the towns of Assur, Dura and other sites to the conquests of Shapur which thus must have changed the face of the Roman-Iranian frontier lands with the consequent end of certain trade routes and roads. The Romans contributed to this too when Aurelian conquered and destroyed Palmyra under Queen Zenobia in 272. Thereafter the Romans, and later the Byzantines, and the Sasanians maintained a system of border buffer states and *limes* between their two empires which were as often at war with each other as not.[18]

Shapur was not only victorious against the Romans but also in the north in Transcaucasia and presumably in the east. According to KZ the Sasanian empire included 'Turan, Makuran, Paradan, India and the *Kushanshahr* right up to Pashkibur and up to Kash, Sogd and Shash'. This passage has been discussed by several scholars, and I would interpret it to mean that first the land of Turan, probably including most of the province of Kalat in present-day Pakistan, was included in the empire. This Turan may well have some relation to the opposition of Iran and Turan in the national epic, especially when we know that many of the stories come from neighbouring Seistan. A further possibility, that the kingdom of Turan was created by invaders from Central Asia, cannot be dismissed. Next comes Makuran which is easily identified and then Paradan which presents a problem since we have no definite literary references to it and cannot locate it. I suggest that it may be located either in Arachosia or at the mouth of the Indus river rather than a small locality in Gedrosia.[19] India or Hindustan is generally recognised as the Indus valley, but I suspect it is only the upper Indus here, north of present Sukkur into the Punjab. Exactly when this area submitted to the Sasanians is uncertain.

The Kushan empire at this time had already passed its prime and according to some numismatists may have split into two kingdoms, a Bactrian and an Indian kingdom, or even into more parts. It is tempting to think that the limits given in Shapur KZ refer only to the extent or boundaries of a northern Kushan kingdom, which submitted to Shapur after a defeat, since there is no evidence that the Sasanian armies actually reached the confines of the Peshawar region, or Kashgar (Kish?), Sogdiana, and Tashkent. It is not certain that Pashkibur is in fact modern Peshawar, but in any case a district or principality rather than the city is meant. The district either was possibly restricted to the Peshawar plain east of the present Khyber pass, or more likely comprised all of the lowlands which were the ancient Gandhara, including present Jalalabad. Kashgar surely means the kingdom which may have extended into Russian Turkestan north of the Oxus river, or we may have in the inscription the actual or the pretended extent of the Kushan empire up to the borders of the state of Kashgar which was more or less restricted to eastern Turkestan. I am inclined to favour this latter view since Sogdiana and Shash were probably states with their centres primarily and respectively in the Zarafshan and Ferghana valleys. In other words the boundaries of the *Kushanshahr* in theory, if not in practice, included the mountainous area of part of the Pamirs and present-day Tajikistan. The scanty archaeological and Chinese literary evidence would not contradict this view.

Thus in the north-east Ardashir and/or Shapur secured the submission of the Kushan state. A good guess would put the first defeat and submission of the Kushans under Ardashir while the incorporation of the *Kushanshahr* in the Sasanian empire would date from Shapur's reign. In all probability the oasis state of Merv marked the military outpost of direct Sasanian rule under Shapur as it did later. In the eyes of the Persians what was beyond was no longer Iran but non-Iran. The archaeological evidence for the destruction of the city of Kapisa (*hodie* Begram) north of Kabul can be neither attributed nor denied to Shapur, but is probably earlier. The extent of Shapur's hegemony in the east, on the whole, is now known from his inscription.

From Shapur's inscription KZ we see that most of Transcaucasia was included in his empire, and from the inscription of Kartir at the same site we learn (line 12) 'the land of Armenia, Georgia, Albania and Balasagan, up to the Gate of

244

the Albanians, Shapur the king of kings with his horse(s) and men pillaged, burned and devastated'.[20] This indicates that Shapur did not inherit these lands from his father but had to conquer them, and for Kartir these are lands of non-Iran (Anirān). Shapur re-created the Achaemenid empire and the Persians again ruled over non-Iranians. Yet Shapur was not the great innovator or organiser that Darius was, since he continued for the most part in the path he had inherited, the legacy of the Parthians. A new feature, however, was the state church which will be discussed below.

The list of notables at the court of Shapur in KZ is both longer and more variegated than that of his father. From this and other inscriptions, the protocol and the social stratification of the Sasanian court are revealed. In the bilingual (Parthian and Middle Persian) inscription of Hajjiabad Shapur tells of an arrow he shot in the presence of the rulers (shahrdār, i.e. the kings of various countries in the Sasanian empire), the royal princes (BR BYT' or vispuhr), the great nobles (vazurkān) and the small nobles (āzātān). In the Paikuli inscription of Narseh we find the expression, 'the Persian and Parthian royal princes, great and small nobles', which reveals the fusion of the Parthian and Persian nobility, perhaps similar to the Medes and Persians in the time of the Achaemenids. The court of Shapur, like that of Ardashir, does not show the developed forms of imperial bureaucracy characteristic of the later empire, for example the offices of the prime minister or chief of priests are not present. The functions of many of the listed posts are not known, but a number of considerations lead one to believe that the court differs little from the Arsacid court. A surprise is the presence of seven satraps, the latest appearance of this title, referring to the districts or provinces as well as the chief city which gave its name to the province. The satrapies depended directly on the king and the central government hence were located in western Iran and not on the frontiers. Subdivisions of provinces existed but apparently neither in a uniform system nor throughout the empire.

Although the Sasanians have been characterised as representing an Iranian reaction to Hellenism, under Shapur we have the last Greek used in inscriptions in Iran, and his patronage of Greek philosophers and savants has come down in Persian tradition. Likewise the mosaics of his new city Bishapur in Fars reveal a strong Western influence not to be attributed

245

solely to artisans among the prisoners from Roman armies.. [21] One may suggest that under Shapur there is really a revival of Greek cultural influences in Iran which, however, hardly survives his death.

As the empire expanded so the bureaucracy also must have grown, but again the old traditions continued. We know from several sources that the royal seals were not personal seals, but were used by various officials of the king as had been true earlier. Just as in Seleucid times Sasanian official seals carried only legends or monograms but no figures. Representations of deities, personal portraits or animals were pictured on private seals. The official seals seem to have been important prerogatives of office, and later we find many seal impressions of *mobads* and other religious dignitaries as well as civil officials. Seals were used for all kinds of business and for religious affairs—for all matters which required identification or any writing. The seals and their impressions provide valuable information on geographical names and offices in the Sasanian empire. [22] Together with the seals should be mentioned the insignia, coats-of-arms or emblems which were used by noble families as their signs of identification. Many of them were really stylised monograms or abbreviations, but Sasanian heraldry is a complicated subject which has been little studied. Insignia already existed in Parthian times and there is an interesting parallel between the signs or coats-of-arms on the headgear of Kushan notables on sculptures from Mathura, India and the signs on the helmets of the notables of Shapur's retinue pictured on the rocks of Naqsh-i Rajab near Persepolis The proliferation of titles and honorifics in the course of Sasanian history was a tendency which lasted down to the twentieth century and the confusion of personal names, offices or titles, and honorifics was a problem for Byzantine writers in their day as it was for more contemporary foreign authors writing about Iran.

Social structure under the early Sasanians again most probably was an inheritance from Arsacid times. Divisions in society were normal in the Near East and by no means restricted to the caste-conscious Indians or the Zoroastrian Iranians. For example, Strabo (XI.501) speaks of four 'castes' among the Georgians: the rulers, priests, soldiers and the common people, and the importance of families where possessions were held in common. When the Zoroastrian church became firmly

246

established in Iran it contributed to the fixing of social classes in accordance with religious tradition. As is well known, society was later divided into four classes, the priests, warriors, scribes and common folk, and this division has been discussed frequently by scholars.[24] The extended family has remained the basic unit of allegiance, trust and authority in Iran down to the present day, and while the centralisation of government in Sasanian Iran was a feature which distinguished it from Arsacid times, none the less the family remained paramount.

Shapur was known for his liberal spirit and in religion, if nowhere else, his liberalism apparently was in contrast to the policy of his successors. It is significant, I think, that the successor of Shapur, Hormizd Ardashir and another son, the future king of kings Narseh, are both mentioned prominently among those members of the royal family for whom special fires were instituted by Shapur; while another son Varahran, king of Gilan, does not have a fire instituted in his honour. The succession of Hormizd Ardashir seems to have been unopposed and under him the policy of Shapur was still in effect, but Hormizd did not rule long and he was succeeded by Varahran, known as Bahram in Islamic sources. A change in religious policy occurred which we shall discuss below and quite probably there were other changes too. Unfortunately our sources tell us little of this period of Sasanian history and Islamic authors give no hint of difficulties or important changes. Varahran was succeeded by his son of the same name, who after a reign of seventeen years was followed briefly by his son, a third Varahran.

Then came a reaction and Narseh, son of Shapur and now surely advanced in years, revolted and seized the throne. Among other actions he had the name of a predecessor, Varahran I, chipped away from an inscription in Bishapur and his own name substituted for it.[25] This, and his toleration of Manichaeism, in which he followed his father, indicate a change in the policy which had been followed by the Bahrams. Under his rule the Romans recouped their lost prestige and also some territory so that future relations were based on a kind of balance of power. The Sasanian empire was now more occupied with internal affairs than with external, and presumably a *modus vivendi* between the great feudal lords and the king of kings had been forged in such a way that a new allegiance to the house of Sasan was accepted by all.

247

Heresies and the Church

The development of the church during the early Sasanian empire is tied to the name of Kartir (to be pronounced Kerdir) who was unknown to history before the discovery of his monolingual inscriptions in the Middle Persian language. One was carved below the Middle Persian version of Shapur on the Ka'bah of Zoroaster, another on the cliff at Naqsh-i Rustam behind the horse of Shapur showing his triumph over the Roman emperor Valerian, a third at Naqsh-i Rajab and a fourth on a mountainside at Sar Mashhad south of Kazerun. At Naqsh-i Rajab accompanying the inscription is presumably the representation of Kartir himself with finger raised in a gesture of respect. At Sar Mashhad Bahram II is shown killing a lion while protecting his queen, and behind her is probably Kartir. The contents of these inscriptions are very much the same, except that Sar Mashhad and Naqsh-i Rustam are longer than the other two, while Naqsh-i Rajab is a kind of abbreviated testament of personal belief. Unfortunately both the Naqsh-i Rustam and the Sar Mashhad inscriptions are badly weathered with large portions illegible. None the less, the story they tell of Kartir reveals a fascinating page of early Sasanian history, the establishment of orthodoxy and a state church.

Before turning to Kartir, an examination of Islamic and Pahlavi sources reveals that the chief religious leader or *mobādan mobad* of Ardashir was a certain Tansar, whose name, as we have said, probably should be read Tosar. He is also called a *herbad* or 'teaching priest' in some sources.[26] There is no indication that Tosar is to be identified with Kartir, but his activities, including making a new recension of the Avesta according to the *Denkart* (ed. Madan IV.412), would make a veritable Kartir of him. The inscriptions, however, are more reliable than literary sources and they tell only of Kartir, although a person called Tosar may have been active under Ardashir before Kartir came to the fore. One might read the name of the chief *mobad* under Ardashir *gāhir* or *māhir*(in Ṭabarī I.816 and the *Mujmil at-tawārikh/* as Kartir, but this is mere surmise and no more. Kartir, however, must be one of the founders of Zoroastrian orthodoxy under the early Sasanian kings.

The longest inscriptions of Kartir are the eighty-one lines of Naqsh-i Rustam and the almost identical fifty-nine lines of Sar Mashhad, the first twenty-five lines of which latter inscription are the same, with a few variants, as the inscription of Kartir Ka'bah of Zoroaster, while lines 52 to the end are almost a verbatim copy

248

of his inscription at Naqsh-i Rajab.[27] In the last part of the inscription of Naqsh-i Rustam and Sar Mashhad Kartir gives what almost seems to be an *apologia pro vita sua*. In spite of much work on the inscriptions much remains enigmatic.[28] Kartir goes to great pains to tell posterity that he first came to power under Shapur when he was a *herbad* and a *mobad*, which implies at least the existence of different kinds of priests already under the early Sasanians in the Zoroastrian religion.[29] Under King Hormizd he was given the title 'mobad of Ahura Mazda', probably the first to hold this later well-attested title. In the reign of Varahran II he received the rank of nobility, the headship of the religion, and was made chief judge of the empire, and chief of the royal fire at Istakhr at the imperial shrine of Anahita. This last dignity may have been the prerogative of the early Sasanian kings which was now given to Kartir by Varahran II. The fact that he is called 'the lord' at the very end of Naqsh-i Rajab and that he notes his elevation to the nobility, further suggests that the nobility were especially powerful in this period. Kartir probably played an important political as well as religious role in the empire.

One should note that in his inscriptions we find mention of the activity of Kartir outside of Iran in trying to establish both fire temples and orthodoxy among the Hellenised Magians and to convert those pagans who followed rites and beliefs similar to those of the Zoroastrians; in other words Kartir was a missionary.[30]

At the same time he reacted strongly against both foreign religions and heresies within Iran, and this may well be one reason why Mithraism as we know it in the Roman Empire is not also found in Iran. Kartir (KKZ 9-10) specifically attacked Jews, Buddhists, Hindus, Nazoraeans, Christians, Mktk (a Mesopotamian religion similar to the Mandaeans?), and Manichaeans, destroying their centres and proscribing them.[31] The work of Kartir apparently was not an innovation, since Armenian and Syriac sources tell of the zeal of Ardashir in establishing fire temples and destroying pagan temples, especially in Armenia. Kartir's action was militant Zoroastrian orthodoxy in Zoroastrianism, for the Magi were organised, heresy was forbidden, and many Varahran fires were instituted. These fires represented the backbone of the Sasanian fire cult for they were centres of teaching as well as rites in the various geographical areas of the land. The work of Kartir was impressive (KKZ, line

249

14) for we see in effect the ordering of the state church in Iran, including the practice of consanguineous marriages, a feature of Zoroastrianism which adversely struck outside observers. He also probably laid the basis for the power of the clergy which was to rival, if not later surpass, that of the nobility.[32]

The fanaticism of the period of Varahran II was tempered in the reign of Narseh (293-302) who refused to accept the accession of the young King Varahran III, who is called the Saka king in Paikuli, and seized power in northern Iran. He marched on Ctesiphon and was met by a party at Paikuli, a site north of present Khaniqin, and there he was proclaimed king of kings, and a bilingual inscription was erected to commemorate this event. In line 16 of Paikuli the name 'Kartir, the *mobad* of Ahura Mazda' appears, but because of lacunae in the inscription one cannot determine the context, but it would seem that he supported Narseh. He was surely quite elderly and must have died or retired shortly afterwards. Since Narseh did not mutilate Kartir's inscriptions, and there is no evidence of a clash between the two, we may assume that Narseh, who mentions in his inscription (Paikuli, line 9) 'Ahura Mazda and all the gods and Anahita called the lady', did not overthrow the work of Kartir. The policy of toleration of Narseh towards the Manichaeans is generally known, but it is possible that a change began at the very end of the reign of Varahran II.[33] The evidence for a complete about-face in religious policy under Narseh and a victory of *herbads* over *mobads* or Anahita over Ahura Mazda, is lacking; rather the change seems to be one of relaxation yet continuity.

The question of heresies within the Zoroastrian religion is complicated because our Pahlavi sources are all post-Islamic in date, when the minority religious communities of the Zoroastrians were more concerned with correct beliefs than in Sasanian times when the religion was upheld by the state. I believe that orthopraxy was more important than orthodoxy under the Sasanians and Zurvanism, or time speculation, was not a heresy in the same manner as Mazdakism, which was a threat to the practices and the organisation of society as well as to the church. But in the early days of the empire the Zandiks, as the Manichaeans were called, were the chief heretics.

The exact dates of Mani's life are uncertain since they are tied to the chronology of Shapur's accession which itself is not certain; but he was killed either in the last year of the reign of Varahran I (274-5) which is likely, or in the early years of his

250

successor (277). Manichaeism has been called an expression of universalism or syncretism in religion and it has been compared with Bahaism of the present day. It is perhaps not as representative of Iranian religious tendencies in its dualism as was the Zoroastrian state religion, but certainly the syncretic and 'international' features of Manichaeism found many ready supporters in Iran. We are not here concerned with the teachings of Manichaeism which are at present better known than before the discovery of original Manichaean writings in Coptic, Parthian, Sogdian and other languages. The Manichaeans suffered the same fate in Iran as in the Christian world; in both the arch-heretics were always Manichaeans and they were accordingly persecuted severely. After Narseh, however, Manichaean communities continued to exist in Iran, especially in eastern Iran, and later, as is well known, Manichaean missionaries reached as far as China.

Perhaps the most striking heresy, if it can be so called, was the social and economic movement led by Mazdak at the very end of the fifth century, about whom much has been written.[34] It would seem that royal opposition to the nobility and their power was an important reason for the support of Mazdak by king Kavad. The Mazdakites preached a form of communism, the division of wealth including wives and concubines, which found support among the poor, but our sources are not clear and are contradictory about the course of events of this revolution. The Mazdakites, however, met the same fate the Manichaeans had suffered at the hands of Kartir and King Varahran. It happened at the end of Kavad's (second) reign, and the Crown Prince Chosroes Anosharvan was the chief instigator of the massacre of the Mazdakites circa 528. The death of their leaders, of course, did not end the Mazdakites as a sect but sent them underground. But a new pejorative had been coined and henceforth any social or religious reformer was usually branded as a Mazdakite by his opponents, and this lasted long into Islamic times when many Iranian revolts against the caliphate or the rule of the Arabs were designated as Mazdakite movements. The Mazdakite movement was known to such Islamic authors as Nizām al-Mulk in his Siyāsatnāme.

Already, from the beginning of the Sasanian period, we are in a new religious world. The cults of the old Mesopotamian gods were long since dead and in their places new gnostic and ritualistic sects had arisen side by side with Christianity, Judaism

251

and Zoroastrianism. Cabalistic beliefs and practices seem to have been widespread, and in the views of most Greek and Roman authors the Persians were the chief believers in magic and unusual religious practices. Zoroastrianism for the classical writers was the epitome of the mysterious, Oriental cult. Yet Kartir and his followers laid the basis for Zoroastrian orthodoxy which probably opposed magic, demon worship, and the like as much as did Christian orthodoxy in the empire of the Caesars.

Belief in divine revelation and the recording of that revelation in books was in the air, and the Christians, of course, were the most widespread propagators of the idea of 'Holy Writ'. It may have been because of the example of the Christians that the Zoroastrian church assembled and canonised its writings. Zoroastrian tradition claims that fragments of the Avesta were assembled and presumably written down in Arsacid times and again under Shapur I. The written Avesta of the early Sasanians must have been really a mnemonic device to aid the memory of the priests who usually recited the Avesta in a traditional Oriental manner. In the beginning of the fifth century the present Armenian alphabet was devised mainly to propagate the Christian religion in that land. Some have conjectured that the present Avestan alphabet was invented about the same time possibly as a forerunner or even as an imitation of the Armenian alphabet although the Avestan alphabet in phonetic completeness is more like the Devanagari alphabet of Sanskrit. It is usual to assume a religious motivation for the creation of this rather late alphabet which, as far as we know, was only used for texts of the Zoroastrian religion. It is a pity that this alphabet did not replace the incomplete Pahlavi alphabet, with its great deficiency of letters to represent sounds, for the Middle Persian language. It must be emphasised that we have no old manuscripts of the Avesta, none earlier than thirteenth or fourteenth century, but the existence of a written Avesta in Sasanian times much as we know it today seems assured in spite of the overwhelming importance of the oral tradition.

From Christian authors writing in Syriac and Armenian it would seem that the Sasanians primarily followed Zurvanism, a Zoroastrian heresy which, after the Islamic conquest, vanished in favour of orthodoxy. I believe, as shown elsewhere, that Zurvanism was not a full-fledged heresy with doctrines, rites and a 'church' organisation separate from the Zoroastrian fold, but rather a movement to be compared perhaps with the Muʿtazilites of Islamic times.[35]   There were basically two features of Zurvanism which have been preserved for us, time speculation (eternity, etc.) and the myth of the birth of both Ohrmizd (Ahura Mazda) and Ahriman from their father Zurvan. The first was widespread and certainly by itself would not form the basis for a separate sect. The Zurvan birth story can be paralleled by the story of Chronos in Greek mythology and again, in my opinion, would not lead to the formation of a sect. Undoubtedly the Zurvan birth story was widespread among 'orthodox' Zoroastrians in Sasanian times, but after the Islamic conquest when Zoroastrians withdrew into tightly knit communities, Zurvanite elements were eliminated from the new orthodoxy which was concerned with 'orthodoxy' as well as 'orthopraxy'. In Sasanian times a Zoroastrian heretic was more one who broke away from orthopraxy and even became a Christian or Manichaean, while in Islamic times a Zoroastrian heretic was primarily a person who also broke with orthodoxy as, for example, Abalish (or ᶜAbdallāh?) a Zoroastrian who became a heretic in the time of the caliph al-Maʾmun in the ninth century, and may have really adopted Manichaean beliefs.[36] Any kind of social heresy, of course, would be the concern of the ruling caliph.

From the acts of the Christian martyrs we learn much especially about the Nestorian communities in the Sasanian empire. In effect the consolidation and growth of the Zoroastrian church in Iran was paralleled by the growth of the Christian church and of the Manichaean communities. Undoubtedly the influx of Christian prisoners in Iran in the wake of both Shapurs' conquests gave a strong impetus to the spread of Christianity, but the religion naturally spread in Mesopotamia among the Semitic peoples. The first great persecution of Christians occurred under Shapur II, beginning about 339, and seems to have had political motivation since it began after Constantine had made Christianity the religion of the Roman Empire. Later there were periods of tolerance followed by more persecution, but after the break away of the Nestorians from other Christians at the end of the fifth century, the condition of Christians in Iran improved. The Nestorians elected a catholicos who had his seat in Ctesiphon and synods usually met there in deciding church problems. The ecclesiastical geography of the Nestorian bishoprics is also of importance for the civil geography of the Sasanian empire since the Church usually followed civil boundaries; thus we gain some knowledge of civil administrative divisions from the acts of the martyrs.

The Christianisation of Armenia and Transcaucasia in the fourth century provided a source of conflict between Armenia and the Sasanians even more than the struggle for influence in those areas between Romans and Persians. In the east, too, Christian missionaries made converts among the Hephthalites and Sogdians, so one may infer everywhere a growing Christian influence at the end of the Sasanian empire. The whole religious picture of Iran, however, was more complicated than we can know from the sparse records, and the interplay of various religions is matched by internal divisions within the Zoroastrian church which we perceive but dimly.

The Glory that was Iran

If one asks an ordinary Persian who had built an unknown, ancient, ruined mosque or other structure in some locality, the chances are great that he would reply it was Shah ʿAbbas, the Safavid ruler who embellished with edifices the city of Isfahan. If the ruins were clearly pre-Islamic the reply might be Khusro or Chosroes Anosharvan 'of the immortal soul', the Sasanian counterpart of Shah ʿAbbas. His very name became, like that of Caesar, the designation of the Sasanian kings for the Arabs (Kisra in Arabic) and almost a synonym for splendour and glory. But Chosroes ruled Iran less than a century before the Arab conquest and, as is not uncommon in history, the seeds of decay already existed in the period of greatest splendour in the Sasanian Empire.

Iran had not fared well in her external relations under the successors of Shapur I; under Varahran II the Romans regained lost territory in northern Mesopotamia as well as hegemony over Armenia. Narseh fared no better and further concessions had to be made to the Emperor Galerius. After him it seemed as though the Romans had regained the dominant position which they had held in Parthian times. Under Shapur II, who had an unusually long rule of seventy years, the Sasanians passed to the offensive both in the west and in the east where the Kushan state and other territories may have proclaimed their independence during the minority of Shapur. On the whole Shapur II was successful in regaining both territory and lost prestige for the Persians. He followed the practice of Shapur I in settling Roman prisoners in various provinces of his empire, according to Ammianus (XX.6.7) who is a valuable source for the history of Shapur II and his wars with the Romans.

After Shapur his weak successors lost much of their imperial authority to the nobility which grew in strength and influence. There are many gaps in our knowledge of the history of these years. We do not even know, for example, whether Ardashir II was the brother or son of Shapur II. The nobility seems to have made and unmade rulers. Although there may be no causal connection it is interesting to note that as royal power declined in favour of the feudal lords, the heroic, or epic tales regarding the reigns of such kings as Varahran V or Bahram Gor (421-439), the hunter of wild asses, increased or came to the fore.[37] One may suspect that titles and offices increased in number and importance during the long period of weak monarchs. Concomitant with the new power of the nobility were struggles over the succession by opposing parties of the feudal lords. Such was the case with the crowning of Varahran V (in 421) and of Peroz (459).

In the fifth century a formidable new enemy appeared in the north-east as successor to the Kushans, a new wave of invaders from Central Asia called the Hephthalites. They are connected with the new order on the steppes of Central Asia which can be characterised best as the rise of the Altaic-speaking peoples or the Hunnic movement. Just as the first millennium BC in Central Asia was considered by classical authors as the period of Scythian dominance in the steppes, so the first half of the first millennium AD is the time of the Huns, while the second half and later is the period of the Turks and the Mongols. Of course the term 'Scythian' continued to be used by classical authors for various steppe peoples well into the Christian era just as the Ottomans were designated 'Huns' by several Byzantine authors. None the less the various terms 'Scythian, Hun and Turk' were general designations of the steppe peoples in Western sources including the Near East, though the Chinese had other names. Obviously not all peoples who lived in, or came from Central Asia into the Near East or eastern Europe in the first half of the first millennium AD were Huns, and the fact that Western and Near Eastern sources call a tribe Hunnic really only means that they came from the steppes of Central Asia, a vast area. The word 'Hun' has caused scholars great trouble as have other problems of Hunnic history, but this is not the place to discuss such questions as, for example, the identity of the Hsiung-nu of

Chinese sources with various 'Huns' of Western, Near Eastern or Indian sources.[38]

Although presumably the name of the Huns appears as early as the geography of Ptolemy (III. 5.10), applied to a tribe in south Russia, we cannot find any other evidence for 'Huns' in the Near East or south Russia before the fourth century AD. The joining of the word 'Hun' to the Kidarites by Priskos is probably an example of the use of the general fifth-century term for an earlier history and no proof that the Kidarites were Altaic-speaking people. Presumably Kidara was the name of a ruler since the name appears on coins, but there is no evidence that he led a new Central Asian horde to conquer the Kushan realm. Several attempts to date a ruler Kidara have not been convincing and we may only hazard a guess that such a reign was in the fourth century.

Another name from eastern Iran or Central Asia seems to indicate a migration or invasion from the north. The newcomers are called Chionites in classical sources. In 359 the king of the Chionites, Grumbates, is mentioned by Ammianus (XIX.1.10) as an ally with Shapur II and his army before the walls of Amida. It is generally believed that the Chionites, with the form OIONO = Hyon = Hun on their coins, were Central Asian invaders of eastern Iran connected with the Hunas of Indian sources and with their successors the Hephthalites. Unfortunately we have no sources for the history of eastern Iran in this period and the many and varied coins present many problems which hardly can be solved without new sources of information from excavations.

From the coins of certain Sasanian Kushan rulers one would conclude that the Persians were at least liege lords of part of the Kushan domains throughout most of Shapur II's rule, if not also before his reign. Some time, probably at the end of the fourth or early fifth century, a new ruler Kidara appears as an independent southern Kushan ruler.[39] The Chionites probably moved into the northern Kushan domains (north of the Oxus river) some years before Kidara whose power seems to have been based mainly in lands south of the Hindu Kush since he has coins with Brahmi legends. This division between lands north and south of the mountains is important. The Chionites probably expanded over Kushan domains and independent rulers of them appeared in Bamiyan, Zabul and elsewhere, the coins of which are very difficult to classify.[40] The confusion in our sources between Kidarites, Chionites and Hephthalites may well reflect a real mixture of peoples and rulers. One may say, however, that the name of the Chionites is followed by that of the Hephthalites in history.

It is difficult to determine the ethnic composition of Chionites or Hephthalites, but there is no evidence that the Chionites were different from the Hephthalites; rather the meagre evidence indicates that the Hephthalites may have stood in the same relation to the Chionites as the older Kushans did to the Yüeh-chih. In other words, the Hephthalites may have been a prominent tribe or clan of the Chionites. One may well expect Altaic, i.e. Hunnic, elements among the Hephthalites, to use the later name, but again the evidence points to a population primarily of Iranians ruled by Huns. It is possible that some of the early rulers were Huns, but there were still many Iranians in Central Asia, and the people of eastern Iran among whom the Hephthalites settled were also Iranian, so we may consider the Hephthalite empire in eastern Iran and north-west India as basically an Iranian one. Zoroastrian as well as Manichaean missions in Central Asia must have increased the West Iranian cultural elements among the people. Undoubtedly by the time of the Arab conquests, however, the Turkic elements among the Hephthalites had increased, but that was after the Turks themselves had appeared in the Near East.[41] It is, of course, possible to construct theories of history and of ethnic relationship on the basis of suggested etymologies of one or two words, but the lack not only of sources but of reliable traditions in the fragmentary information about Central Asia and eastern Iran in classical sources makes any theory highly speculative.

The Persians in the last half of the fifth century suffered a series of defeats at the hands of the Hephthalites and King Peroz lost his life in 484 in battle with them. After him the nobles waxed even stronger, placing several rulers on the throne in succession and finally Kavad I, who then maintained his throne only with Hephthalite aid. This was a period of low ebb for the Sasanians when their eastern neighbours seem to have exercised influence even in internal affairs. The Mazdakite revolution already has been mentioned, but the great change or revolution in Iran came with Chosroes I who, as we have said, was the greatest pre-Islamic ruler in the minds of the Persians.

The far-reaching reform of taxation under Chosroes has been discussed by several scholars, notably F. Altheim, whose merit was to show repeatedly that the model for the new system of taxation was the system in force in the eastern Roman Empire which in turn had been built on the reforms of Diocletian.[42] The unrest and social changes of the Mazdakite period made a new assessment of property and of taxes necessary, but we cannot say with certainty what the situation was before Chosroes. What is reported by later authors regarding Sasanian times refers to the post-Chosroes period. We may assume that Chosroes wanted stability, and in terms of taxation, of course principally on the land, a fixed sum rather than a yearly variation according to the yield, which seems to have been the old system. A survey of the land was made including a census and a counting of date palms and olive trees. The land tax of the later Roman empire was based on the land unit the *iugum*, but the amount of taxation was already determined by the *indictio* and divided among the various plots of land. This became the system of Sasanian Iran, of course with many different details into which we cannot go. The Sasanian head tax, like the Roman *capitatio*, was under Chosroes assessed in a number of fixed categories according to the productive capacity of a man. In both empires state employees were exempt from paying the head tax, and in Iran the Magi, soldiers and the high nobility were exempt as well. Certain details of the taxation are disputed but the main lines are clear; Chosroes sought stability and a fixed income for government coffers.

From the Talmud, however, we learn that ancient practices in regard to the payment of taxes still continued under Chosroes. If one could not pay his land tax and another paid it, the latter received the land. By paying the land tax of someone who could not pay, one could obtain the debtor as a bondsman or slave. According to one source (*Nedarim* 62b) if a Jew declared he was a Zoroastrian he could escape the head tax. This was rather a special tax, or heavier head tax, placed on Jews, Christians and other minorities. The bishop for the Christians and the head of the Jews for the Jewish communities collected taxes from their followers. This continuity of tax practices in Iran continued into Islamic times. The Sasanian system provided the background of the well-known but also in part different and complicated system of the Islamic *kharāj* and *jizya*.

In addition to a tax and financial reform, there was a social and bureaucratic revolution, but again many details escape us or are subject to various interpretations. Certain innovations may be the work of Chosroes' predecessors, but one may say that after him they appear as a characteristic feature of Sasanian Iran. The most important was perhaps the growth of the lower nobility or the *dihqāns* (literally village lord) as the Arab conquerors called that backbone of Persian provincial and local administration. This lower nobility really possessed and ruled the land at the end of the Sasanian empire and it would seem that they owed their positions to the ruler and were an effective counter-weight to the few great families who became progressively less important. In line with his policy of stability Chosroes may have sought religious support for a social stratification of four classes or castes, which, however, may have developed throughout earlier Iranian history so that by the time of Chosroes it was full-fledged.

There is considerable material in Islamic works, such as the *Kitāb al-Tāj* of Jāhiz, and countless anecdotes and stories which refer to the activities of Chosroes I. The sources agree in their assessment of the empire of the Sasanians after Chosroes as a tightly organised structure with the king supreme at the top of the hierarchy. The 'mystique' of the king of kings was reinforced, and books of protocol, mirrors of princes and other writings, laid down the duties of monarchs to their subjects and subjects to their ruler. It would seem that there was a considerable activity in fixing rules of behaviour, prerogatives and obligations for various classes of society in this period. The offices of *mobadān-mobad* or chief of the clergy, *dabirān-dabir*, or chief of the scribes, and similar titles, in imitation of the king of kings, indicate the ordering of society by imperial and religious sanction. The fascinating picture of society under the later Sasanians is one of a people who have seemingly reached a social and religious stability in religion, class structure and general culture but continuing with the seeds of decay in the resultant stagnation.

The age of Chosroes was one of conquest too. Antioch was briefly captured in 540 and in the east the Hephthalite power was crushed by a joint Persian and Turkish attack *circa* 558 when the Western Turkish khanate and the Sasanians ended a united Hephthalite rule replacing it with at least nominal Turkish hegemony north of the Oxus river and Sasanian overlordship over many of the Hephthalite principalities south of the Oxus. Chosroes, as Shapur I and II, was known also for his systematic transport and settlement of prisoners of war in various parts of Iran, an age old custom followed in Iran by Shah ⁺Abbas and Reza Shah in more recent times. It was under Chosroes that the unusual but not really important Sasanian conquest of Yemen took place which had echoes in the Quran. Under Chosroes we

259

find the frontiers of the empire secured by a system of *limes* in the Syrian desert, in the Caucasus by Derbend and east of the Caspian Sea in the steppes of Gurgan. The institution of a system of four *spāhbads* or generals of the realm in north, south, east and west is also attributed to Chosroes, and one hears more of the importance of *marzbāns* or 'wardens of the marches' in this later period of Sasanian history. The city building activity of Chosroes already has been mentioned. One town he built with the aid of Byzantine prisoners was the better Antioch of Chosroes near Ctesiphon, with a name similar to the better Antioch of Shapur I or Gundeshapur. The figure on the seal of Chosroes was a wild boar which symbol was very widespread in Sasanian art (figs. 7 and 8). The reorganisation of the bureaucracy by means of a system of *divans* or ministries by Chosroes is generally regarded as the prototype of the 'Abbasid *divans* by many Islamic authors and while proof of direct continuity is sometimes difficult to establish beyond doubt, there were many influences.

There is so much written about Chosroes that one may omit a discussion here and refer to various writings about him.[43] The internal reforms of the king of kings were more important than external changes in the frontiers, and their overall result was a decline in the power of the great nobility and the sub-kings in favour of the bureaucracy. The army too was reorganised and tied to the central authority more than to the local officers and lords. While one could continue with a long list of reforms attributed to Chosroes, some of the lesser known developments in that period of Sasanian history might be of interest.

It is well known that names which we find in the national epic appear at the end of the fifth and the beginning of the sixth century among the royal family and presumably also among the nobility although we hear little about the latter.[44] The old title of *kavi* in its Middle Persian form *kay*, written *kdy*, appears on coins of Peroz and Kavad, another indication of an antiquarian revival.[45] It is highly probable that the lays and legends of ancient Iran were gathered together in the days of Chosroes I and that the national epic as we know it in Firdosi was much the same then as now. Whether there was any great remaking of the epic, such as weaving events of Chosroes' life into those of Kai Khusro, cannot be proved but it is not impossible. Some scholars would even attribute the introduction of the highest offices of the empire, such as *mobadān-mobad*, first to the reign of Chosroes, but the wholesale assignment of innovations to him is probably an exaggeration. Likewise the contention that Chosroes founded a new hierarchy of fire temples with the introduction of a Gushnasp fire, tied with the crowning of the king in Shiz or Ganzak, is possible but unproved.[46]

Chosroes' name is also connected with a revival of learning with both Greek and Indian influences coming into Persian intellectual activities. Agathias (II.30) has a well-known passage about the Greek philosophers (presumably neo-Platonists) who came to the Persian court after the closing of their academy in Athens in 529 and who were well received. The question of the extent of Sasanian learning is unsettled in its details, some scholars attributing a Persian origin to much of later Islamic science and learning, others denying the existence of a large Pahlavi scientific literature. We know of Burzoe, the famous physician of Chosroes, who reputedly was sent to India by the king and brought back the game of chess plus many Sanskrit books such as the fables of Bidpay and works on medicine which he translated into Pahlavi. Other Persian authors are known only by later references. Many Arabic and New Persian works on astronomy such as star tables (especially the *zīj-i Shahriyar*) betray Sasanian prototypes, and one may suspect that much Pahlavi profane literature was lost because the *mobads* were not concerned to preserve it, while men of learning were content to use Arabic rather than the difficult Pahlavi form of writing for their works of science and literature.

On the other hand it is virtually certain that various Greek scientific works were translated into Pahlavi and then later from Pahlavi to Arabic, an indication of the existence of scholarly activity in Pahlavi.[47] This learning, however, would seem to be more compilation than original, and the literary renaissance in the time of Chosroes also was primarily concerned with writing down and fixing various stories and legends including the national epic. The letter of Tansar (Tosar), which has been mentioned, the *Kar Namak* of Ardashir and other tracts of Pahlavi literature have been attributed to this period.[48] Some scholars have maintained also that the Avestan alphabet was created under Chosroes rather than earlier. The changes and additions which must have occurred in both epic and religious literature make datings difficult, but the great activity under the rule of Chosroes cannot be denied.

Sasanian art can be characterised as the culmination of a millennium of development. For one may discern Greek and

261

Roman elements, ancient Oriental archaising motifs and purely Iranian subjects, such as the investiture of the king on horseback, in later Sasanian art. The brief Greek revival under Shapur I hardly interrupts the development of Iranian art from the Parthian period and Ardashir down to Chosroes. Just as in late Gandharan art so in Sasanian art stucco and plaster are supreme as the medium of expression. The widespread use of monograms, symbols and complicated designs is typical of late Sasanian art and as such is a forerunner of Islamic art. The more naturalistic emphasis in earlier Sasanian art seems to give ground before more stylised and even geometric art at the end of the period. The anthropomorphic representation of the god Ahura Mazda, perhaps a residue from the 'messianic period' of the religions of the Near East, is not attested at the end of the empire. Ancient motifs of the hunt, investiture of the king or battles on horseback, appear on rock carvings or on the wonderful silver platters, and they are all distinctive and could not be mistaken for anything other than Sasanian. The Sasanian hallmark or 'stamp' may be considered another evidence of the freezing of culture and society. What has remained of the architecture, sculpture, metalwork, ceramics and silks of the Sasanian period, however, is enough to testify to the grandeur and richness of Iranian culture.

The Sasanian empire seemed stronger than ever after Chosroes but in spite of his changes and reforms the age was not one of innovation. Rather the period in a truer perspective might be characterised as a summation of the past, of gathering-in and recording, when history becomes important as a justification for the state and the religion. The past which was revived in epic, in traditions and in customs, however, was a heroic past of great and noble families and of feudal *mores*, not of centralised, bureaucratic state which Chosroes wanted to establish. Were the successors of Chosroes somewhat like Don Quixote while the common people were ready for the new message of the followers of Muhammad? The noble families kept alive the heroic traditions of Iran and they survived the Islamic onslaught while the empire went down in ashes. Local self-interest and fierce individualism have been both the bane and the glory of Iran throughout its history, but through triumph and defeat the culture and the way of life of the Persians have unified the population of the country more than political or even religious forms unless they too were integrated into the heritage of Persia.

1 This inscription, in Greek, Parthian and Middle Persian, will be referred to hereafter as (Shapur) KZ. The last translation was by the late A. Maricq in *Syria*, 35 (1958), 295-360, where a bibliography is given. Foreign sources on the Sasanians are usually quite hostile, different from Herodotus and his contemporaries, who merely regarded the Persians as barbarians.

2 E. Sachau, *'Die Chronik von Arbela', Abhandlungen der Akad. der Wiss.* (Berlin, 1915), 56, 60.

3 B. Simonetta, *'Vologese V, Artabano V e Artavasde una revisione di fatti e di ipotesi', Numismatica*, 19 (1953), 1-4.

4 R. Ghirshman in *Revue des Arts Asiatiques*, 10 (1937), 123, German translation by O. Hansen in *ZDMG*, 92 (1938), 441-442. The date of the inscription would be 263 or 266, the first year of Ardashir beginning at the end of either 223 or 226 and the first year of the Sasanian era (the first date) 205 or AD 208. This last date could well be that of the accession of Papak or of his revolt against his Parthian overlord (see note 6). It should be noted that the Arsacid kings also probably had their royal fires, according to a seal from Nisa.

5 On the other hand, it is significant to note that each Varahran (Bahram) fire was established by a ruler (*dahyupat*). Cf. *Bundahishn*, ed. B. T. Anklesaria (Bombay, 1908), 127-128. The converse, that each ruler created his own and only Varahran fire, does not follow. Cf. S. Wikander, *Feuerpriester in Kleinasien und Iran* (Lund, 1946), 14, 157.

6 W. B. Henning, *'The Dates of Mani's Life'*, Asia Major, 6 (1957), 119.

7 A. Maricq, *'Classica et Orientalia', Syria*, 25 (1958), 344-348 summarises the different views and argues well, but not with convincing proof, that the later dates have more plausibility than those of three years earlier. Cf. Frye, *'The Cologne Greek Codex about Mani', Geo Widengren Festschrift* 1 (Leiden, 1972), 424-9.

8 Ardashir's queen of queens presumably was his sister or half-sister Denak. Since Shapur did not have a sister, his daughter Adur Anahit was his 'queen of queens'. This custom may be the result of a combination of a Hellenistic (best known are the Ptolemies) royal practice of brother-sister marriage with a religious Zoroastrian approval of next-of-kin marriage.

9 Cf. note 61 of Chapter 5. A good summary of the office of *bitaxš* with bibliography may be found in B. Metzger, *'A Greek and Aramaic Inscription Discovered at Armazi', JNES*, 15 (1956), 21. To it one should add A. Pagliaro's opinion that the title derived from the Achaemenid office 'eye of the king', on which see above. Many etymologies have been proposed but the one of Pagliaro is uncertain.

10 See the names in Justi, *Iranisches Namenbuch*, 349. At the end of the Sasanian empire, however, the name, which means 'boar', is found frequently in eastern Iran where it may represent the same family with Hepththalite ties. I am not convinced that all of the instances of compound names with *varaz* given by A. Christensen, *L'Iran sous les Sassanides* (Copenhagen, 1944), 410, are just honorifics.

11 The Andegan family is also well known (Justi, *op. cit.*, 16) but the primary seat of their holdings has not been located. Also the expression 'lord of the A' leads one to suppose this may have been a tribal designation

possibly to be located at the head of the Persian Gulf down to Bushire, according to Henning in *BSOAS,* 14 (1952), 510. There are other possible references to the family such as the *Hnduk* of Moses Daskhurantsi in C. Dowsett, *The History of the Caucasian Albanians* (London, 1961), 92, where variants of the texts are given. Compare also the Beth Hendoye of the acts of the Martyrs translated by O. Braun, *Ausgewählte Akten* (Munich, 1915), 275.

12 Apursam was probably the honoured elder statesman or councillor of Ardashir in his younger days, but not a prime minister in the later sense of the institution. The interpretation of the honorific as 'friend' proposed by O. Klima *'Iranische Miszellen', Archív Orientální,* 26 (1958), 610, corresponding to the Hellenistic *philos,* is also possible. On the (*A*) *spahpat* house cf. Marquart, *Ērānšahr,* 71-72. On the rulers of Demavend see W. Eilers, *'Der Name Demawend', Archív Orientální,* 22 (1954), 268.

13 One uncertain title is that of *m'dknpt* 'chief of *maygan'* 'steward' or 'chief of savings' according to Maricq (note I), 324, note 10. I had suggested 'chief of the immortals' or better 'chief of the bodyguard', but all suggestions are mere surmises. Is this title related to the *maipet* of Armenian sources which can hardly be 'lord of Media'?

14 R. Göbl, *'Investitur im sasanidischen Iran', Wiener Zeitschrift für die Kunde des Morgenlandes,* 56 (1960), 37 foll. sees in an eagle headdress the crown connected with Anahita and her cult while others believe it is the headgear of the crown prince.

15 *Les prairies d'or,* ed. et trans. C. Barbier Meynard et P. de Courteille, 2 (Paris, 1863), 153.

16 In *Bibliotheca Orientalis,* 8 (1951), 103-106, where a bibliography is given. The information on the captures of Antioch by the Persians is summarized by G. Downey in his *A History of Antioch* (Princeton, 1961), 587-595.

17 B. C. Macdermot, *'Roman Emperors in the Sassanian Reliefs', Journal of Roman Studies,* 44 (1954), 76-80.

18 The Roman *limes* in the desert in Syria are well known, but the system of fortifications and border guards on the Sasanian side is less known. Cf. H. S. Nyberg, *'Die Sassanidische Westgrenze und ihre Verteidigung', Studia Bernhardo Karlgren Dedicata* (Stockholm, 1959), 316-326.

19 The last attempt to locate it, as far as I know, was by Herzfeld, *Paikuli,* glossary 230, where he summarises previous work and concludes that Paradan or Paradene was the Surat district north of Bombay. Surat, however, is too far to the east. In addition to the Paradene of Ptolemy in Gedrosia, we have Parazene on the Helmand river; see K. Miller, *Itineraria Romana* (Stuttgart, 1916), 787, and J. Schnetz trans. *Ravennas Anonymous Cosmographia* (Uppsala, 1951), 24, and the frequently used term Paraitakene applied to the Helmand. Then there is the city of Parti in Sind in *Cosmas Indicopleustes* ed. E. O. Winstedt (Cambridge, 1909), 322. I do not think that all of Arachosia was included in the *Kushanshahr,* and the land of the lower Indus is also not represented in that empire. Presumably both were included in the Sasanian empire. One must admit the evidence is not encouraging for any proper identification.

20 There are four matters to be clarified in this translation: Georgia,

Albania, Balasagan and the Gate of the Albanians. For the first, the inscription says *wlwc°n* or Varuchan 'Iberia', which may not have included all of present Georgia. Albania is written here *'l'ny* which is confused with 'Alan' and in the name of the pass 'Gate of the Albanians' = Derbend. We should read Albanian in both cases and not 'Gate of the Alans' = Darial as does M. L. Chaumont in *JA* (1960), 361. Balasagan was the territory on the Caspian Sea coast from Derbend southward including the steppes of Mughan.

21 Cf. R. Ghirshman, *Bichapour* 2, (Paris, 1956).

22 Cf. R. N. Frye, *'Die Legenden auf sassanidischen Siegelabdrücken' WZKM*, 56 (Vienna, 1960), 32-35.

23 For example, Procopius, *Wars*, 1.13.16, understands the title *pityaxes* as a personal name and *mirranes* (the personal name Mihran) as a title. The confusion is quite common elsewhere too.

24 E.g. A. Christensen, *L'Iran sous les Sassanides*, 98.

25 *Paikuli*, 120. The name of Narseh has been substituted for Varahran as can be seen in the inscription while the headgear is that of Varahran I. For a photograph of the relief see F. Sarre and E. Herzfeld, *Iranische Felsreliefs* (Berlin, 1910), plate 41.

26 The problem of the various functions of *'herbad'* is not satisfactorily resolved. Cf. S. Wikander, *Feuerpriester* (note 5), who discusses this in detail. It would seem that in the Sasanian empire *mobad* was the generic term for all priests of the Magian religion, while the word *'mogh'* finally became a designation for any Zoroastrian; compare Sogdian *mwg'nch dynh* 'the Magian religion'. The word *herbad* probably had a narrower, more technical meaning, while the title of *herbadān herbad*, which we find later in the Sasanian epoch, was probably only an honorary title, as explained by M. L. Chaumont in *'Recherches sur le clergé zoroastrien: Le herbad'*, *Revue de l'histoire des religions*, 158 (Paris, 1960), 161-179. I fail to see any conflict between *mobads* and *herbads*, correlated with orthodox dualism versus Zurvanite monism, in Sasanian times.

27 A concordance of the inscriptions of Kartir with bibliography may be found in P. Gignoux, *'Etude des variantes textuelles des inscriptions de Kirdir Genèse et Datation'*, *Le Muséon*, 86, (Louvain, 1973), 193-216.

28 For Sar Mašhhad see P. Gignoux, *'L'inscription de Kartir à Sar Mašhad'*, *JA* (Paris, 1969), 387-418, and for Nagsh-i Rustam his *'L'inscription de Kirdir à Nagš-i Rustam'*, *Studia Iranica*, 1 (Paris, 1972), 177-205.

29 Just how far this fortifies the theory of Wikander (note 26) that the *mobads* were the priests of northern Iran with the centre at Shiz-Ganzak while the *herbads* were the Anahita priests of southern Iran with their centre at Istakhr I cannot say. Some sort of distinction between northern and southern, or Parthian and Persian, religions may well have existed, but the details probably should not be elaborated as much as Wikander has done.

30 See the article by J. de Menasce, *'La conquête de l'iranisme et la récupération des mages hellénisés'*, *Annuaire de l'école pratique des hautes études* (Paris, 1956), 3-12 and M.-L. Chaumont, *'Conquêtes Sassanides et Propagande Mazdéenne IIIéme Siècle'*, *Historia*, 22 (Wiesbaden, 1973), 664-710. The existence of Magi in the Byzantine empire in the time of Justinian is attested by the treaty between the Byzantines and the Persians, reported by Menander Protektor by which the Greeks promised not to force Zoroastrians in their territories to convert to Christianity.

31 The text has (KKZ, line 10, SM 14) *yḥwdy W šmny W blmny W n᾿cl᾿y Wklsṭyd᾿n Wmkṭky Wzndyky,* literally Yahudi, S(r)aman, Braman, Nasra, Kristiyan, Mktk and Zandik. All of these words present some problems, but they were all religions of the land (*BYN štry*) which meant all areas ruled by the Sasanians and not just those of the heartland of Iran. It may be conjectured that Nasra and Kristiyan go together as do Mktk, and Zindik, Sraman and Braman. Nasra might refer to a number of Christian or semi-Christian sects, or even to followers of John the Baptist, but it is difficult to determine what Kristiyan and Nasra designate. On a distinction between Nazoraeans and Nasareans see C. Clemen, *Religions-geschichtliche Erklärung des neuen Testaments* (Giessen, 1924), 202. See also G. Wiessner, *Zur Märtyr-überlieferung aus der Christenverfolgung Schapurs II* (Göttingen, 1967), 70-1, note 10. The term Zindik was ordinarily used of Manichaeans although it was also applied to any heretic by Zoroastrians and was taken up by the Muslims with an even wider usage. *Mktk* then should refer to a religion or sect of Mesopotamia. On a similar list of religions combatted by the Christians of Mesopotamia see the martyrdom of Mar Simon, ed. Bedjan II, 150; ed. Kmosko 824, and translated by O. Braun, *Ausgewählte Akten persischer Märtyrer* (Munich, 1915), 19.

32 Cf. on the rise of the Magi Agathias, IV.25, ed. B. G. Niebuhr (Bonn, 1828), 261-262, and ed. R. Keydell (Berlin, 1967), 154-5.

33 Cf. W. Seston, *'Le roi sassanide Narsès, les Arabes et le Manichéisme',* Syria (1939), 229.

34 O. Klima, *Mazdak* (Prague, 1957), and F. Altheim, *Ein asiatischer Staat* (Wiesbaden, 1954), 189 foll. Several articles by Soviet scholars have also appeared about Mazdak.

35 *'Zurvanism Again',* Harvard Theological Review, 52 (1959), 63-73, and *'Die Wiedergeburt Persiens um die Jahrtausendwende',* Der Islam, 35 (1959), 50.

36 Cf. J. Tavadia, *Die Mittelpersische Sprache und Literatur der Zarathustrier* (Leipzig, 1956), 53, for further references. J. de Menasce suggests that his name was ῾Abdallāh. Cf. note 30 of chapt. 7.

37 It is tempting to explain the appellation *gor* 'onager' as a later misreading of the title *gul ⟨ gula ∼ vula,* a Central Asian word for king as proposed by O. Hansen, *'Tocharische-iranische Beziehungen',* ZDMG, 94 (1940), 162.

38 In my opinion the word 'Hun', whatever its etymology, early came to have the general sense of fierce or terrible people. In the dictionary of Asadī Ṭūsī, *Lughat-i Furs,* ed. ῾Abbās Iqbāl (Tehran, 1941), 367, the word *hun* is explained as 'enemy' which may be our ethnic name. On the name 'Hun' see the works of the specialist on the Huns O. Maenchen-Helfen, e.g. his *'Huns and Hsiung-nu',* Byzantion, 17 (1944), 222-243, and *'Pseudo Huns',* Central Asiatic Journal, 1 (1955), 101, especially his book, *The World of the Huns* (California, 1973), also W. Samolin, *'Hsiung-nu, Hun, Turk',* CAJ, 3 (1957), 143-150, and F. Altheim, *Geschichte der Hunnen,* 4 vols, (Berlin, 1959-62). On the etymology see O. Pritsak *'Xun',* CAJ; 5 (1959), 27-35.

39 Cf. M. F. C. Martin, *'Coins of Kidāra and the Little Kushans',* Journal of the Royal Asiatic Society of Bengal, 3 (1937), 2 (Numismatic Supplement 47), 23-50, and A. D. H. Bivar, *'The Kushano-Sassanian Coin Series',* Journal of the Numismatic Society of India, 18 (1956), 13-36, and R. Göbl, *Dokumente zur Geschichte der iranische Hunnen,* 4 vols (Wiesbaden, 1967), where other references may be found.

40 An attempted preliminary classification of the Chionite coins may be found in R. Göbl, *'Neue Zuteilungen zur Münzprägung der Chioniten',*

Palaeologia, 4 (Tokyo, 1955), 274-279. The Hephthalite coins have been studied by R. Ghirshman, *Les Chionites-Hephtalites* (Cairo, 1948), but I cannot accept many of his conclusions. The seventh-century (?) ruler of the present Kohistan-Kabul-Ghanza area, many of whose coins have been found, called 'Napki MLK', presents many problems not the least of which is the reading of his name which I cannot accept. I suggest the name is to be read Nēzak which name applied to a series of rulers of the mountainous area of the Hindu Kush. See my *'Napki Malka and the Kushano-Sasanians'*, in *Near Eastern Numismatics, Studies in Honor of George Miles*, ed. D. K. Kouymjian (Beirut, 1974), 115-22.

41 See K. Enoki, *'On the Nationality of the Hephthalites'*, *Memoirs of the Research Department of the Toyo Bunko*, 18 (Tokyo, 1959), 1-58. Sources and references to other theories can be found here. I cannot follow Enoki's theory of the homeland of the Hephthalites in the Badakhshan area. The etymology of 'Hephthalite', and of the ruler 'Axšundar' can be explained as Iranian, while the Turkish etymology of the latter as *axsung er* (Kāshgharī 1. 106.3) is hardly convincing. The name of another Hephthalite king, Varz, possibly should be read Varaz since this name appears frequently at the time of the Arab conquests presumably held by various Hephthalite princelings on the Sasanian-Hephthalite frontier of Merv and Merv-i Rud. The name of the Sasanian feudal family of Varaz mistaken as a title by Greek authors also comes to mind. Turkic problems of Avars, Khazars and the like, are beyond the scope of this book.

42 In the main I follow A. Christensen's, *L'Iran sous les Sassanides* and Altheim's *Ein Asiatischer Staat* (Wiesbaden, 1954), 129-255. Cf. his *Geschichte der Hunnen*, 2, 182-191, where further bibliography is given.

43 For a general account of his reign see Christensen, *L'Iran*, 363-440. On the *limes* see H. S. Nyberg (note 18), and J. H. Kramers in *BSOS* (1936), 613-616.

44 Names such as Kavad, Jamasp, Kaus and Khusro were noted by T. Noeldeke in his translation of Ṭabarī (Leiden, 1879), 147.

45 The title *kay* spread outside of the Sasanian empire as evidenced by coins from Transoxiana, according to Henning, *'Mitteliranisch'*, in *Handbuch*, 27, 53. I prefer to read the legends on *early* coins as 'Bukharan king Kana' rather than the last word the Sogdian title *kay/k'w'* (Henning) or *k'wy* (Altheim), first because *k'n'* in the *earlier* coins occupies the place of *k'y* 'king?' on the later coins, second because older *k'y* (not *kdy*) would hardly become younger *k'w'* (or *k'wy*) in Sogdian, and finally one would normally expect the name of the ruler after the title 'king'. I only know of one example of the legend *pwy'r k'y* on a coin (see Henning, *loc. cit.*), and do not believe this is the *earliest Bukharan* coinage from which the later form *k'w'* developed. Furthermore, there was a ruler of Bukhara called Kānā according to the Persian history of the city by Narshakhi; see my *The History of Bukhara* (Cambridge, Mass., 1954), 35. New finds may change the above remarks.

46 Wikander, *Feuerpriester* (note 5), 151-2.

47 C. A. Nallino, *'Tracce di opere greche giunte agli Arabi per trafila Pehlevica'*, *A Volume of Oriental Studies presented to E. G. Browne* (Cambridge, 1922), 345-363. The *Fihrist* of Ibn al-Nadīm also lists books in Pahlavi which were translated into Arabic.

48 T. Noeldeke, *Das iranische Nationalepos* (Heidelberg, 1920), sections 6 and 7. W. Barthold, *'Zur Geschichte des persischen Epos'*, ZDMG, 98 (1944), 136.

7 THE PERSIAN CONQUEST OF ISLAM

Disintegration of the Old Order

After Chosroes Anosharvan Sasanian society ever more exalted
the heroic age of the past with its traditions and symbols; but that
old world had been turned upside down by the Mazdakite revolt
and the reforms of the same Chosroes. [1] This does not mean,
however, that urbanisation, for instance, now flourished at the
expense of a feudal countryside; quite the contrary. After
Chosroes the large class of *dihqāns* built small castles all over the
empire where they held land, but this was not the same as the old
courts of the subkings and the great families. Furthermore, the
end of the Sasanian empire did not witness a growth of cities, for
poor economic conditions and constant warfare did not favour
commerce and the growth of cities. It seems that Iran after an
initial period of strength and centralisation under Chosroes I and
II, during the last years of the empire became more fragmented
than ever before, to such an extent that once the king of kings was
gone there were no great feudal lords or feudal armies to
effectively organise resistance against the Arabs. It may well be
that each *dihqān* imagined himself a Rustam, or even a Parthian
Suren or Karen, but the ideals of the past were not the realities of
the present. What were the conditions of life in the last century of
the empire?

The great number of coins found of Chosroes I and especially
of Chosroes II paralleled the increase in taxes. Gold coinage was
rare, mainly anniversary and commemorative issues, and these
coins were similar to the Roman *aurei* and not related to the
dominant silver system of Persia. The Sasanian silver *drachme*
had a characteristic form, and especially after Chosroes I the flat,
thin coin was the only type minted. [2] The standardisation of the
coinage with the stamping of dates and mint marks shows that
the state exercised more control over the later issues than earlier

in Sasanian history. After Chosroes I the reduction of copper coinage in favour of silver further indicates the end of local autonomy and the decline of provincial commercial interests in favour of centralisation and this tendency was not reversed with the political decline of the central government. Neither from this, nor from the existence of an important barter economy, nor from apparently well-developed economic features such as bills, cheques or letters of credit, can we conclude that the later Sasanian empire was economically flourishing. The frequent wars and conquests of the Persians sometimes brought significant funds into the state treasury, for war booty was an important source of revenue in antiquity. But wars were also costly and destructive and the last years of the empire were full of them. No material is at hand to determine the relative prosperity of the last century of Sasanian rule in comparison with earlier times. If the Byzantine empire after Justinian provides a comparison we may suspect that economic conditions were far from good in the late Sasanian state. On the other hand, the riches and luxury of the court of Chosroes II Aparvez impressed the Byzantines under the emperor Heraclius when they sacked his palace, as well as later Muslim authors who have many anecdotes about them. 3 The rise in taxes and frequent warfare, especially under Chosroes II, cannot have helped merchants or lower classes of society and one may assume that the perhaps increased wealth of royalty and nobility was not matched in the bulk of the population.

The last decades of the Sasanian empire, after the death of Chosroes II reveal the decline of central authority in favour of the generals. The policy of Chosroes I ultimately had led to a weakening of royal prerogatives, since the old balance of power among the great families had been replaced by a bureaucracy and a military aristocracy only too eager to assert their power against the ruler. Some of the top offices of the bureaucracy were held by religious leaders though the scribes on the whole were not *mobads* or religious officials. 4 It might be said that the generals and the top religious and bureaucratic officials rather than the king ruled the Sasanian empire just before it fell to the Arabs. They in turn were supported by the *dihqāns*, the scribes and, of course, the army.

One may discern a more rigid class or caste system in this period since the religion sanctioned the ordering of society along such lines. The priests belonged to one class or order, and other Persians fell into various groups, all based on a theoretical, religious ordering of society into priests, warriors, scribes and common folk. Christians and followers of other religions also fell into groupings similar to the later *milet* system of the Ottoman empire.[5] This ordering of society no doubt contributed to a certain stability, but it did not favour co-operation between various groups or any common public responsibility of everyone in the empire towards the ruler or to persons in other 'castes'. Therein lay a great weakness which aided the Arabs in their conquests. Much has been written about the development of Zoroastrianism at the end of the empire, most of it based on rational theories or surmises, but the real source material unfortunately is scanty or ambiguous. Some scholars have postulated a victory of northern *mobads* who were Zurvanites over *herbads* who were orthodox Zoroastrians, from the early times of the Sasanian empire, but I personally must confess to an inability to see the evidence for this.[6] It would seem that the Zoroastrian religion under the later Sasanians could be characterised by the decaying ritualism of a state church as well as by the growth of speculative, gnostic thought in it. Zurvanism, to be sure, would fit into a prevailing pessimism in philosophy. It is highly probable that sects of Zoroastrianism existed in Sasanian times, but in an empire where state and church went hand in hand, orthopraxy more than orthodoxy, in my opinion, determined sect or heresy.

Many times in the acts of the Christian martyrs Christian prisoners are urged to perform certain acts such as to eat fresh meat rather than prepared flesh, or to honour the sun by performing a rite, for which act they will be set free. Procopius (*Wars*, II.28.25) said that the Persians were excessively rigid as regards the routine of daily life, and we know also from him (I.11.35) and other writers that burial customs, once varied among Persians, were now restricted to exposure of the corpse with the bones collected in *astodans* or ossuaries which were then put in caves or rock-hewn holes in mountains.[7] The evidence, then, for great concern regarding orthopraxy in Sasanian Iran is convincing, but when we turn to the spiritual or the intellectual side of Zoroastrianism we are not on such solid ground.

The fact that later Islamic writers mention various 'sects' of Zoroastrianism would imply that they also existed in Sasanian times. Yet the differences between the 'sects' are wholly philosophical or 'cosmological'. For example, Shahristānī, writing in the twelfth century, speaks of the Zurvanite 'sect', the followers of which believed in Ohrmizd and Ahriman as two sons of Zurvan 'eternal time', while the 'Mazdaeans' believed in a strict dualism of the first two without a common origin. The problem of the origin of evil, of Ahriman, was undoubtedly a contested point in Zoroastrianism as in other religions, but there is no evidence of separate sects as we know them, based on different concepts of the origin of evil and contending for adherents in Sasanian Iran. Perhaps there were different schools of *mobads* concerned with 'scholastic' differences rather than well-defined sects, while the existence of a northern or Parthian and a southern or Sasanian school or tendency may have been the only real division in the Zoroastrian church.[8]

Various popular and philosophic beliefs, of course, were held by Zoroastrians in Sasanian times. Astrology was widespread while magic and demonology flourished among the masses. The great continuity in such beliefs down to the present time in Persia has been shown many times and need not detain us here.[9] More difficult to trace are gnostic, theosophical, docetic, messianic, or other movements, which may be called 'intellectual' trends, in Sasanian Iran. They surely existed and many of them continued into Islamic times, but certain religious problems are common to many religions and it is difficult to find in them Zoroastrian influences on Islam rather than simply parallel developments. We cannot speak here of mysticism or Zoroastrian theosophy and relations with later Islamic Sufism or the *Ishrāqī* philosophy of Suhrawardī and his school. The work of Henry Corbin has shown that certain motifs or symbolism in Zoroastrianism found echoes in the ideas of some Muslim writers.[10] In the angelology of Zoroastrianism he finds parallels with Islamic concepts while the idea of a saviour in both, particularly in Shi'ite Islam, is striking.[11] These are matters for another book on the Zoroastrian religion, but we may conclude that later Zoroastrianism was rich in scholastic philosophy and probably also in mysticism, both of which were by no means Islamic creations.

The feature of Zoroastrian rites which most attracted the atttention of foreign observers in Sasanian times was the fire system. Later Islamic authors were impressed with the numbers of fire temples or *ateshkade* which they found all over Persia. It is true that most of them were simple, mere domes upon four pillar-like walls (the *chahār tāq)*, but others were impressive in size as was their very number. It seems that the endowment of a fire temple was considered a pious act, as among the modern Parsis, and many of them were named after their donors. Undoubtedly

271

much land and wealth was associated with the fire temples, but in the eyes of the Arabs their general simplicity must have been conspicuous compared with the gilded and resplendent Christian churches.

Generally, from the Achaemenid period onward, the fire rites were either performed in the open on hill-tops or on platforms, or in enclosed temples, and the *chahār tāq* may have been a compromise between the two in Sasanian times. As the ritual and practices of the Zoroastrian state church in the Sasanian period became canonised, the religious architecture also became standardised.[12] But the network of fire temples was the most interesting feature of the church and if we correctly interpret our sources, they tell us that this network was a hierarchical arrangement like the hierarchy of church or of state officialdom. We have noted that each king had his royal fire, and there were at least three great fires corresponding to the three original classes or castes of society, the Farnbag fire for the priests, the Gushnasp fire for the warriors and the Burzin Mihr fire for farmers and common folk. We know of no fire for the scribes, i.e. bureaucrats, doctors, poets, etc., and it is possible that the assignment of each fire to a class is just a scholastic construction with no real significance in the rites or in the care of the various fires, or in the style of temples and other buildings. The Varahran or Bahram fires seem to have been the most widespread and the backbone of the fire system, perhaps equivalent to provincial fires. Below them were fires in every city, then in the village and finally in the home. There was a prescribed ritual of renewing the home fire from the city fire and the city fire from the Bahram fire at certain times, and this, together with the rites of purification, must have kept the Zoroastrians on their toes.[13] The numerous admonitions and prohibitions of the Zoroastrian religion in the later Sasanian empire, as one learns from Pahlavi books, reveal a religion far more concerned with rites and practices than beliefs, a formalistic society perhaps similar to the Hindu caste society of India or to Mandarin China.

The Zoroastrian religion was probably on the defensive at the end of the empire, for as the state declined so did the religion which was inextricably tied to it. Not only was the religion weakened internally, however, but external forces were working against it. Manichaeism had never died or suffered extinction at the hands of the *mobads;* indeed it gained new adherents especially in Central Asia. More significant was the spread of

Christianity. The Nestorian church had bishoprics all over the empire and our sources are full of stories of prominent Persians who embraced Christianity and even suffered martyrdom for their new faith. The last century of Sasanian rule saw the growth of Monophysite Christianity, mainly at the expense of the Nestorians, but in any case Christianity grew so much that some have speculated that Christianity might have displaced Zoroastrianism had not Islam appeared. Consequently the state of the official church of Persia was not as flourishing at the end as it had been several centuries previously. The rapid success of the Arabs was perhaps unexpected, but from the view-point of religion the success of Islam may not have been as miraculous as has been supposed.

It was not primarily religious problems which made the victories of the Arabs seem so easy, but the exhausted and chaotic state of the Sasanian government during and after Chosroes II. Chosroes II Aparvez came to the throne in 590 or 591 with the aid of Byzantine troops sent with him by the emperor Maurice against the usurper Bahram Chobin who, incidentally, has occupied an important place in Persian folklore and later even in messianic eschatology. A decade later the death of Maurice at the hand of Phocas gave Chosroes an opportunity to open hostilities with Byzantium. The Sasanian troops found little opposition, partially because of the internal conflicts in the Byzantine empire, Antioch, Jerusalem and finally Alexandria were taken, a veritable restoration of the Achaemenid empire. Finally Persian troops appeared before Constantinople, the capital itself and it seemed as though the Persians would conquer their ancient foes. But in a few years the roles were reversed.

The new Byzantine emperor, Heraclius, sailed with an army into the Black Sea and eastward while the Persian army was on the Asiatic shore of the Bosporus. Landing in the Caucasus region he marched into Armenia and Azerbaijan striking for the heart of the Sasanian empire. This amazing military feat has been studied by several scholars but the details of Heraclius' movements are not all clear.[14] He captured Shiz, the important religious centre in Azerbaijan in 624, and defeated the Persians. In 628 Heraclius captured the royal residence of Chosroes at Dastagird near Ctesiphon, but Chosroes still refused to make peace. The Persian generals revolted and Chosroes was seized and slain. His son and successor Kavad II lasted only six months and died of poison or sickness.

273

The rulers followed one another in rather rapid succession. They included the general who had captured Jerusalem, Shahrvaraz, 'the boar of the state' who ruled a few months before he was assassinated, and two princesses Boran and Azarmidukht. After four years of internal warfare and many murders the last Sasanian, a young prince related to Chosroes II, was raised to the throne by the nobles. Yazdagird III was much like the last of the Achaemenids, and if he had had time perhaps he might have saved Persia from the Arabs. It was too late; the Arabs were already united under the banner of Islam ready to embark on the conquest of both the Sasanian and Byzantine empires.

Islam versus Iran

The Arabs of the Arabian peninsula had been in contact with Mesopotamia and Egypt for more than a millennium before Muhammad, and in southern Arabia high civilisations had flourished and died by the time of Alexander the Great. We know little about southern Arabia, in spite of inscriptions and archaeological remains, but even less about northern Arabia until the rise of the Nabataeans. They apparently expanded northward in the Hellenistic era settling in Transjordan and northwestern Arabia and dominating trade between Arabia and the eastern Mediterranean. The Nabataeans were sedentary and have left many remains including the red rock city of Petra, at present a famous tourist site. The Nabataean state flourished under the Roman empire and their merchants went far to the west, but about AD 106 Trajan destroyed the Nabataean kingdom. In southern Arabia the Himyarites were the counterparts of the Nabataeans in the north, but after the fall of the Nabataean kingdom trade declined and Arabia underwent a bedouinisation. Towns were abandoned or declined and the period from the fourth to the seventh century AD has been called the 'Dark Age' of Arabia.

Arabs had infiltrated the Fertile Crescent before Christ and had even established kingdoms in Edessa, where the Arab Abgar kings ruled until the rise of the Sasanids, and also in Hatra, Palmyra and elsewhere. The most famous of the Arab kingdoms, however, were the Ghassanids, clients of the Byzantine empire in the Syrian desert and the Lakhmids with their capital in al-Hira on the Euphrates. Both kingdoms were formed by settled Arab tribesmen; the Ghassanids, on the whole, adopted Monophysite

Christianity while the Lakhmids generally followed Nestorianism. These two buffer states served the Byzantine and Sasanian empires well until the beginning of the seventh century when Chosroes II deposed Nu'man, the Lakhmid king (602), and ended the dynasty, while the Ghassanids fell at the time of the Persian invasion under Chosroes II.[15] The wars between the Ghassanids and Lakhmids are known not only from Byzantine sources but also from Arabic poetry. The fighting was frequently fierce and cruel. The elimination of these two principalities exposed both the Byzantine and Sasanian empires to direct attack by the bedouins of Arabia proper. This too was a factor in the success of Islam.

A foretaste of the power of united Arab tribes came to the Persians at the battle of Dhū Qār, located between the later cities of Kufa and Wasit c. 611, where the Sasanians were completely defeated by the bedouins. Arab poets naturally praised this victory in many compositions. Once the nomadic Arabs had been united by a new religious fervour they became irresistible. The sequence of events is well known, but their dramatic suddenness leaves one in wonder at the rise of Islam in the full light of history. We can only repeat the dates and battles to show the speed of Arab conquest. The town of al-Hira capitulated to a Muslim force in 633, but it was only after Syria had fallen to the Arabs that the main bedouin forces were sent against the Persians. In May 637 the Sasanian army was annihilated and the Persian commander Rustam killed at al-Qadisiyah. Ctesiphon was captured within a short time. A second conflict at Jalula at the end of the year also ended in a Persian defeat and all of Iraq (the low lands) submitted to the new conquerors. In 642 the power of the Sasanians was broken in their homeland by the Arab victory at Nihavend. The following year Hamadan fell to the invaders, and it became a centre for further expeditions northward into Azerbaijan or south into Isfahan and south-east into Kirman. Muslim armies, however, did not stop at the central deserts but continued into Khurasan. The establishment of the Umayyad caliphate and the history of Islam are not our concern, but the changes in Persia are part of the story of the ancient heritage of that country.

Yazdagird, like the last Darius a millennium previously, fled to Khurasan before the invaders and he too was murdered by his own people in Merv in 651. With his death the central authority of the Sasanian empire perished and local princes or governors faced the Arab conquerors. There is evidence from Arabic works that many *dihqāns* and leaders among the Persians accepted Islam, but this was generally over a long period since there was no immediate reason for conversion at the time of the conquests. At first, the Arabs made separate treaties with each town or district ruled by the elders of the city or by a feudal lord, and tribute rather than conversion was the watchword of the day. The disappearance of the top echelons of the state and church of the Sasanians, however, left a vacuum into which the Arab conquerors came only slowly. Yet the transition from Persian to Arab rule apparently was neither a great upheaval nor a great innovation. Instead of Ctesiphon Medina and then Damascus became the official capital, but Persia was governed by the local authorities as before under the Sasanians. Of course, all of the imperial paraphernalia of Sasanian rule fell to pieces; whatever unity had existed was only gradually transferred to the new caliphate, but this really happened only under the 'Abbasids a century after the Arabs conquered Persia. One of the chief characteristics of Persia under the century of Umayyad rule (*circa* 660-750) was the re-assertion of local loyalties and provincialism. It became more and more apparent to the Persians, however, that the road to advancement lay in co-operation with the Arab conquerors, and this surely stimulated conversions to Islam, especially among the *dihqāns*, though mostly for political reasons.

The local tax structure and the local social order remained, except for the new foreign class of warriors frequently settled in the towns of Persia as garrisons. Not until the Arabs organised their rule on an imperial basis, however, did the situation begin to change in Persia. The scribes and local bureaucracy worked as they had under the Sasanians, reporting and turning over money to the new rulers.

In 696 the caliph, 'Abd al-Malik, decided that it was intolerable that records should be kept in Greek or in Pahlavi rather than in Arabic, and in the following year Arabic became the language of the chancellery everywhere save in Khurasan where the reform did not come into effect until *circa* 741. The scribes on the whole were not happy with the change, but most of them seem to have adapted themselves to the new conditions rather well, and this class provided the people who translated from Greek, Syriac or Pahlavi into Arabic.

The role of Persians in the history of Arabic literature,

276

especially philology and grammar, is too well known to be catalogued. The earliest writers of Arabic grammars, such as Sibawaih, were Persians. In the decree of 741 not only were the records ordered in Khurasan to be kept in Arabic but only Muslims were to be employed, a measure which again caused many conversions to Islam.[16] Classical Arabic had become a *lingua franca* as well as the language of the new religion and the Persians reacted as they had to Aramaic and Greek in the past; those who learned to read and write learned Arabic, for Pahlavi was becoming a language used only by the Zoroastrian priesthood. The Persians, of course, continued to speak Persian although many undoubtedly could also speak Arabic. Under the later Sasanians a Middle Persian *koine* had not only spread all over the empire, but also had become popular outside the boundaries of the empire in Central Asia and Afghanistan. The Arab conquerors in dealing with all of their Iranian subjects in Persia and in Central Asia used this *koinē* as the medium of communication, together with Arabic. In my opinion the Arabs themselves contributed to the spread of Persian in the east at the expense of local languages such as Sogdian, or dialects. Refugees from Persia must have also helped in the spread of Persian in Central Asia. This *koinē*, of course, was the father of New Persian which we shall discuss below.

Not only did the class structure of four estates in Persia continue under Islam, as we learn from such books as Naṣīr al-Dīn Ṭūsī's *Akhlāq-i Nāṣirī*, but the towns remained the same with their separated quarters of Christian, Jewish and other communities. Only now the Muslims took over the role of the Zoroastrians who had been the rulers, and the Zoroastrians retreated into ghettos. It is interesting that the writing or copying of Pahlavi books and other activities of the Zoroastrian priesthood seem to have taken place more in the villages rather than in cities under Islam.[17] This coincides with the general growth of autonomy of villages in Persia in the early Islamic period when decentralisation became prominent.

Not only did the tax system of Sasanian Persia continue into Islamic times, but also the old Sasanian coins were minted by Arab governors of the caliphs with Arabic inscriptions beside the representation of a fire altar. When Islamic coinage and taxation do come into existence they are still a continuation of the Sasanian models. Even if the words *vizier* 'minister' and *divan* 'bureau' were not Persian in origin the institutions at least under the ʿAbbasids were Sasanian in inspiration. Where else would the caliphs find models for the protocol and the ceremonial of their courts? After all the Arabs conquered only some provinces of the Byzantine empire, but they conquered *all* of the Sasanian empire with *all* of its imperial traditions. The association of state and religion implicit in Islam found an imperial model in the Sasanian empire as well as an exposition of the theory in later Persian books of *Andarz* or 'counsel' derived from Sasanian originals. The list of Sasanian influences on all phases of Islamic culture and civilisation would be too long to include here.

While many *dihqāns* became Muslims they also preserved the old traditions and epic literature of Persia. Their patronage of the arts and of minstrels, in short their customs, were Persian not Arab. They preserved their social position, and Islam weighed lightly upon them. Throughout the Umayyad caliphate the Persian Muslims were clients or *mawalt* of various Arab families or tribes. The Abbasid revolution ended not only the influence of the Arab tribes, but also the division of Muslims between Arabs and their clients. One need not repeat the clichés about the Arab kingdom of the Umayyads and the Persian empire of the ʿAbbasids. The ʿAbbasids did not solve the problems inherent in an 'Arab' Islam, but under them conditions were ripe for the changes in Islamic culture which made it more than an Arab faith and way of life. At the time when Islam was becoming an 'international' religion and culture, the Persians developed their own language and Islamic tradition, and oddly the Persians played the leading role in both the internationalisation of Arabic and, of course, in the Persian renaissance.

There was a literary movement in the time of the ʿAbbasids which was called the *Shuʿūbiyya*, or the 'nationalist' school. There are several views about the *Shuʿūbiyya*, either that it was only active among the literati with small importance for the masses, or that it was of profound social significance, a struggle to determine the destinies of Islamic culture as a whole.[18] I believe the problem has been approached with a misleading emphasis, as though the philo-Persian literati were trying to wreck the structure of Islam when they introduced Persian ideas and institutions into Islamic culture, or Persian words into Arabic. By the time of the ʿAbbasids the question at stake was not Islam or Iran, but rather a Persianised, international Islam or a narrow Arab Islam. The philo-Persians were reading the signs of the time; they were the wave of the future, while narrow Arab

278

interests were provincial and in a sense reactionary against the real destiny or genius of Islam. H. A. R. Gibb made an acute observation, when he said that the issue at stake was whether the new Islamic society 'was to become a re-embodiment of the old Perso-Aramaean culture into which the Arabic and Islamic elements would be absorbed, or a culture in which the Perso-Aramaean contributions would be subordinated to the Arab tradition and the Islamic values'.[19] In the case of Persia there was no question, but that the former view should prevail, while in the Arabic-*speaking* parts of the caliphate it would seem the latter triumphed.

A sign of the division of the Islamic world into these two camps, in my opinion, was the rise of the New Persian language in the tenth century and the breakdown of classical Arabic at about the same time. The Arabic language of intercourse had separated from classical Arabic to such an extent that even grammarians did not use the classical tongue in conversation, while common folk had long gone their own ways with dialects.[20] Thus conditions were ripe for the development of a New Persian literature. Before we turn to the renaissance of New Persian, however, an examination of certain ethnic and religious problems of the Umayyad and early 'Abbasid periods will be useful.

Central Asian Particularism

Central Asia was called *ma wara'l-nahr*, 'the other side of the (Oxus) river', by the Arabs, and this reflects a Sasanian tradition, for the military centre for the Sasanian frontier was at Merv as it was for the Arabs. These lands had not been under Persian control, but were ruled by many local princes, some of whom in present Afghanistan may have been tributary to the Sasanian monarch. The most important people in the area were the Sogdians who had had extensive trade relations with China for over half a millennium before the Arab conquest. The most important city of the Sogdians was Samarkand, but Sogdian merchants and colonists were found as far apart as Mongolia and Merv.[21] We know from Menander Protektor that Sogdians had served on missions from the Turks to Byzantium and were known for their trading activities. Their role in the spread of Iranian culture to the Turks is also amply attested by Sogdian words in Old Turkish, their spreading of Manichaeism among the nomads, and other indications.

279

Both in Sogdian documents and from archaeological excavations we find a corroboration of Arabic accounts on the numerous local rulers in Central Asia. [22] There were, it seems, a series of small city states maintaining courts and a way of life with many affinities to the society portrayed by the Iranian national epic, a kind of knighthood in flower. Christianity had more or less ended the heroic tradition of the *gusan* (minstrel) in Armenia and under the Sasanian state church a similar fate had befallen them in Persia. In Central Asia, however, at the small courts of the princelings the feudal, chivalric society continued to exist, if not to flourish as it had in the past. Eastern Iran was then the refuge of the old traditions which provided the background for Firdosi and his *Shahname.*

The Arabs in their conquests of these small states in Central Asia made use of the tactics of *divide et impera* among the various princes, as well as in relations with the Sogdian-Turkish allies. They also did something else, for in the armies of Qutaiba ibn Muslim, the great Arab general (died 715), were many Persian clients who were garrisoned with the Arabs in Bukhara, Samarkand and other cities. These Muslim Persians, together with non-Muslim Persian refugees from the Arab invasion who had settled in Central Asia, provided a large Persian-speaking element in the towns where Sogdian dialects in the course of two centuries were replaced by Persian as the language of intercourse. [23] In Khwarezm, according to al-Bīrūnī, Qutaiba destroyed the people who knew the old Khwarezmian language, literature and traditions. The information of al-Bīrūnī, himself a native of Khwarezm, may be correct since S. P. Tolstov and other archaeologists have found many fragmentary documents of leather and wood with Khwarezmian writing, either in a cursive alphabet on the former or in block letters on wood. [24] The Khwarezmians, both before and after Islam, played the same role of merchants to south Russia and the Volga region that the Sogdians did with regard to China.

The Hephthalite princes south of the Oxus river too felt the weight of Arab rule, and the ancient city of Balkh, or for a time Bārūzān a neighbouring town, was a centre of Arab military rule in the area. The Hephthalites north of the Hindu Kush mountains were associated with the Sogdians while those south of the Hindu Kush were connected with Seistan in the plans of Arab conquest. The mountainous centre of present Afghanistan was Indian in culture as well as apparently also in the majority of the population, attested by the flourishing Buddhist shrines of Bamiyan and the Hindu Shahi rulers of Kabul who traced their lineage back to the Kushans. The Hephthalites in the north, too, were in many ways successors of the Kushans. They continued using the Greek alphabet, which had been modified for use with an Iranian language first, probably in the reign of Kanishka, and much of the organisation, protocol and titulary of their predecessors remained under the Hephthalites. The *kanārang*, or 'warden of the marches' was probably a Kushan title adopted by both the Hephthalites and the Sasanians, since the Arabs found a *kanārang* in Ṭūs at the time of the conquest. Other local titles of rulers or officials may be found in Arabic geographies.

The Arabs came to terms with the local merchants and commercial agents, and much of late Umayyad and early 'Abbasid policy in Khurasan and Central Asia can be better understood as the conflict of economic interests, rather than just the quarrels of Arab tribesmen among the garrison troops. The 'Abbasid revolt was not only a political and religious movement, but also an economic affair since many local native supporters of Abu Muslim, as well as Arabs, followed him out of resentment at Umayyad economic policy as much as for political reasons. Trade between the Near East and China was important for many Sogdian and Hephthalite merchants and a sympathetic and liberal policy on the part of the caliphate was greatly desired. It is impossible here to investigate these important facets of Islamic history, which are discussed in my book *The Golden Age of Persia*.

From Arabic sources we learn that there was considerable opposition to Arab rule, but the frequent revolts were local and usually restricted to a city where the Muslim garrison was massacred or expelled. Of course, outside intervention by the Türgesh Turks, the successors of the West Turkish empire in Central Asia, or coalitions of local princes caused great difficulties for the Islamic armies. But religious or mass movements in the countryside are not recorded under the early caliphs or under the Umayyads. On the whole Arab rule was light although cases of local governors oppressing the local population are not unknown.[25] Central Asia, after all, was a frontier area of the Islamic world and rebels, both Iranian and Arab, did not have far to flee to escape caliphal control.

The success of the 'Abbasid revolution launched a series of popular religious movements in Khurasan and Central Asia which were dangerous both to the Muslims and established government and to the orthodox Zoroastrian community which had established a *modus vivendi* with the Arab rulers. The first of these movements, *circa* 746, was led by a certain Bihafrid in eastern Khurasan, who claimed to be a prophet of Zoroastrianism, but preaching a negation of many of their practices such as next-of-kin marriages and the recitation of prayers.[26] The Zoroastrian religious leaders persuaded Abu Muslim, the 'Abbasid leader in Khurasan, to kill Bihafrid which he did *circa* 749. Although it would seem that the followers of Bihafrid adopted some Islamic practices, they were hated by both Muslims and orthodox Zoroastrians. None the less his partisans continued to flourish long after his death.

Another such person, Sunpad, was a follower of Abu Muslim who rebelled after his death in Khurasan and apparently exalted Abu Muslim to the role of a hidden messiah, although we cannot exactly determine his religious preachings. He was killed a short time after he revolted and was followed by Ishaq 'the Turk' in Transoxiana who likewise preached a faith in Abu Muslim till Ishaq's death *circa* 758. His work and that of Bihafrid was continued by the heresiarch Ustadsis in the Herat area and eastern Khurasan until his capture and execution by caliphal forces in 768. He was followed by the most successful of the religious rebels, Muqanna', who taught the doctrine of the migration of souls through various prophets and through Abu Muslim to himself. He had many followers in Transoxiana until his destruction *circa* 785. Some later authors called his revolt a revival of the ancient Mazdakite movement.

There were other movements but the point of interest is that all of these religious uprisings occurred in Khurasan or Transoxiana, while we hear of none in Fars or elsewhere in western Persia. The conclusion one might draw would be that eastern Iran and Central Asia were prone to dissatisfaction and heresy to a much greater extent than western Persia; that is, the former Hephthalite and Sogdian domains had not had the same religious unity as the state church of Sasanian Persia. Whether Islamic heresies, too, flourished more on the frontiers of the caliphate than in the west is a moot point, but not improbable, according to scattered and uncertain evidence. One could say that the religious situation in eastern Iran and Central Asia ran parallel to the local regionalism or political fragmentation, for not only was Zoroastrianism present particularly in various local forms, but the same was true of Manichaeism, Nestorian Christianity, Buddhism and local cults of the ancestors. A heroic cult of Siyavush, another of an unidentified goddess, and other cults flourished there. [27] Likewise political rule was characterised by local autonomy, where the cities had self-government to a greater degree than in western Persia. In Fars province the situation was different.

Orthodoxy in Fars

According to Yaqut, a thirteenth-century geographer, Fars in Abbasid times was divided into five *ostans* or districts, each of which was composed of *rustāqs*. Each *rustāq* was sub-divided into a number of *tassūj*, which in turn was merely a group of villages. [28] This reflects Sasanian organisation, its religious network of fire temples as well as its political divisions. From various Islamic sources we know that Istakhr in Fars, which had been one of two centres of Zoroastrianism in Persia under the Sasanians, the other being Shiz in Azerbaijan, continued to flourish under Islam. Gradually the network of fire temples fell to pieces as the number of Zoroastrians declined, but Fars remained predominantly Zoroastrian down to the tenth century and with substantial numbers of Zoroastrians even in the time of the Turkish Seljuk conquests in the eleventh century.

We have a fascinating account of struggles between Muslims and Zoroastrians within the city of Kazerun in the life of the famous founder of a Sufi or dervish order, Abu Ishāq Ibrahīm b. Shahriyār al-Kāzerūnī, who died 1034. Many Zoroastrians were converted to Islam by the shaykh, but none the less the strong position of Zoroastrianism is clear from this book as well as from other Islamic sources. [29] The governor of Kazerun under the Boyid dynasty, which ruled Fars at that time, was a Zoroastrian called Khorshīd who held the high esteem of the Boyid ruler in Shiraz, so much so that the Boyid prince ordered Shaykh Kāzerūnī to appear before him where he was reprimanded for disturbing the peace with his proselytising activities (Meier, pp. 117-121).

The Muslims and the Zoroastrians were the two main communities in Fars for the Christians and Jews were insignificant in numbers. While there were Shi'ites and Sufis as well as Sunnites among the Muslims, the Zoroastrian community seems to have been relatively stable and orthodox. Its main activity, which we can find in the sources, is not disputes over heresy, although these were not absent, but rather an intellectual renaissance of Zoroastrianism in the ninth and early tenth centuries.[30] What brought about this literary activity shortly before the rapid decline of Zoroastrianism, migrations to India and conversions to Islam?

There is no direct answer to the reason for the Zoroastrian renaissance, when the Pahlavi *Denkart, Bundahishn,* and many other books were written, but one may make informed surmises. First, the times not only permitted but provoked such writings. The Muʿtazilites, or Islamic free-thinkers, many of whom were Persians, had created an atmosphere of free debate and interest in philosophical and theological questions. Muslim literary activity was great and interest in other religions was high and the age was one of free inquiry and stimulus to write religious tracts. Second, the Zoroastrians were losing ground and they passed from a militant defiance of Islam or the Arabs to an intellectual defensive. This may be seen in the number of apologetic works written at this time such as the *Shkand Gumanik Vičar* or the *Denkart*. One may suspect that the Zoroastrian community followed a parallel road to the Islamic development, which was first a liberal policy under the Muʿtazilite impetus followed by an orthodox reaction of Hanbali Sunnism, theologically grounded by al-Ashʿarī (died 936), but this is difficult to prove. Certainly after the Zoroastrian literary renaissance of the ninth century a somewhat sterile orthodoxy became the rule. Third, it would seem that the Zoroastrian church even in Sasanian times relied more on the oral transmission of the religion with all of its ramifications rather than on written treatises. Now the need for writing became acute.

Among the titles of Pahlavi books translated into Arabic, as found in the *Fihrist* of Ibn al-Nadīm as well as other authors, are many 'scientific', ethical-didactic works and 'mirrors of princes', but no religious tracts. This is, of course, understandable, but one may none the less wonder whether there were many religious works to translate. Writing was probably never as important to religious leaders in ancient Persia as has been supposed, but under the new circumstances of Islamic rule, with the prestige of the written word of God and the impetus to imitate Muslim literary prolixity in the religious sphere, Zoroastrian religious leaders reacted with a religious renaissance of their own. For the Pahlavi books of the ninth century were probably all composed by

284

mobads. It is clear that Arabic had completely taken over the Pahlavi secular literary tradition.

As a matter of fact the geographer Iṣṭakhrī, writing in the tenth century, says (137, line 16) that in Fars province the people used three languages. The first was Persian or Farsi *spoken* by everyone and understood by all, save for dialectical divergences. The second was Pahlavi in which the accounts of the ancient Persians were written, as well as contemporary Zoroastrian books, a language which ordinary people could not understand without an explanation. Finally there was Arabic in which the correspondence of the ruler and the bureaux of state was written and which some common folk also employed. I believe this passage not only describes the linguistic situation in Fars, but also the social and cultural divisions. Everyone *spoke* Persian, but the Zoroastrians among themselves employed Pahlavi as their written language, while the Muslim community was served by Arabic. Some of the Muslim Persians spoke Arabic as well, but less frequently after the decline of classical Arabic in favour of Arabic dialects in the Arabic speaking areas of the ʿAbbasid caliphate. Further, the situation in Fars province was much the same as elsewhere in Persia, though all over the caliphate Arabic was the language of state, of course, and still a *lingua franca* as well as the language of learning and science.

During the first two centuries of the ʿAbbasid caliphate in Persia, Arabic had completely displaced Pahlavi as the language of learning, so that Pahlavi finally remained the province of the *mobads* alone, while Arabic translations of secular Pahlavi works were made, after which the Pahlavi originals were discarded and lost. Even Iranophile literati of the *Shuʿūbiyya* movement wrote in Arabic attacking the Arabs. The dominance of Arabic probably provided a strong incentive for Persian intellectuals to convert to Islam, or to go, at least nominally, with the tide.

As Islam grew in scope and richness Sufism, Shiʿism and other Islamic movements provided a haven for Persians who could no longer follow the sterile, orthodox Zoroastrianism. When Persian leaders from Daylam, a Caspian Sea area, newly converted to Shiʿite Islam, wrested political control of western Persia from the caliphs and eventually took Baghdad the capital in 945, the end was in sight for Zoroastrian Persia. Here was the Boyid dynasty of Persians upholding Islam and the Arabic language, because both had become internationalised while Zoroastrian Persian culture had retreated into a ghetto. The

Shi'ite Boyids on the whole seem to have been relatively tolerant of other beliefs, for they retained the Sunnite caliphs and many Sunnite officials. We have already mentioned the Zoroastrian governor of Kazerun among other similar officers under them. The Boyids, however, were more interested in the Arab traditions of the family of 'Alī and general Islamic culture as a reality than they were in the past glories of Persia. It is true that they had an antiquarian interest in the past; for example, one of the Boyid princes 'Aḍud al-Daulah in 955 had an inscription carved at Persepolis in Arabic telling how he visited the ruins and had Marāsfand, the *mobad* of Kazerun, interpret for him the Pahlavi inscriptions from the time of Shapur II. [31]

The time was ripe for the New Persian renaissance, but it came in the east rather than in western Iran. Perhaps the basic reason for this may be found in a remark of the geographer al-Maqdisī who said (440, line 2) that the scholars were respected in the east, but in Fars the secretaries or scribes.

The New Persian Renaissance

For some cultures language is more important that religion or society in the continuity or preservation of that culture. This, I believe, is true of Persia for the linguistic continuity from Middle to New Persian is undeniable, yet the two are not the same. The most striking difference between Pahlavi and New Persian is the introduction of an immense Arabic vocabulary into the latter, which made New Persian a world language with a famous literature which its predecessor had not been. It was really Arabic which gave New Persian the richness which engendered the flowering of literature, primarily poetry, in the late Middle Ages. New Persian represented a new tradition formed by Muslim Persians well versed in Arabic, but with a love for their own spoken language. The New Persian language written in the Arabic alphabet was formed in the ninth century in eastern Iran and came to flower in Bukhara, the capital of the Samanid dynasty. How did this happen?

The general spoken language of the Sasanian court and the Sasanian administration in provincial centres of Iran was called *Darī*, 'the court language', by many Arabic writers after the Islamic conquest. This language was imperfectly recorded in the Pahlavi alphabet, but as Arabic took its place, it continued to be preserved in a stultified *written* form by the *mobads* almost as an hieratic written language which modern scholars call Book Pahlavi. All over Iran various Iranian dialects were spoken not written, fascinating examples of which are given by the geographer al-Maqdisī. [32] But the proper, standardised Persian spoken by the upper classes and in cities was *Dari*. *Dari* then was simply a special style of Persian not a dialect or a language. This tongue even spread to Central Asia outside of the old boundaries of the Sasanian empire, and this process had begun in pre-Islamic times, because of the prestige of the Sasanians and because Persian merchants settled in cities like Bukhara and maintained their own language, while the Sogdian merchants used Persian in their dealings in Sasanian domains. Likewise the Sasanian troops stationed on the frontiers contributed to the spread of the common Persian tongue.

After the Arab conquest Persians fled to Transoxiana, but even more important for the spread of Persian was the mass of Persian clients who accompanied the Arab troops during their conquests. Undoubtedly the Arabs themselves used Persian as the language of communication with the many Sogdian, Hephthalite and other princelings. It was under Arab rule that local Sogdian and other Iranian dialects gave way to Persian, although the dialects were still spoken in the countryside just as in Persia local dialects continued down to the present day. The dominance of Persian over the local dialects was especially strong in the fragmented Hephthalite domains, and both Balkh and Bukhara became centres of correct Persian, as they did of correct Arabic (Maqdisī, 32, line 8) because they were great commercial and cultural centres. In my opinion the points made above provided the basis for the development of Persian in Central Asia and Afghanistan, with the result that today we still have Persian dialects Tajiki and Afghan Persian spoken there.

To return to the rise of New Persian literature in the Arabic script, we can make some reasonable assertions about its beginnings. We are not concerned here with the nature of Middle Persian verse, whether it was based on a syllabic or an accentual principle. [33] In the formation of New Persian poetry the old system was harmonised with the quantitative prosody of Arabic, and the result was a wonderful expansion of forms, perhaps the earliest and best example of which is Firdosi's *Shahname*, written in *mutaqarib* metre. If we can detect the time of this change in the fragments of early Persian poets which have survived, then that date is approximately when the 'Arabicisation of Persian poetry' began.

Roughly from about 850 to 900, from the poetry of Muḥammad-i Waṣīf and Bassām-i Kurd to that of Ḥusain-i Khārajī, we find a mixture of Arabic and Persian features in poetry. Before this time, in the fragment of Abū Ḥafṣ-i Sughdī we find Middle Persian verse forms. So the creation of a New Persian poetry probably coincides with the dynasty of the Tahirids (*circa* 821-873) in Khurasan. Whether later tradition is correct, in claiming that ʿAbbās-i Mervī wrote a *qasida* in New Persian in honour of the arrival of the Caliph Ma'mun in Merv in 809, saying that 'before him no one had recited such poetry' is uncertain. [34] The beginnings of written New Persian may well have been the introduction of Persian words into Arabic poetry, and later the idea of writing the spoken Persian language in Arabic letters spread. We know that the Tahirids favoured the use of Arabic at their court at Nishapur, and the last member of the dynasty was noted for his fine Arabic style. [35] At the same time they were independent Persian dynasts, although they paid lip-service to the caliph, and they spoke Persian in their courts surely with pre-Islamic overtones.

Perhaps the Saffarid dynasty in Seistan, which rose from humble origins, called forth New Persian since its founder Yaʿqūb knew no Arabic, and according to tradition he wanted poetry recited in a language he understood, not Arabic. [36] In any case the writing of Persian in Arabic characters seems to have started in the middle of the ninth century, but it was under the Samanids that the literary flowering occurred.

The Samanids were in origin a noble Iranian family which came from the Termez area and claimed to descend from the Sasanian general Bahram Chobin. [37] The Samanids held to the customs of the *dihqāns* with their interest in epic tales sung by minstrels and in the art of pre-Islamic times. The rise to power of the Samanids in Transoxiana corresponded to the decline of the central power of the caliphate. The landlord class in eastern Iran too became more prominent at this time.

In the Samanids who ruled Central Asia and eastern Iran from 892 (the coming to power of Ismaʿīl the real founder of the kingdom) to 999, the poets and other literati found excellent patrons. It was at the Samanid court of Bukhara that Rūdakī and Daqīqī composed their poetry in Persian. The renaissance had begun. It is significant, however, that the earliest Persian prose was entirely translated from Arabic, such as the Persian

288

translation of Ṭabarī's history and his commentary to the Quran. The renaissance, however, was based on Islam; the old order was dead and the *Shuʿūbiyya* movement was out of date. The Arabic prose works were translated into Persian since the people were too lazy to read Arabic, as one translator expressed it. There was no revolt against either Islam or Arabic in the New Persian literary renaissance which might better be termed a *naissance* since a new Islamic Persian culture was being created. The Zoroastrian elements in the poetry represented the mode of the time and should not be considered as expressions of true Zoroastrian belief. Nostalgia for the past existed, especially among poets where one is likely to find such sentiments, but there was no turning back.

New Persian was now a language of Islam side by side with Arabic, and Islam had definitely outgrown its Arab background. It had become a multi-national, multi-lingual universal culture and faith and Iran played the leading role in this transformation. In a sense Islam had to change before the Persians accepted it, but one might also say that just as Greek civilisation served as a vehicle for Christianity, so did Iranian civilisation for Islam.

Islamic Persia was launched on its wonderful course with its Hafiz, Saʿdi, Omar Khayyam and a myriad of writers and artists down to the present day. But behind the poems, the rugs and the art which are known all over the world today there is the heritage of the past, a glorious heritage which has maintained a continuity and an influence down to the present, sometimes unseen but none the less present. May it long continue.

NOTES

1 History and epic fiction were frequently confused, and the messianic or apocalyptic features of later Sasanian literature have been described by several authors; see, for example K. Czeglédy, *'Bahrām Chōbīn and the Persian Apocalyptic Literature'*, *Acta Orient. Hungarica*, 8 (Budapest, 1958), 21-43.

2 Later called *dirhems*, the origin of this word is uncertain as is its presumed source the Greek word *drachme*. For example it may be Greek meaning 'handful' . The weight of the Sasanian *drachme* varied from 3.65 to 3.94 grams. Copper coins followed the silver standard.

3 References in Christensen, *L'Iran*, 453-455 and 464-469. The Pahlavi text on *King Husrav and his Boy*, ed. and trans. by J. M. Unvala (Paris, 1924?), tells of a page at the court of Chosroes II from the district of Eran Vīnārt Kavād 'Kavad put in order Iran', Qum north of Isfahan, who had the proper training of a young nobleman, the description of which is a testimony to the elegance and opulence of the times.

4 For example, in the Syriac act of martyrdom of Mar Aba a certain priest Kardag, the *ainbad* 'chief of protocol', one of the notables among the

Magian priests under Yazdagird I was active. Other cases are known, but not many. The bureaucracy, including scribes and tax-collectors, however, was a separate class or caste. Cf. M. Sprengling, *'From Persian to Arabic'*, *American Journal of Semitic Languages*, 56 (1939), 190, 196.

5 The order of Magian priests and of Christians is mentioned in the account of the martyrdom of Mar Aba; cf. Braun, *Ausgewähte Akten* (Munich, 1915), 212, 231. The fourfold division of society is well known from Mas'udī and other Islamic authors; cf. E. Benveniste, *'Les classes sociales dans la tradition avestique'*, *JA* (1932), 117.

6 G. Widengren, *'Stand und Aufgaben der iranischen Religions-geschichte'*, *Numen* 2 (1956), 144.

7 The problem whether modes of burial were related to Zoroastrianism or not is vexing, but I propose a general hypothesis that exposure of the dead to vultures and the subsequent interment of the bones in ossuaries was a general Central Asian custom which spread to Persia where it was promulgated as a religious duty by the *mobads*. Previous to the Sasanians various burial customs obtained in Mesopotamia and in western Iran. The evidence for this is not only literary but archaeological, since many more ossuaries were found in Central Asia than in Persia and apparently they date from an earlier period in Central Asia. Most relevant reports of excavations in Soviet Central Asia contain information about ossuaries. The existence of exposure among the Magi from early times does indicate a parallel development in Media, but the relationship between priestly practice in western Iran and seemingly popular usage in Central Asia is not clear. The general principle of keeping a corpse from defiling the earth could be maintained by enclosing it in wax, stone or otherwise, as well as by exposure on stone slabs.

8 The matter is disputed; cf. M. Molé, *'Le problème Zurvanite'*, *JA* (1959), 467, and my *'Zurvanism Again'*, *The Harvard Theological Review*, 52 (1959), 63-73, where further references may be found.

9 Present-day practices at *Noruz* 'New Year's day', the regard for fire and countless other popular beliefs and practices, which are pre-Islamic survivals, can be cited as evidence of the strong Zoroastrian influence on daily life both in Sasanian times and later. The extensive messianic or apocalyptic literature, both in Pahlavi and later in New Persian, indicates the great importance of messianic beliefs at the end of the Sasanian empire. One of the most famous hero-messiahs was Vahram-i Varjavand, the mythical prototype of Bahram Chobin who was known for his chivalry and exploits. The same tendency to identify popular heroes with messiahs is found later in Islamic times, the most famous of whom was Abu Muslim, the subject of many romances and apocalyptic works. Someone should write a detailed study on the 'messiah in Persian history', from early times.

10 Cf. especially his *Les motifs zoroastriens dans la philosophie de Sohrawardi* (Tehran, 1946) and *'Le temps cyclique dans le mazdéisme et dans l'ismaélisme'*, *Eranos Jahrbuch*, 20 (Zurich, 1952), 149-217.

11 H. Corbin, *Terre céleste et corps de résurrection de l'Iran Mazdéen à l'Iran Shı'ite* (Paris, 1961), 15.

12 K. Erdmann, *Das iranische Feuerheiligtum* (Leipzig, 1941), 32, 62, and K. Schippmann, *Die Iranischen Feuerheiligtümer* (Berlin, 1971).

13 Erdmann *Ibid.*, 43.

14 Cf. V. Minorsky, *'Roman and Byzantine Campaigns in Atropatene'*, *BSOAS*, 11 (1945), 248, with references.

15 Cf. G. Rothstein, *Die Dynastie der Lahmiden in al-Hira* (Berlin, 1899), 119. 'Amr the king of the Lakhmids, is first mentioned in the Paikuli inscription from the time of Narseh. See also T. Noeldeke, *Die*

Ghassanischen Fürsten aus dem Hause Gafna's (Berlin, 1887).
16 Details and sources may be found in M. Sprengling, *op. cit.*, (note 4), 214.
17 Cf. J. Tavadia, *'Zur Pflege des iranischen Schrifttums'*, ZDMG, 98 (1944), 337.
18 For the first point of view cf. B. Spuler, *'Die Selbstbehauptung des iranischen Volkstums im frühen Islam'*, *Die Welt als Geschichte*, 10 (1950), 189, and I. Goldziher, *Mohammedanische Studien*, 1 (Halle, 1889), 155. For the second position see H. A. R. Gibb, *'The Social Significance of the Shuʿūbtyya'*, *Studia Oriential Ioanni Pedersen* (Copenhagen, 1954), 105-114.
19 Gibb *Ibid.*, 108.
20 On this question cf. J. Fück, *Arabiya* (Berlin, 1950), 78.
21 On Sogdian colonies in the Far East see E. G. Pulleyblank, *'A Sogdian Colony in Inner Mongolia'*, *T'oung Pao*, 41 (1953), 317-356. On Sogdians in Merv we have Sogdian inscriptions on potsherds, together with Arabic and Pahlavi, now in the museum at Tashkent.
22 On the important Sogdian documents from Mt. Mug, see the *Sogdiiskii Sbornik* (Leningrad, 1934), and a series of older articles by A. Freiman in *Vestnik Drevnei Istorii* and more recent and better articles by V. Livshits in *Problemy Vostokovedeniya* no. 6 (1959), 123, and no. 6 (1960), 116, and *Sovetskaya Etnografiya* (1960). The archaeological work is reported in volumes 15 and 37 of *Materialy i Issledovaniya po Arkheologii SSSR* plus special subjects such as the fascinating volumes on the paintings and sculptures of Panjikant.
23 We know of the activities of Sasanian princes and Persian leaders from literary sources, while on a Sogdian letter (A14-2) from Mt. Mug speaks of a Persian general, presumably operating against the Arabs: cf. Livshits, *The Sogdian Letters from Mt. Mugh*, Twenty-fifth International Congress of Orientalists (Moscow, 1960), 5. The letters have been published by Livshits, *Yuridicheskie Dokumenty i Pis'ma* (Moscow, 1962), and by M. N. Bogolyubov and O. I. Smirnova, *Khozyaistvennye Dokumenty* (Moscow, 1963).
24 S. P. Tolstov, *Trudy Khorezmskoi Arkheologo-Etnograficheskoi Ekspeditsii* (Moscow, 1958), 207-212. Interesting Khwarezmian coins were also found. I cannot follow Tolstov, however, in all of his theories *ad majorem gloriam Chorasmianorum*.
25 E.g. the *Ta'rtkh-i Sistan*, ed. M. Bahar (Tehran, 1936), 92; yet on the preceding page the author tells how many Zoroastrians were converted to Islam because of the missionary efforts of the Arab governor.
26 Information and a bibliography of sources on all these 'heresies' may be found in G. H. Sadighi, *Les mouvements religieux iraniens au IIᵉ et au IIIᵉ siécle de l'hégire* (Paris, 1938), 111-286.
27 Material on the political and religious situation in Central Asia on the eve of the Arab conquest has been conveniently summarised with references in A. Dzhalilov, *Sogd Nakanune Arabskogo Nashestviya* (Stalinabad, 1960), esp. 73-81.
28 *Kitāb Muʿjam al-buldān*, ed. F. Wüstenfeld, I (Leipzig, 1866), 40. The etymologies of the various words cannot be discussed here.
29 *Firdōs al-Murshidiyya* or *Die Vita des Scheich Abū Ishāq al-Kāzarūnī*, ed. F. Meier (Leipzig, 1948), 30, 197, *et passim*.
30 On the discussions of a Zoroastrian heretic with Muslim, Christian, Jewish and orthodox Zoroastrian leaders at the court of the caliph al-Ma'mun see A. Barthelemy, *Gukjastak Abalish* (Paris, 1887). The

Denkart is full of attacks on heretics or *ashamog.* Cf. note 36 of Chapt. 6.

31 Photographs of two similar Kufic Arabic inscriptions from Persepolis may be found in E. Schmidt, *Persepolis,* I (Chicago, 1953). A third inscription has been published in G. Wiet ed., *Répertoire chronologique d'épigraphie arabe,* 4 (Cairo, 1933), 135, no. 1475. The last line should be corrected to read *wa Marāsfand al-mūbad al-Kāzarūnī.*

It is interesting that the first large migration of Zoroastrians to India is dated *circa* 936, while a Zoroastrian rebellion which was suppressed occurred in Shiraz under the Boyids in 979. Cf. J. C. Tavadia, *op. cit.,* 304, 331.

32 Ed. M. J. de Goeje (Leiden, 1877), 334-336, 369, 398.

33 On the syllabic principle see E. Benveniste, *'Le mémorial de Zarer',* *JA* (1932), 245-293, and C. Rempis, *'Die ältesten Dichtungen in Neupersisch',* *ZDMG,* 101 (1951), 220-248. For the accentual principle see W. B. Henning, *'A Pahlavi Poem',* *BSOAS,* 13 (1950), 641-648, and S. Shaked, *'Specimens of Middle Persian Verse',* *W. B. Henning Memorial Volume* (London, 1970), 395-405.

34 Rempis, *op. cit.,* 221, where data on the early poets may be found.

35 On this cf. Frye, *'Die Wiedergeburt Persiens',* *Der Islam,* 35 (1960), 47.

36 For references see Henning, *'Mitteliranisch',* *op. cit.,* 87.

37 A. A. Semenov, *'K voprosu o proiskhozhdenii Samanidov',* *Trudy Instituta Istorii i tnografii Akad. Nauk Tadzhikskoi SSR,* 27 (Stalinabad, 1954), 4.

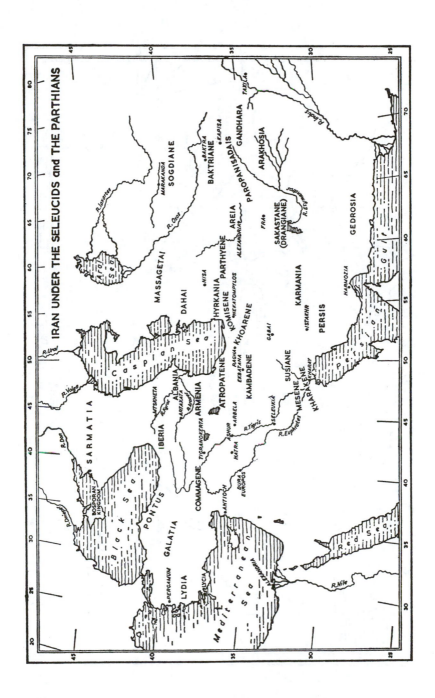

IRAN UNDER THE SELEUCIDS and THE PARTHIANS

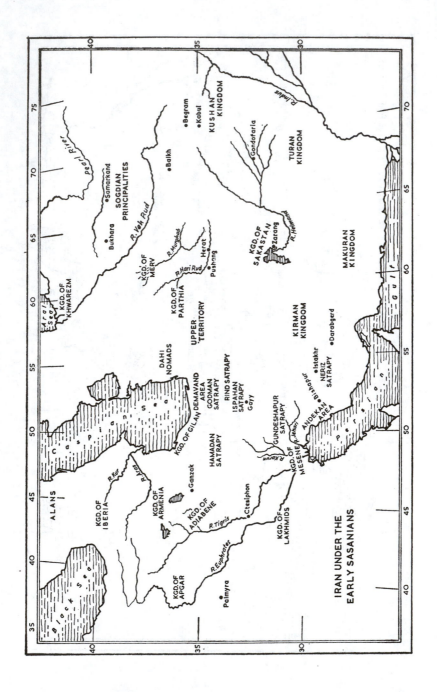

IRAN UNDER THE
EARLY SASANIANS

Black Sea

ALANS

KGD. OF
IBERIA

R.Kur

R.Aras

KGD. OF
ARMENIA

Ganzak

KGD. OF
ADIABENE

R.Tigris

Ctesiphon

KGD. OF
LAKHMIDS

R.Euphrates

KGD. OF
AFGAR

Palmyra

Caspian Sea

DAHI
NOMADS

KGD. OF GILAN

DEMAVAND
AREA

GODMAN
SATRAPY

HAMADAN
SATRAPY

RIND SATRAPY

ISPAHAN
SATRAPY

Gay

GUNDESHAPUR
SATRAPY

KGD. OF
MESENE

R.Jehazi

R.Karun

ANDEKAN
AREA

Bishapur

Istakhr

NERIZ
SATRAPY

KIRMAN
KINGDOM

Darabgerd

Persian Gulf

Aral Sea

KGD. OF
KHWAREZM

R.Veh Rud

Bukhara

Samarkand

SOGDIAN
PRINCIPALITIES

Pearl River

Balkh

KGD. OF
MERV

R.Murghab

R.Hari Rud

Herat

Pushang

KGD. OF
PARTHIA

UPPER
TERRITORY

KGD. OF
SAKASTAN

Zarang

R.Helmand

Begram

Kabul

KUSHAN
KINGDOM

Gondofaria

TURAN
KINGDOM

R.Indus

MAKURAN
KINGDOM

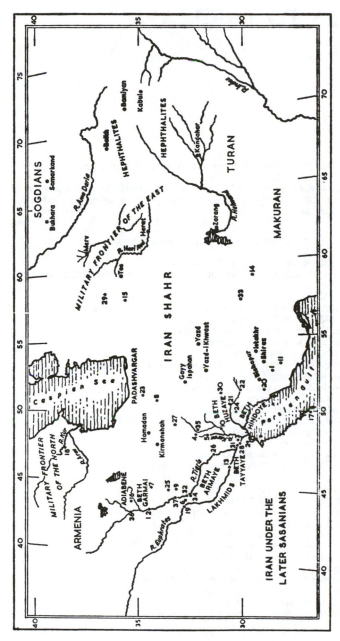

For names of numbered sites see page 296.

NOTES TO THE MAPS

The spelling of names on the maps may vary slightly from the usually simplified forms in the text.

On map one, the locations of Thatagush- and Akaufachiya are uncertain. The locations of the following areas on map three are uncertain: Godman satrapy, Rind satrapy, Andekan area.

LIST OF CITIES UNDER THE LATER SASANIANS

1 Ardashir Khwarreh or Gor (Firuzabad).
2 Astarabad Ardashir, or Wahishtabad Ardashir or Karka de Maishan (in Mesene).
3 Abaz Kawad or Abad Kawad or Nehargur (Madhar) near Ahwaz.
4 Eran Asan Kart Kawad or Karka de Redan (Ivane-e Karkha).
5 Eran Khwarreh Shahpuhr (Susa under Shahpuhr II).
6 Eran Khwarreh Khusro (near Ctesiphon?).
7 Eran Shad Kawad (near Khaniqin).
8 Eran Vinart Kawad (Qum).
9 Dastagerd-e Khusro or Dastagerd-e Malik (Eski Bagdad).
10 Hormizd Ardashir (Ahwaz).
11 Kawad Khwarreh (south of Gor, Karzin?).
12 Karkha de Peroz (north of Samarra).
13 Khusro Shad Hormizd (Uruk?).
14 Nev Hormizd Ardashir or Narmashir (in Kirman east of Bam?).
15 Nev Shahpuhr or Abrshahr (Nishapur).
16 Nod Ardashir (near Arbela).
17 Panyat or Pasa Ardashir (Khatt or al-Qatif).
18 Peroz Kawad (Bardha or Perozapat in Armenia).
19 Peroz Shahpuhr or Faishabur (al-Anbar).
20 Ram Ardashir or Ramishn Ardashir (Tawwaj).
21 Ram Hormizd (Ardashir) (Ramuz in Khuzistan).
22 Vam Kawad, also called Weh Amid Kawad (Arrajan).
23 Ram Peroz (near Rayy).
24 Rew Ardashir (Rishahr in Khuzistan or al-Rumiyya).
25 Roshan Kawad or Roshan Khurso, or Khusro Roshan Kawadi (Zengabad on the Diyala River).
26 Roshan Peroz (in the Kashkar district of Iraq).
27 Shahpuhr Khwast (south of Khurramabad in Luristan?).
28 Shad Shahpuhr or Rema (ʿUbulla).
29 Shahr Ram Peroz (near Abiward).
30 Wahisht Hormizd (near Malamir in Khuzistan).

31 Wahman Ardashir or Prat de Maishan (near Basra).
32 Weh Ardashir (Seleukia on the Tigris).
33 Weh Ardashir or Bardashir (Kirman).
34 Weh Antiok Khusro or Rumagan or Rumiyan (near Ctesiphon).
35 Weh Antiok Shahpuhr or Gundeshapur.
36 Weh Hormizd Kawad (Mosul), the same as Weh Kawad on Tigris?
37 Wuzurg Shahpuhr ('Ukbara).

Other sites include Kam Peroz between Kazerun and Firuzabad, Mihragan Katak in Media between Hamadan and Hulwan, Khusro Shad Peroz at Tureng Tepe in Gurgan, Rustaqobad or Rustam Kawad, which is Askar Mukarram in Khuzistan, and Abadan Peroz (or Shahram Peroz) in Ardebil.

APPENDIX I

GENEALOGY OF THE ACHAEMENIDS

(After Kent, *Old Persian*, 158 with chronological revisions)

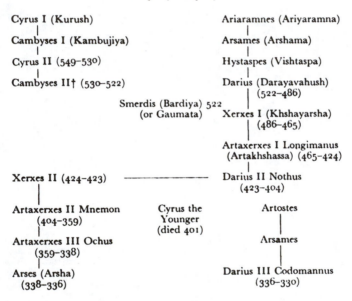

Achaemenes (Hakhamanish)

Teispes (Chishpish)*

Cyrus I (Kurush)
    |
Cambyses I (Kambujiya)
    |
Cyrus II (549–530)
    |
Cambyses II† (530–522)

Ariaramnes (Ariyaramna)
    |
Arsames (Arshama)
    |
Hystaspes (Vishtaspa)
    |
Darius (Darayavahush)
    (522–486)

Smerdis (Bardiya) 522
(or Gaumata)

Xerxes I (Khshayarsha)
    (486–465)

Artaxerxes I Longimanus
(Artakhshassa) (465–424)

Xerxes II (424–423) ——————— Darius II Nothus
    (423–404)

Artaxerxes II Mnemon   Cyrus the   Artostes
    (404–359)   Younger
    | (died 401) |
Artaxerxes III Ochus   Arsames
    (359–338)
    |
Arses (Arsha)   Darius III Codomannus
    (338–336)   (336–330)

* The introduction of another Cyrus and another Teispes into the genealogy of Cyrus I (his grandfather and father respectively) is said to be necessary for chronological reasons, but there is no evidence for this ; cf. E. Cavaignac in *Journal Asiatique*, 239 (1951), 364.

† The naming of a child after his grandfather was known among other Indo-European peoples.

APPENDIX 2

TENTATIVE GENEALOGICAL TABLE OF THE ARSACID KINGS

Arsaces I (*'ršk*) 247–? – – – – –   Tiridates (*tyrdt*) *ca.*?–211 BC

                              Artabanus I (*'rtpn*) *ca.* 211–191 BC

                  —————————Priapatius (*prypt*) *ca.* 191–176 BC

Mithradates I (*mtrdt*)   – – – – Phraates I (*prṱh* or *prdty*) *ca.* 176–171 BC
ca. 171–138 BC

Phraates II *ca.* 138–128 BC – – – ? Sinatrukes (*sntrwk*) *ca.* 77–68? BC
                     Gotarzes I (*gwtrz*) *ca.* 91–80? BC
                     Orodes I (*wrwd*) *ca.* 80–77 BC

Artabanus II *ca.* 128–123 BC   Phraates III *ca.* 68–57 BC

Mithradates II *ca.* 123–87 BC
          Orodes II *ca.* 57–37 BC – – – – ·Mithradates III *ca.* 57–54 BC

Tiridates II   Phraates IV *ca.* 38–2 BC
ca. 30–25 BC
          Phraataces (*prdtk*) *ca.* 2 BC–AD 4 – – – Vonones I (*whwnm*?) *ca.*
                                          AD 7–12

Orodes III *ca.* AD 4–7

        Artabanus III *ca.* AD 12–38   Tiridates III *ca.* AD 36
        Vardanes (*wrt'n*) *ca.* AD 39–47   – – – – Gotarzes II (*gwtrz*) *ca.* AD 38–51

        Vonones II *ca.* AD 51

        Vologeses I (*wlgš*) *ca.* AD 51–80
                               Pakores (*pkwr*?) *ca.* AD 79–105
                               Oroses *ca.* AD 109–128

        Artabanus IV *ca.* AD 80–81 ?
        Vologeses II *ca.* AD 105–147   Mithradates IV *ca.* AD
                                     128–147?

        Vologeses III *ca.* AD 148–192

        Vologeses IV *ca.* AD 191–207

        Vologeses V *ca.* AD 207–227 (?)
                     – – – – Artabanus V *ca.* 213–224
                                   Artavasdes (*'rtwzd*) *ca.* 226–
                                   227?

Vertical lines mean father to son succession while horizontal lines mean blood or adopted brothers.

THE DYNASTY OF THE SASANIANS*

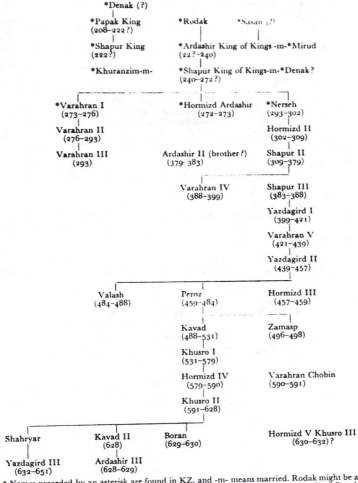

* Names preceded by an asterisk are found in KZ, and -m- means married. Rodak might be a name in the *Shahname* (Calcutta ed. 1.1365) where *rūdyāb* is given as the patronymic of Papak unless a common noun meaning 'seized liver' i.e. 'troubled' or 'agitated' is meant.

BIBLIOGRAPHY

BIBLIOGRAPHY

For an extensive bibliography on Zoroastrianism the reader is referred to R. C. Zaehner, *The Dawn and Twilight of Zoroastrianism* (Weidenfeld and Nicolson, London, 1961), 339-348, and J. Duchesne-Guillemin, *La religion de l'Iran ancien* (Paris, 1962) and it is superfluous to repeat the material already found there. Here we shall present a bibliography following the chapters of our book but omitting those works dealing with Zoroastrianism. For a useful bibliography see W. G. Oxtoby, *Ancient Iran and Zoroastrianism* in *Festschriften* (Waterloo, Ontario, 1973). A general work is M. M. Dyakonov, *Ocherk istorii drevnego Irana* (Moscow, 1961). Specialised works, mentioned in the footnotes, generally will not be repeated in this bibliography which is mainly general in character.

CHAPTER 1

Most general works on Persia give a survey of the land and people, but there is no one book dealing with the human and natural geography of the country. The best gazetteer, though unfortunately with inaccuracies, is the ten-volume Persian language *Farhang-i Jughrāfiyā-yi Irān*, edited by General Razmārā (Tehran, 1950-1954). The best general, natural, economic, and political geography of the country is probably the three-volume work by Mas'ūd Kayhān, *Jughrāfiyā-yi mufaṣṣal-i Irān*, 3 vols. (Tehran, 1937). The Islamic geography of Iran is treated in G. LeStrange, *Lands of the Eastern Caliphate* (Cambridge, 1930), and by P. Schwarz, *Iran im Mittelalter* (Leipzig, 1929 foll.), both of which are valuable reference works

303

also for Sasanian geography, which is also the subject of J. Markwart, *The Provincial Capitals of Eranshahr* (Rome, 1931), a translation with commentary of a Pahlavi text. The same author's *Ērānšahr* (Berlin, 1901) is a similar study based on an Armenian geography.

Ethnography is not well represented. Perhaps the most comprehensive study of the peoples of Iran including Afghanistan is S. P. Tolstov ed., *Narody Perednei Azii*, 53-308 (Moscow, 1957).

For further general information on the land and people consult the bibliography in V. V. Bartold, *Istoriko-geograficheskii obzor Irana* (St Petersburg, 1903), reprinted in his *Sochineniya*, 7 (Moscow, 1971), 29-225.

CHAPTER 2

The fundamental old work on Indo-European philology is still the five-volume comparative grammar by Karl Brugmann, which has appeared in many editions and in a French translation. It is, of course, much in need of revision. Unfortunately the series *Indogermanische Grammatik* of the Carl Winter Verlag is incomplete, but the volumes already published by Kurylowicz and Watkins show the progress made since Brugmann. The Indo-European comparative dictionary is by P. Walde and J. Pokorny (Berlin, 1928 foll.), in 3 vols. with a revision of it by Pokorny entitled *Indogermanisches Etymologisches Wörterbuch* (Bern, 1959). Needless to say, scholars do not agree on many of its etymologies. This is not the place to list contributions to Indo-European philology by A. Meillet, E. Benveniste, J. Kurylowicz and many others, for ample bibliographies may be found in such journals as *Kratylos, Indogermanisches Jahrbuch* and *Linguistic Bibliography*. A good survey of the question of an Indo-European *Ursprache*, homeland and culture may be found in the article of A. Scherer, *'Indogermanische Altertumskunde (seit 1940)'*, *Kratylos*, 1 (1956).

The Indo-Europeans in the ancient Near East have been discussed many times, and several accounts are M. Mayrhofer, *Die Indo-Arier im alten Vorderasien* (Wiesbaden, 1966), and A. Kammenhuber, *Die Arier im vorderen Orient* (Heidelberg, 1968).

On Zoroaster one need only add to Zaehner's exhaustive

bibliography the book of W. Hinz, *Zarathustra* (Stuttgart, 1961), which contains a new translation of the Gathas, and M. Molé, *La légende de Zoroastre, selon les textes pehlevis* (Paris, 1967). Regarding the pre-Islamic epic literature of Iran and the East-Iranian sagas the article by Mary Boyce in the volume on literature of the *Handbuch der Orientalistik*, ed. B. Spuler (Leiden, 1968), is the best survey available. For a shorter survey see the article on *'Iranian Literature'*, by I. Gershevitch in E. B. Ceadel, *Literatures of the East* (London, 1953). The classic study on Firdosi's *Shahname* is by T. Noeldeke in the *Grundriss der iranischen Philologie*, 2 (Strassburg, 1904). This may be supplemented by the small book of A. Christensen, *Les gestes des rois dans les traditions de l'Iran antique* (Paris, 1936). A guide to Pahlavi literature is found in the book of J. Tavadia, *Die mittelpersische Sprache und Literatur der Zarathustrier* (Leipzig, 1956), and M. Boyce, '*Middle Persian Literature*', *Handbuch der Orientalistik* (Leiden, 1968), 31-66.

The book *Saka-Studien* by J. Junge (Leipzig, 1939) is a useful survey of ancient north-eastern Iran but it must be used with caution. The monumental but outdated studies of F. Spiegel, *Eranische Altertumskunde*, 3 vols. (Leipzig, 1871-1878), and W. Geiger, *Ostiranische Kultur in Alterthum* (Erlangen, 1882) still may be used to orient oneself with profit.

The social structure of the ancient Iranians is discussed by E. Benveniste in *'Les classes sociales dans la tradition avestique'*, *Journal Asiatique* (1932), 116-134. The book by A. A. Mazaheri, G. Perikhanyan, *'Agnaticheskie gruppy v drevnem Irane'*, *Vestnik Drevnei Istorii*, 3 (Moscow, 1968), 28-53. Among the many Soviet publications one may note E. A. Grantovskii, *Rannyaya Istoriya Iranksikh Plemen Prednei Azii* (Moscow, 1970).

CHAPTER 3

The Elamites are still an enigmatic people despite the long excavations of the French at Susa. Further study of Elamite texts, both early texts from the Susa area and later texts from Persepolis should help to elucidate Elamite history. The former normally would be published in the *Memoirs* of the French mission to Susa, and the latter in the *Journal of Near Eastern*

Studies. Until then G. Cameron's *Early History of Iran* (Chicago, 1936), is still a useful survey, but it has been replaced by W. Hinz, *Das Reich Elam* (Stuttgart, 1964). The Elamite tablets from Persepolis are a prime source of history. See R. T. Hallock, *Persepolis Fortification Tablets* (Chicago, 1969), X, where references are given to the Treasury tablets and other publications.

For the Assyrians the survey by H. Schmökel, *Geschichte des alten Vorderasien*. together with R. Borger, *Einleitung in die assyrischen Königsinschriften* both in the series *Handbuch der Orientalistik* (Leiden, 1957 and 1961), is convenient. The book by B. B. Piotrovskii, *Vanskoe Tsarstvo* (Moscow, 1959) is, I believe, the best general work on the Urartians while the corpus of inscriptions by Melikishvili (Moscow, 1960) is the most complete collection of texts. On the Medes the book by I. M. Dyakonov, *Istoriya Midii* (M., 1956) is better than that of I. Aliev, *Istoriya Midii* (Baku, 1960), though the latter also may be used with profit. Of special importance are the reports of excavations at Takht-i Sulaiman in the *Archäologischer Anzeiger* (Berlin), where references to further publications may be found. The publication of the results of excavations at Hasanlu in Azerbaijan by the University of Pennsylvania should also throw much light on the culture of the Mannai. Cf. R. Dyson, *'Problems on Protohistoric Iran as seen from Hasanlu'*, *Journal of Near Eastern Studies*, 24 (Chicago, 1965), 193-217, and L. D. Levine, *'Geographical Studies in the Neo-Assyrian Zagros II'*, *Iran*, 12 (London, 1974), 99-124.

On the Magi see the two studies, G. Messina, *Der Ursprung der Magier* (Rome, 1930), corrected by E. Benveniste in his *Les Mages dans l'ancien Iran* (Paris, 1938). The etymology and development of the word is still uncertain. In M. Ehtecham's *L'Iran sous les Achemenides* (Fribourg, 1946), the organisation of the empire and the provinces is discussed. The book by M. Dandamaev, *Persien unter den ersten Achämeniden* (Wiesbaden, 1975) is especially valuable for social and economic questions. Until E. Benveniste publishes his translation of the Old Persian cuneiform texts in the Corpus Inscriptionum Iranicarum, the standard work is by R. Kent, *Old Persian* (New Haven, 1950), although the glossary in *Handbuch des Altpersischen*, by W. Brandenstein and M. Mayrhofer (Wiesbaden, 1967), contains a number of additional reconstructed words, or those attested in Aramaic. For titles the book of W. Eilers, *Iranische*

Beamtennamen in der keilschriftlichen Überlieferung (Leipzig, 1940) is valuable, as is E. Benveniste, *Titres et noms propres en iranien ancien* (Paris, 1966). See also M. Mayrhofer, *Onomastica Persepolitana* (Vienna, 1973). The results of the excavations at Persepolis (three volumes published) by E. Schmidt at the University of Chicago are extremely important for Achaemenid history. In passing it may be noted that Plato, *Laws* III, in discussing the Achaemenid government, probably gives the current version of the end of Cambyses, that the eunuch *(Smerdis)* and the Medes usurped the power from the Persians and Darius overthrew them, restoring Persian power.

CHAPTER 4

The ideological and political changes in the aftermath of Alexander's conquests in the Near East have been narrated in a semi-popular book by S. K. Eddy, *The King is Dead, Studies in Near Eastern Resistance to Hellenism* (Lincoln, Nebraska, 1961). The standard works on the Seleucids are still those quoted in the footnotes, E. Bevan, *The House of Seleucus* (London, 1902), A. Bouché-Leclercq, *Histoire des Séleucides* (Paris, 1914), and E. Bikerman, *Institutions des Séleucides* (Paris, 1938). The general works on Hellenism by Tarn, Rostovtzeff, P. Jouget, and Eduard Meyer are well known and valuable for a picture of the entire Near East of that time. The prolific author Franz Altheim has many interesting publications dealing with this period of history. One comprehensive work is by E. Will, *Histoire politique du monde hellénistique,* 2 vols. (Nancy, 1966).

L'Iran extérieur is treated by many scholars. Soviet publications on the Greeks and their neighbours in south Russia continue at an accelerated pace, such that it is difficult to keep up with them. Among recent studies in Western European languages, the following may be mentioned: for south Russia, M. Gimbutas, *The Prehistory of Eastern Europe,* 2 vols. (Cambridge, Mass., 1956, 1962). The art of the Scythians is discussed in a popular work *The Scythians* (London, 1957) by T. T. Rice. The archaeology of the eastern steppes and the area of Altai mountains are treated in an interesting manner by K. Jettmar, '*The Altai before the Turks*', *Bulletin of the Museum of Far Eastern Antiquities,* 23 (Stockholm, 1951), 135-223, also his '*Mittelasien und Sibirien im Vortürkischer Zeit*', in *Handbuch* der *Orientalistik* (Leiden, 1966), 1-105. General works include J. M. Cook, *The Greeks in the East* (London, 1962), and D. Schlumberger, *L'Orient hellénisé* (Paris, 1970).

The Graeco-Bactrians are known primarily from their coins, the catalogues of which are valuable sources. The British Museum collection was published by P. Gardner in 1886, the Calcutta Museum collection by V. A. Smith in 1906, and the collection of the Punjab Museum in Lahore by R. B. Whitehead in 1914. The general survey of pre-Islamic Oriental coins by J. de Morgan, *Manuel de numismatique orientale* (Paris, 1936), may be used, but with caution. On Kushan art *The Dynastic Arts of the Kushans* by John Rosenfield (U. of California Press, 1967) is a good summary of what we know of the culture and civilisation of the Kushans.

CHAPTER 5

The Parthians are still little known and general books about them such as N. Debevoise, *A Political History of Parthia* (Chicago, 1938), are less than one would like. *The Parthians* by M. A. R. Colledge (London, 1967), surveys what we know about them. See also G. A. Koshelenko, *Kultura Parfii* (Moscow, 1966). Many studies exist on the martial relations between the Romans and the Parthians, but they tell us little of internal Parthian affairs. The publications based on the Soviet excavations of Nisa are of great importance in reconstructing a picture of the Parthian homeland. The Dura-Europos excavations, and those at Hatra and Assur in Mesopotamia, on the other hand, are all peripheral, but none the less important for Parthian history in revealing what their subjects or allies did. See also *The Cambridge History of Iran*, vol. 3.

The best survey of Parthian and Sasanian inscriptions, plus a discussion of linguistic matters, may be found in W. B. Henning, 'Mitteliranisch', *Handbuch der Orientalistik*, I, 4 (Leiden, 1958), and probably the best catalogue of Parthian coins is the *Sammlung Petrowicz, Arsakiden Münzen* (Vienna, 1904). The coins of minor dynasties are described by G. F. Hill, *Catalogue of the Greek Coins of Arabia, Mesopotamia and Persia* (London, 1922). See also G. Le Rider, *Suse sous les séleucides et les parthes* (Paris, 1965).

CHAPTER 6

The basic work on Sasanian Iran remains A. Christensen. *L'Iran sous les Sassanides* (Copenhagen, 1944), supplemented by numerous detailed studies by the same author. T. Noeldeke's translation of Ṭabarī, *Geschichte der Perser und Araber* (Leiden, 1879) is also a classic in this domain. Sasanian art is surveyed in K. Erdman, *Die Kunst Irans zur Zeit der Sasaniden* (Berlin, 1943), while all of pre-Islamic archaeology is discussed in the useful handbook by L. Vanden Berghe, *Archéologie de l'Iran ancien* (Leiden, 1959). In the latter book references to sites and monuments may be found. Two works by V. G. Lukonin should be noted: *Iran v epokhu Sasanidov* (Leningrad, 1961), and *Kultura sasanidskogo Irana* (Moscow, 1969). *The Cambridge History of Iran* vol. 3 provides a useful summary of Sasanian history.

The best survey of Manichaeism, I believe, is H. C. Puech, *Le Manichéisme* (Paris, 1949), while titles on Sasanian Zoroastrianism may be found in the publications of Zaehner and Duchesne-Guillemin.

CHAPTER 7

The basic handbook, with a formidable bibliography on Iran in early Islamic times is B. Spuler, *Iran in frühislamischer Zeit* (Wiesbaden, 1952). This has now been superseded by *The Cambridge History of Iran,* vol. 4 (Cambridge, 1974) and by R. N. Frye, *The Golden Age of Persia* (London, 1975). Still useful for a survey of Persian-Arab interaction especially in literature is E. G. Browne, *Literary History of Persia,* vol. 1 (London, 1908). The various heresies and sects in Iran in the early Islamic period are discussed by G. H. Sadighi in his *Les mouvements religieux iraniens au IIᵉ et au IIIᵉ siècle de l'hégire* (Paris, 1938).

On the Zoroastrian literary activity of the ninth century see H. W. Bailey, *Zoroastrian Problems in the Ninth-Century Books* (Oxford, 1943), which is concerned with philological problems and J. P. de Menasce, *Škand-Gumānīk Vičār* (Fribourg, 1945), which is the edition and translation of an apologetic text, with religious problems also discussed.

Journals which are of special concern to our subject are the organs of the various national Orientalist societies, as well as

The *Bulletin of the School of Oriental and African Studies*, and the *Journal of the Royal Asiatic Society* both in London, the *Messenger of Ancient History (Vestnik Drevnei Istorii)* in Moscow, the *Indo-Iranian Journal*, published in the Hague, *Iranica Antiqua*, published in Leiden, as well as *Persica*, published in The Hague, *Studia Iranica*, edited in Paris, and *Iran*, the organ of the British Institute of Persian Studies, published in London, and various journals devoted to Oriental art or to philology.

INDEX

INDEX

Abaev, 176
Abalish, 253
'Abbas, see Shah 'Abbas
'Abbas-i Mervi, 288
'Abbasid, xi, 260, 276, 278-9, 281, 283
'Abdallah, 253
'Abd al-' Malik, 276
Abgar, 206, 209, 274
Abgarids, 209
Abivard, 203
Abkhazian, 73
Abū Hafs-i Sughdī, 288
Abu Mûslim, 281
Achaemenes, 86
Achaemenid, passim
Adad Nirai II, 63
adhyaksha, 110
Adiabene, 209, 210, 213, 237
Adityas, 26
'Adud al-Daulah, 286
aes, 19
Aeschylus, 97
Afanasier, 179
Afghan, 8, 12, 48, 287
Afghanistan, 3, 8, 33, 51, 111, 112, 158, 162, 178, 185, 188, 191, 224, 277, 279, 280, 287
Afrayasib, 43, 44
Africa, 10, 119, 134, 174, 177
Afshars, 14
Agamtanv, 85
Agathangelos, 170
Agathias, 7, 236, 261
Ahriman, 270-1
Ahura Mazda, 34, 35, 39, 44, 75, 96, 97, 101, 113, 125, 126-8, 136, 165, 220, 226, 227, 249-50, 253, 262
aika, 24
aios, 17
Airarat, 72

Airya, 42
airyaman, 54
Airyāna Vaējah, 32
Akes, 41
Akhlāk-i Nāsirī, 277
Akkad, 64, 65, 87, 89
Akkadian, 6, 55, 66-7, 78, 81-2, 85, 89, 91, 94, 99, 110-12, 113, 115, 120
al-(Arabic prefix; ignore in alphabetical order)
Alan(s), 174, 176, 177, 178-9, 209
Alarodi, 72
Albania, 244
Albanian(s), 19, 73, 209, 245
Alexander the Great, 4, 7, 30, 31, 46, 47, 49, 52, 53, 66, 68, 82, 90, 94, 99, 105, 108, 129, 131, 132, 133, 135, 143-51, 153, 158-9, 161, 165-6, 167, 168, 171-3, 182, 185, 200, 201, 206, 221, 274
Alexander (Seléucid governor), 203, 211
Alexandria, 166, 168, 273
Alexandria in Asia, 152
Alexandria-Antioch, 206
'Ali, 286
Alp Er Tonga, 43
Alpines, 11
Altai, 174, 178, 179, 180
Altaic, 20, 29, 179, 181, 255-7
Altheim, 257
Amardoi, 48
Amarna, 23
Amazons, 54
America, 10
Amesha Spenta, 44
Amestris, 131
Amida, 256
Ammianus Marcellinus, 7, 160, 238, 254, 256

Ammon, 95
Amu Darya, see Oxus, 48
Amul, 48
Amyrgoi, 45
Anabasis, 87, 117, 118, 132
Anahita, 84, 104, 128, 129, 135, 170, 222, 227, 238, 250
Anatolia, 14, 66, 74, 78, 80, 88, 123, 131, 132, 135, 136, 151, 156, 172, 181, 190, 242
Anavon, 51
Anaximenes of Lampsakos, 90
Andarz, 278
Andegan (Indegan), 239
Andragoras, 184, 201, 202
Andronova, 179
angareion, 110
angarya, 217
An-hsi, 187
Anirān, 245
anšahrik, 217
Anshan, 66, 67, 77, 85-6
an-siək = *aršak,* 187
Antony, see Marc Antony
Antigonids, 173
Antigonos, 147, 150-1
Antimachus I, 184, 185
Antioch, 151, 203, 242-3, 259, 260, 273
Antiochia (Margiana), 151, 211
Antiochus (of Commagene), 165
Antiochus I, 151, 155, 158-60, 164, 182, 183, 201
Antiochus II, 153
Antiochus III, 153-5, 160, 184, 203, 208, 211
Antiochus IV, 159, 203, 227
Antiochus, 161, 206
Anzan, 77
āpadana, 107
Apamea, 151
Aparnak, 201
Aparni, 52
Aparshar, 201
Aphrodite, 128, 129
Apivahu, 39
Apocrypha, 136
Apollo, 159, 171
Apollodotus, 183, 188
Appian, *Syriake,* 150-1, 160
Apursam, 240
Arab(s), xi, 2, 4, 6, 15, 48, 64, 209, 210, 215, 219, 254, 257, 270, 272, 273-6, 278, 281, 282, 284, 287, 289

Arabia, 10, 274, 275
Arabic, xi, 4, 7, 29, 38, 52, 214, 219, 240, 254, 261, 274, 276-81, 285, 286, 288, 289
Arachosia, 13, 51, 93, 98, 108, 155, 187, 205, 207, 213, 243
Aral Sea, 45, 46
Aram, 72
Aramaean, 63, 64, 77
Aramaic, 55, 64, 73, 81, 82, 96, 105, 109, 110-11, 113, 115, 120, 122, 131, 135, 161-2, 163, 204, 210, 215, 219, 222, 226, 238, 277
Ararat, 71
Araxes, 81
Arbela, 209, 237
Ardashir, 87, 200, 206, 210, 221, 227, 228, 236-41, 243-5, 248, 262
Ardashir II, 255
Ardini, 72
Ardoxsho, 224
Ardvisura, 33, 43
Areia, 53
Areioi (Arioi), 53
arasā, 202
Argishti, 72, 73
Aria, 53
Ariane, 3, 53, 205
Ariaramnes, 82, 86
Arios, 53
Aristotle, 148
Arizantoi, 81
Arkadrish, 90
arkapatēs, 215
urkhos, 215
Arm-, 73
Armenia, 7, 71, 72, 88, 98, 110, 135, 146, 154, 158, 159, 170, 203, 208, 209, 213, 239, 241, 244, 249, 254, 273, 280
Armenian(s), 7, 9, 19, 28, 72, 73, 74, 78, 101, 112, 135, 170, 201, 209, 214, 221, 249, 252
Armenoids, 11
Arrian, 7, 46, 202
Arsaces, 184, 201-2, 204, 205, 236
Arsacid(s), 202, 204-5, 208, 212, 214, 218, 227, 237, 239, 252
Arsames, 82, 86, 93, 115, 120, 122, 131
Arshak, 202
Arsham, 122
aršan, 202
Arshan, 39
arshtā-, 113

314

arsin, 181
arta-, 127
Artabanus I, 206
Artabanus II, 186
Artabanus III, 207, 211, 218
Artabanus V, 237
Artabarzanes, 203
Artakhsharakan, 202
Artakhshassa, 104
Artashés, 208
Artavahishtak, 204
Artavasdes, 208, 237
Artaxata, 209
Artaxerxes, 104, 107, 131-2, 226
Artaxerxes II, 87, 107, 109, 123, 128,
    132, 145, 202, 227
Artaxerxes III, 132-3
Artaxias, 208
Artemis, 129, 170
Aryaman, 26
Aryan(s), 2, 3, 17, 21, 22-7, 28, 33,
    34, 35, 36, 39, 42-3, 54-6, 63, 83,
    92, 101, 104, 111, 112, 113, 124,
    127, 129, 145, 221
aryanam khsháthram, 3
Aryanshahr, 51
Arzanene, 209
As, 176
Asaak, 205
asabara, 116
Asagarta, 77
Asarhaddon, 64, 65, 78, 79
asha, 34, 35
Ashcarī, 284
ashovan, 42
Ashkabad, 46, 163, 204
Ashkenaz, 45, 71
Ashkuz, 45
Ashur, 74, 80
Asia, 93, 102, 118, 132, 134, 144,
    146, 151, 157, 161, 169, 174, 176,
    178, 179, 180-1, 182, 184, 188-90,
    213, 218-19, 223, 226, 243, 255-7,
    272, 277, 279-82, 287
Asia Minor, 123, 132, 148, 152, 154,
    221, 223
Asianoi, 181
Asoka, 31, 130, 135, 161, 162
Assara Mazash, 101
Assur, 101, 222
Assurbanipal, 64, 65, 68, 101
Assurnasipal, 63
Assyria, 63-5, 66, 68, 71, 74, 76, 77,
    78, 79-81, 88, 190

Assyrian(s), 40, 49, 50, 63, 68, 70,
    71, 72, 75, 76-8, 84, 92, 110-11,
    114, 118, 121, 151
astodans, 205, 270
Astyages, 85-8, 93
Atar, 224
ateshkade, 271
Athens, 133, 261
Atossa, 98
Atradates, 87
Atropatene, 146, 203, 209, 214
Atropates, 146
Attalids, 173
Attic, 159
Aurelian, 243
aurei, 268
Autophradates, 226
Avars, 175
Avesta, xi, 6, 23, 24, 29, 32, 39,
    40, 42, 43, 47, 49, 53, 54, 55, 82,
    83, 105, 113, 126, 128, 129, 172,
    182, 220, 248, 252
Avestan, 18, 23, 24, 25, 27, 33, 38,
    44, 46, 50, 51, 54, 183, 202, 261
Avroman, 158, 218
āyadana, 99, 100, 222
áyas, 19
ayazan, 222
Azarmidukht, 274
āzāta(n), 214-15, 245
Azerbaijan, 7, 9, 12, 28, 32, 67, 73,
    77, 79, 81, 159, 203, 239, 273,
    275, 283
Azes, 188
Azilises, 188

Baba Kamma, 221
Babili, 89
Babylon, 64, 65, 67, 71, 77, 88, 89,
    106, 108, 109, 120, 128, 133
Babylonia, 63, 64, 68, 80, 89, 94-5,
    98, 100, 115, 120, 121, 122, 150,
    151, 157, 158, 163, 172, 206
Babylonian(s), 62, 64, 65, 76, 77, 80,
    85, 99, 100-1, 108, 112, 117, 121,
    127, 131, 134, 169
Bacasis, 213
Bactria, 12, 32, 40, 41, 42, 50, 51,
    53, 88, 93, 108, 118, 145, 150, 155,
    158, 160, 163, 170, 173, 181,
    182-3, 185-7, 191, 203, 205, 213,
    223, 224
Bactrian(s), 40, 47, 49, 129, 160,
    163, 185, 201, 217, 244

Bactrus, 48
Badakhshan, 8, 49
Baga-stāna, 95
Bagayadi-, 97
Baghdad, 3, 7
Bagoas, 133
Bahaism, 251
Bahram, 170, 247-8, 272
Bahram Chobin, 273, 288
Bahram Gor, 255
Bailey, 44, 45
bāji, 121
bājikara, 121
Bakhtiyari, 14
Bākhtri-, 48
Baktra, 152, 159, 160, 184
Balasagan, 244
Balkans, 130
Balkh, 12, 32, 280, 287
Baltic, 19
Balto-Slavic, 19
Baluch(i), 8, 14
Baluchistan, 43, 48, 211
Bam, 8
Bamiyan, 14, 256, 281
bandak(a), 120, 217
bant, 45
Bardesanes, 221
Bardiya, 96-100
barīd, 110
Bariz, 52
Bārūzān, 280
Basque(s), 28
Bassām-i Kurd, 288
batēsa, 215
Bazrangi, 227
bdeašx, 216
Begram, 224, 244
Behistun, 45, 55, 71, 75, 78, 81-3,
   90, 95-6, 98-9, 101, 106, 111, 127,
   130, 160, 213, 237
Bel, 165
Benveniste, 154
Berossos, 128, 166, 172
Bessus, 145
Beth Arbaya, 209
Beth Garme, 210
Beth Nohadre, 209
Beth Qardu, 209
Bethlehem, 207
bg, 120
Biainili, 72
Bible, 45, 63, 71, 78, 79, 112
Bidpay, 261

Bihafrid, 282
Bikni, 63
Birjand, 215
Bīrūnī, al-, 30, 50, 200, 280
Bishapur, 238, 242, 245, 247
Bit Khamban, 77
bitaxš, 110, 216, 239
Black Sea, 7, 12, 72, 173, 174, 177,
   273
Boghaz Köy, 23
Boran, 274
Bosphoran, 174, 177, 180
Bosphorus, 173, 273
Boudioi, 81
Bousai, 81
Boyid, 283, 285-6
Brahmi, 256
Brahmins, 21, 26, 35
Brahui, 8, 14, 28
BR BYT', 105, 245
BRH, 226
British, 157
Buddha, 31, 35, 224
Buddhism, 283
Buddhist(s), 185, 225, 249, 281
Bug river, 177
Bukhara, 7, 13, 40, 47, 280, 286-7,
   288
Bundahisn, 31, 200, 284
Burushaski, 28
Burzin Mihr, 272
Burzoe, 261
Byarshan, 39
Byzantine, 243, 246, 255, 269, 273,
   274, 275, 278
Byzantium, 273, 279

Cabalistic, 252
Caducians, 81, 87
Caesar, 252, 254
Cambyses, 85, 93, 94-101, 117, 120,
   129
capitatio, 258
Cappadocia, 78, 135, 165, 221, 242
Carchemish, 80
Carmania, *see* Kirman, 90
Caria, 114
Carpathians, 174
Carrhae, 208, 214
Caspar, 189, 207
Caspian, 81
Caspian Gates, 12
Caspian Sea, 7, 9, 13, 43, 48, 52, 70,
   73, 78, 93, 160, 182, 211, 260, 285

cataphractii, 218
Caucasian, 28, 175
Caucasoid, 10, 11
Caucasus, 9, 12, 23, 28, 38, 45, 73, 76, 78, 88, 175, 178, 179, 209, 218, 260, 273
Celts, 21, 176, 180
Central Asia, *see* Asia
centum, 19, 180
Chaeronea, 133
Chahār tāg, 271-2
Chaldean, 64
Chaman, 51
Chandragupta, 150, 151
Ch'ang ch'ien, 186
Characene, 206, 210
Chares, 37
Charlemagne, 6
Cheikho, 236
Chersonesos, 177
chiliarch, see *khhiliarchos,* 239
China, 7, 8, 13, 45, 47, 48, 174, 178, 179, 180, 190, 272, 279, 280-1
Chinese, 46, 47, 48, 166, 174-5, 176, 180, 181, 185-7, 226, 256
Chinese Turkestan, 45, 170, 179, 180-1, 184, 186, 207, 218
Chionites, 256-7
Chishpish, 86
Chitral, 14
Choshoes I (Anosharvan), 240, 251, 254, 257-62, 268-9
Chosroes II (Aparvez), 268-9, 273-5
Christ, 36, 157, 165, 178, 274
Christensen, 38
Christian(s), 22, 135, 180, 189, 249, 258, 270, 272, 283
Christianity, 5, 25, 84, 126, 135, 169, 172, 251, 253, 273, 275, 280, 283, 289
Chronos, 253
Cilicia, 88, 115, 121
Cimmerian, 69, 72, 78, 173, 175
Circassian, 73
clibanarii, 218
Columbus, 174
Commagene, 165, 190, 221
Constantine, 253
Constantinople, 273
Coptic, 251
Corbin, Henry, 271
Corinth, League of, 143
Crassus, 214
Crimea, 173, 176, 177

Croesus, 88, 93
Ctesias, 40, 41, 85, 86, 87, 90, 94, 97, 99
Ctesiphon, 3, 7, 210, 212, 250, 253, 273, 275-6
Cunaxa, 132
Curtius, 90
Cyaxares, 79, 80
Cyrus I, 49
Cyrus II, 41, 42, 45, 46, 48, 77, 82, 85-95, 97, 100-1, 112, 116, 129-30, 135, 227, 236
Cyrus the Younger, 132

Daas, 52
dabirām dabir, 259
Dacia, 177
Dadikai, 49
daevic, 223
Daha (Dahae, Dahi), 42, 43, 52, 201
Dahistan, 52
dahyu-, 54
daiva, 126-8
Damascus, 63, 64, 276
Damghan, 205
Daniel, 107
dahyu, 54
Dagīgī, 288
Dardic, 27, 49, 181
Dari, 286-7
dari-, 123
daric, 123-4, 147
Darius, 6, 30, 41, 44, 45, 48, 49, 51, 52-3, 54, 67, 75, 81, 86, 91, 93 95-6, 97-101, 104, 105, 106-9, 112, 113-16, 119, 129-31, 155, 165, 202, 226, 245
Darius II, 107, 121, 132
Darius III Codommanus, 133, 144-6
Dasa, 43
dasarum, 108
Dasht-i Kavir, 7
Dasht-i Lut, 7
Dastagird, 273
dāta-, 112
databara, 112
David, 64, 144
Dayaukku, 77-8, 79
Daylam, 285
dayyan, 113
Dead Sea, 71, 136
decima, 155
degel, 117
Deioces, 77

deiwos, 20
Demaratos, 136
Demavend, 9, 63, 240
demes, 152
Demetrius I, 150, 184, 206
Demetrius II, 184-5, 206
Demodamas, 182
Denak, 237
denarius, 224
Denkart, 221, 248, 284
Denmazdak, 204
Derbend, 260
Derbikes, 94
dev, 127
Devanagari, 252
devas, 127
Dhū Qar, 275
Diadochi, 150, 173, 183
Diarbakr, 209
dies, 20
Digor, 178, 179
dihgān, 259, 268, 269, 276, 278, 288
Dio Cassius, 209
Diocletian, 258
Diodorus Siculus, 88, 112
Diodotus, 184, 202
Diogenes the Stoic, 166
divan, 260, 277
dmōs, 55
Dnieper, 175-6
Dniester, 177
Domitian, 177
Don river, 175-7
Don Quixote, 262
Dorians, 20
drachme, 147, 158, 268
drauga, 113
Dravidian, 8, 28
drogvant, 42
Druids, 21
drywhwš, 104
dtbry ', 112
Dumézil, 21, 55, 56
Dura-Europos, 214-16, 242-3
Dyakonov, 81
dyáus pitǎ, 20
dyāuš, 25
dyzpty, 216

East Indies, 10
Ebirnari, 89
Edessa, 206, 209, 210, 274

Egypt, 7, 36, 64, 68, 88, 95, 96, 100-1, 103, 104, 106, 110, 111, 112, 114, 115, 119, 120, 123, 130, 131, 132-3, 143, 144, 151, 168, 171, 274
Egyptian(s), 30, 46, 49, 62, 79, 80, 95, 108, 118, 127, 131, 168, 170
eisangeleus, 105
Ekbatana, 87, 88, 89-90, 106, 109, 128, 150, 160, 161, 203
ekuos, 19
Elam, 49, 64, 66-8, 77, 79, 85, 92
Elamite(s), 6, 11, 28, 32, 55, 63, 66, 67-8, 70, 72, 76, 77, 78, 82-4, 90, 92, 100-2, 104, 108, 109, 111, 123, 127, 129, 163
Eiburz, 9, 12, 211
Elephantine, 111, 117
Ellipi, 70, 77
Elymais, 70, 206, 210
Enoch, 172
Epiphaneia, 203
epiphanēs, 159, 171
epistolographos, 154
Eranshahr, 3, 241
Eratosthenes, 53, 166, 205
Erech, 42
Esther, 106, 111-12
Ethiopia, 108
ethnē, 154
Etruria, 74
Euager, 150
Euclid, 166
Eucratides, 185, 203, 205
Euphrates, 2, 7, 9, 89, 151, 154, 208, 209, 210, 214, 242, 274
Eurasia, 174, 189-90
Europe, 84, 93, 125, 129, 164, 173, 177, 190
Euthydemids, 173
Eutychius, 236
Euthydemus, 184, 185, 203
eva, 24
Ezra, 89, 106, 112, 135

Farah, 8, 51
Far East, 176
Farnbag, 204, 272
fars, 50
Fars, 3, 11-12, 13, 49, 50, 51, 67, 76, 86, 121, 155, 170, 210-11, 236, 243, 245, 282, 283, 286

Ferghana, 13, 45, 47, 181, 184, 225, 224
Fertile Crescent, 62, 64, 80, 115, 120, 174
Fihrist, 284
Finno-Ugrian, 174
Firdosi, 39, 42, 199-200, 219, 236, 260, 280, 287
Frada, 98
Frangrasian, 43
frataraka, 210-11, 226
Fravardin, 238
French, 17, 42, 67, 189
Fryana, 35

Galatians, 154
Galerius, 254
Gamirkᶜ, 78
Gandhara, 51, 108, 130, 175, 185, 189, 190, 244
Ganges, 2
ganzabara, 122
Ganzak, 261
gard-, 90
Gari-Ardashir, 215
Garmapada, 96
Gathas, 23, 24, 33, 34, 42, 83, 125
Gathic, 33, 35, 54
Gaugamela, 144-5, 146
Gaumata, 95, 96-100, 106
gaushaka, 110
gara, 47
Gazaka, 159
GDH, 44
Gedrosia, 205, 211, 243
genus, 25
Georgia, 158, 161, 208, 244
Georgian(s), 9, 73, 209, 246
Germani, 90
Germanic, 18, 178
Germans(s), 174, 176
Getai, 46
Gev, 214
Ghassanids, 274, 275
Ghazni, 13
Ghirshman, 69, 70
Ghorband, 49
Gibb, H. A. R., 279
Gilan, 159, 211, 247
Gilgamesh, 69
Gilgit, 186
Gimirrai, 78
Gobryas, 89
Gochihr, 227

Godard, 69, 70
Godarz, 38
Golden Horde, 175, 187
Goliath, 144
Gomer, 78
Gondophares, 188-9, 207
gopat shah, 47
Gordian, 242-3
Gordvene, 209
Gorno-Attai, 179
gōsān (gusan), 219
Goths, 173, 177
Graeco-Bactrian, 176, 180, 182-5, 187, 212, 225
Graeco-Iranian, 191
Graeco-Macedonian, 182
Graeco-Roman,169, 172
Granicus, 144-5
grda-, 55-6
Greece, 2, 131, 133, 136, 149, 171, 189-90, 201, 261
Greek, *passim*
Grumbates, 256
Gubaru, 89, 95
Gundeshapur, 243, 260
Gupta, 226
Gurgan, 214, 260
Gushnap, 238, 261, 272
Guti, 66 68, 70
Gutium, 89
*gwshky*ʾ, 110

Hadhaiyab, 209
hadish, 107-8
Haetumant, 51
Hafiz, 289
Hai-sa, 73
Hajjiabad, 245
Haloun, 181
Halys, 80
Ham, 42
Hamadan, 7, 12, 63, 78, 79, 82, 90, 96, 106, 203, 275
Haman, 111
hamārakara, 122
Hammurabi, 23, 62, 67
Hamun, 13, 51, 207
Hamza al-Isfahani, 200
Han, 47, 181, 187, 190, 218
Han-shu, 187, 223
Hanbali Sunnism, 284
haoma, 27, 45, 102
Haoshyanka, 39
Harahuvati, 13, 51

Haraiva, 3, 52
harāka, 121
Harappa, 27
Hari-Rud, 12, 41, 48
Harmatta, 177
Harpagos, 86-8
Harran, 80, 88
Hatra, 210, 238, 243, 274
hatru, 120-1
haumavarga, 45, 46
Hausravah, 39
Hayy, 73
hazārapati, 105
hazārpat, 239
Hebrew, 29, 30, 101, 112, 126
Hecataios, 41, 46
Hecatompylos, 13, 150, 205
hegira, 34
Heliocles, 188, 206
Hellenes, 150
Hellenism, 135, 143, 157, 158, 161,
    163, 165-6, 170, 172-3, 200,
    201, 245
Hellenistic, 83, 143, 151, 154-6, 158,
    161, 169-71, 173-4, 183, 189, 190,
    212
Helmand, 13, 51, 52
Henning, 41, 181
Hephaestus, 110, 224
Hephthalite, 189, 225, 254-7, 259,
    280, 282, 287
Heracles, 170-1, 219, 224
Heraclius, 269, 273
Herat, 7, 12, 32, 33, 41, 42, 48, 52,
    53, 81, 152, 184, 186-7, 205, 282
herbad, 200, 248-9, 270
Hermaeus, 188
Hermias, 154
Hermitage Museum, 176
Herodotus, 3, 7, 41, 44, 46-7,
    49, 51, 53, 70, 72, 78-88, 90, 93-4,
    95, 97-8, 105-6, 108 114, 116, 117,
    118, 119, 121, 123, 129, 130, 131,
    136, 175, 176, 180, 181, 215
Hertel, 22
Herzfeld, 50, 70, 207
Himalaya, 27
Himerus, 213
Himyarites, 274
Hindu, 130, 249, 272
Hindu Kush, 8, 13, 27, 28, 48, 49,
    184, 185, 187, 188, 256, 280
Hinduism, 84
Hippostratos, 188

Hira, al-, 274, 275
Hittite(s), 17, 23, 62, 65, 69, 75
hmrkr, 122
Hormizd Ardashir, 247, 249
Hoshang, 39
hotar, 34
hsi-hou, 223
Hsiung-nu, 181, 186, 223
hštrp, 215
hšyty wzrk, 226
Huja, 66
Hun, 175, 179, 255-7
Hunas, 256
Hungary, 177, 179
Hunnic, 179, 181, 255, 257
Hunza, 28
(h)*urart*-, 71
Hurrian, 23, 28, 32, 62, 70-2, 75
Husain-i Khārajī
hutukhshān, 55
hu-varza-ka, 106
Huvishka, 223, 225
hvarnah, 43, 44
Hydarnes, 136
Hyrcania, 41, 52, 81, 146, 153, 160,
    211
Hyspaosines, 206
Hystaspes (*see* Vishtaspa), 86, 93-4

Iazyges, 177
Iberia, 208
Ibero-Caucasian, 73
Ibn al-Athir, 236
Ili, 186
Il-Khanid, 79
ilku, 120
India, 2, 3, 7, 15, 23, 27, 28, 36, 53,
    54, 103, 110, 116, 123-4, 130, 135,
    146, 150, 157, 162, 175, 178, 180
    182, 185, 186-8, 189-90, 205, 207,
    223, 225-6, 242-4, 246, 256, 261,
    284
Indian(s), 5, 15, 21, 23, 24, 27, 36,
    51, 55, 123, 130, 134. 135, 162,
    181, 189, 244, 246, 256, 261
Indian Ocean, 3, 8, 52, 119, 130
indictio, 258
Indo-European, 2, 5, 17-22, 24-5,
    26, 28, 36, 50, 54, 55, 62, 66,
    73, 102-3, 112, 113, 174, 180
Indo-Greeks, 185
Indo-Iranian, 8, 14, 17, 19, 21, 24,
    28

Indo-Parthian, 188, 202, 206, 221, 225, 227
Indra, 23, 25, 26-7
Indus, 4, 7, 8, 10, 14, 52, 53, 119, 130, 150, 243
Indushushinak, 67
Ionia(n), 65, 88, 92, 114, 115, 118, 119, 132, 151, 175, 182
Ipsus, 151
Iran, *passim*
Iranians, *passim*
Iranoids, 11
Iraq, 215
Iron (Ossetic), 178, 179
Iron Age, 40
Isaiah, 80
Isfahan, 8, 12, 254, 275
Ishaq 'the Turk', 282
Ishkata, 49
Ishkuza, 78
Ishpakai, 79
Ishrāqī philosophy, 271
Ishtumegu, 85
Isidore of Charax, 51, 160, 204, 205, 207, 227
Islam, xi, 2, 4, 5, 157, 273, 274, 275, 277-9, 281, 284, 289
Islamic, 51, 52, 101, 200, 217, 225, 227, 240, 247, 248, 252-3, 262, 271, 279, 281, 282
Ismaʿil, Samanid, 288
Israel, 63, 135
Issedones, 180-1
Issus, 144-5
Issyk Kul, 186
Istakhr, 227, 236, 238, 283
Italian, 17
Italo-Celts, 21
Italy, 74, 166, 174, 177
iugum, 258
Izates, 209, 210
Izates, 209

Jāhiz, 259
Jalalabad, 50, 244
Jalula, 275
jánah, 25
jantu, 25
Japan, 36
Japheth, 42
Japhetic, 28, 66
Jeremiah, 71, 80
Jerusalem, 273, 274

Jews, 89, 112, 117, 135, 221, 249, 258, 283
Jhelum, 188
jizya, 258
Josephus, 99, 177, 209
Judaism, 126, 135-6, 209, 251
Jupiter, 20
Justin, 7, 150, 182, 183, 203, 208, 213, 214
Justinian, 269
Jut, 52

Kaʿbah of Zoroaster (KZ), 100, 109, 215, 226, 237, 241, 248
Kabul, 13, 14, 49, 184, 187, 224, 225, 244, 281
Kafir, 8, 27
Kai Khusro, 260
Kal-i Janggāh, 215
Kalat, 8, 243
Kambojas, 94
Kambūjia, 94
kanārang, 281
Kandahar, *see* Qandahar
Kanishka, 163, 223-6, 281
kāra, 103
Kansu, 187
Kao-fu, 187
Kapisa, 244
karapan, 39
Karasuk, 179
Karen, 38, 214, 240
kariz, 10
Kharka, 70
Kharmir Blur, 73
Kar Namak, 238, 261
Kartir, 127, 242, 244-5, 248-9, 251, 252
Karun, 11
kas-, 70
Kash, 243
Kashan, 66
Kashgar, 184, 186, 225, 244
Kashtaritu, 79
Kassi, 70
Kassites, 63, 66, 68, 69, 70
kath, 94
katoikia, 152, 157
Kavad I, 251, 257, 260
Kavad II, 273
Kavata, 39
kavi, 37, 39-40, 54, 219
kay, 260

321

Kayanian, 37, 38, 219
Kazerun, 248, 283, 286
Kāzerūnī, al-, 283
Kent, 108
keraga, 217
Khabur, 209
Khaldi, 72, 74, 75
Khanigin, 250
kharaj, 121, 258
Kharoshthi, 135, 162, 185, 188, 223
khiliarchos, 105
Khiva, 46
Khodjent, 151
Khorshīd, 283
Khotan, 186
Khotanese Saka, 6
khshassa-, 54, 104
khshassapavan, 81
khshathra, 44, 54
khshathapavan, 81
khshayathiya, 84
Khurasan, 8, 12, 14, 32, 40, 52,
    160, 201, 203, 205, 214, 239,
    275-7, 281, 282, 288
Khusro, see Chosroes
Khuzistan, 11, 66, 91, 108, 118, 155,
    160, 210, 243
khvaētu, 54
khvarənah, 44
khvarrah, 44
Khwarezm, 40, 43, 47, 108, 179,
    204, 224, 225, 280
Khwarezmian, 6, 41, 42, 44, 46-7,
    48, 50, 133, 280
Kidara, 256
Kidarites, 256
Kikkuli, 23
Kirkuk, 210, 237
Kirman, 8, 52, 90, 108, 160, 211,
    239, 275
Kirmanshah, 7, 49, 77
Kiselev, 179
Kish, 66, 244
Kishmar, 32
Kisra, 254
Kissi, 70
Kitab al-Tāj, 259
Kizil Irmak, 80
klēros, 152, 157
Kohistan, 9
komē, 152
Kordvene, 209
kerys, 45
Kossai, 66, 68, 70

Kuban, 175
Kuei-shuang, 223
Kufa, 275
Kuh-i Khwaja, 207
Kujula Kadphises, 188, 223
Kura, 72
Kurdistan, 68, 70, 126, 158
Kurds, 9
kurgan, 175, 179
Kurkath, 94
kur-tash, 55
Kushan, 163, 176, 178, 182, 187,
    189-90, 204, 207, 212, 221, 223-6,
    241, 244, 246, 254-7, 281
Kushanshahr, 243, 244
kyn'k, 117
kyrbasia, 45
Kyreskhata, 94
Kyropolis, 94

Laghman, 122, 162
Lakhmids, 274-5
Laodicea, 160
Latin, 7, 17, 20, 25, 125, 215
Lebanon, 108, 123, 134
Leningrad, 176
Lithuanian, 21
London, 124
Lucian Macrobius, 227
Lullubi, 66, 68
Luristan, 66, 68-70, 76
Lurs, 9, 14
Lydia(n), 80, 82, 88, 93, 108, 123

Macedonia, 132-3
Macedonian(s), 119, 133, 143-4, 146,
    150, 151, 153, 164-5
Madan, 248
Maeotic, 175
Magan, 68
Magi, 33, 35, 82-4, 86, 220, 222
    249, 258
Magian, 96-101, 124-6, 128-9, 221,
    249
Magnesia, 203
Magoi, 81
magophonia, 99, 101
Magousai, 221
Mahasena, 224
Maka, 51
Makran (Makuran), 28, 51, 68,
    160, 241, 243
Ma' mun, al-, 253, 288

Mandaeans, 249
Mandane, 87
Manesus, 215
Manetho, 166
Mani, 250
Manichaean(s), 201, 249-51, 257
Manichaeism, 6, 247, 250, 272, 279, 283
māniya, 55-6
Mannaean, 28, 66, 68, 69, 70-1, 76, 77, 78, 80, 81, 82
Mannai, see Mannaeans
Mānne, 55
Maqdisi, al-, 286-7
Maraphioi, 90
Marāsfand, 286
Marathon, 129
Marc Anthony, 208, 209
Marcian Heracleensis, 90
Marcus Aurelius, 177, 212
Mard(o)i, 48, 87
Mardonius, 105
Mardos, 97
Marduk, 65, 67, 88, 89
Margiana (see Merv), 98, 151
Margu- (see Merv), 48
Markwart, 41, 42, 43, 48, 90, 201, 210
Marquart, see Markwart
Marv Dasht, 66, 109
marīka, 55
maryaka, 55
marzbān, 216, 260
Mashhad, 12
Masjid-i Sulaiman, 74, 91
Maspioi, 90
Massagetai, 43, 46, 50, 93-4, 179
Masson, M.E., 204
Masʿūdī, 200, 240
masya, 46
Mathura, 225, 246
Mattiwaza, 23
Manes, 186, 187-8
Maurice, 273
Maurya, 135, 150, 161
Mā warā'l-nahr, 279, 280
Mazanderan, 159, 211
Mazar-i Sharif, 12
Mazdaeans, 271
Mazdak, 251
Mazdakism, 250
Mazdakite, 251, 257-8, 268, 282
Mazdayasnian, 125-6, 221, 238
Mede(s), 3, 4, 28, 32, 33, 40, 41, 45,

49, 71, 73, 74, 76, 77, 78, 80-5, 92-3, 101, 106, 108, 112, 114, 116, 126, 135, 237, 245
Media, 10, 12, 40, 41, 42, 45, 48, 50, 53, 69, 77, 78, 79, 81, 85, 96, 97, 98, 102, 129, 146, 150, 151, 154, 155, 159-61, 205-6, 213-14
Media Minor, 159
Median, 126, 159
Medikon, 166
Medina, 276
Mediterranean, 4, 62, 119, 123, 132, 166, 169
Mediterraneans, 11
Megasthenes, 166, 182
Meier, 283
Meillet, 20, 21, 22
Melikishvili, 71
Memphis, 95
Menander, 185, 279
Menni, 71
Menua, 72
meridarch, 185
Merv, 7, 13, 32, 40, 41, 48, 151, 207, 211, 218, 239, 244, 275, 279, 288
Mesene, 210, 227
Mesopotamia, 2, 3, 7, 9, 11, 23, 24, 27, 30, 33, 36, 49, 50, 55, 62, 63, 64, 66, 69, 70, 74, 89, 91, 93, 96, 102, 112, 115, 120, 121, 129, 156, 158, 160, 161-2, 164, 167, 168, 169-70, 172, 190, 205, 206, 208, 210, 213, 214, 215, 217, 218, 221, 222, 223, 241, 253, 254, 274
Midas, 78
Middle Ages, 173, 178, 286
Middle Iranian, 128, 135, 161, 162
Middle Persian, 6, 7, 44, 127, 214, 215, 226, 238, 245, 248, 252, 260, 277, 286, 287, 288
Mihran, 214
Mihrbozan, 222
Mihrdatak, 222
Mihrfarn, 222
milet, 221, 270
Milindapana. 185
Minni, 71
Mitusinsk, 179
Mitanni, 23, 63, 72
Mithra, 32, 33, 49, 84, 110, 113, 125, 127, 128, 135, 173, 222-4, 227
Mithradates Callicinus, 165
Mithradates Eupator, 173-4, 177

Mithradates I, of Parthia, 185, 204-6, 212
Mithradates II, 204, 206, 208, 212-13, 218, 240
Mithradatkirt, 204
Mithraism, 83, 128, 172, 249
Mithras, 172-3
Mithrenes, 146
mitra, 21, 26
mitra, 21, 23, 26
Miyaneh, 77
Mktk, 249
MLK, 226
mobad, 200, 240, 246, 248-50, 261, 269, 270, 271, 272, 285, 286
mobādān mobad, 259, 260
Mohenjo-Daro, 10, 27
Molon, 203, 211
Mongolia(n), 29, 44, 279
Mongols (s), 10, 45, 79, 175, 176, 179, 186, 255
Mongoloid, 10, 179
Monophysite, 273, 274-5
Morgenstierne, 49
Moses, 87
Moses of Khorene, 78
Mtskheta, 162, 209
Muhammad, 262, 274
Muhammad-i Wasif, 288
Mujmil at tawārikh, 248
Mugan, 79
Müller, Max, 20
Muqanna°, 282
Murashu, 122
Murghab, 90
Murtaq, 186
Musasir, 72
Muslim, xi, 4, 5, 164, 275, 277-8, 281, 282-3
mutaqarib, 287
Muʿtazilite, 252, 284
Mykoi, 51
Mytilene, 37

Nabataean, 274
Nabonidus, 85, 88-9
Nabopolassar, 80
Nadim, al-, 284
Nahria, 71
Nahum, 79
Nairi, 71
nakhodar, 209
Nana, 67, 129

Nanai, 170, 222
Napoleon, 143
Naqshi-i Rajab, 246, 248-9
Naqshi-i Rustam, 67, 75, 91, 100, 108-9, 129, 130, 215, 226, 240, 242, 248-9
Narain, 183, 186, 187
Narseh, 245, 247, 250-1, 254
Nāsatyas, 23
Nasīr al-Dīn Tūsī, 277
Nazoreans, 249
naxarar, 216
Near East, 4, 20, 23, 24, 30, 45, 49, 62, 63, 64, 65, 75, 78, 79, 89, 102, 104, 111, 112, 119, 124, 129, 131, 143, 166, 174, 178, 180, 190, 220, 242, 246, 255, 256-7, 262
Nebuchadnezzar, 80
Negritos, 10
Negroid, 10
Nehemiah, 135
Neo-Persian art, 190
Neo-Platonists, 261
Nergal, 65
Nero, 208
Nestorian, 253, 273, 275, 283
New Persian, 4, 7, 35, 38, 261, 277, 279, 286, 287, 288, 289
New York, 124
nḥwdr, 215
Nicholas of Damascus, 85, 87
Nihavend, 66, 160, 214, 275
Nikanor, 150
nikatör, 153
Nile, 95, 117, 131
Nimrud, 70
Nimrud, Dagh, 165, 204
Nineveh, 64, 79, 80, 84
Nisa, 163, 170, 202, 204, 216, 218, 219, 222
Nishapur, 13, 201, 288
Nisibis, 209
Nizām al-Mulk, 251
nmāna, 54
Noeldeke, 241
Nogay, 45
nohodar, 215
nomos, 155
Nordics, 11
Nubia, 117
Nuʿmán, 275
Numenius, 227
Nuristan, 14

Occident, 148
Ochus, 132
Octavian, 208, 209
Odatis, 37
Odenath, 242
Oesho, 224
Ohrmizd, 222, 253, 270
Oibaras, 87
oikos, 153
OIONO, 256
Olbia, 177
Old Indian, 18
Old Persian, 3, 6, 17, 18, 23, 24,
   47-9, 51, 52, 53, 54, 55, 75, 79,
   81-2, 84-6, 90, 91, 94, 102-3, 105,
   108, 112, 116, 121, 122, 123, 125,
   126, 128, 130, 226, 237
Old Testament, 64, 89, 108, 112, 136
Omar Khayyam, 289
Opis, 89
Ordos, 174
Orient, 134, 135, 148, 150, 165, 166,
   172, 201, 221, 238
Origen, 221
Orontes, 146
arosangai, 106
Orroei, 209
Orthagnes, 207
Orthokorybanti, 45
orthos, 45
Osroene, 209
Ossete(s), 9, 38, 178
Ossetic, 50, 176
ostān, 283
Ostrogoths, 174
Ottoman, 107, 221
Outioi, 51
Oxus, 12, 41, 46, 48, 187, 188, 189,
   223, 226, 244, 256, 259, 279,
   280

Pahlava, 207
pahlavān, 199
Pahlavi, 6, 29, 38, 47, 55, 220-1,
   236, 248, 250, 252, 261, 272,
   276-7, 284-7
pahlavik, 222
Paikuli, 241, 245, 250
pakhatu, 81
Pakhto, 14, 24, 50
Pakistan, 8, 49, 243
Pakores, 207
Paktyes, 49, 50
Palaeo-Caucasian, 28

Palestine, 7, 64, 65, 89, 126, 217
Pallas Athena, 183
Palmyra, 189, 210, 242, 243, 274
Pamir, 24, 45, 55, 186, 244
Panjshir, 49
Panticapaeum, 173
Papak, 227, 236-7, 239
Paradan, 243
paradrya, 45
parakshe, 50
Parapotamia, 215
parasang, 110
paraśū-, 50
Paretakenoi, 81
Parikani, 48, 51
Parikhan, 47, 52
Paris, 124
Parmys, 98
Parni, 149, 201, 212
Paropanisadai, 49, 188
Pars, 44
Parsa, 44, 49, 50, 52, 54, 76, 85,
   90, 109, 121
parsava, 50
Parsi, 271
parskaden, 222
Parsua, 49, 50, 76-7, 79, 81
Parsumash, 76
Parswana, 49
Partatua, 79
partēz, 135
Parthaunisa, 204
Parthava, 52
Parthia, 52, 81, 98, 146, 149, 155,
   170, 184, 185, 190, 201, 203, 207,
   208, 212, 217, 243
Parthians, passim
Parthian Stations, 51, 160
Parthica, 202
Parutas, 49
Parysatis, 132
pasā-, 90
Pasargadai, 54, 82, 85, 86, 89-92,
   104, 105, 107, 128
pasārkadrish, 90
Pashkibur, 243, 244
Pashto, see Pakhto
Pasiani, 50
pasti-, 116
pasuka, 123
Pataliputra, 185
Pathans, 14, 49
patikospān, 216
Patrocles, 182

325

patyakhsh, 110
Pazyryk, 179
Peloponnesian War, 132
Perdikkas, 150
pərəṣu, 50
perk, 50
Perkunas, 21
Peroz, 255, 257, 260
Persepolis, 55, 67, 74, 75, 82-3,
    90-2, 101, 104-5, 107-9, 111, 117,
    123, 124, 126, 129, 130, 131, 163,
    165, 168, 227, 236, 246
Persia, 1-2, 3, 6, 8-15, 199
Persian(s), *passim*
Persian Gulf, 8, 52, 68, 160
Persis, 3, 11, 44, 76, 77, 83, 85, 86,
    91, 92, 93, 96, 98, 105, 155, 160,
    165, 212, 226-8
Perun, 20
Peshawar, 50, 244
Petra, 274
Peukestas, 150
phalerae, 180
Pharasmanes, 209
Philip the Arab, 242-3
Philip of Macedonian, 133, 143,
    147
philoi, 153
Phocas, 273
Phoenicia, 115, 118, 132, 134
Photius, 87
Phraates I, 212
Phraates II, 186, 206
Phraortes, 79, 81
Phrataphernes, 146
Phrygia, 78
piorun, 21
Piotrovskii, 73
Pishdadian, 39
Pishinah, 39
Pithon, 150
Plataia, 129
Plato, 134
Pliny, 48; 150, 160, 182, 205, 209,
    211, 222, 227
Plutarch, 104, 128, 150, 214, 217,
    218
polis, 149, 156-7
politeuma, 152, 157
Polybius, 10, 159, 164, 176, 182,
    184
Polynesia, 10
Pompeius Trogus, 7
Pompey, 177

Pontus, 165, 221
Portuguese, 17
praetor, 117
Prakrit, 112, 162, 188
prirk, 117
Prisk, 105, 256
prithivi-, 50
Procopius, 166, 270
proskynesis, 103
Prussia, 6
Ptolemies, 153, 158, 171, 173
Ptolemy I, 147, 151, 183, 184
Ptolemy (geographer), 7, 53, 81,
    160, 177, 203, 205, 256
Pul-i Darunta, 162
Punjab, 130, 185, 241, 243
Pyrenees, 28
Pythagoreanism, neo-, 172

Qadisiyah, al-, 275
qanat, 10
Qandahar, 7, 8, 13, 51, 112, 158,
    161, 162, 207
Qarakhanid, 43
Qara Kum, 46
Qashqais, 14
qashtu, 120
Quchan, 46
Quintus Curtius, *see* Curtius
Qumran, 71
Quran, 259, 289
Qutaiba ibn Muslim, 280

Raga, 32, 152
rājan, 22
Ravi river, 185
Rayy, 32, 205, 214
Red Sea, 119
Renaissance, 134
rex, 22
Reza Shah, 13, 259
rī, 22
Rig Veda, 26, 27, 29, 34, 43, 44
Roman(s), 82, 83, 128, 133, 155,
    166, 169, 171, 172, 174, 189, 203,
    208, 209, 211-12, 216-18, 223,
    225, 241-3, 246, 247, 249, 253,
    258, 262, 274
Romance languages, 17
Rome, 2, 17, 143, 169, 177, 201,
    208, 209
Romulus-Remus, 86
Roshnani, 186

Rostovtseff, 163, 180, 190
Roumania(n), 17, 130
Rovanduz, 72
Roxane, 146
Roxolani, 176, 177
ṛta, 34
Rūdaki, 288
Rusa, 72, 77, 78
Russia, 43, 45, 69, 78, 130, 173, 174, 175, 176-80, 187, 189, 256, 280
Rustam, 38, 51, 207, 219, 275
rustāg, 283

Sa'di, 289
Safavid, 87, 254
Saffarid, 288
Sagartia(ns), 77, 98
Sai, 181
Saini, 42, 43
Sairima, 42
sak-. 44
Saka, 44-6, 51, 88, 94, 130, 175, 178, 180, 181, 185-8, 206-7, 219, 221, 224, 250
Sakaraukai, 45
Sakkis, 70
Salamis, 129
Salm, 42
Salmanasar III, 63, 68, 72, 76
Samanids, 286, 288
Samaria, 65
Samarkand, 7, 13, 47, 94, 279, 280
Sanabares, 207
Sanatrug, 210
Sandrakottos, 150
Sanherib, 64, 65
Sanskrit, 19, 20, 25, 29, 50, 51, 53, 55, 252
Sar Mashhad, 248-9
Sarangians, 41
sarasvati-, 51
sárati, 53
Sardis, 88, 108, 110
Sarduri II, 72
Sargon II, 64, 71, 72, 77, 87
Sarmatia, 177
Sarmatian, 43, 69, 174-9, 190
Sasan, 227, 236-7, 247
Sasanian, passim
Satan, 136
satem, 19
satrapēs, 81
Sattagydia, 49, 50, 51
Sauromatians, 176

Saxons, 6
Schlumberger, 189, 190-1
Scylax of Caryanda, 119, 130
Scythian(s), 11, 14, 38, 45, 52, 69, 70, 72, 73, 75, 78, 80, 130, 174, 175-9, 255
Scytho-Sarmatian art, 190
Sebeos, 238
Seistan, 7, 13, 28, 32, 38, 41, 51, 52, 186-7, 205, 207, 214, 239, 243, 280, 288
Seleucia on the Tigris, 151, 154, 159, 160, 166, 168, 206, 210, 213
Seleucid(s), 31, 53, 149-72, 182, 183-4, 202-3, 211-12, 214, 217-18, 222, 224, 226, 238, 246
Seleucus I, 147, 150-1, 153, 159, 160, 182, 183, 201, 215
Seleucus II, 184, 202
Seleucus (geographer), 166
Seljük, 283
Semitic, 5, 66, 113, 121, 168, 253
Sennacherib, see Sanherib
Septimius, Severus, 208, 212
Serapis, 224
Seric, 166
Shah 'Abbas, 254, 259
Shahan Shah, 44
Shahi kings, 225, 281
Shahname (Book of Kings), 35, 36, 37, 207, 287
shahrdār, 245
Shahristanī, 270
Shahrvaraz, 274
shaknu, 121
Shamash, 74
Shami, 204
Shapur I (Shahpuhr), 43, 190, 210, 215, 225, 236-7, 240, 241-53, 254, 259-62
Shapur II, 225, 238-9, 253-6, 259-60, 286
Shash, 243, 244
shekel, 123-4
Shem, 42
Shi-chi, 47, 181
Shi'ite, 271, 283, 285-6
Shiraz, 283
Shivini, 74
Shiz, 261, 273, 283
Shkand Gumanik Vičar, 284
shkudha-, 78
Shustar, 243
Shutruk-Nakhunte, 67

327

Shuʿūbiyya, 278, 285, 289
Sibawaih, 277
Siberia, 174, 178, 179, 180, 181, 190
Sidon, 132
siglos, 123
Sikayahuvati, 97
Simonetta, 183
Sind, 28, 108
Sindi, 175
Sippar, 89
Siva, 170, 224
Siyāsaināme, 251
Siyavush, 283
Skudra, 130
Skunkhaʁ 45
Slavic, 18, 19, 20
Slavs, 176
Smerdis, 97
Sogdian, 6, 44, 46-8, 50, 99, 117, 170, 180, 181, 207, 221, 251, 254 277, 279-82, 287
Sogdiana, 44, 47, 48, 94, 108, 179, 182, 184, 223, 225, 244
soma, 27
Soma, 27
Sophagasenus, 184
Sophene, 209
sōtēr, 153, 171
South Russia, see, Russia
Soviet, 45, 47, 71, 149, 166, 174, 191
spāda, 116
spāhbad, 260
Spahpat, 214, 240
Spain, 174, 177
Spako, 86
Spalahora, 188
Spalirises, 188
Spandarmatak, 204
Spandiyad, 214
Spanish, 17
Sparda, 88
Spartans, 136
Spartocids, 173
Spartok, 173
Spasinv Charax, 206
Spontadata, 100, 104
Sphendadates, 99, 100
Spitama, 29
stater, 123
Stephan of Byzantium, 203
Stoicism, 148, 166
Strabo, 7, 47, 52, 53, 70, 101, 102, 129, 153, 159, 182, 185, 201, 205, 213, 222, 226, 227, 246

stratēgos, 155, 182, 185, 215
Stroukhates, 81
Sublime Porte, 107
Suez Canal, 119
Sufi, 283
Sufism, 271, 285
Sugd, 47
Suhrawardt
Sukkur, 243
Sumer (ian), 50, 64, 65, 66, 89
Sunnite, 283, 286
Sunpad, 282
Suppiluliuma, 23
Suren, 38, 207, 214, 239
Surkh, Kotal, 189, 204, 225
Susa, 64, 65, 66, 67, 68, 107-8, 110, 120, 128, 133, 146, 155, 165, 168, 210
Swat, 14, 185-6
Sweden, 25
Syennis, 115
synedrion, 213
Syr Darya, 182
Syria, 63, 64, 72, 77, 80, 93, 115, 150, 151, 152, 158, 169, 184, 208, 210, 215, 242, 260, 275
Syraic, 7, 210, 237, 249, 252, 276
Syarvarshan, 39
Syro-media, 81

Tabari, 239, 241, 248, 289
Tabaristan, 48
tachara, 107, 108
tacharapati, 108
Tacitus, 211, 222
Tagar, 179
tʿagawor, 135
Tahirids, 288
Ta-hsia, 186-7, 223
Tajiki, 287
Tajikistan, 244
Takht-i Sulaiman, 159
talent, 123
Talmud, 217-18, 221, 258
Taman, 175, 177
tamgas, 178
Tanaoxares, 97
Tang-i Sarwak, 210
Tansar, 240, 248, 261
Tapuria, 185
Taq-i Bustan, 237
Tarn, 148, 154, 173, 183, 206
Tashkent, 244

328

tassūj, 283
taumā-, 54
Ta wan, 48
Taxila, 112, 162, 185, 187-8
Tehran, 7, 12, 32, 63, 152, 203, 214
Teishebaini, 73
Teispes, 86
Tejen, 41
Tepe Giyan, 66, 75
Tepe Sialk, 66, 75
Termez, 288
Teshup, 63
Thamanaeans (Thamanai), 41, 51
Thatagu-, 49
Theophylactus Simocatta, 216
theos, 153, 159
Thieme, 54
Thracian, 73, 118, 130, 173, 175, 176, 180
Thraco-Phrygian, 78
Thraetaona, 36
Tiberius, 208
Tibetan, 47
Tiflis, 209
Tiglathpileser I, 63
Tiglathpileser III, 63, 72
tigrakhaudra, 45
Tigranes the Great, 208, 209
Tigranocerta, 209
Tigris, 7, 89, 151, 154, 159, 160, 163, 166, 209, 210, 213
Timarchus, 203, 205
Tiridates, 202, 209
Tokharian, 55, 180, 181
Tolstov, S.P., 46, 225, 280
Tomyris, 94
Tonga, 43
topos, 155
Toprak Kale, 204
Torah, 135
Tornberg, 236
Tosar, 240, 248, 261
Traitaná, 36
Trajan, 177, 206, 208, 212, 274
Transcaucasia, 3, 158, 177, 209, 216, 242, 243-4, 254
Transjordan, 274
Transoxiana, 32, 182, 282, 287, 288
Transylvania, 130, 179
Traxiane, 185
Tscherikower, 160
Tuch, 42
tugr, 181
Tumshug, 186

Tur, 42, 43
Tura, 42
Turan, 43, 207, 241, 243
Türgesh, 281
Turkestan (Russian), 12, 46, 179, 181, 201, 244
Turkish, 29, 67, 175, 259, 280
Turkmenistan, 43, 46, 163, 202
Turko-Mongolian, 20, 174, 178
Turks, 10, 11, 14, 20, 42-3, 45, 176, 179, 187, 223, 255, 279, 281
Tūs, 281
Tushpa, 64, 72, 73
twgrn, 43
Tyche, 171

Udyana, 186, 187
ueik, 20
Ugbaru, 89
Uighur, 181
Uja, 66
Umman-Manda, 76, 85
Umayyad, 48, 276, 278-9, 281
United States, 166
uoikos, 20
uparisaina-, 49
Ural, 174
Urartian, 28, 62, 68, 70-5, 77, 80, 81, 84, 114
Urartu, 63, 64, 66, 71, 72, 73-4, 76, 77, 78, 79, 81, 91
Urashtu, 71
Urmia, 12, 70, 71, 72, 76, 91
Uruk, 67, 163, 168
Usadan, 39
Usrushana, 94
Ustadsis, 282
Urakhshtra, 79
Uzar, 39
Uzii, 66

Vahagn, 170
Vahyazdata, 98
Valakhsh, 222
Valerian, 242-3, 248
Van, 64, 71, 72, 73, 74, 209
Vandals, 173
Varahran I, 247, 250
Varahran II, 247, 249-51, 254
Varahran III, 247, 250
Varahran V, 255
Varaz, 239
varəzāna, 54
varuṇa, 26

Varuṇa, 21, 23, 24, 26
vāstryōshān, 55
Vasudeva, 225
vazurkān (RB'n), 214, 245
Vedas, 23-4, 26, 34, 84
Vedic, 29, 32
Vendidad, 33, 113, 126, 172, 223
Verethragna, 170, 224
Vespasian, 177
veśzpats, 20
vicus, 20
Videvdat, see Vendidad
Vima Kadphises, 223, 224
vis-, 54
Vishtaspa, 31, 32, 34, 35, 39, 41, 42,
    54, 100, 104, 219
Visigoths, 174
visō puthra, 105
viśpáti, 20
vispuhr, 245
vith-, 54
Viyakhna, 96
Volga, 218, 280
Vologeses I, 210, 211, 217, 222
Vologeses IV, 237
Vologeses V, 237
Vologesokerta, 210
Vorones I, 188, 207, 211
Vṛtra, 27

Wasit, 275
Widengren, 103
World War I, 107
World War II, 70, 204
Wu-sun, 180, 181, 186
wyršn, 208

Xanthos, 29, 82
Xenophon, 7, 86, 87, 97, 117,
    118-19, 132
Xerxes, 6, 29, 52, 86, 105, 106, 108,
    111, 112, 126, 127, 130, 131-2,
    136, 144

yabghu, 223
yad-, 100
yaj-, 100
Yama, 36
Yaʿqūb, 288
Yāgūt, 283
Yasht, 42, 43, 49, 110, 128, 172

Yasna, 35, 42
Yautiyā, 51, 52
yavuga, 223
yaz-, 100
Yazdagird II, 222, 238
Yazdagird III, 274, 275
Yemen, 259
Yenisei, 179
Yidgha, 186
Yima, 36
Younger Avesta, see Avesta
Yüeh-chih, 181, 185-7, 206, 223, 257
Yuti, 52

Zab, 72
Zabdicene, 209
Zabul, 256
Zaehner, 173
Zagros, 9, 12, 14, 68, 69, 75, 77, 210
Zamua, 81
Zandik, 250
zantu, 25, 54
zaotar, 34
Zarafshan, 244
Zarang, 51
Zaranka, 51
Zarathushtra, see Zoroaster
Zariadres, 37
Zek, 214
Zeno, 148
Zenobia, 243
Zeus, 101, 159, 165
zij-i Shahriyār, 261
Zikertu, 77
Ziwiye, 70
Zoroaster, xi, 28-42, 44, 75, 82-4,
    100, 101, 109, 124, 126-7, 173,
    200, 215, 219, 226, 237, 240, 241,
    248
Zoroastrian(s), 6, 22, 29, 31, 39, 42,
    43, 44, 51, 53, 55, 57, 67, 82-4,
    100-2, 104, 125, 126-9, 199, 200,
    204, 221, 227, 228, 246, 248-9,
    252, 257, 258, 271, 272, 277, 282,
    283-4, 286, 289
Zoroastranism, x, 38, 127-9, 169,
    170, 173, 207, 220, 249-52, 270-1,
    273, 282-5
Zrangai, 51
Zurvan, 253, 271
Zurvanism, 250, 252-3, 270
Zurvanites, 270
Zutt, 52